# Investing in Youth: Tunisia

## STRENGTHENING THE EMPLOYABILITY OF YOUTH DURING THE TRANSITION TO A GREEN ECONOMY

OECD
BETTER POLICIES FOR BETTER LIVES

**Please cite this publication as:**
OECD (2015), *Investing in Youth: Tunisia: Strengthening the Employability of Youth during the Transition to a Green Economy*, OECD Publishing, Paris.
*http://dx.doi.org/10.1787/9789264226470-en*

ISBN 978-92-64-19082-5 (print)
ISBN 978-92-64-22647-0 (PDF)



**Photo credits:** Cover © Lars Lindblad/Shutterstock.com, ©Rido - Fotolia.com, ©Inmagine LTD/Blend Images.

Corrigenda to OECD publications may be found on line at: *www.oecd.org/about/publishing/corrigenda.htm*.

# Foreword

Four years after the start of the so called *Jasmine Revolution*, the Tunisian nation has been transformed, driven by the will for change of a whole generation of young Tunisians that took the streets to build a brighter future. The early results of this social and political metamorphosis, despite the costs, the pain and the risks that it implied, have been impressive.

By 2012, Tunisians had held successful democratic elections, passed a law on associations that triggered a blooming of non-governmental organisations and think-tanks, and approved another key law on access to information. These represent a significant step in the direction of increased transparency, while Tunisia's joining of the Open Government Partnership in early 2014 was another important signal. By early 2014, Tunisians had passed a new constitution, setting the course for the country's future, while parliamentary and Presidential elections were successfully held under this framework in late 2014. A great deal of these achievements can be attributed to Tunisian youth. Despite these encouraging achievements, there is no cause for complacency. There is still a lot to be done to build a strong, sustainable and inclusive Tunisian economy that offers the opportunities that the youth demand and deserve.

As confirmed by this OECD report, *Investing in Youth: Tunisia – Strengthening the Employability of Youth during the Transition to a Green Economy,* tackling youth labour market challenges remains urgent in Tunisia, and is indeed one of the country's top priorities. Some two out of five young Tunisians in the labour force are unemployed, and one in four youths are neither in employment, nor in education or training (NEET) – nearly twice the rate in most OECD countries. Some groups fare even worse, particularly women and those from the more deprived Centre West and Southern regions. Failure to tackle now the long-standing structural obstacles that prevent youth in Tunisia from gaining access to productive and rewarding jobs can undermine political support for the transition to a stable, fairer, and democratic society.

The report is the response to a request for collaboration made by the Tunisia Government to the OECD in May 2013. The OECD is proud to contribute to Tunisia's endeavour to design and execute a comprehensive approach for improving the employability of younger generations.

*Investing in Youth: Tunisia* puts forward specific policy options, based on the practices and reforms that have worked well in other countries. It provides an in-depth analysis of the obstacles to improve labour market outcomes in the formal sector for Tunisia's youth and discusses the most promising labour market and social policies to remove them. The report also proposes viable policy strategies for promoting employment and employability among those young people under-represented in the labour market, notably women. Furthermore, it identifies cost-effective policy options to strengthen the vocational education and training system and to move towards effective entrepreneurship support programmes. The report also lays the ground to support Tunisia's youth in the transition towards a green economy, which is a key priority for the country.

In 2013, the OECD launched the *OECD Action Plan for Youth*, which provides a new framework for consolidating its experience on youth issues by assessing youth challenges from a concerted strategic perspective to develop education systems and labour market arrangements that work together well. The OECD is working closely with countries to implement the comprehensive measures of the *Action Plan for Youth* in their national and local contexts and to provide peer-learning opportunities for countries to share their experience of policy measures to improve youth employment outcomes. *Investing in Youth: Tunisia* is the second report to extend the *Action Plan for Youth* to emerging economies, following Brazil.

The report has been prepared with financial support from the Middle East and North Africa (MENA) Transition Fund, which the OECD gratefully acknowledges. Several projects are being undertaken by the OECD to underpin the main objective of the MENA Transition Fund, which is to provide Arab countries in transition with a framework to strengthen governance for transparent, accountable governments and provide an economic framework for sustainable and inclusive growth. We look forward to continuing a fruitful collaboration with the MENA Transition Fund.

The OECD is ready to continue supporting the reform agenda of Tunisia, as well as that of the other MENA countries in transition, by helping design, develop and deliver "Better Policies for Better Lives".

Angel Gurría

Secretary-General of the OECD

# *Acknowledgements*

This report is the outcome of a collective effort and reflects the contribution of a team of policy analysts, from various OECD directorates co-ordinated by the OECD Directorate for Employment, Labour and Social Affairs, under the supervision of Alessandro Goglio (Counsellor). Chapters 1, 2 and 3 were prepared by Stijn Broecke (from the Employment Analysis and Policy Division – EAP – in the OECD Directorate for Employment, Labour and Social Affaires), with research assistance from Elkefi Rahmani (secondee to the OECD from the *Observatoire National de l'Emploi et des Qualifications*), and Alessia Forti, as well as statistical assistance from Paulina Granados-Zambrano. Andrea Bassanini (Senior Economist, ELS/EAP) calculated and provided the employment protection legislation indicators for Tunisia used in Chapter 2. Chapter 4 was prepared by Pauline Musset and Hendrickje Windisch, under the supervision of Simon Field from the Skills beyond School Division (SBS) of the OECD Directorate for Education and Skills, and Chapter 5 was prepared by Stuart Thompson from the Local Economics and Employment Development (LEED) Division of the OECD Centre for Entrepreneurship, SMEs and Local Development (CFE). Additional inputs on entrepreneurship were provided by David Halabisky (CFE/LEED). Editorial assistance was provided by Monica Meza-Essid and Marlène Mohier (ELS). The report also benefited from useful comments provided by Stefano Scarpetta (ELS Director), Mark Keese (ELS/EAP Head of Division), Sylvain Giguere (CFE/LEED, Head of Division) and Deborah Roseveare (EDU/SBS Head of Division).

To prepare the report, a team from the OECD Secretariat visited Tunisia in December 2013 and engaged in wide-ranging discussions with ministries, senior officials, experts and social partners. The OECD Secretariat would like to thank the *Ministère de la Formation Professionnelle et de l'Emploi* (MFPE) of Tunisia for the excellent support in carrying out this project and for organising the initial fact-funding mission in Tunis, a seminar to discuss the report's preliminary findings and recommendations in October 2014, as well as the final dissemination seminar in early 2015. In particular, Imed Turki, Mariem Lissari, Nizar Ata and Youssef Naouar deserve special thanks for their considerable contribution to ensuring a successful completion of this project. The Secretariat would also like to thank all parties met during and after the fact-finding mission for their time and useful insights. The Secretariat is grateful for the many replies to requests for additional information and comments on the report that were provided by many officials from both MFPE and other ministries and organisations in Tunisia. Thanks are due in particular to Chokri Hammami from the Ministère des Affaires Sociales for his help with analysing the Tunisian Labour Code and collating the information on sector minimum wages. Further thanks are due to colleagues from the International Labour Organization for their help with analysing the School-to-Work Transition Surveys (Yves Perardel and Sara Elder). This report has been produced with the financial assistance of the Middle East and North Africa (MENA) Transition Fund, which provides grant funding to address the thematic areas covered by the G8 Deauville Partnership. The contents of this report are the sole responsibility of the OECD and can in no way be taken to reflect the views of the Transition Fund or the G8 Deauville Partnership members.

# Table of contents

**Figures**

## Tables

# Acronyms and abbreviations

| | |
|---|---|
| AfDB | African Development Bank |
| ALMP | Active Labour Market Programme |
| AMG | *Assistance Médicale Gratuite* (Free Medical Assistance) |
| AMG1 | *Carte de Soins Gratuits* (Free Health Care Card) |
| AMG2 | *Carte de Soins à Tarifs Réduits* (Subsidised Health Care Card) |
| ANETI | *Agence Nationale pour l'Emploi et le Travail Indépendant* (National Employment and Self-Employment Agency) |
| ATFP | *Agence Tunisienne de la Formation Professionnelle* (Tunisian Agency for Vocational Training) |
| AVFA | *Agence de la Vulgarisation et de la Formation Agricole* (Agricultural Extension and Training Centre) |
| BFPME | *Banque de Financement de Petites et Moyennes Entreprises* (Small and Medium Enterprise Financing Bank) |
| BTP | *Brevet de Technicien Professionnel* (Professional Technician's Certificate) |
| BTS | *Banque Tunisienne de Solidarité* (Tunisian Solidarity Bank) |
| BTS | *Brevet de Technicien Supérieur* (Advanced Technician's Diploma) |
| CAIP | *Contrat d'Adaptation et d'Insertion Professionnelle* (Adaptability and Employability Contract) |
| CAP | *Certificat d'Aptitude Professionnel* (Vocational Aptitude Certificate) |
| CC | *Certificat de Compétences* (Competence Certificate) |
| CEFE | *Création d'Entreprise Formation d'Entrepreneurs* (Business Start-up Entrepreneur Training) |
| CENAFFIF | *Centre National de Formation de Formateurs et d'Ingénierie de Formation* (National Centre for Training of Trainers and Pedagogy) |
| CES | *Contrat Emploi Solidarité* (Employment Solidarity Contract) |

| | |
|---|---|
| CFA-F0/CFA-F4 | *Certificat de Fin d'Apprentissage* (Apprenticeship Certificate) |
| CGTT | *Confédération Générale des Travailleurs Tunisiens* (General Confederation of Tunisian Workers) |
| CIDES | *Contrat d'Insertion des Diplômés de l'Enseignement Supérieur* (Higher Education Graduates Insertion Contract) |
| CITET | *Centre International des Technologies de l'Environnement de Tunis* (Tunis International Center for Environmental Technologies) |
| CNAM | *Caisse Nationale d'Assurance Maladie* (National Health Insurance Fund) |
| CNDD | *Commission Nationale de Développement Durable* (National Commission for Sustainable Development) |
| CNFCPP | *Centre National de la Formation Continue de la Promotion Professionnelle* (National Centre for Continuing Training and Career Development) |
| CNQ | *Classification Nationale des Qualifications* (National Qualifications Framework) |
| CNRPS | *Caisse Nationale de Retraite et de Prévoyance Sociale* (National Pension and Social Contingency Fund) |
| CNSS | *Caisse Nationale de Sécurité Sociale* (National Social Security Fund) |
| CPI | Consumer Price Index |
| CREE | *Créez Votre Entreprise* (Set Up Your Business) |
| CRES | *Centre de Recherches et d'Études Sociales* (Centre for Social Research and Studies) |
| CRVA | *Contrat de Réinsertion dans la Vie Active* (Contract for the Reintegration into Working Life) |
| CWP | Community Work Programme |
| DFEB | *Diplôme de Fin d'Études de l'Enseignement de Base Générale* (General Basic Education School Leaving Certificate) |
| DFEBT | *Diplôme de Fin d'Études de l'Enseignement de Base Technique* (Technical Basic Education School Leaving Certificate) |
| ECEC | Early Childhood Education and Care |
| ENEL | National Electricity Board |
| ENPE | *Enquête Nationale sur la Population et l'Emploi* (National Population and Employment Survey) |
| FIAP | *Fonds d'Insertion et d'Adaptation Professionnelle* (Insertion and Professional Adaptation Fund) |
| FONAPRAM | *Fond National de la Promotion de l'Artisanat et des Petits Métiers* (National Fund for the Promotion of Crafts and Small Enterprises) |

| | |
|---|---|
| GDP | Gross Domestic Product |
| GIZ | German Federal Enterprise for International Cooperation (*Deutsche Gesellschaft für Internationale Zusammenarbeit*) |
| GTZ | Agency for Technical Co-operation (*Gesellschaft für Technische Zusammenarbeit*) |
| ILO | International Labour Organization |
| INOFCA | *Institut National Pédagogique et de Formation Continue Agricole* (National Institute for Agricultural Education and Continuing Training) |
| INS | *Institut National de la Statistique* (National Institute of Statistics) |
| IRPP | *Impôt sur le Revenu des Personnes Physiques* (Personal Income Tax) |
| ISET | *Institut Supérieurs d'Études Techniques* (Institute of Technological Studies) |
| IYF | International Youth Foundation |
| MANFORME | *Mise à Niveau de la Formation Professionnelle et de l'Emploi* (Strenghtening Vocational Training and Employment) |
| MAS | *Ministère des Affaires Sociales* (Ministry of Social Affairs) |
| MDCI | *Ministère de Développemment et de la Coopération Internationale* (Ministry of Development and International Co-operation) |
| MENA | Middle East and North Africa |
| MFPE | *Ministère de la Formation Professionnelle et de l'Emploi* (Ministry of Vocational Education and Employment) |
| MORAINE | *Méthode Originale de Recherche Active d'Idées Nouvelles pour Entreprendre* (Original and Active Research Method for New Entrepreneurship Ideas) |
| MW | Minimum wages |
| NEET | Neither in Employment, nor in Education or Training |
| NGO | Non-Governmental Organisation |
| NRR | Net Replacement Rate |
| OECD | Organisation for Economic Co-operation and Development |
| ONTT | *Office National du Tourisme Tunisien* (Tunisian National Tourism Office) |
| OTT | *Organisation Tunisienne du Travail* (Tunisian Labour Organisation) |
| PAPPE | *Programme d'Appui aux Promoteurs des Petites Entreprises* (Small Entrepreneur Support Programme) |
| PC50 | *Prise en Charge par l'État de 50% des Salaires Versés* (50% Wage Subsidy) |
| PCGD | *Plan de gestion des déchets* (Waste management plans) |

| | |
|---|---|
| PCRD | *Programme des Chantiers Régionaux de Développement* (Regional Public Works Development Programme) |
| PDI | *Programme de Développement Intégré* (Integrated Development Programme) |
| PEE | *Programme d'Encouragement à l'Emploi* (Employment Incentive Programme) |
| PES | Public Employment Services |
| PISA | Programme for International Student Assessment |
| PNAFN | *Programme National d'Aide aux Familles Nécessiteuses* (National Support Programme for Disadvantaged Families) |
| PRONAFOC | *Programme National de la Formation Continue* (National Programme for Continuing Education) |
| PSNP | Productive Safety Net Programme |
| RPL | Recognition of Prior Learning |
| SCV | *Service Civil Volontaire* (Voluntary Civil Service) |
| SGIDD | *Stratégie de Gestion Integrée et Durable des Déchets* (Strategy for integrated and sustainable waste management) |
| SIVP | *Stage d'Initiation à la Vie Professionnelle* (Initiation to the World of Work Internship) |
| SMAG | *Salaire Minimum Agricole Garanti* (Agricultural Minimum Wage) |
| SMIG | *Salaire Minimum Interprofessionnel Garanti* (Non-Agricultural Minimum Wage) |
| SSC | Social Security Contributions |
| SWTS | School-to-Work Transition Survey |
| TFP | *Taxe à la Formation Professionnelle* (Taxation scheme for Vocational Education and Training) |
| TIE | *Trouvez une Idée d'Entreprise* (Find a Business Idea) |
| TND | Tunisian dinar |
| TWA | Temporary Work Agency |
| UGTT | *Union Générale Tunisienne du Travail* (Tunisian General Labour Union) |
| UNESCO | United Nations Educational, Scientific and Cultural Organization |
| UNICEF | United Nations International Children's Emergency Fund |
| UTICA | *Union Tunisienne de l'Industrie, du Commerce et de l'Artisanat* (Tunisian Union of Industry, Commerce and Crafts) |
| UTT | *Union des Travailleurs Tunisiens* (Tunisian Workers Union) |
| VET | Vocational Education and Training |

# Executive summary

Despite years of strong economic growth prior to the revolution, Tunisia experienced growing inequalities in opportunities to obtain good jobs, translating into rising unemployment among young people in particular – a situation which further deteriorated in the wake of the global economic crisis and during the transition to democracy.

A key priority for policy makers is to set the country on a path of economic recovery, grounded in a new, more sustainable and inclusive growth model, which will generate productive employment opportunities, and tackle regional disparities and other inequalities head-on.

Policy makers will also need to factor in the additional challenge of climate change and environmental pressures as they tackle youth unemployment, since these are likely to change demand for both skills and employment. As this report argues, a well-functioning labour market together with an effective safety net will be essential in this transition to a greener economy, as will a high quality vocational education and training system and strong entrepreneurship support structures.

Boosting youth employment in Tunisia will first of all require improving the country's record on job creation. This means implementing a mixture of appropriate macroeconomic policies and addressing a range of structural weaknesses that have to date prevented economic growth from being inclusive. The latter must include action to bring down structural labour market barriers that affect the willingness and ability of employers to hire youth.

Social protection systems will also need to be strengthened, given the key role they play in providing an adequate safety net for youth who are out of work. Such policies shield youth from poverty and enable them to look for new and productive employment – a process which can be reinforced further by effective public employment services. Even though Tunisia has a comprehensive social insurance system in place, high unemployment and informality rates mean that a large portion of youth are not contributing to – and therefore cannot benefit from – such protection.

The school-to-work transitions of young people can further be improved through an effective vocational education and training (VET) system, particularly where it contains a strong element of work-based learning. In the context of a greening economy, a well-functioning VET system can also help young people acquire the necessary skills to seize opportunities in areas where rapid employment growth is expected, such as clean technology, energy, tourism, agriculture, and waste and recycling.

Similarly, effective entrepreneurship support structures can help young people make the most of the new opportunities that green growth is likely to bring. While a relatively well-developed support system is already in place in Tunisia, with the provision of information, training, finance and follow-up services, significant scope for improvements remains.

Many of the recommendations in this report rely, for their effective development and implementation, on a successful partnership between stakeholders. This is of particular importance in Tunisia, where responsibility for labour market, VET and entrepreneurship policy is highly fragmented.

## Key recommendations

**Make hiring young people more attractive**

- Be more sparing in the use of wage subsidies to encourage hiring and target them more on the disadvantaged, the low-skilled and the long-term unemployed.
- Future sectoral wage negotiations should carefully consider the situation of youth by setting wages for younger workers that more accurately reflect their productivity.
- Reduce differences in remuneration and benefits between the public and private sectors, and resist the urge to use public sector job creation as a means of social appeasement.
- Reduce the gap in employment protection between permanent and temporary contracts.

**Raise the employability of youth through effective social and labour market policies**

- Set up an unemployment insurance system.
- Extend and better target non-conditional cash transfer programmes (*Programme National d'Aide aux Familles Nécessiteuses*) to offer a basic safety net of last resort.
- Revive public works programmes that can provide an insurance function to the unemployed.
- Develop a comprehensive strategy to tackle informality.
- Strengthen the capacity of the public employment services, through a mixture of additional investment, expansion of the system, and closer collaboration with the non-governmental sector and private employment agencies.
- Improve social policies to help young families balance work and caring responsibilities more effectively.

**Improve the effectiveness of vocational education and training to smooth school-to-work transitions**

- Make vocational education and training more attractive to prospective students, by making it easier to switch between academic and vocational tracks and improving the quality of options at the upper secondary level.
- Further strengthen the links between the vocational education and training system and social partners to ensure that the mix of provision becomes more demand-driven.
- Make mandatory work-based learning the standard.
- Improve advice and guidance for prospective students.

**Further strengthen entrepreneurship support**

- Develop a general strategy that clearly defines roles of stakeholders as well as short- and long-run objectives in developing entrepreneurship supports.
- Improve the co-ordination between training centres and business start-up support structures and address the duplication in the provision of entrepreneurship support services.
- Equalise the quality and accessibility of entrepreneurship training across regions.
- Provide more support for business start-ups in the medium- to long-term.
- Provide additional support to potential female entrepreneurs.

**Key recommendations** *(cont.)*

**Act to stimulate green employment opportunities for youth**

- Expand the existing and successful Prosol initiative to other areas of renewable energy.
- Ensure appropriate support for social enterprise to stimulate employment opportunities in the fields of waste recycling and of local energy production.
- Create cost-effective strategies to facilitate the development of eco-tourism, export of organic agricultural products, and the upgrading of skills in construction.

**Improve co-ordination to develop an effective policy response**

- The Ministry of Vocational Education and Training and the Ministry of Social Affairs, both responsible for different aspects of labour market policy, should work together more closely.
- The various ministries and bodies responsible for VET will need to develop a coherent strategy to address the overall needs of the labour market.
- The roles of various ministries and other organisations in entrepreneurship support would equally benefit from clear strategic direction.

# Assessment and recommendations

## Tunisia faces a unique window of opportunity to set the country on a new and inclusive growth path, but time is pressing

While the road travelled by Tunisia since the revolution has been bumpy and will in all likelihood continue to be so in years to come, much has been achieved since January 2011. Two rounds of democratic elections have been successfully held in October 2011and in October 2014. In 2014, Tunisia achieved another landmark by passing a new constitution, which has set the course for the country's future. The enactment of the 2011 Law on Associations has fuelled a mushrooming of non-governmental organisations and think tanks, while the Law on Access to Information represents a significant step in the direction of increased transparency.

Nevertheless, despite these achievements and the changes brought about by faster communications, social media and a more vocal civil society, restoring trust and confidence in the future remains challenging. Indeed, in some respects the general mood in the country has not ceased to deteriorate. Since 2010, Tunisians' optimism for the future has suffered a dramatic decline – second only to that observed in Syria over the same period (Figure 0.1).

**Figure 0.1. Optimism for the future, Tunisia, OECD, selected emerging and MENA countries, 2010[a]-13[b]**

Percentage of respondents with a positive attitude for the future

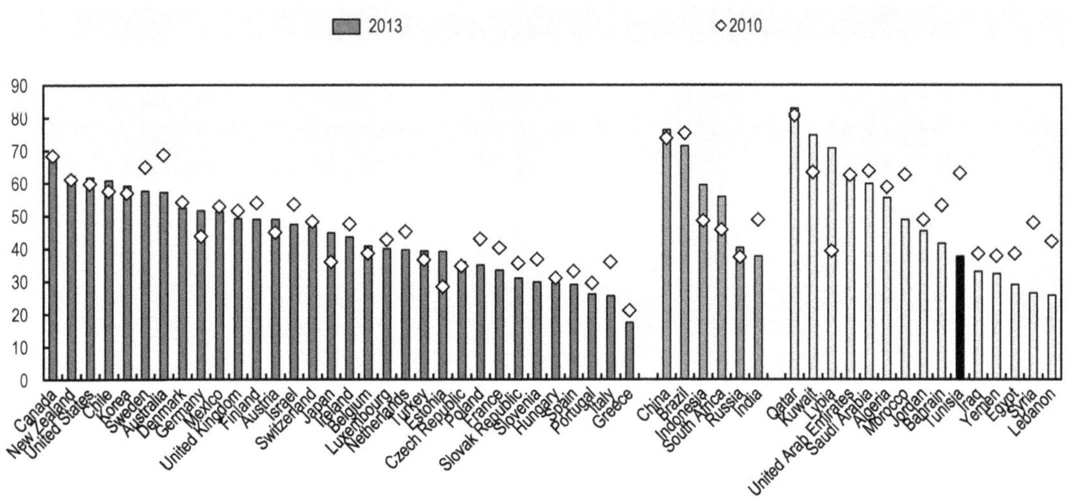


*a)* 2009 for Algeria, Bahrain, Estonia, Iraq, Kuwait, Libya, Morocco, Qatar, Switzerland and United Arab Emirates.

*b)* 2012 for Algeria, Bahrain, Chile, China, Iraq, Israel (Information on data for Israel: http://dx.doi.org/10.1787/888932315602), Japan, Kuwait, Libya, Morocco, South Africa, Korea, Qatar, Switzerland, United Arab Emirates and United States.

*Source*: OECD calculations based on Gallup World Poll 2010-2013.

This largely reflects the fact that some of the main problems that led to the revolution remain unresolved, while the economic and employment situation has continued to worsen. A key priority for policy makers now is to set the country on a path of economic recovery, grounded in a new, more sustainable and inclusive growth model. This would generate productive employment opportunities for the large part of the labour force, and tackle regional disparities and other inequalities head on.

## Youth unemployment remains the thorn in the country's side

Prior to the revolution, Tunisia experienced years of strong economic growth. Despite this, inequalities in income distribution and opportunities to obtain good jobs increased (INS, 2012; Boughzala and Hamdi, 2014; Ghali et al., 2014). This lack of inclusive growth has probably found its most troubling expression in the extremely poor (and worsening) labour market outcomes for youth, which were a key contributor to the general social unrest that led to the revolution in 2010-11. Subsequently, in the wake of the revolution and the global financial crisis, the situation only deteriorated further – albeit with signs of improvement in more recent times. Chapter 1 of this report provides an overview of the labour market outcomes of youth in Tunisia, as well as an analysis of their school-to-work transitions. It shows that around two out of five Tunisian youths are unemployed, and one in four young Tunisians are neither in employment, nor in education or training (NEET) – nearly twice the rate encountered in the average OECD country. An additional concern is that these statistics conceal considerable heterogeneity across groups:

- Young women have much lower employment rates than young men (13.3% versus 30.3%) resulting primarily from higher labour market inactivity rates (77.2% versus 52.9%).
- Youth with tertiary education face a much higher risk of unemployment than their peers with lower educational attainment.
- Outcomes for young people living in the more deprived Centre West and Southern regions of the country are particularly dire (Figure 0.2).

Even when youth are in employment, it is frequently in poor quality jobs: an estimated one in two employed youths in Tunisia work informally, with little or no protection and/or job security while, of those working with a contract, half have a temporary one.

**Figure 0.2. Youth unemployment by governorate, Tunisia, 2012**

Percentage of the labour force in each governorate

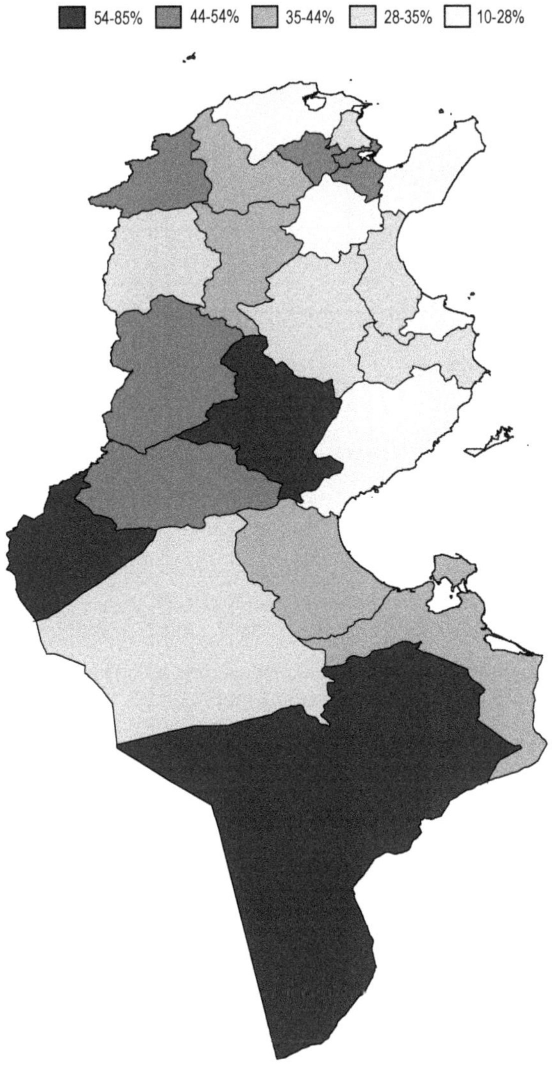


*Source*: OECD calculations based on the *Enquête Nationale sur la Population et l'Emploi* (ENPE) [National Population and Employment Survey].

## Poor labour market outcomes translate into low levels of well-being

The lack of good employment opportunities for youth is closely associated with their financial and more general well-being. 34% of Tunisian youth say they find it difficult or very difficult to get by with their present household income (as opposed to living comfortably or getting by) – compared to 20% of youth in OECD and 30% in large emerging economies, respectively (Figure 0.3). This inability to cope financially translates into low levels of well-being: based on their self-reported life satisfaction, only 21% of Tunisian youths can be considered to be "thriving" (as opposed to "struggling" or "suffering").[1] This is low by OECD (56%), but even by large emerging economy (28%) and MENA (27%) standards (Figure 0.4).

**Figure 0.3. Youth perceptions about household income, Tunisia, OECD, selected emerging and MENA countries, 2013[a]**

Percentage finding it difficult/very difficult to cope[b]

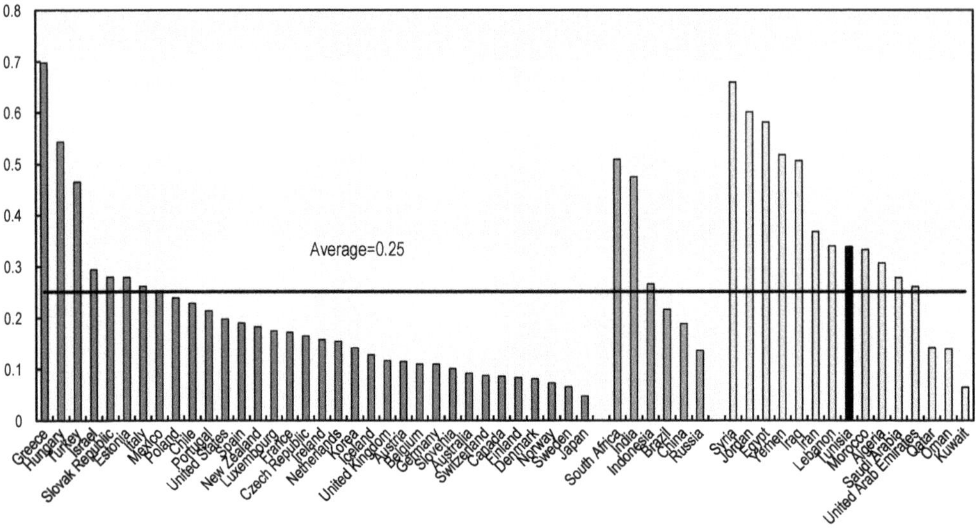


*a)* 2012 for Algeria, Chile , China, Iraq, Israel (Information on data for Israel: http://dx.doi.org/10.1787/888932315602), Japan, Kuwait, Morocco, Norway, Qatar, South Africa, Korea, Switzerland, United Arab Emirates, United States; 2011 for Oman.

*b)* Response options include: living comfortably on present income; getting by on present income; finding it difficult on present income; finding it very difficult on present income; do not know; refused.

*Source*: OECD calculations based on Gallup World Poll 2011-2013.

**Figure 0.4. Youth life satisfaction, Tunisia, OECD, selected emerging and MENA countries, 2013[a]**

Percentage thriving[b]

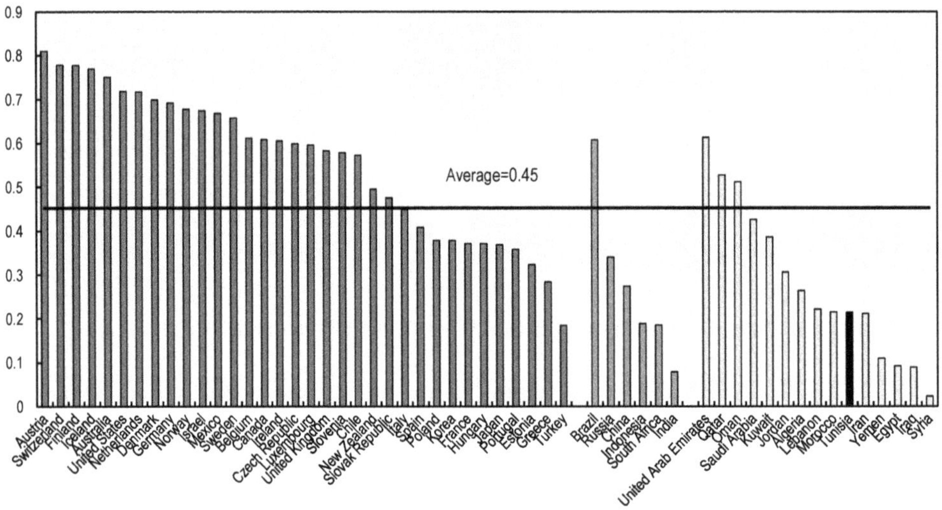


*a)* 2012 for Algeria, Chile , China, Iraq, Israel (Information on data for Israel: http://dx.doi.org/10.1787/888932315602), Japan, Kuwait, Morocco, Norway, Qatar, South Africa, Korea, Switzerland, United Arab Emirates, United States; 2011 for Oman.

*b)* Response options include: thriving; struggling; suffering.

*Source*: OECD calculations based on Gallup World Poll 2011-2013.

## Tunisian policy makers recognise that helping youth get a better start in the labour market is a key priority

Action is needed both to bring immediate results in alleviating the current situation of high un- and underemployment, and to produce better outcomes for youth in the longer run by equipping them with relevant skills for the future and removing barriers to their employment. A *Plan d'Urgence pour l'Emploi* [Employment Emergency Plan] was drawn up shortly after the revolution (March 2011) based on four key priorities: i) job creation; ii) the promotion of entrepreneurship; iii) the protection of existing and threatened jobs; and iv) boosting the employability and the activation of young people. Following national consultations, the emergency plan was replaced by the *Stratégie Nationale pour l'Emploi 2013-2017* [National Employment Strategy] in December 2012, containing six strategic objectives: i) employment-oriented macro-economic policies based on social dialogue; ii) additional support for employment generating sectors; iii) private sector development (including policies to tackle informality and boost self-employment/entrepreneurship); iv) regional development and female employment; v) enhancing the employability of the workforce (with particular focus on smoothing school-to-work transitions and building a training system responsive to the needs of the economy); and vi) improving the operation of the labour market by adopting a labour legislation that better balances the need for flexibility with protection for workers, as well as active labour market programmes targeted on the most vulnerable. The issue of youth employment also featured centrally in the *Contrat Social* [Social Contract] signed on 14 January 2013 between the government and the main social partners.

## The economic climate remains unfavourable to job creation and the fiscal space is getting tighter

Economic growth will be essential for job creation and bringing down youth unemployment in Tunisia. However, although the country initially weathered the global financial crisis relatively well, its economic performance deteriorated sharply in the aftermath of the revolution, as both tourism and foreign direct investment fell and the crisis in neighbouring Libya had important spill-over effects (World Bank, 2012). These crises also diminished the possibility for migration to act as a pressure release valve to reduce Tunisian unemployment, with many European countries taking tougher stances on in-migration and tens of thousands of Tunisian migrant workers returning home from Libya (AfDB and IOM, 2013). These developments underscore that tackling youth challenges is also essential to strengthen the resilience of the Tunisian economy in the face of future adverse shocks.

While there are some positive signs with the European market slowly recovering and tourism, exports and remittances improving, much uncertainty persists due to heightened security tensions and political uncertainty related to the impending elections. As a result, the recovery of the Tunisian economy remains timid. Real growth was estimated at 2.7% in 2013 and is expected to reach 3.0% in 2014 (Figure 0.5). Despite a sign of recovery, such growth rates are still too mild to make a significant dent in unemployment. Indeed, a return to higher growth rates will depend critically on important structural reforms to remove barriers to private investment and entrepreneurship, including strengthening the banking sector and financial markets, and creating a more transparent and competitive environment for doing business (ILO, 2011; OECD, 2014a). The fiscal space to act is however shrinking. While the central government deficit is widening (Figure 0.6), this deterioration only reflects central government accounts and negative budgetary pressures outside central government are significant – with a pension system in structural deficit, a financing crisis in public hospitals and a need to recapitalise banks. On the external side, the IMF expects some reduction of the current account deficit in relation to 2013, but it nevertheless remains large (Figure 0.6).

**Figure 0.5. Tunisia's GDP, constant prices, 2006-15**

Percent change on previous year

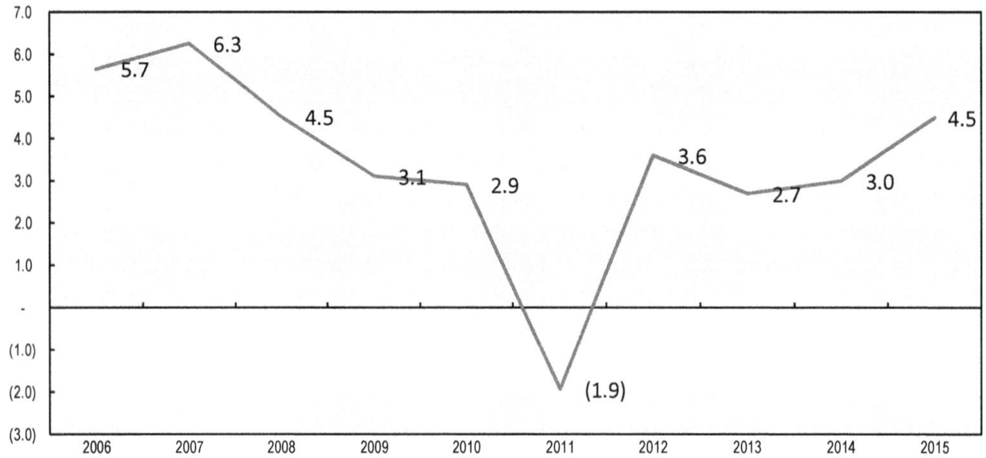


*Source*: International Monetary Fund, World Economic Outlook Database, April 2014, www.imf.org/external/pubs/ft/weo/2014/01/weodata/index.aspx.

**Figure 0.6. Central government deficit and current account deficit, Tunisia, 2010-14**

Percentage of GDP

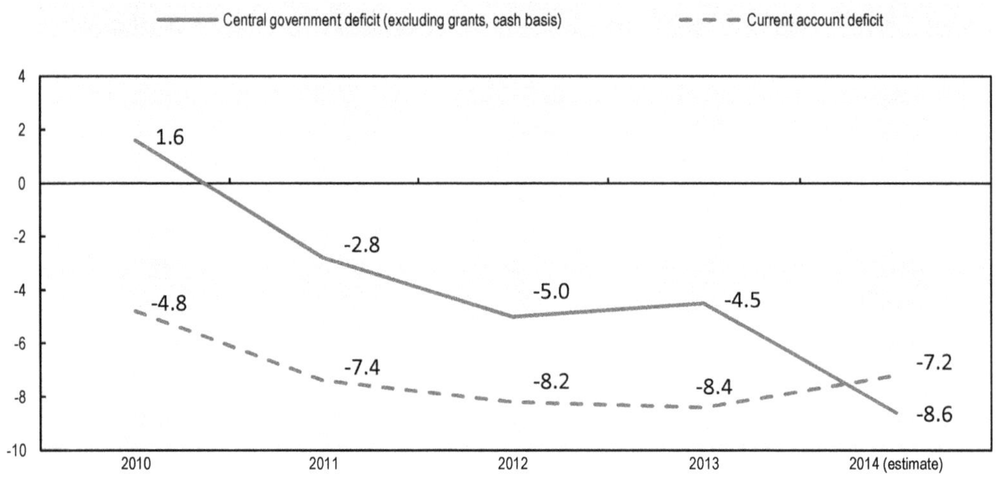


*Source*: IMF (2014), "Tunisia: Third Review Under the Stand-by Arrangement, Request for Modification of Performance Criteria and Waivers of Applicability", *IMF Country Reports*, No. 14/123, International Monetary Fund, Washington, DC.

## Reforms to labour market and social policies will be essential to achieve inclusive and sustainable growth, including a smooth transition towards a greener economy

While a brighter economic outlook will help, it will not solve all of the difficulties that youth face in gaining access to productive and rewarding jobs. Actions are also needed on the side of employment and social policy that will bear immediate fruits, such as providing adequate income support, effective employment services and other active labour market measures. These immediate interventions, in turn, must be buttressed by action which will address structural labour market and social barriers to youth entering productive and rewarding jobs, including policies and institutions that affect the cost of hiring and the ability of employers to adjust flexibly to changing economic circumstances. Attention should also be focused on the most disadvantaged groups of youth, such as the low-skilled, who face the greatest risk of becoming permanently marginalised from the labour market and society.

Reforms to improve labour market and social policies/institutions will also be essential to achieve a smooth transition towards a green economy. Indeed, as this report (and in particular Chapter 5) will demonstrate, a successful transition towards a low-carbon and resource-efficient economy will reshape the labour market in ways that create new opportunities for workers, but also new challenges. Labour market policies have a role to play by facilitating the reallocation of labour across sectors of the economy, while at the same time helping to maximise the benefits from this transition for workers, and assuring a fair sharing of the unavoidable adjustment costs.

### *Demand-side barriers to youth employment need to be removed*

Chapter 2 of the report analyses the demand-side barriers to youth employment in Tunisia such as the cost of hiring (as determined by minimum wages, non-wage costs and collective bargaining institutions) and employment protection legislation. It also discusses policies currently in place to tackle such barriers (including wage subsidies) and offers a range of policy options to create more favourable conditions for employers to hire youth, while still ensuring decent wages as well as an adequate level of protection for workers.

#### *The cost of hiring is raised by sector wage agreements and high public sector pay and benefits*

High labour costs can be a barrier to (formal) employment, especially for those who are low-skilled and lack work experience (including youth). This can result from a mandatory minimum wage that is set at a high rate relative to average earnings and/or from high employer social security contributions that add to wage costs. However, neither minimum wages nor employer social security contributions in Tunisia appear to be set at particularly high levels relative to median wages by OECD standards. Despite this, wage subsidies (including reductions in social security contributions) have been, and continue to be, widely used to address youth unemployment. While there is some evidence that these programmes might be having an effect, it is also clear that they are frequently badly designed and implemented: targeting is poor and deadweight losses are high. To be more effective, the focus of such subsidies should be on those youth encountering the greatest labour market difficulties only. One challenge to youth employment is likely to come from sector wage agreements, which set starting wages considerably above the national minimum wage and as such insufficiently consider the situation of youth, especially the low-skilled and less experienced. The government should also aim to contain, if not reduce, the gap between public and private sector wages and benefits which leads to a rise in reservation wages and results in public sector queuing. This, in turn, renders hiring in the private sector at the going wage rate more difficult (Box 0.1).

**Box 0.1. Key recommendations: Cost of hiring**

Policies should ensure that workers get paid decent wages, but also that the cost of hiring does not hinder demand for the least-skilled and most inexperienced workers, or encourage firms to hire them informally. Therefore:

- While the real value of the minimum wage should not be allowed to erode in years to come, important (real) increases should be avoided in the near future.
- Future sector wage negotiations need to carefully consider the situation of youth, and should set wages for younger workers that more accurately reflect their productivity in order to encourage firms to hire them.
- Differences in remuneration and benefits between the public and private sectors should be reduced, and the urge to use public sector job creation as a means of social appeasement should be resisted.
- Wage subsidies and/or reductions in social security contributions to encourage hiring should be used more sparingly and targeted much more on the disadvantaged, the low-skilled (i.e. non-graduates) and the long-term unemployed.

### *A dual labour market traps youth in precarious working relationships*

Employment protection legislation plays a critical role in shielding workers from the negative consequences of arbitrary actions by employers (e.g. loss of income and depreciation of human capital) and makes firms internalise at least some of the costs of labour turnover (e.g. the public provision of job-search assistance and active labour market programmes). It may also encourage longer working relationships with workers, thereby facilitating industrial stability, the build-up of firm-specific human capital and innovation. When employment protection is too rigid, however, it undermines firms' ability to respond quickly to changes in technology or consumer demand. Overly strict regulations reduce job flows, have a negative impact on employment of some groups of workers (notably youth), encourage labour market duality and hinder productivity and economic growth (Box 0.2).

Tunisia combines strict protection on regular employment with extremely light legislation on temporary work, resulting in a "dual" labour market which traps young workers in precarious employment relationships, reducing their career opportunities and undermining their skills – with wider implications for both job quality and productivity. Employees on regular contracts benefit from high levels of protection against individual dismissal, resulting from: the difficulty of dismissing workers for reasons other than economic or serious misconduct; high severance pay stipulated by collective sector agreements; and high compensation in the case of unfair dismissal combined with uncertainty in jurisprudence around what constitutes fair dismissal. Legislation on temporary contracts, on the other hand, is very lax, and employers can essentially carry out permanent activities through the endless use of fixed-term contracts with different workers, and at a much lower cost. In addition, while temporary agency work (TWA) is authorised in Tunisia, it is only very loosely regulated with very few restrictions imposed on its use. This gap in protection between permanent and temporary contracts has led to the very widespread use of the latter in Tunisia (see Chapter 1). Yet, despite the increase in precariousness that this brings, employment services and social protection to help workers who lose their job smooth consumption and find new work remain inadequate (see Chapter 3).

**Box 0.2. Key recommendations: Employment protection legislation**

The gap in protection between permanent and temporary contracts should be reduced:

- Protection provided by permanent contracts should be reduced. In particular, firing regulations should be eased: i) the definition of fair dismissal should be extended to cover dismissal on capability grounds; ii) in deciding on whether dismissal for economic reasons was fair, legislation should be clarified so that judges stick to assessing whether or not the dismissal was truly for economic reasons or not, rather than calling into question the need for the dismissal from a managerial perspective; and iii) the level of compensation following unfair dismissal should be reduced. The latter recommendation may be particularly important for small firms.
- At the same time, employment protection on fixed-term contracts should be increased, for instance by introducing identical severance pay provisions to those of permanent contracts. Other (but not necessarily mutually exclusive) options include making it more expensive to hire on fixed-term contracts (e.g. through higher social security contributions) or providing financial incentives for conversion to regular contracts.
- The use of non-regular contracts needs to be better regulated, in particular the cases in which Temporary Work Agency (TWA) employment is allowed, as well as the number of renewals of such contracts. The labour code should explicitly require equality of pay and working conditions between TWA and regular workers exercising similar activities.

### *Social and labour market policies have an important role to play in boosting the employability of youth*

While Chapter 2 of this report discusses potential demand-side barriers to youth employment in Tunisia, including the cost of hiring and employment protection legislation, Chapter 3 takes a look at the supply-side of the equation and asks how labour market and social policies can best promote the employability of youth. In this respect, social protection systems can play a key role in providing an adequate safety net for youth who are out of work, not only in shielding them from poverty but also in giving them the means to look for new and productive employment – a process which can further be reinforced by effective public employment services (PES). The chapter also pays considerable attention to the employability of young women, and on how social policies could be improved to help young families better balance work and caring responsibilities, thereby boosting female labour force participation.

#### *Youth are likely to fall through the social safety net, with negative consequences for their employability*

Adequate social protection systems are needed not just in a pursuit of social justice and equity, or to provide all citizens with a minimum acceptable livelihood and protection against risk; but also because they can support the emergence of a dynamic and inclusive labour market, where individuals are empowered and encouraged to pursue productive opportunities when they arise. Even though Tunisia has a comprehensive social insurance system in place, high unemployment and informality rates mean that up to two thirds of youths will not be contributing, and therefore benefiting, from such protection. Even youth who are covered by social insurance are unlikely to receive unemployment benefits in the case of job loss, as eligibility criteria for the current scheme are very strict and therefore very few youth (or even adults) are likely to be entitled. Unconditional cash transfers and free/subsidised health care for the poor exist, but are aimed predominantly at families (and, even then, are poorly targeted). In this context, public works programmes could serve as a useful safety net for the young – however some of these programmes have become defunct or are poorly targeted and/or implemented (Box 0.3).

**Box 0.3. Key recommendations: Social protection**

The government should ensure that youth receive the necessary social protection to enable them to seek, or engage in, productive employment:

- Free basic health care should be provided to all citizens, including the unemployed and those active in the informal sector, and regardless of previous work history and/or social security contributions.
- An unemployment insurance system to help individuals and households smooth consumption when they become unemployed through no fault of their own.
- In addition, in the case of youth (who are less likely to be covered by traditional unemployment insurance systems due to a lack of necessary contributions or sufficiently long employment history), special financial support to assist them in the job-seeking process (a jobseeker's allowance) could be introduced.
- The *Programme National d'Aide aux Familles Nécessiteuses* (PNAFN) – an unconditional cash transfer programme, eligibility for which is not based on work history but instead on income and assets – could play a critical role in offering a basic social safety net of last resort for the poorest in society. However, to in order to fulfil this function adequately, the PNAFN would need to be much better targeted than it currently is. Public works programmes (or even employment guarantees) could be used to provide an essential insurance function to the unemployed, while also providing work experience and training.

Informality in Tunisia is high and reflects a complex set of causes – many of which go beyond the realms of labour market and social policy. The report argues that for many Tunisian youth, informality does not represent a choice and is more likely to be related to a scarcity of formal jobs. Given high levels of unemployment, the bargaining power of employees is weak and they accept whatever job is offered to them. Indeed, youth working informally tend to earn significantly less than their peers in formal jobs. That said, there are also incentives inherent in the Tunisian tax-benefit system that encourage some young people to choose informality. Amongst these incentives are: public sector recruitment rules that have favoured the long-term unemployed (and therefore incited youth to work informally while queuing); high income tax rates; as well as inequalities and gaps between taxes and social security contributions paid on the one hand, and the benefits and public services received, on the other (Box 0.4).

**Box 0.4. Key recommendations: Informality**

The government should put in place a comprehensive and evidence-based strategy to tackle informality. As part of this strategy:

- Better monitoring of compliance with the law is needed, while ensuring that vulnerable workers do not have their livelihoods put at risk by overly vigorous enforcement activities. The focus should not merely be on inspecting and sanctioning, but also on trying to find durable solutions in partnership with the firms/individuals concerned.
- Income tax bands and rates should be revised so that formal work pays and individuals do not seek to remain undeclared because of high marginal tax rates.
- At the same time, the tax regime for the self-employed needs to become less generous and brought more in line with that of dependent workers, in order to reduce the incidence of false self-employment as well as avoid resentment on the part of wage earners who pay much higher taxes.
- The link between taxes/social security contributions and benefits needs to be improved, alongside a more general effort to improve trust in government as well as the quality of public services.

### *Employment services remain incapable of providing youth with the employability support they need*

Effective employment services can play a key role in helping youth into work, both through the delivery of active labour market programmes that can raise the employability of youth as well as through core services like counselling, job search assistance, and matching and placement support. However, very few youth say they found work through ANETI, Tunisia's public employment service (PES). The vast majority of active labour market programmes (ALMPs) provided are aimed at university graduates, which lowers ANETI's attractiveness to non-university graduates. Lower-skilled youth are therefore much less likely to register with the PES. ANETI also lacks the capacity to provide high quality counselling, job search assistance, and matching and placement support. The geographical reach of the service is limited and most staff are submerged in administrative tasks. While laudable efforts have been made after the revolution to increasingly involve non-governmental organisations in the delivery of ALMPs, private employment agencies in Tunisia are prohibited by law (although, in practice, they do exist), which closes one additional avenue for improving capacity and the delivery of employment services (Box 0.5).

**Box 0.5. Key recommendations: Employment services**

The capacity of the public employment service needs to be boosted to allow it to fulfill its key role in supporting youth to find work. This will include:

- Additional investments in ANETI as well as a geographic expansion of its network, but also a better use of its existing resources (e.g. delegating administrative tasks away from counsellors to appropriately qualified staff; virtual access to employment services in more remote areas; and merging the specialised PES offices dedicated to higher education graduates with the standard PES offices).
- Efforts made to work closer with NGOs in the delivery of ALMPs should be stepped up.
- In addition, Tunisia should legalise and regulate private employment services. On the one hand, this would clarify the rights and obligations of all parties involved and thereby reduce abuse. On the other, it would allow ANETI to exploit possible complementarities by entering into public-private partnerships and outsource some of its activities to firms that have the skills and expertise to deliver such services more effectively.
- In both cases, the outsourcing of activities should be accompanied by careful performance management arrangements.

### *Female labour force participation is hampered by a lack of support to help young families balance work and caring responsibilities*

Female labour force participation remains low in Tunisia, despite tremendous progress in recent decades. Given their higher educational attainment, low female labour force participation represents a significant waste of human capital. There is ample scope in Tunisia to improve social policies to help women participate more actively in the labour market and allow them to combine work with caring responsibilities more effectively. Both paid maternity (30 days) and paternity (one day) leave are extremely low in Tunisia and mothers have no additional unpaid leave entitlement – meaning that childbearing is likely to force discontinuities in women's working careers and could lead to their permanent exit from the labour market. In addition, little support exists to help parents meet the costs of childcare and, as a result, a relatively low proportion of young children are enrolled in early childhood education and care (ECEC). Part-time employment is available, but few youths work part-time. Finally, the tax-benefit system has a tendency to cast women in the role of second earners or carers and as such does not help in promoting female labour force participation (e.g. incentives for women, but not men, to work part-time and care for children; extension of family allowances if young women, but not young men, care for their younger siblings; young women, but not young men, considered to be dependent for health insurance purposes until they are married; etc.) (Box 0.6.).

**Box 0.6. Key recommendations: Family policies**

Young families should be given more support to help them juggle work and family responsibilities. In particular:

- Maternity and paternity leave entitlements should be increased. Paid leave is too short in Tunisia, while unpaid leave is inexistent and should be introduced.
- The government should do more to help parents (in particular the poorest) to meet the relatively high costs of childcare, as well as to extend provision.
- Men and women should be given the same incentives to take up paid employment by the tax-benefit system.

## Strengthening the employability of youth will also require a strong VET system and effective entrepreneurship support programmes

Setting Tunisia on a path of more sustainable and inclusive growth also requires the support of both skills and entrepreneurship policies. In Tunisia, like in many other countries, vocational education and training (VET) has for long been a neglected part of the education system and has found itself overshadowed by the higher education sector. Yet the international evidence shows that well-designed vocational programmes, including apprenticeships which link work-based and classroom learning, can equip young people with the skills that employers need, help to match young people to jobs, and form an important part of an effective skills strategy (OECD, 2010; OECD, 2013). In the context of a greening economy, a well-functionning VET system can help young people acquire the necessary skills to seize opportunities in areas where there is a potential for new employment opportunities. Similarly, entrepreneurship can offer an alternative option for young people to enter the labour market. Developing the entrepreneurial skills of youth and providing them with the necessary support in setting up their own business can also help therefore to ensure a more fluid transition into the labour market.

### *The attractiveness of VET needs to be improved and closer links with employers are required*

#### *Tunisia has implemented some important reforms of its VET system*

Chapter 4 of this report shows how Tunisia has undertaken a number of successive reforms of its education and vocational training system since the 1990s, and can therefore build upon a number of strengths in further developing the system. There is a substantial post-secondary VET sector in Tunisia, with more than half of university students taking *licences appliqués* [professional bachelors]. Some VET programmes, such as apprenticeships and courses offered in *alternance* [dual training], boast a strong work-based learning component and there have also been efforts to formalise informal apprenticeship arrangements to make them lead to recognised qualifications. A national qualifications framework has been introduced to make the system more transparent for students, employers and other stakeholders. Efforts have been made to promote the recognition of prior learning, thereby reducing the direct and opportunity costs of formal learning and improving the efficiency of the labour market by making acquired skills more transparent. Finally, through the *chèques de formation* [training cheques] Tunisia has introduced an innovative way to expand provision of VET in the private sector where labour market demand is high.

### *VET is widely seen as a marginal and low status option*

Despite these strengths, Chapter 4 also shows that Tunisia's VET system faces a number of significant challenges, including its lack of attractiveness to prospective students. From a very young age onwards, students are tracked between *collèges techniques* [technical colleges] and general lower secondary education, and the lack of articulation arrangements offer little opportunity of transition between the two systems later on. This significantly reduces the attractiveness of VET to prospective students, particularly in a context where academic qualifications are widely perceived as leading to better employment outcomes, including much-coveted public sector jobs, and VET is primarily seen as a fall-back option for the academically weaker students. At upper secondary level, the VET sector remains small, covering only around 10% of the cohort and, while the post-secondary VET sector is more developed, the *licences appliquées* [professional bachelors] lack a work-based learning component. In addition, careers guidance is a neglected area, meaning that students are often not well-informed about what VET programmes offer. More generally, inadequate monitoring and evaluation mechanisms hinder the ability of policy makers to make evidence-based interventions to improve the quality and attractiveness of the system.

### *Links with employers are weak*

Another major weakness of the VET system in Tunisia is the generally weak link with employers and social partners, who are not systematically involved in the development of course content. In addition, employers play only a limited role in determining the number of training places in different institutions and at the different levels, meaning that the mix of provision is determined primarily by existing capacity and, to a lesser extent, student preferences. This lack of employer engagement is partly the result of a highly centralised approach to managing the VET system. As a consequence, some employers have voiced concern about their ability to recruit individuals with specific skills – an issue which might grow in importance as Tunisia moves towards a greener economy (see below). Indeed, the shift towards greener production practices will lead to changes in skill requirements across the economy. These green skills that new labour market entrants will require largely can be acquired by incremental enrichment of established vocational education and training programmes, combined with top-up training, the latter tailored to the needs of experienced workers (Box 0.7).

**Box 0.7. Key recommendations: Vocational education and training**

The VET system should be made more attractive to students and the social partners involved more closely:

- The lower secondary technical track should be integrated into general lower secondary education.
- VET at the upper secondary level should be strategically expanded, linked to strong quality assurance mechanisms.
- Mandatory work-based learning should be extended to the *licences appliquées*.
- Careers guidance should be introduced in all lower secondary schools and better data should be made available to support students' choice.
- The articulation between VET qualifications and academic programmes should be improved (in particular between the BTS and the *licences appliquées*).
- Stronger mechanisms are needed to engage employers and achieve a better balance between existing capacity, student preferences and employer needs in determining course provision.
- The *Centre National de Formation de Formateurs et d'Ingénierie de Formation* (CENAFFIF) [National Centre for Training of Trainers and Pedagogy] should review all curricula from the point of view of green employment, seeking to introduce appropriate green skills and through this the adaptability of the workforce.
- Set up a self-evaluation monitoring approach to better inform the decision-making process.

## *Entrepreneurship support is relatively well-developed, yet more can be done*

### *The basic building blocks are in place*

In response to growing labour market challenges, entrepreneurship has become a policy priority in Tunisia in recent years and a relatively well-developed support system is already in place, with the provision of information, training, finance and follow-up services in the first two years of operation. Entrepreneurship training and support is provided in both VET and higher education, and programmes also exist to help the unemployed set up their own business. As discussed in Chapter 4 of this report, a number of international projects carried out in the 1990s and 2000s left a solid base of support structures and institutions in place for entrepreneurship training within the VET system. Since 2008, entrepreneurial competences and skills have been key learning outcomes of formal education in Tunisia and students are typically introduced to entrepreneurship during their training. Similarly, in higher education, entrepreneurship education is already an important feature of the activities of institutions, who offer start-up support activities through, for example, university incubators (OECD, 2012b). Beyond the education system, additional mechanisms are in place to assist the unemployed set up their own business – notably the entrepreneurship support delivered by ANETI (Tunisia's public employment service) through its *Programme d'Appui aux Promoteurs des Petites Entreprises* (PAPPE) [Small Entrepreneur Support Programme] which provides jobseekers who want to set up their own business with the necessary information, training, advice and counselling, as well as financial support (Chapter 3).

### *Further strengthening of the system is needed with a clear strategic vision*

There are a number of aspects of the entrepreneurship support system in Tunisia where there is room for improvement. In particular, learning materials are in urgent need of updating and the government should strive to equalise the quality and accessibility of such training across regions. Co-ordination between training centres and business start-up support structures should be improved, and the duplication that currently exists in the provision of entrepreneurship support services addressed. This wastes scarce resources and makes it more difficult for young people to understand where they can get the necessary support. For business start-ups, more support should be available in the medium- to long-term (e.g. continued coaching) so as to raise survival rates, and potential female entrepreneurs should be given additional support to realise their business ideas. There is little agreement on the objectives of entrepreneurship support: for most, the promotion of self-employment is the ultimate goal, while the enhancement of capabilities and competences to recognise opportunities and turn them into actions are not considered to be an objective. More generally, the development and provision of entrepreneurship support services would benefit from a general strategy that clearly defines roles as well as short- and long-run objectives (Box 0.8). Such a strategy should be orientated towards sectors where there are opportunities for growth, for example in the transition to a green economy.

**Box 0.8. Key recommendations: Entrepreneurship support**

Tunisia should maintain and fine-tune its efforts to support young entrepreneurs as an important tool for tackling youth unemployment. In particular:

- A national strategy should be developed to guide the improvement of entrepreneurship support services in VET and higher education, clearly defining roles as well as short- and long-run objectives, and encompassing different levels of support for different groups of potential entrepreneurs.
- The various structures (*Espaces Entreprendre*, business centres, *Espaces Tremplin*, incubators) providing entrepreneurship support services should be rationalised in an effort to reduce duplication and get the most out of the scarce resources available.
- Entrepreneurship training should go beyond the provision of introductory modules on entrepreneurship to support learners in developing entrepreneurial mind-sets and increasing their opportunities to practice entrepreneurial behaviours.
- More support should be made available to trainers by making entrepreneurship training more available and by improving teaching material. Training for trainers should be available as part of ongoing career development training as well as initial training for trainers. This should be complemented by creating mechanisms that facilitate the exchange of good practices among trainers and by them with additional supports such as teaching manuals.
- For business start-ups, more support should be available in the medium- to long-term (e.g. continued coaching) so as to raise survival rates.
- Given the additional barriers they face as well as their low labour force participation rates, potential female entrepreneurs should be given additional and targeted support. Setting up a single body responsible for co-ordinating the promotion of women's enterprise development could help in this respect. Better family policies, as outlined above, would also help in promoting female entrepreneurship in Tunisia.

## The greening of the economy offers opportunities to create jobs for youth, but also brings additional challenges

Chapter 5 of this report shows that the greening of the economy, although not a major deciding factor in addressing youth unemployment, nonetheless offers opportunities for the creation of new jobs – particularly in specific areas like energy, waste and recycling, tourism, agriculture, construction, and innovation/clean technology. Indeed, given the new and emerging skills requirements that these will bring, youth may be particularly well-placed to gain from such new opportunities given the comparative advantage that their more recent education and training will give them over more experienced workers. Capitalising on such opportunities will require an overall strategy which affects all ministries, meaning further elaboration of the existing *Stratégie Nationale du Développement Durable* [National Sustainable Development Strategy] and better clarity regarding institutional co-ordination.

However, the greening of the economy will also bring important challenges that need to be overcome. While additional employment may be created in certain sectors, some jobs will become obsolete and the skill requirements of others will change. This implies that, on the whole, the effects on employment from a transition to a green economy are likely to be relatively small (OECD, 2011; OECD, 2012a; OECD, 2014b), while the reallocation of jobs across sectors will be much more important. Furthermore, since the most affected industries tend to have the highest shares of low-skilled workers, the greening of the economy will also entail important distributional concerns, as specific segments of the economy and their workers will bear a disproportionate part of the adjustment costs.

These challenges clearly reinforce the central policy messages of the present report: to successfully strengthen the employability of youth in the context of a transition to a green economy, a well-functioning labour market will be an essential prerequisite, buttressed by effective social safety nets, employment services and activation policies that work, as well as a VET system that is able to adjust to current skills needs and anticipate skills demands, and entrepreneurship policies that help individuals spot and capitalise on new opportunities. In addition, a key ingredient needed to put such a policy package in place will be constructive social dialogue, which will also ensure that unavoidable adjustments costs in the transition to a green economy are shared fairly (Box 0.9).

### Box 0.9. Key recommendations: Opportunities for the creation of green jobs

- There are a number of specific areas where action could be taken to improve green employment and entrepreneurship, specifically:
  - ***Energy.*** The existing and successful Prosol initiative could be continued and expanded to other areas of renewable energy. Barriers to the production of energy at a municipal level need to be considered.
  - ***Innovation and a clean-tech cluster.*** Further actions can be taken to encourage graduate entrepreneurship, and to seek spin-outs from universities and research institutes. Opportunities to develop or attract businesses connected with existing green investments need to be explored more fully.
  - ***Waste and recycling.*** Greater involvement of social enterprises in recycling and reuse could both increase employment and be used for training unemployed youth. Issues related to the legal status of non-profit organisations need to be finally resolved.

**Box 0.9. Key recommendations: Opportunities for the creation of green jobs** *(cont.)*

- ***Tourism.*** Efforts to make existing tourism more sustainable need to be reinforced in the light of external pressures. Development of eco-tourism can bring employment to more remote areas, but requires better organisation and an overall strategy.
- ***Agriculture.*** Organic agriculture represents an opportunity for both the environment and employment. Tunisia has an existing organic sector, but with appropriate public support its size and export potential could be increased.
- ***Construction.*** Although there is likely to be little net growth in employment in the construction sector as a result of green growth, policies to upgrade skills will play a key role, while better management of resources (recycling of waste, and improving energy efficiency) will generate positive feedback effects on jobs creation in other sectors.

- Maximising opportunities from the transition to a green economy will require an overall strategy which affects all ministries, meaning further elaboration of the existing National Sustainable Development Strategy and better clarity regarding institutional co-ordination.
- It will also require looking at ways to build an effective social dialogue, which will have a key role to play in developing green growth policies and smoothly adapting labour markets to this emerging reality.

## Developing a successful policy response will depend critically on the effective co-ordination between different stakeholders

One key obstacle identified by this report is the extent of fragmentation of responsibility and the challenges that this will bring for co-ordinating an effective policy response to the youth employment problem in Tunisia. Such co-ordination problems affect labour market, VET, entrepreneurship and sustainable development policy alike.

### *Labour market policy is spread across two different ministries*

In Tunisia, responsibility for labour market policy is spread across two different ministries, with very little co-ordination between the two. The *Ministère de la Formation Professionnelle et de l'Emploi* (MFPE) [Ministry of Vocational Education and Employment] is responsible for the public employment service (ANETI) and active labour market programmes, including entrepreneurship support. However, many of the policies and institutions that determine the functioning of the labour market are under the responsibility of the *Ministère des Affaires Sociales* [Ministry of Social Affairs] that uses these tools for a very different purpose. Minimum wage policy, unemployment benefits, social security contributions, collective sector agreements and the Labour Code are all under the auspices of the Ministry of Social Affairs, yet have important implications for the functioning of the labour market. If employment is to be treated as a key government priority, then it will need a whole-of-government approach and, in particular, close collaboration between the two aforementioned ministries, so that both social and labour market policies are closely attuned to one another and work in harmony to achieve the desired goals.

### *Governance of the VET system is highly centralised, yet very fragmented*

The effectiveness of the vocational education and training system in Tunisia is reduced by both its high level of centralisation as well as its fragmentation. Indeed, the governance of the VET system is very centralised (design of the programme, curriculum development, and implementation) – which reduces the involvement of the local authorities in the management and administration of the system. In addition, at the central level, many different ministries are responsible for different aspects of the system, while responsibilities for course design and delivery are frequently delegated to separate bodies/institutions. Such fragmentation results in a lack of clarity for both students and employers, complicates the issue of articulation and transitions between different institutions and programmes, and generates obstacles to developing a coherent strategy to address the overall needs of the labour market.

### *There are also challenges in co-ordinating entrepreneurship activities*

There are a large number of ministries and agencies involved in supporting entrepreneurship in Tunisia, which creates a challenge for implementing and co-ordinating activities. For example, entrepreneurship support services in Tunisia are provided by: *Centres d'Affaires* [Business Centres], *pépinières* [incubators], *Espaces Tremplin* [Springboard to Entrepreneurship] and *Espaces Entreprendre* [Entrepreneurship Spaces] – but in practice there is often very little difference in the support provided by these different structures and there are no mechanisms ensuring that young entrepreneurs get appropriate support at the appropriate time. In addition, there are very few examples of good linkages between providers of training and business start-up support structures, meaning that learners generally have a low level of awareness about all of the support that is available to them.

### *Implementing the Sustainable Development Strategy will require effective co-ordination*

As mentioned above, maximising opportunities from the transition to a green economy will require an overall strategy which affects all ministries and greater clarity regarding institutional co-ordination. Indeed, the transition towards a green economy will involve a number of important trade-offs between different aspects of sustainable development (economic growth, environmental protection and social development) that need to be recognised explicitly and require appropriate mechanisms (stakeholder for a, inter-ministerial committees) where they can be discussed and resolved (Box 0.10).

**Box 0.10. Key recommendations: Policy co-ordination**

- The MFPE and MAS should work more closely together, in particular in deciding on " social" policies that may affect the workings of the labour market, including: minimum wage policy, unemployment benefits, social security contributions, collective sector agreements and the Labour Code.
- A co-ordination body should be set up to reduce the fragmentation of VET across ministries and improve the responsiveness of the system.
- A more federated governance structure for the VET sector should be envisaged.
- The MFPE should work with other ministries, ATFP and ANETI to improve the co-ordination of public business development services and strengthen linkages with training centres and universities.
- Appropriate co-ordination mechanisms and institutions should be set up to guarantee the effective implementation of the Sustainable Development Strategy.

## Investing in youth must be a key policy objective for achieving better long-term economic and social outcomes in Tunisia, even though given the tight fiscal space, difficult choices will need to be made

Investing in youth and giving them a better start in the world of work should remain a key policy objective for Tunisia. Otherwise, there is a high risk of persistence, or even growth, in the hard-core group of those who are left behind, facing poor employment and earning prospects. While the present report aims to be comprehensive in its analysis and concrete measures put forward, these have to be addressed taking into account the limited fiscal space within which Tunisia currently finds itself. That said, some of the proposals made have the potential to generate important savings (e.g., better targeting of wage subsidies; rationalisation of entrepreneurship support programmes; abolition of the dedicated public employment service for university graduates; etc.) which could be re-directed into areas where new investment is required. In addition, many recommendations are costless, including: employment protection legislation reforms; changes in governance and co-ordination arrangements; the legalisation and regulation of private employment services; greater engagement of employers in the VET system; etc. Some elements of prioritisation will nevertheless be necessary where additional resource is required. With this in mind, the short-run priority should be to lay a basic protection floor for the large numbers of youth out of work, which can be best achieved through the extension and better targeting of unconditional cash transfers (PNAFN), as well as the revival of public work programmes. At the same time, the long-run employment prospects of youth need to be strengthened, so that they will be in a position to take advantage of the opportunities arising as the economic recovery gathers pace. Investments to strengthen and expand the VET system will be essential in this regard, as well as maintaining a strategic focus on the transition towards "green growth".

## Note

1. Gallup measures life satisfaction by asking respondents to place the status of their lives on a "ladder" scale with steps numbered from 0 to 10, where 0 indicates the worst possible life and 10 the best possible life. Individuals who rate their current lives a "7" or higher AND their future an "8" or higher are "thriving." Individuals are "suffering" if they report their current AND future lives as a "4" and lower. All other individuals are "struggling".

## *References*


AfDB – African Development Bank, and IOM – International Organization for Migration (2013), *Migration of Tunisians to Lybia: Dynamics, Challenges and Prospects*, International Organization for Migration and African Development Bank, Tunis.

Boughzala, M. and M.T. Hamdi (2014), "Promoting Inclusive growth in Arab Countries: Rural and Regional Development and Inequality in Tunisia", *Global Economy and Development Working Papers*, No. 71, Brookings, Washington, DC.

Ghali, S., S. Mouley and S. Rezgui (2014), *Potentiel de Croissance et Création d'Emplois*, Institut Arabe des Chefs d'Entreprises.

ILO – International Labour Organization (2011), *Tunisia: A New Social Contract for Fair and Equitable Growth*, Studies on Growth with Equity, International Labour Organization, Geneva.

IMF – International Monetary Fund (2014), "Tunisia: Third Review Under the Stand-by Arrangement, Request for Modification of Performance Criteria and Waivers of Applicability", *IMF Country Reports*, No. 14/123, International Monetary Fund, Washington, DC.

INS (2012), *Mesure de la Pauvreté: Des Inégalités et de la Polarisation en Tunisie 2000-2010* [Measuring Poverty: Inequalities and Polarisation in Tunisia 2000-2010], Institut National de la Statistique, Tunis.

OECD (2014a), "Tunisia: Better Policies Series", OECD Publishing, Paris, forthcoming.

OECD (2014b), *Greener Skills and Jobs*, OECD Publishing, Paris, http://dx.doi.org/10.1787/9789264208704-en.

OECD (2013), "The OECD Action Plan for Youth – Giving Youth a Better Start in the Labour Market", Free Brochure, OECD Publishing, Paris, June, www.oecd.org/els/emp/Youth-Action-Plan.pdf.

OECD (2012a), "What Green Growth Means for Workers and Labour Market Policies: An Initial Assessment", *OECD Employment Outlook 2012*, OECD Publishing, Paris, http://dx.doi.org/10.1787/empl_outlook-2012-en.

OECD (2012b), "Promoting Graduate Entrepreneurship in Tunisian Universities", *OECD Local Economic and Employment Development (LEED) Working Papers*, No. 2012/18, OECD Publishing, Paris, http://dx.doi.org/10.1787/5k913fsjhkd8-en.

OECD (2011), *Towards Green Growth*, OECD Green Growth Studies, OECD Publishing, Paris, http://dx.doi.org/10.1787/9789264111318-en.

OECD (2010), *Learning for Jobs*, OECD Publishing, Paris, http://dx.doi.org/10.1787/9789264087460-en.

World Bank (2012), *Interim Strategy Note for the Republic of Tunisia for the Period FY13-14*, Report No. 67692-TN, World Bank, Tunis.

# *Chapter 1*

# Youth employment in Tunisia: The challenge

*This chapter provides an overview of youth in the labour market in Tunisia and highlights some of the key challenges facing policy makers in the country. The labour market has had significant difficulty absorbing large and increasingly educated cohorts of young people, resulting in particularly low employment rates which are the combination of both high unemployment and low participation rates. School-to-work transitions are challenging and one in four young people are neither in employment, nor in education or training (NEET). Women and young people from the more deprived Centre West and Southern regions are particularly at risk. Even when Tunisian youth are in employment, it is frequently in poor quality jobs: informal employment is common, affecting an estimated one in two young workers, and the share of temporary contracts is high. Furthermore, working hours are long and the incidence of low-pay amongst youth is common.*

The statistical data for Israel are supplied by and under the responsibility of the relevant Israeli authorities. The use of such data by the OECD is without prejudice to the status of the Golan Heights, East Jerusalem and Israeli settlements in the West Bank under the terms of international law.

## Introduction

With 25% of youth (aged 15-24)[1,2] neither in employment, nor in education or training (NEET), the challenge facing policy makers in Tunisia is immense. Yet this figure understates the true scale of the problem since, even where youth are in employment, the quality of their jobs often leaves much to be desired: an estimated 50% of employed youth in Tunisia work informally – with little, or no, protection and employment security, while many others work on temporary contracts. The employment situation of youth in Tunisia therefore presents a true social tragedy that urgently needs to be addressed. This chapter provides an overview of youth in the labour market in Tunisia, covering basic demographic and labour market indicators, but also measures of the quality of jobs and a detailed analysis of school-to-work transitions. The chapter takes an internationally comparative perspective, with OECD countries as well as selected large emerging economies and MENA countries as comparators. In addition to the findings outlined above, this chapter shows that:

- While high, the share of youth in the working age population is falling – which could release at least some pressure on the youth labour market in years to come.
- Youth in Tunisia face both high inactivity (64.9%) and unemployment (37.6%) rates.
- Young women (41.8%), graduates (62.3%) and those from the poorer Centre West and Southern regions are particularly likely to be unemployed.
- Although university graduates have high unemployment rates, they are significantly less likely to be NEET. In absolute numbers, they also represent a relatively small share of the total unemployed youth.
- Long-term unemployment is also high, and affects more than one in three unemployed youth.
- School-to-work transitions in Tunisia are a challenge, and many youth (particularly women and those from the less advantaged regions) never transition into employment.
- In addition to high informality rates and a large share of temporary employment, youth experience low pay and long working hours.

## Youth make up a large, but falling share of the working age population

Over a quarter of Tunisia's working age population (ages 15-64) is young (15-24) compared to under a fifth on average among OECD countries (Figure 1.1). While the share of youth in the working age population in Tunisia is expected to fall rapidly to just under 20% by 2050, this will still be relatively high by OECD standards (where it is expected to be 17.8%) although slightly lower than what is forecast for the largest emerging economies (20.5%), and certainly at the low end for the selected MENA countries included in Figure 1.1.

**Figure 1.1. Share of youth in the working age population, Tunisia, OECD, selected emerging and MENA countries, 2010-50**

Population aged 15-24 as a percentage of population aged 15-64

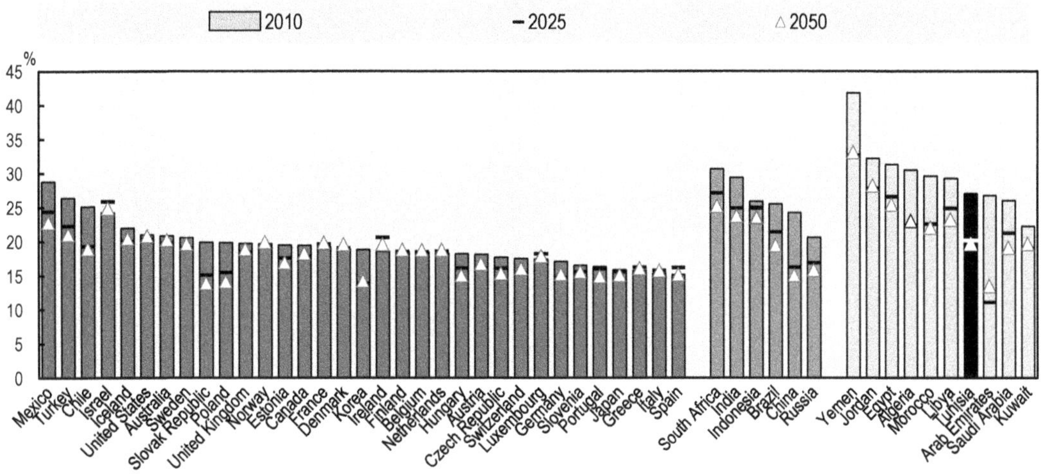


*Source*: OECD calculations based on United Nations, Department of Economic and Social Affairs, Population Division (2011), *World Population Prospects: The 2012 Revision.*

Tunisia's rapid demographic transition can be traced back to family planning policies introduced in the 1960s (Haouas et al., 2012) which contributed to the crude birth rate falling from 50.3 in 1961 to 18.6 in 2011 (World Development Indicators). At the same time, and as a result of advances in health and education, life expectancy rose from 42.6 to 74.8 years over the same period (World Development Indicators). As a consequence of these developments, the proportion of youth in the working age population reached a peak in the early 1980s and has been falling ever since (Figure 1.2). The proportion of youth in the working age population is expected to reach a historical low in 2020 (at just over 20%) and remain relatively stable afterwards. The continued fall in the share (and number) of youth in the working age population between now and 2020 will ease some of the pressure on the labour market for youth in years to come.

**Figure 1.2. Share of youth in the working age population, Tunisia, 1950-2050[a]**

Population aged 15-24 as a percentage of population aged 15-64

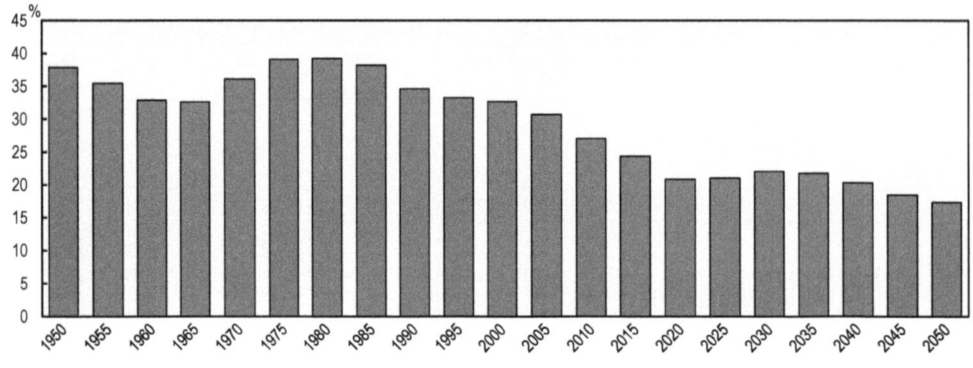


*a)* Medium-fertility assumption: total fertility is assumed to converge eventually toward a level of 1.85 children per woman.

*Source:* OECD calculations based on United Nations, Department of Economic and Social Affairs, Population Division (2011), *World Population Prospects: The 2012 Revision.*

## Tunisian youth fare poorly in the labour market

The youth employment rate in Tunisia is particularly low. In 2012, only 21.9% of youth were in employment, compared to 37.8% across the OECD (Figure 1.3). This low employment rate cannot just be attributed to the high share of youth in the working age population. Indeed, Turkey and Mexico, countries with very similar shares of youth in the working age population, have youth employment rates of 31.5% and 43.1%, respectively. In Tunisia, youth face both a high inactivity rate (64.9% compared to 53.6% across the OECD) as well as a high unemployment rate (37.6% compared to 20.3% across the OECD). Amongst OECD countries, only Greece and Spain fare worse than Tunisia on both employment and unemployment indicators and, among the large emerging economies included in Figure 1.3, only South Africa has poorer labour market outcomes for youth than Tunisia. Even by MENA standards, Tunisia performs poorly, particularly with regards to youth unemployment rates.

In the wake of the global economic and financial crisis and the revolution of January 2011, and exacerbated by the crises in neighbouring countries (especially Libya), the labour market in Tunisia deteriorated rapidly after 2010 – particularly for youth. Youth unemployment rates hovered just below the 30% mark in the six years running up to the revolution, but soared to over 42% in 2011 (Figure 1.4).[3] Since then, they have started declining somewhat again (down to nearly 38% in 2012,The unemployment rate of prime age workers also increased in the year after the revolution, but much less so, while the unemployment rate of older workers remained low. The inactivity rates of all age groups remained mostly unaffected while the employment rates experienced small dips – although again this fall was greater for youth than it was for the other age groups.

**Figure 1.3. Labour force status of youth (15-24), Tunisia, OECD, selected emerging and MENA countries, 2012[a]**

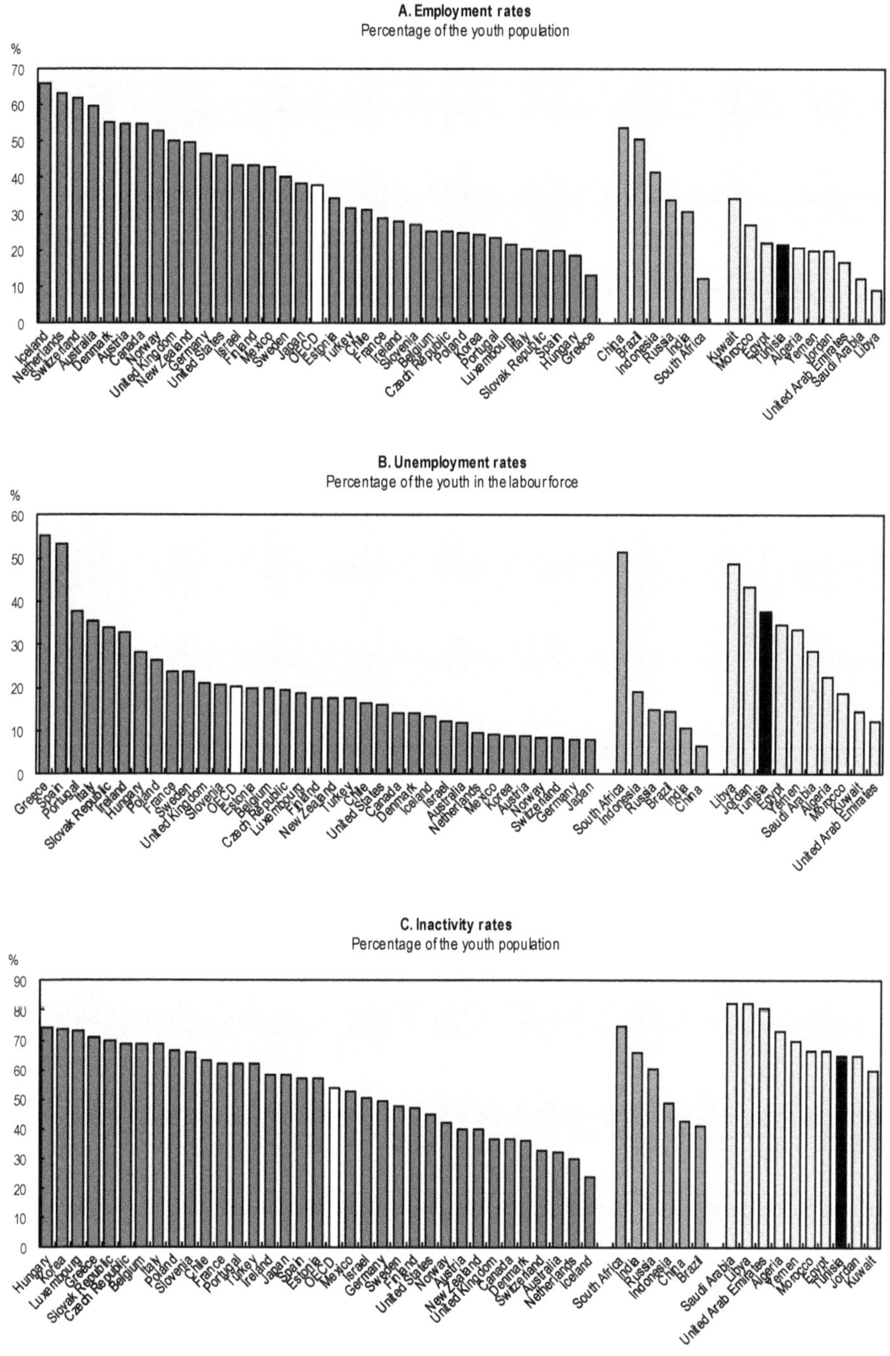


*a)* Data for Jordan correspond to 2004; United Arab Emirates, 2008; China and Yemen, 2010; Algeria and Kuwait, 2011. The "working age population aged 15-24" needed to calculate employment and inactivity rates for Kuwait and UAE corresponds to United Nation estimates (2010 for Kuwait; the average between 2005 and 2010 for UAE).

*Source*: *OECD Employment and Labour Market Statistics*, www.oecd-ilibrary.org/employment/data/oecd-employment-and-labour-market-statistics_lfs-data-en; *ILO Annual Indicators Dataset*, 1% sample of Census data for China, OECD estimates based on labour force survey for Indonesia.

**Figure 1.4. Labour force indicators by age group, Tunisia, 2005-12**

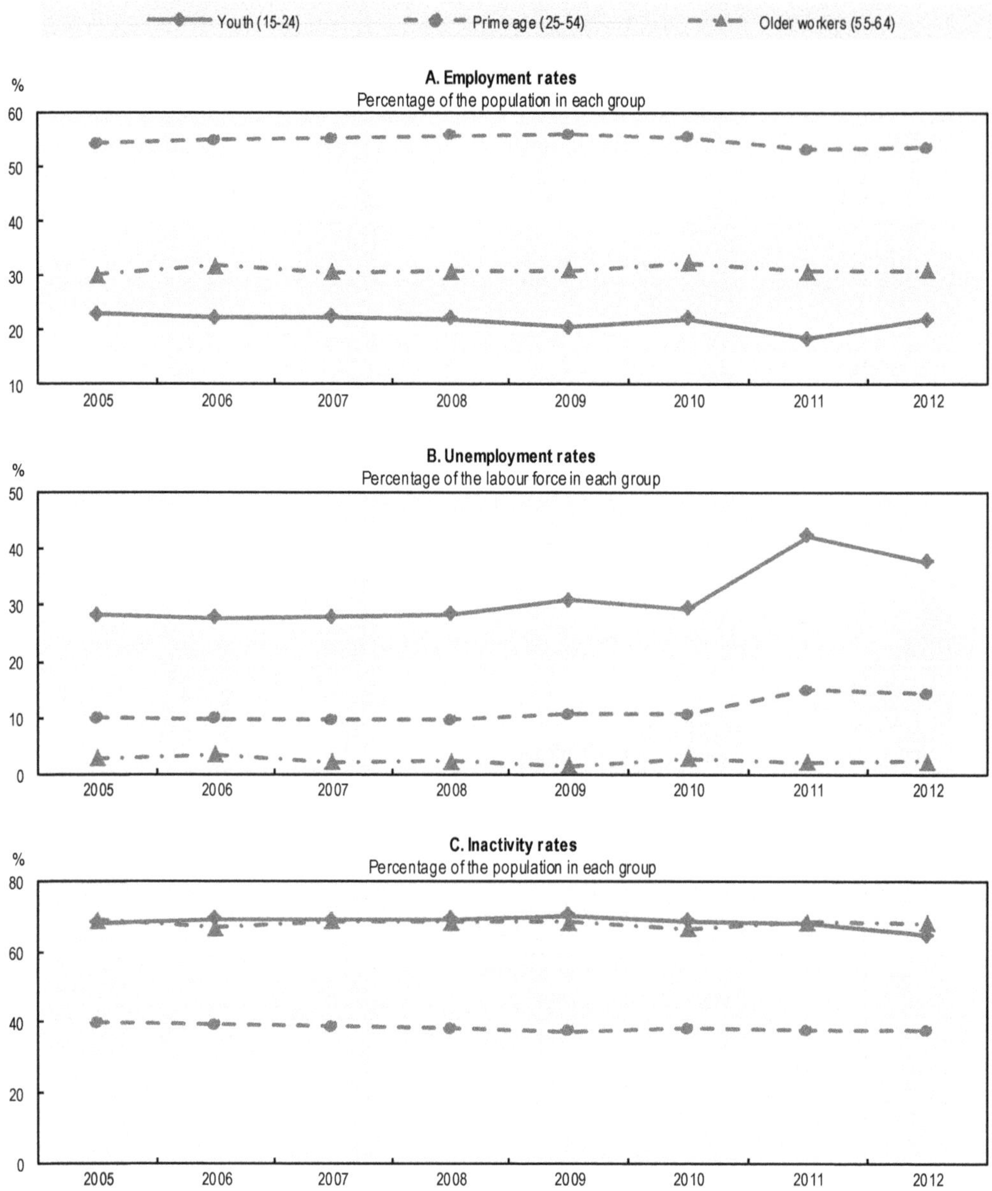


*Source*: OECD calculations based on the *Enquête Nationale sur la Population et l'Emploi* (ENPE) [National Population and Employment Survey].

## Some youth fare far worse than others

Labour market outcomes are not equal across groups of Tunisian youth (Figure 1.5). Importantly, young women have considerably lower employment rates than men (13.3% versus 30.3%) resulting primarily from higher inactivity rates (77.2% versus 52.9%) – although their unemployment rates are also higher (41.8% versus 37.7%). In addition, the labour market varies significantly by region, with outcomes far worse for young people living in the more deprived Centre West and Southern regions of the country.

**Figure 1.5. Youth labour market outcomes by socio-demographic characteristics, Tunisia, 2012**

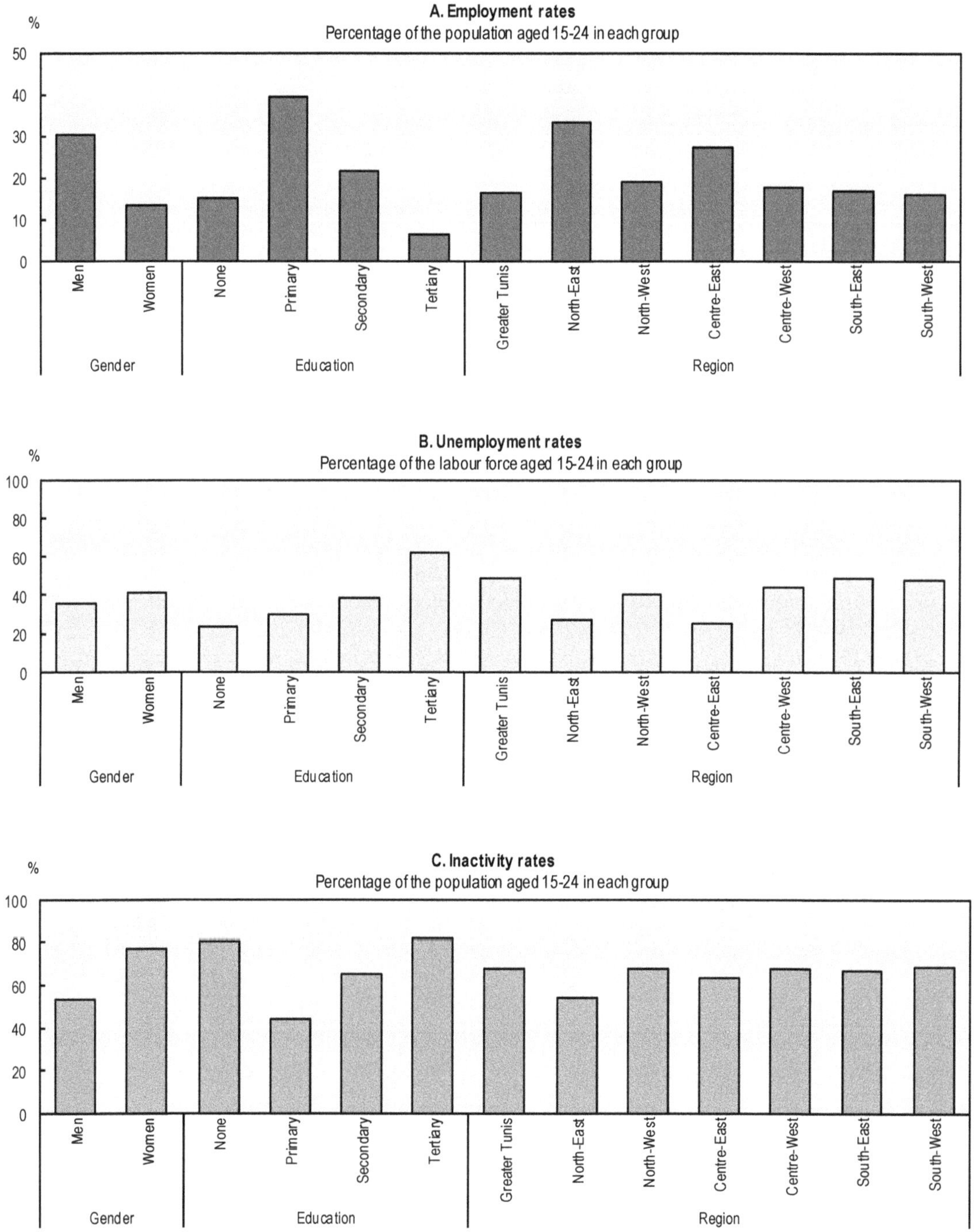


*Source*: OECD calculations based on the *Enquête Nationale sur la Population et l'Emploi* (ENPE) [National Population and Employment Survey].

One of the most striking aspects of the youth labour market in Tunisia is how labour market outcomes deteriorate with educational attainment – a feature it shares with many other Arab countries (Assaad, 2013). In particular, youth with tertiary education face a much higher risk of unemployment than their peers with lower educational attainment: in 2012, 62.3% of young tertiary graduates were unemployed, up from 47.1% in 2005.[4] The graduate unemployment rate has increased rapidly over the past decade, closely mirroring the surge in the number of students graduating with tertiary education qualifications (see Box 1.1 on the issue of over-qualification in Tunisia.[5]

**Box 1.1. Over-qualification and skills shortages in Tunisia**

An over-supply of university graduates in relation to demand may be expected to lead to a considerable degree of over-qualification as highly educated young people are forced to accept positions that require less education (at least in the short-run, before firms have had the chance to adapt their productive processes to make the best use of the available human capital). However, convincing evidence of over-qualification in Tunisia is lacking. When young people are asked directly about whether they feel over-qualified for the job they perform, 75% of youth feel that "their past studies/training are useful/appropriate for carrying out their current job", whilst only 28% self-report as over-qualified and 5% say they "have gaps in [their] knowledge and skills [...] need additional training" (OECD calculations based on the ILO's School-to-Work Transition Survey for Tunisia, 2013). This level of over-qualification is consistent with estimates obtained using different methods (Ministère de l'Emploi et de l'Insertion Professionnelle des Jeunes and World Bank, 2009). Although comparisons with other countries are difficult because of differences in methodology, the extent of over-qualification in Tunisia appears on the low side compared to estimates for Europe and other OECD countries (Quintini, 2011a; Quintini, 2011b). One possible explanation for this might be that, despite high levels of education, the quality of education received by Tunisian youth is relatively low so that the actual skills possessed by youth do not adequately reflect their level of qualification. In other words: despite being over-qualified on paper, they are in fact well-matched to their current jobs on the basis of the skills they possess.

On the other hand, the over-supply of university graduates combined with high unemployment rates imply that employers have little difficulty filling vacancies. Evidence from the public employment service (ANETI) indicates that vacancies are quickly filled: about 87% of all job vacancies published throughout 2013 had been filled, while only 5% were still open (the remaining 7% having been cancelled/suspended). Among the vacancies that were filled, over 85% were filled within one month of posting. Evidence from an employer survey corroborates the conclusion that skills shortages may not be a significant issue in Tunisia: only 6% of employers said they had any difficulties in the recruitment of certain professions in 2010 (CRES and ILO, 2012). Although methodological differences exist, the Manpower Group (2013) Talent Shortage Survey suggests that, in OECD countries, around 31% of employers report such recruitment difficulties.

Despite these higher unemployment rates, it should be remembered that university graduates represent a minority of the young unemployed: in 2012, only 15.1% of unemployed youth had a tertiary qualification, compared to 23.7% and 60.0% with primary and secondary qualifications, respectively. As the next section will show, university graduates are also significantly less likely to be neither in employment, nor in education or training (NEET) than those with less education. Furthermore, despite high unemployment rates, research on the returns to education indicates that obtaining a tertiary qualification in Tunisia is still worth the investment (Barouni and Broecke, forthcoming).[6] Finally, although the oversupply of university graduates may be one reason why their unemployment rates are higher, there is also some evidence that an element of choice may be involved as young people queue for better rewarded public sector jobs (see Chapter 3 for a discussion of this issue).

## A high proportion of youth is neither in employment, nor in education or training (NEET)

The NEET rate offers a much better insight into how well countries manage the transition between school and work – better than unemployment and inactivity rates, which do not explicitly take into account the proportion of youth studying. The high unemployment and low labour force participation rates of Tunisian youth discussed in the previous sections translate into a very high NEET rate: in 2010, approximately one in four Tunisian youth were NEET (Figure 1.6).[7] This compares to an OECD average of 12.6%. Amongst OECD countries, only Turkey has a higher NEET rate than Tunisia, however South Africa and Egypt fare even worse.

**Figure 1.6. NEET rates, Tunisia, OECD, selected emerging and MENA countries, 2012[a]**

Percentage of the population aged 15-24

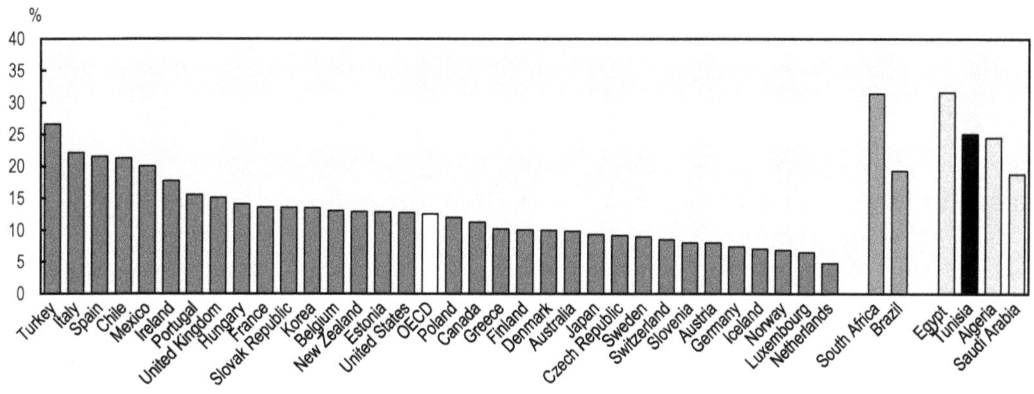


*a)* Data for Algeria and Tunisia correspond to 2010.

*Source*: OECD (2014), *Education at a Glance – OECD Indicators*, http://dx.doi.org/10.1787/eag-2014-en; *ILO Annual Indicators Dataset* for Algeria, Egypt, Saudi Arabia and South Africa. For Tunisia, OECD calculations based on the *Enquête Nationale sur la Population et l'Emploi* (ENPE) [National Population and Employment Survey].

Not surprisingly, NEET rates also vary significantly across groups of young people (Figure 1.7). Nearly one in three young women in Tunisia are neither in employment, nor in education or training, and the NEET rate is also significantly higher in the Centre West (37.9%) than it is in Greater Tunis (19.3%). It has already been pointed out that, although youth with tertiary qualifications have the highest unemployment rates, they actually represent only a small part of the total unemployed youth population. In addition, youth with tertiary qualifications have a significantly lower NEET rate (16.2%) than youth with no qualifications at all (79.7%) – partly reflecting the fact that they are considerably more likely to continue studying.

**Figure 1.7. NEET rate by socio-demographic characteristics, Tunisia, 2010**

Percentage of the population aged 15-24 in each group

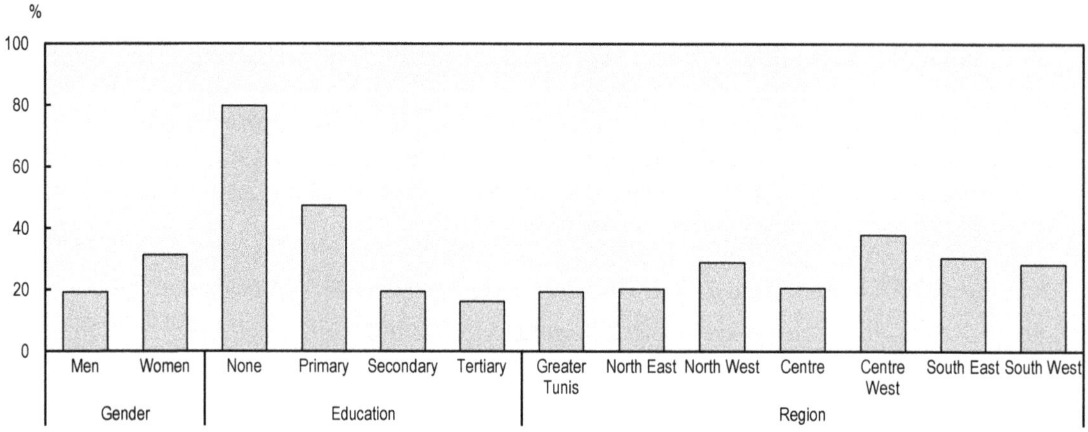


*Source*: OECD calculations based on the *Enquête Nationale sur la Population et l'Emploi* (ENPE) [National Population and Employment Survey].

## More than one in three unemployed youths have been unemployed for over a year

Long-term unemployment (one year or more) affects 36.3% of unemployed youth in Tunisia (Figure 1.8). This is considerably higher than what is observed in OECD countries on average (22.4%) – but in some countries the incidence of long-term unemployment is much higher still (particularly in MENA countries, but also in some large emerging economies and OECD countries).

**Figure 1.8. Incidence of long-term unemployment,[a] youth aged 15-24, Tunisia, OECD, selected emerging and MENA countries, 2012[b]**

Percentage of youth (15-24) unemployed

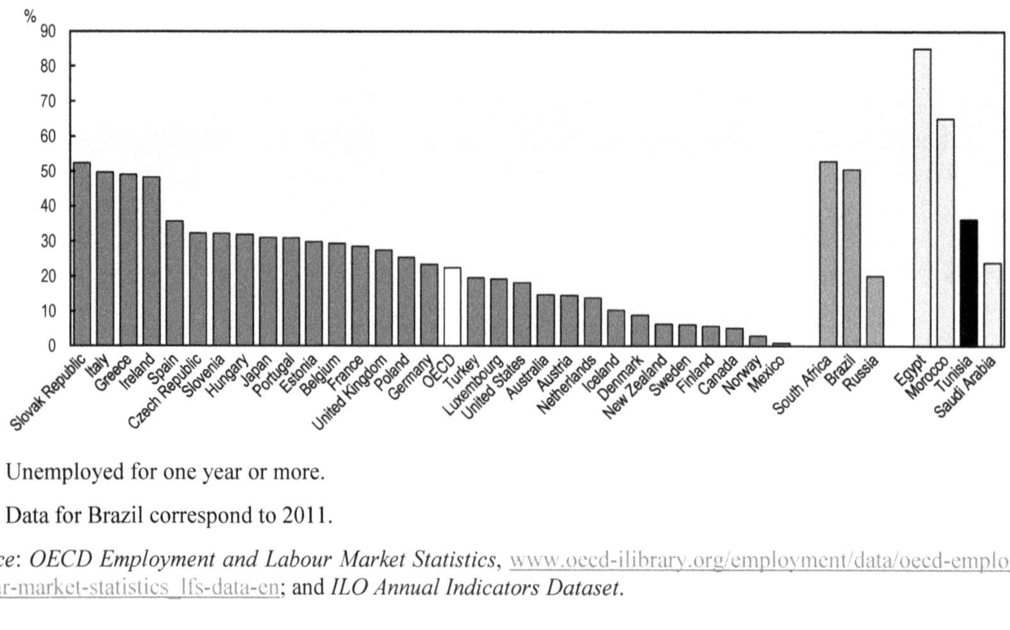


*a)* Unemployed for one year or more.

*b)* Data for Brazil correspond to 2011.

*Source*: *OECD Employment and Labour Market Statistics*, www.oecd-ilibrary.org/employment/data/oecd-employment-and-labour-market-statistics_lfs-data-en; and *ILO Annual Indicators Dataset*.

## School-to-work transitions are a challenge

Figure 1.9 illustrates the activity status of youth (15-29) by single year of age for a number of advanced and emerging economies, including Tunisia. Among the emerging economies, Tunisia stands out by the fact that its youth stay in education for longer on average. Indeed, the age at which 50% of youth have left education is 20.4 in Tunisia – which is much closer to what is generally observed amongst the advanced countries than amongst the emerging economies. This, of course, is reflected in the relatively high educational attainment of Tunisian youth (see Chapter 4). It is in terms of what happens to them after leaving education that the paths taken by Tunisian youth are very different from what happens to youth in more advanced economies. Indeed, very few youth in Tunisia enter employment, and NEET rates are high. Another striking fact about the school-to-work transition in Tunisia is that very few youths combine study and work (1.5% according to ILO and ONEQ, 2014) – while the available evidence clearly demonstrates that models that combine study and work achieve a smoother transition from school to work than those taking a *study first, then work* approach (OECD, 2010). It is interesting that the countries in Figure 1.9 with the largest proportion of youth entering NEET status after leaving education are also the countries with the lowest proportion of youth combining work and study (e.g. India, Indonesia and South Africa).

**Figure 1.9. Activity status by single year of age, Tunisia, selected OECD and emerging countries, 2011[a]**

Percentage

**A. Advances economies**

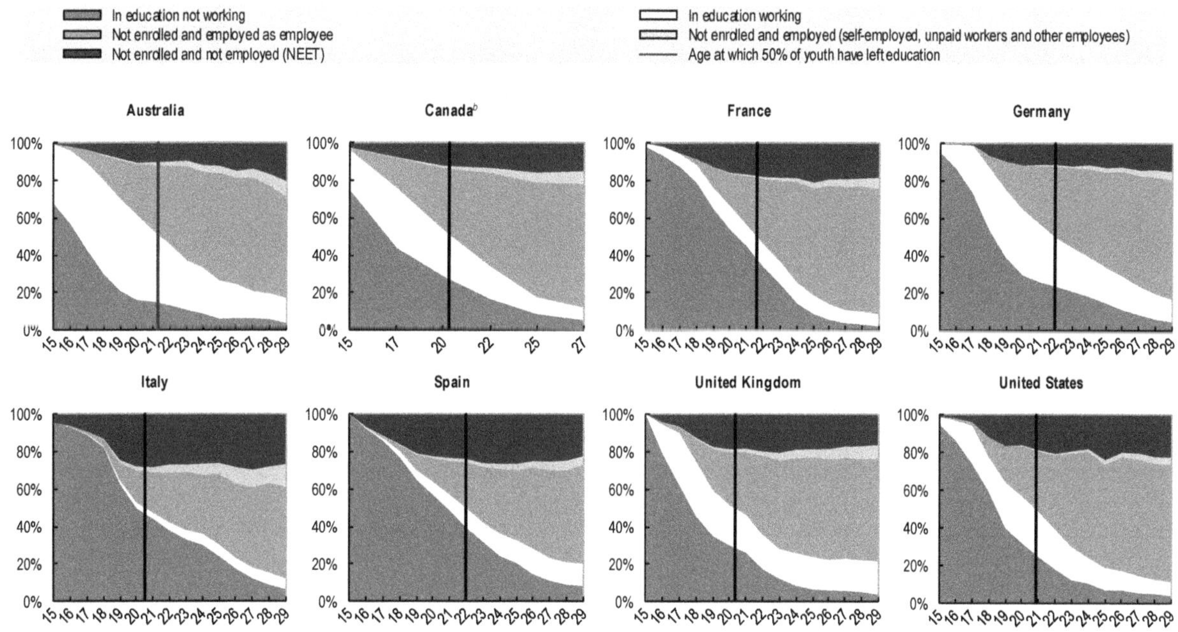


*a)* Data for Indonesia correspond to 2004; 2008 for Korea; 2009 for Australia and Chile; 2009/10 for India; and 2010 for South Africa and Tunisia.

*b)* Age in two and three year groups for Canada.

**Figure 1.9. Activity status by single year of age, Tunisia, selected OECD and emerging countries, 2011[a] *(cont.)***

Percentage

**B. Emerging economies**

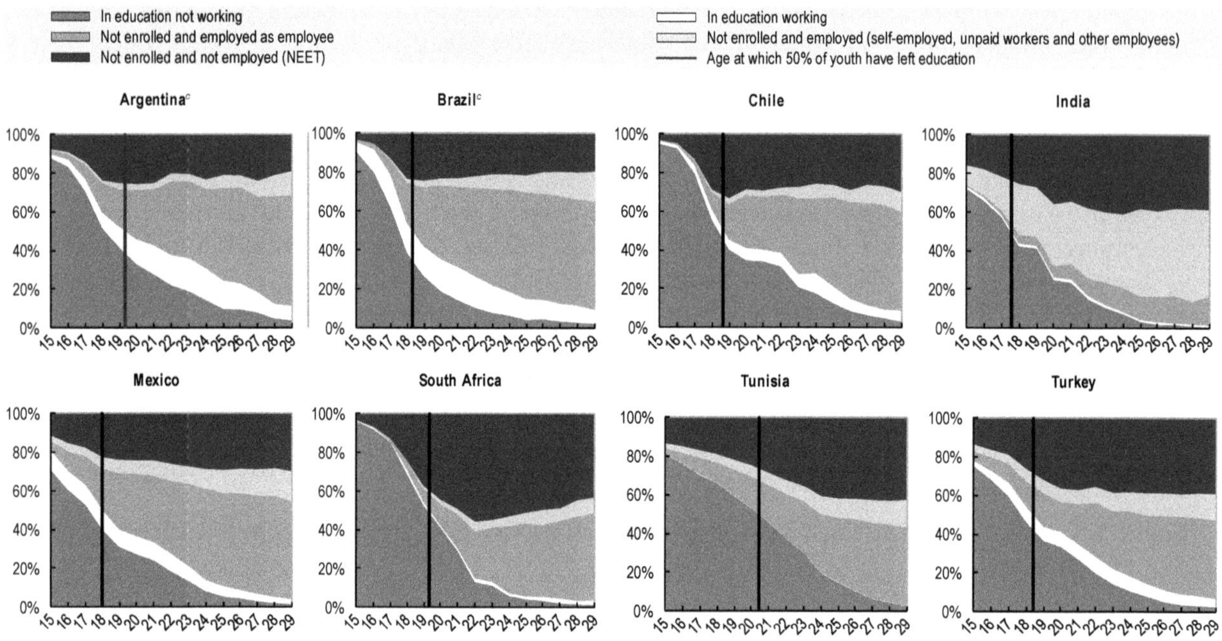


*c)* Selected urban areas only.

*Source*: Quintini, G. and S. Martin (2014), "Same Same But Different: School-to-Work Transitions in Emerging and Advanced Economies", *OECD Social, Employment and Migration Working Papers*, No. 154, OECD Publishing, Paris, http://dx.doi.org/10.1787/5jzbb2t1rcwc-en. For Tunisia, OECD calculations based on the *Enquête Nationale sur la Population et l'Emploi* (ENPE) [National Population and Employment Survey].

Calculating the length of school-to-work transitions (i.e. the time it takes young people to find work after leaving education) would require longitudinal data on individuals (i.e. data which follow the same individuals over time). In most countries such data are not available, including in Tunisia (see above Box 1.1). As a proxy, the difference between the average school-leaving age and the average age at which 50% of youth are in employment can be used. These calculations are presented in Table 1.1. The average length of transitions in Tunisia is estimated at six years – a figure considerably higher than what is seen in most other countries, with the exception of Turkey (7.6 years) and South Africa (8.3 years).

The burden of difficult school-to-work transitions in Tunisia falls disproportionately on women (Figure 1.10) and youth from the most deprived regions. While the average length of school-to-work transitions for men is 3.6 years, an equivalent figure for women cannot be calculated because, even by age 29, only one-third of women are in employment. Differences are also manifest by region. In Greater Tunis, the average length of school-to-work transitions is 4.0 years, while in the North West it is 8.8 years and in the Centre West and the Southern regions, fewer than 50% of youth are in employment even at age 29.

**Table 1.1. Average duration of school-to-work transitions, Tunisia, OECD and other selected countries, 2011[a]**

Number of years

| | School leaving age[b] | Age of entry into work[c] | Length of school-to-work transition |
|---|---|---|---|
| | A | B | B-A |
| Argentina* | 19.7 | 24.9 | 5.2 |
| Australia | 20.4 | 22.1 | 1.7 |
| Brazil* | 18.3 | 21.7 | 3.4 |
| Canada[d] | 21.0 | 22.6 | 1.7 |
| Chile | 18.7 | 24.6 | 5.9 |
| France | 21.6 | 23.5 | 1.8 |
| Germany | 22.0 | 24.2 | 2.3 |
| India | 17.6 | 23.8 | 6.2 |
| Indonesia | 17.4 | 22.0 | 4.6 |
| Italy | 20.5 | 26.3 | 5.9 |
| Mexico | 18.0 | 22.7 | 4.7 |
| South Africa | 19.3 | 27.7 | 8.3 |
| Spain | 22.0 | 26.7 | 4.7 |
| Tunisia | 20.4 | 26.7 | 6.3 |
| Turkey | 18.4 | 26.0 | 7.6 |
| United Kingdom | 20.3 | 22.8 | 2.5 |
| United States | 20.8 | 22.9 | 2.1 |

* Selected urban areas only.

*a)* 2004 for Indonesia, 2009 for Australia and Chile, 2009/10 for India, 2010 for South Africa and Tunisia.

*b)* Age at which 50% of youth are enrolled in education or training.

*c)* Age at which 50% of youth are employed and no longer enrolled in education or training.

*d)* Age is defined in two or three-year groups for Canada and the calculation is based on the average age in each class.

*Source*: Quintini, G. and S. Martin (2014), "Same Same But Different: School-to-Work Transitions in Emerging and Advanced Economies", *OECD Social, Employment and Migration Working Papers*, No. 154, OECD Publishing, Paris, http://dx.doi.org/10.1787/5jzbb2t1rcwc-en. For Tunisia, OECD calculations based on the *Enquête Nationale sur la Population et l'Emploi* (ENPE) [National Population and Employment Survey].

**Figure 1.10. Activity status by age and gender, Tunisia, 2010**

Percentage by single year of age

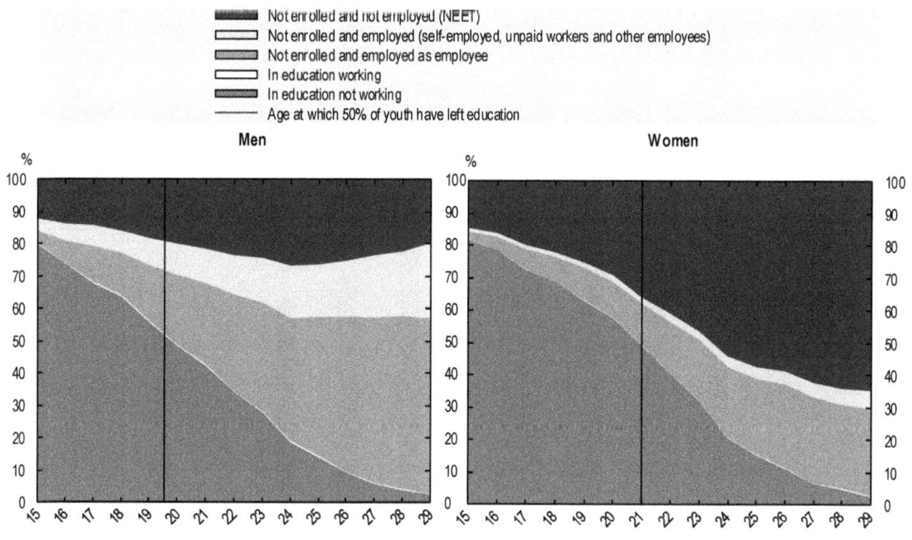


*Source*: OECD calculations based on the *Enquête Nationale sur la Population et l'Emploi* (ENPE) [National Population and Employment Survey].

## Box 1.2. School-to-work transitions in Tunisia: Evidence from retrospective data on employment history

Ideally, school-to-work transitions are studied using longitudinal data (i.e. data tracing the same individuals over time). In the absence of such data, the analysis presented in this chapter has relied on cross-sectional data to calculate proxies for the length of school-to-work transitions in Tunisia. This box analyses school-to-work transitions using a newly available data source: the ILO's School-to-Work Transition Survey (SWTS) carried out in Tunisia in 2013 (February-March). Although the SWTS is not a longitudinal survey as such, it does contain retrospective data on the individual's employment history. While it is well-known that respondents to such surveys tend to misreport their past choices in order to make them appear more consistent with their current choice, the ILO's SWTS allows a more accurate picture of school-to-work transitions in Tunisia to be built than what can be achieved with cross-sectional data alone. In addition, because the SWTS was carried out in a number of other countries using the same methodology, the data allow for some international comparisons on a consistent basis. The target population for the SWTS was 15-29 year-olds. In the case of Tunisia, it collected information on 1 545 and 1 445 young men and women, respectively, representative of the national population.

In the analysis that follows, the ILO's definition of labour market transitions is used, which distinguishes between: individuals already working in stable or at least satisfactory jobs; individuals still in transition; and those who never started the transition process:

- Youth who have *transited* are considered to be those currently employed in a stable[1] job, in a satisfactory[2] but temporary job, or are satisfactorily self-employed.
- Youth still *in transition* are those currently unemployed (relaxed[3] definition), currently employed in non-satisfactory temporary jobs/self-employment, or inactive not in education or training, with the aim of looking for work later.
- Youth whose *transition has not yet started* include inactive students, and inactive non-students with no intention of looking for work.

### How does Tunisia compare?

Figures A and B compare labour market outcomes and school-to-work transitions in Tunisia with those in ten other countries that participated in the SWTS in 2012 and 2013, covering Asia and the Pacific (Cambodia), Eastern Europe and Central Asia (Armenia, the Former Yugoslav Republic of Macedonia and the Russian Federation), Latin America and the Caribbean (Peru), the Middle East and North Africa (Egypt and Jordan), and Sub-Saharan Africa (Liberia, Malawi and Togo). Tunisia has one of the lowest labour force participation rates for youth aged 15-29 years, together with the second highest unemployment rate (37.4%) and the highest NEET rate (almost 31%) (Figure A).

**Figure A. Labour market outcomes of youth (15-29), Tunisia, selected developing and emerging economies, 2012/13**

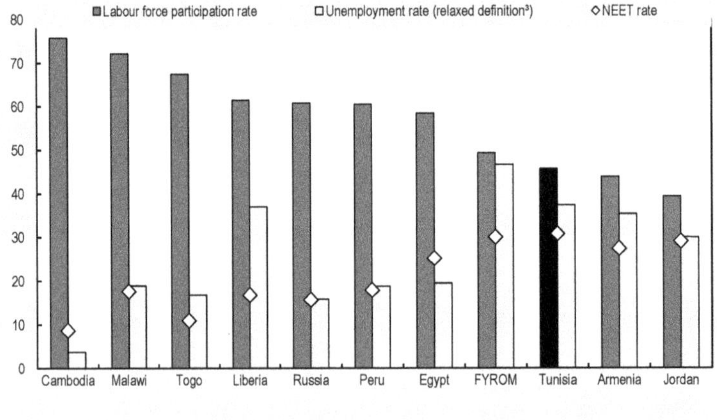


*Source*: ILO (2013), *Global Employment Trends for Youth 2013*, Geneva; and OECD calculations based on the ILO School-to-Work Transition Survey for Tunisia (2013).

## Box 1.2. School-to-work transitions in Tunisia: Evidence from retrospective data on employment history *(cont.)*

In terms of transition stages (Figure B), Tunisia has the lowest proportion of youth already transited to stable or satisfactory work (26%) and one of the highest shares of youth whose transition has not yet started (45%). Although this will partly reflect a relatively high propensity to stay in school for Tunisian youth, almost 20% of the "not yet transited" group in Tunisia corresponds to inactive non-students with no intention of looking for work.

**Figure B. School-to-work transitions of youth (15-29), Tunisia, selected developing and emerging economies, 2012/13**

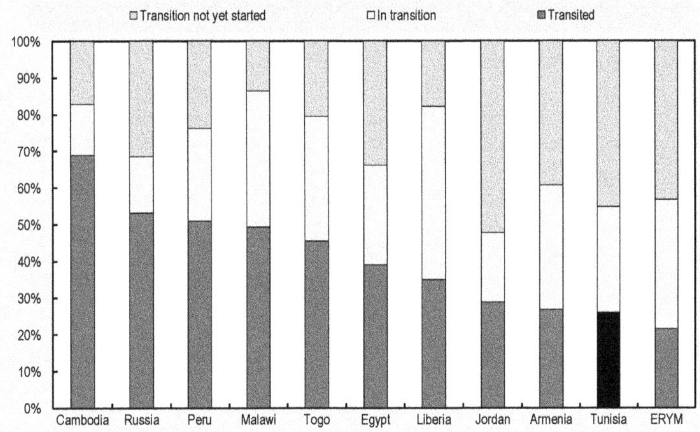


*Source*: ILO (2013), *Global Employment Trends for Youth 2013*, Geneva; and OECD calculations based on the ILO School-to-Work Transition Survey for Tunisia (2013).

### Differences in school-to-work transitions by socio-demographic characteristics

Figure C analyses school-to-work transitions in Tunisia by gender, educational attainment, civil status and region:

- Men (37%) are significantly more likely than women (15%) to have transited successfully, while a larger portion of women (55%) than men (35%) had not yet started their transition. A small part of this difference can be explained by the slightly greater propensity of women to stay in education for longer, however the bulk of the difference is explained by women being less likely to look for work.
- Those with primary education are more likely to have made a successful transition than those with secondary and tertiary qualifications – but this will partly reflect the length of time which has elapsed since graduation.
- While there is no difference between married and single young people in the proportion who have successfully transited, married individuals are slightly more likely to be in transition, and slightly more likely to have started their transition, than single individuals. However, the reason for transitions not having started yet is very different between married and single individuals: in the case of married individuals not having started a transition, the vast majority never intends to look for a job, while for single individuals it is the opposite (most of them are still studying).
- While the proportion of individuals who had already transited to stable or satisfactory jobs is relatively similar across the various regions (around 25%), there are more important differences in the percentages who had not yet started their transition. In particular, these are highest in Greater Tunis and in the South East, but in the latter a much larger portion never intends to look for work than in Greater Tunis, where the vast majority is still studying.
- Finally, it is interesting to note that the average monthly (gross) wage for youth who have already transited to work is TND 425, compared to TND 300 for those still in transition – demonstrating the importance of achieving successful school-to-work transitions for the economic well-being of young people.

## Box 1.2. School-to-work transitions in Tunisia: Evidence from retrospective data on employment history *(cont.)*

**Figure C. School-to-work transitions of youth (15-29) by socio-demographic characteristics, Tunisia, 2013**

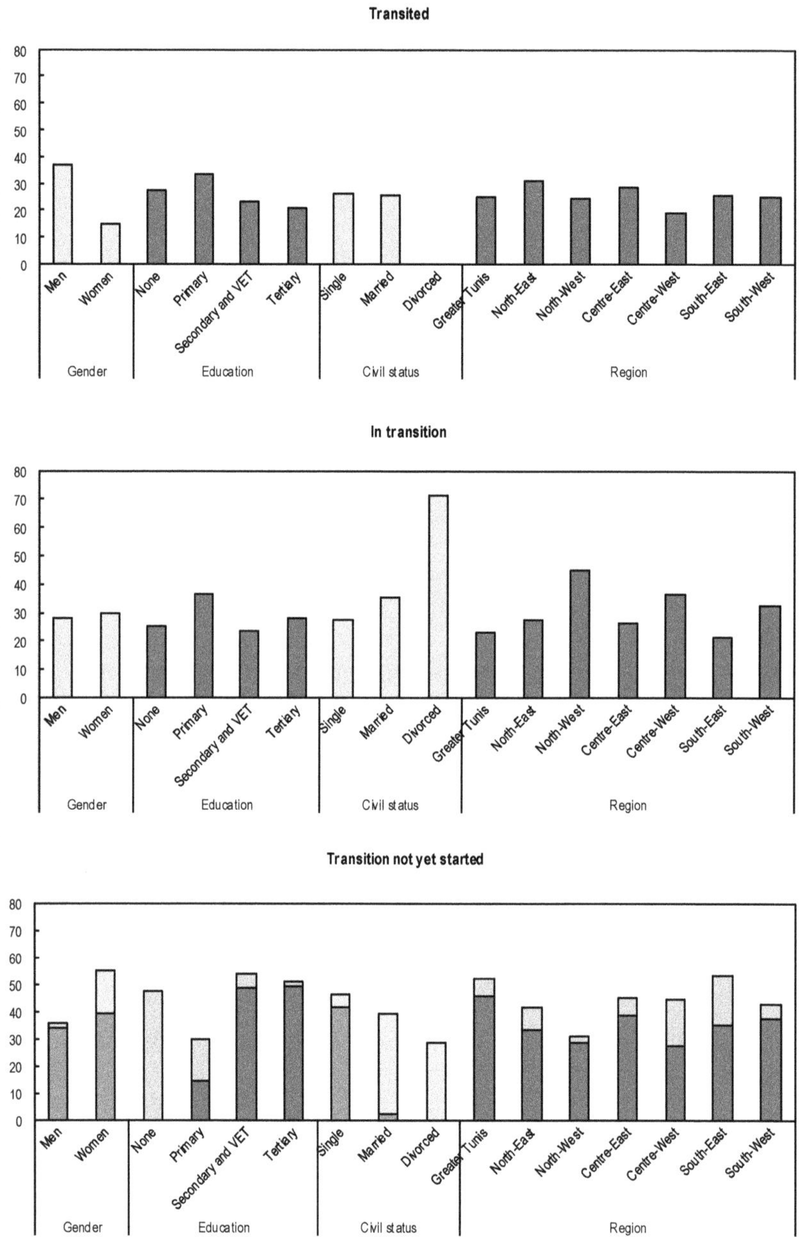


*Source*: OECD calculations based on the ILO School-to-Work Transition Survey for Tunisia (2013).

1. Stable employment includes those with a contract agreement (oral or written) lasting more than 12 months.

2. Satisfactory is defined based on the job-holder's self-assessment with respect to how satisfied they are with their main job.

3. The main difference between the "relaxed" definition of unemployment and the "strict" (and standard) definition is the relaxation of the "seeking work" criterion ("actively sought for work in the past 30 days").

## For those in employment, the quality of jobs is frequently poor

Not only are employment rates for youth low in Tunisia, even when in a job, the quality of that employment is frequently poor. Indeed, informality is high – many youth work with no or little protection in case of sickness or work accidents – and temporary employment is relatively common among those who do manage to obtain a formal job. This means that many youth are subject to precarious working conditions. In addition, working hours tend to be long and the incidence of low-pay is high.

Although official estimates of the degree of informality for youth are not available (see Chapter 3 for a more detailed discussion), the indication is that a large portion of youth in Tunisia is employed in informal jobs. A number of proxies are generally used to measure informal employment, including: work without a contract; lack of social protection coverage; self-employment; or work in a microbusiness. Figure 1.11 shows the proportion of youth who work: i) without a contract (24%); ii) in an unregistered firm (40%); iii) in a micro-business (five or fewer employees) (56%); and iv) without contributing to social security (53%). Where informality is not a choice, this often means they work in precarious and poorly paid employment, with no social security coverage or protection provided by labour contracts (i.e. minimum wages, employment protection or occupational health and safety standards), on top of having less access to training and career advancement than formal workers.

**Figure 1.11. Informality in Tunisia, 2013**

As a proportion of employed youth (15-29)

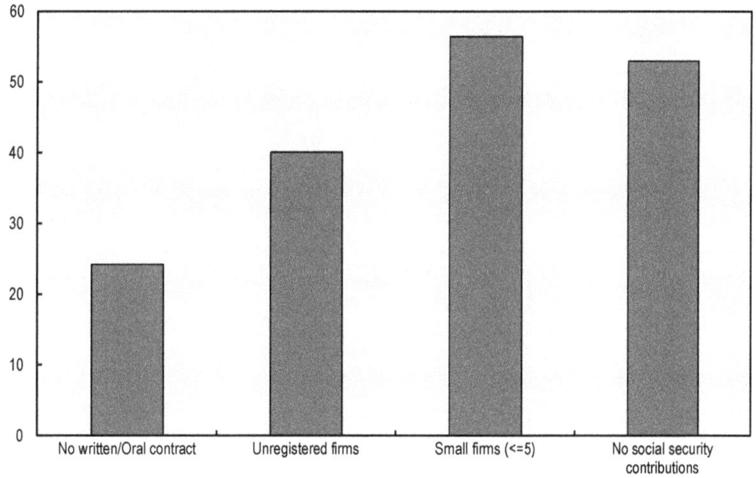


*Source*: OECD calculations based on the ILO School-to-Work Transition Survey for Tunisia (2013).

Figure 1.12 provides an international comparison of the prevalence of temporary employment among youth. Half of Tunisian youth who work for a contract have a temporary one, compared to 36.6% of youth across the OECD on average.[8] Temporary contracts are often thought to be a stepping stone to more stable employment, particularly for those with limited skills and experience, but the risk is that they remain trapped in insecure working conditions: when employment protection regulations and social security coverage differ substantially between permanent and temporary workers, they can create a two-tier or segmented labour market. These issues will be further explored in Chapter 3 of this report.

**Figure 1.12. Share of temporary employment[a] for youth, Tunisia and selected OECD countries, 2012[b]**

As a percentage of employees with a contract, youth aged 15-24

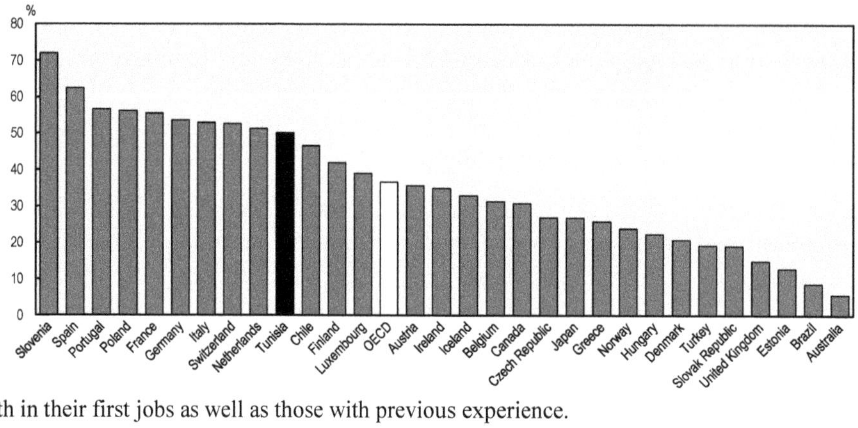


*a)* Includes youth in their first jobs as well as those with previous experience.

*b)* Data for Tunisia correspond to 2010.

*Source: OECD Employment and Labour Market Statistics*, www.oecd-ilibrary.org/employment/data/oecd-employment-and-labour-market-statistics_lfs-data-en. For Tunisia, OECD calculations based on the *Enquête Nationale sur la Population et l'Emploi* (ENPE) [National Population and Employment Survey].

The incidence of low-pay is also relatively common amongst Tunisian youth, with approximately one-third (35%) of young workers earning less than two thirds of the median wage, as well one in eight young workers not employed in the agricultural sector earning less than the *Salaire Minimum Interprofessionnel Garanti* – SMIG (non-agricultural minimum wage) and one in ten of all young workers earning less than the *Salaire Minimum Agricole Garanti* – SMAG (agricultural minimum wage) (Figure 1.13).

**Figure 1.13. Wage distribution of young workers, Tunisia, 2013**

Youth aged 18-29

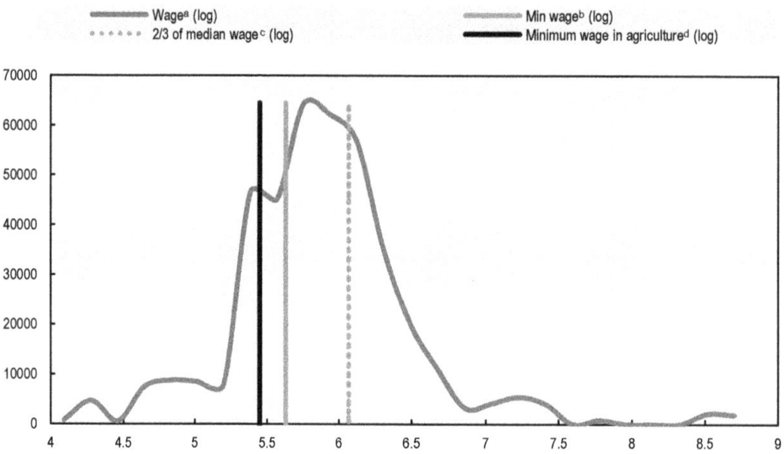


*a)* Wage data have been trimmed at the 1st and 99th centiles to eliminate outliers and are presented in logarithmic form.

*b)* Minimum wages are for July 2012.

*c)* Gross median wages are calculated using net median wages of TND 422 for full-time private sector workers as calculated by CRES and ILO (2012), "Enquête sur la Structure des Salaires, Tunisie 2011, Rapport Final", CRES, Tunis; and estimating the social security contributions and income tax rate assuming a single person without children. These have then been uprated by inflation to March 2013 prices using the consumer price index – giving a gross median wage of TND 674.27.

*d)* The equivalent monthly agricultural minimum wage was calculated using the daily rate assuming 20 days per month.

*Source*: OECD calculations based on the ILO School- to-Work Transition Survey for Tunisia (2013).

Another aspect of job quality is the number of hours worked. Tunisian youth work long hours in comparison to young people in most OECD countries (Figure 1.14): nearly 48 hours per week compared to just under 34 hours in OECD countries. Long working hours are a common feature of labour markets in emerging economies, where they likely reflect economic necessity as well as low productivity. Few young workers in Tunisia (18%) said they would have liked to work longer hours (Tunisia School-to-Work Transition Survey 2013). At the same time, very few youth work part-time in Tunisia, despite special incentives in place to encourage women to take on part-time work (see Chapter 3).

**Figure 1.14. Average usual weekly hours worked on the main job for the youth (15-24) by gender, Tunisia and OECD countries, 2011[a]**

Percentage of individals in dependent employment

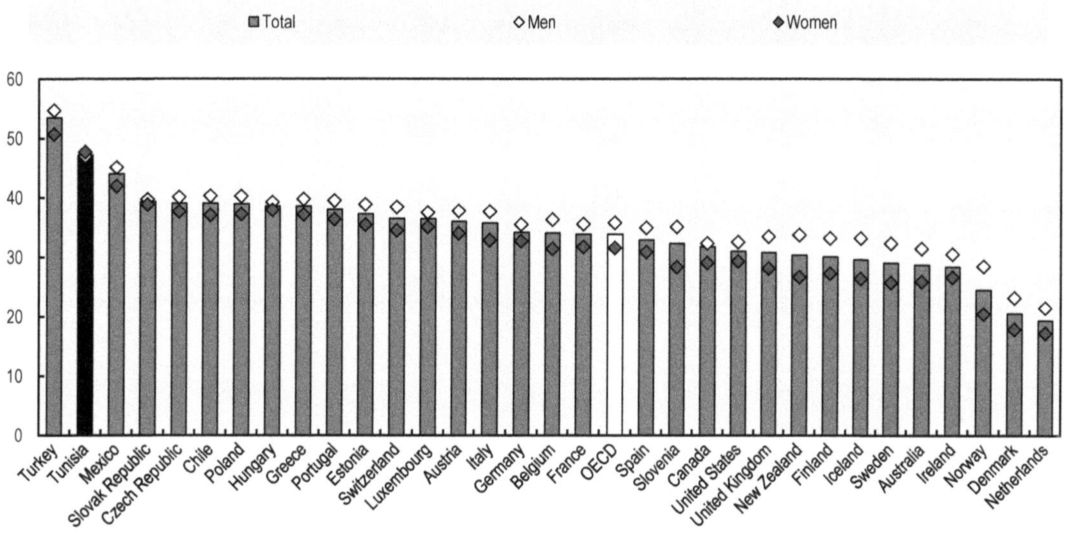


*a)* For Tunisia, the data correspond to the hours worked the week before the date of the interview.

*Source*: *OECD Employment and Labour Market Statistics*, www.oecd-ilibrary.org/employment/data/oecd-employment-and-labour-market-statistics_lfs-data-en; For Tunisia, OECD calculations based on the *Enquête Nationale sur la Population et l'Emploi* (ENPE) [National Population and Employment Survey].

Not surprisingly, given the evidence presented so far, a very low proportion (16%) of employed Tunisian youth is satisfied with the job they are currently in (Figure 1.15). While this is average for MENA countries, it is low by large emerging economies standards (26%) and even lower compared to OECD countries (35%). As a result, a relatively large proportion of youth in Tunisia expresses a desire to change employment (46.9%).[9] While this is similar to the proportion of youth wishing to change jobs in Egypt, Iran and Algeria, it is considerably higher than the proportions encountered in Morocco. The main declared reasons for wanting to change jobs are: the temporary nature of current employment (28.2%), followed by working conditions (25.4%) and low pay per hour worked (22.6% – Tunisia School-to-Work Transition Survey 2013). Relatively few youth in Tunisia cite mismatch as an important reason for wanting to change jobs (unlike youth in Egypt). Compared to these other MENA countries, however, working conditions and the temporary nature of employment are major concerns.

**Figure 1.15. Job satisfaction amongst youth, Tunisia, OECD, selected emerging and MENA countries, 2013[a]**

Percentage satisfied[b]

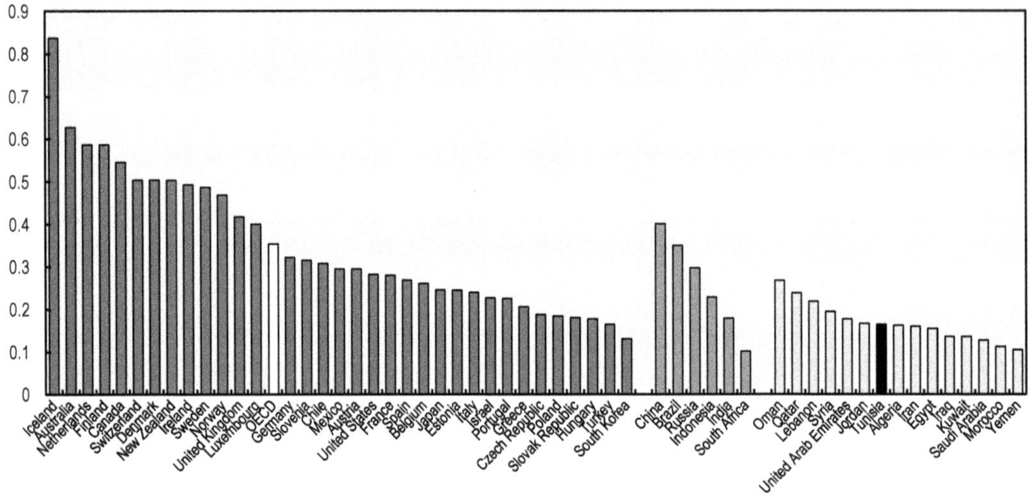


*a)* 2012 for Algeria, Chile , China, Iraq, Israel, Japan, Kuwait, Morocco, Norway, Qatar, South Africa, South Korea, Switzerland, United Arab Emirates, United States; 2011 for Oman.

*b)* Response options include: satisfied; dissatisfied; do not know; and refused.

*Source*: OECD calculations based on Gallup World Poll 2011-2013.

# Notes

1. The focus in this report is on youth aged 15-24, unless otherwise stated. The age limits chosen correspond to those used in standard definitions of youth. Because of lengthy school-to-work transitions in Tunisia, there may be an argument to focus on the 15-29 age group to give enough time to observe actual labour market outcomes. However, while this is true, from an international comparative perspective, looking at the 15-24 age group underscores the relative difficulty of school-to-work transitions in Tunisia.

2. This estimate is for 2010. Given the rise in unemployment since 2010, the current figure is likely to be higher.

3. Part of the surge in unemployment after the revolution can be explained also by large numbers of previously inactive youth registering as unemployed with the public employment service: i) in order to benefit from a newly introduced programme (*Amal*), which provided unemployed university graduates with a monthly stipend of TND 200; and ii) in response to Decree No. 2011-32 which opened up a public sector recruitment round to unemployed individuals registered with the public employment service. Chapter 3 provides further details.

4. The very high unemployment rate for 15-24 year-olds with tertiary qualifications will reflect the fact that very few of this age group will have completed tertiary education and that, if graduated, they will have entered the labour market only very recently. The equivalent unemployment rates for tertiary graduates aged 15-29 and 15-64 in 2012 were 50.3% and 26.1% respectively.

5. OECD estimates based on the *Enquête Nationale sur la Population et l'Emploi* [National Population and Employment Survey] suggest that the number of graduates in Tunisia increased from just under 700 000 in 2005 to over one million in 2011 – an increase of more than 50% in just six years. This is equivalent to an average of around 52 000 graduates entering the labour force annually, while only around 21 000 graduate jobs were created every year.

6. This research accounts for the higher unemployment rates of university graduates, as well as for the opportunity cost (earnings foregone) of studying.

7. The most up-to-date NEET estimate is for 2010 because the latest release of the *Enquête Nationale sur la Population et l'Emploi* [National Population and Employment Survey] (2012) does not contain information on whether individuals are currently studying or not.

8. ILO and ONEQ (2014) show also that a very large proportion of youth (aged 15-29) work without an oral contract.

9. This figure and the calculations that follow are based on the ILO's School-to-Work Transition Surveys for Tunisia and comparator countries.

## *References*

Assaad, R. (2013), "Making Sense of Arab Labor Markets: The Enduring Legacy of Dualism", *IZA Discussion Papers*, No. 7573, IZA, Bonn.

Barouni, M. and S. Broecke (forthcoming), "The Returns to Education in Africa: Some New Estimates", *Journal of Development Studies*.

CRES – Centre des Recherches et des Études Sociales, and ILO – International Labour Office (2012), *Enquête sur la Structure des Salaires, Tunisie 2011, Rapport Final* [Salary Survey, Tunisia 2011, Final Report], Centre des Recherches et des Études Sociales, Tunis.

Haouas, I., E. Sayre and M. Yagoubi (2012), "Youth Unemployment in Tunisia: Characteristics and Policy Responses", *Topics in Middle Eastern and African Economies*, Vol. 14/September, Middle East Economic Association and Loyola University, Chicago, pp. 395-415.

ILO – International Labour Office (2013), *Global Employment Trends for Youth 2013*, ILO, Geneva.

ILO – International Labour Office and ONEQ – Observatoire National de l'Emploi et des Qualifications (2014), *Transition vers le Marché du Travail des Jeunes Femmes et Hommes en Tunisie* [School-to-Work Transitions of Young Women and Men in Tunisia], *Work4Youth Publication Series*, No. 16, ILO, Geneva.

ManpowerGroup (2013), *2013 Talent Shortage Survey: Research Results*, ManpowerGroup, Milwaukee.

Ministère de l'Emploi et de l'Insertion Professionnelle des Jeunes and World Bank (2009), *L'Insertion des Jeunes Diplômés de l'Enseignement Supérieur – Promotion 2004 : Analyse Comparative des Résultats de Deux Enquêtes (2005 et 2007)* [The School-to-Work Transition of Young Higher Education Graduates – the Class of 2004 : Comparative Analysis of the Results of Two Surveys (2005 and 2007)], Tunis.

OECD (2010), *Off to a Good Start? Jobs for Youth*, OECD Publishing, Paris, http://dx.doi.org/10.1787/9789264096127-en.

Quintini, G. (2011a), "Right for the Job: Over-qualified or Under-skilled?", *OECD Social, Employment and Migration Working Papers*, No. 120, OECD Publishing, Paris, http://dx.doi.org/10.1787/5kg59fcz3tkd-en.

Quintini, G. (2011b), "Over-qualified or Under-skilled: A Review of Existing Literature", *OECD Social, Employment and Migration Working Papers*, No. 121, OECD Publishing, Paris, http://dx.doi.org/10.1787/5kg58j9d7b6d-en.

Quintini, G. and S. Martin (2014), "Same Same But Different: School-to-work Transitions in Emerging and Advanced Economies", *OECD Social, Employment and Migration Working Papers*, No. 154, OECD Publishing, Paris, http://dx.doi.org/10.1787/5jzbb2t1rcwc-en.

United Nations, Department of Economic and Social Affairs, Population Division (2011), *World Population Prospects: The 2012 Revision*.

## Database references

OECD Employment and Labour Market Statistics, www.oecd-ilibrary.org/employment/data/oecd-employment-and-labour-market-statistics_lfs-data-en.

# *Chapter 2*

## Removing demand-side barriers to youth employment in Tunisia

*This chapter discusses demand-side barriers to youth employment in Tunisia such as the cost of hiring (as determined by minimum wages, non-wage costs and collective bargaining institutions) and employment protection legislation. It also discusses policies currently in place to tackle such barriers (including wage subsidies) and offers a range of policy options to create more favourable conditions for employers to hire youth, while still ensuring decent wages as well as an adequate level of protection for workers. Key challenges identified in this chapter include: high wage floors introduced by sector wage agreements; a large gap in the level of remuneration and benefits between the public and private sectors, which causes public sector queuing and raises reservation wages; and very rigid employment protection legislation on permanent contracts combined with extremely flexible legislation on temporary contracts, resulting in a dual labour market, with temporary work acting as a trap rather than a stepping stone into more stable employment for Tunisian youth.*

The statistical data for Israel are supplied by and under the responsibility of the relevant Israeli authorities. The use of such data by the OECD is without prejudice to the status of the Golan Heights, East Jerusalem and Israeli settlements in the West Bank under the terms of international law.

## Introduction

Addressing high levels of youth unemployment in Tunisia will need, in the first instance, the creation of a sufficient number of jobs, in particular for skilled workers. This will require a mixture of appropriate macroeconomic policies and addressing a range of structural weaknesses that have to date prevented economic growth from being inclusive. However, such action must be accompanied by interventions aimed at tackling structural labour market barriers that affect the willingness and ability of employers to hire youth – including policies and institutions that have an impact on the cost of hiring and employment protection legislation which determines the ability of employers to adjust flexibly to changing economic circumstances. This will be particularly important in the context of Tunisia's transition to a green economy. Indeed, as Chapter 5 of the present report will make clear, greening the economy is likely to alter the sectoral composition of employment. If employers face significant demand-side barriers, like overly strict employment protection legislation, then this could hinder the smooth reallocation of labour from more polluting to environmentally-friendly firms. It is these demand-side barriers to youth employment that will be the subject of the present chapter.

The main findings are:

- ***The cost of hiring***. Neither minimum wages nor employer social security contributions in Tunisia appear to be set at particularly high levels by OECD standards. Despite this, wage subsidies (including reductions in social security contributions) have been, and continue to be, widely used to try and address youth unemployment in Tunisia. While there is some evidence that these programmes might be having an effect, it is also clear that they are frequently badly designed and implemented: targeting is poor and deadweight losses are high. To be more effective, the focus of such subsidies should be on those youth encountering the greatest labour market difficulties only. One challenge to youth employment is likely to come from sector wage agreements, which set starting wages considerably above the national minimum wage, and future such agreements should more carefully consider the situation of youth. The government should also aim to contain, if not reduce, the gap between public and private wages and benefits which leads to a rise in reservation wages and results in public sector queuing. This, in turn, renders hiring in the private sector at the going wage rate more difficult.
- ***Employment protection legislation***. Tunisia combines strict protection on regular employment with extremely light legislation on temporary work, resulting in a "dual" labour market which traps young workers in precarious employment relationships, reducing their career opportunities and undermining their skills – with wider implications for both job quality and productivity. Employees on regular contracts benefit from high levels of protection against individual dismissal, resulting from: the difficulty of dismissing workers for reasons other than economic or serious misconduct; high severance pay stipulated by some collective sector agreements; and high compensation in the case of unfair dismissal combined with uncertainty in jurisprudence around what constitutes fair dismissal. Legislation on temporary contracts, on the other hand, is very lax, and employers can essentially carry out permanent activities through the endless use of fixed-term contracts with different workers, and at a much lower cost. In addition, while temporary agency work (TWA) is

authorised in Tunisia, it is only very loosely regulated with very few restrictions imposed on its use. This gap in protection between permanent and temporary contracts has led to the very widespread use of the latter in Tunisia (see Chapter 1). Yet, despite the increase in precariousness that this brings, employment services and social protection to help workers who lose their job smooth consumption and find new work remain inadequate (see Chapter 3).

**Box 2.1. Key recommendations**

Given these outstanding challenges, the OECD suggests that:

- Policies should ensure that workers get paid decent wages, but also that the cost of hiring does not hinder demand for the least-skilled and most inexperienced workers, or encourage firms to hire them informally. Therefore:
  - While the real value of the minimum wage should not be allowed to erode in years to come, important (real) increases should be avoided in the near future.
  - Future sector wage negotiations need to carefully consider the situation of youth, and should set lower wages for younger workers that more accurately reflect their productivity in order to encourage firms to hire them. Greater weight should also be given to firm-level negotiations to allow the Tunisian economy to respond more flexibly to changing economic circumstances.
  - Differences in remuneration and benefits between the public and private sectors should be reduced, and the urge to use public sector job creation as a means of social appeasement should be resisted.
  - Wage subsidies and/or reductions in social security contributions to encourage hiring should be used more sparingly and targeted much more on the disadvantaged, the low-skilled (i.e. non-graduates) and the long-term unemployed. The experience with the *Programme d'Encouragement à l'Emploi* provides an important targeting precedent on which the government should continue to build in designing future subsidy programmes. Limits on the consecutive number of programmes that young people can participate in should be set and no distinction should be made in the stipend paid to graduates and non-graduates. Training as well as requirements to recruit at the end of the subsidy should be enforced, and employers monitored more closely.
- Employment protection legislation should protect workers from abuse by employers, as well as make the latter internalise the social cost of dismissals in their decisions. At the same time employers should be given the necessary flexibility to adjust rapidly to changing economic circumstances, and the gap in protection between permanent and temporary contracts should be reduced:
  - Protection provided by permanent contracts should be reduced. In particular, firing regulations should be eased: i) the definition of fair dismissal should be extended to cover dismissal on capability grounds; ii) in deciding on whether dismissal for economic reasons was fair, legislation should be clarified so that judges stick to assessing whether or not the dismissal was truly for economic reasons or not, rather than calling into question the need for the dismissal from a managerial perspective; and iii) the level of compensation following unfair dismissal should be reduced. The latter recommendation may be particularly important for small firms.
  - At the same time, employment protection on fixed-term contracts should be increased, for instance by introducing identical severance pay provisions to those of permanent contracts. Other (but not necessarily mutually exclusive) options include making it more expensive to hire on fixed-term contracts (e.g. through higher social security contributions) or providing financial incentives for conversion to regular contracts.
  - The use of non-regular contracts needs to be better regulated, in particular the cases in which Temporary Work Agency (TWA) employment is allowed, as well as the number of renewals of such contracts. The labour code should explicitly require equality of pay and working conditions between TWA and regular workers exercising similar activities.

## Guaranteeing decent wages while containing the cost of hiring

High labour costs can be a barrier to (formal) employment, especially for those who are low-skilled and lack work experience (including youth). This can result from a mandatory minimum wage that is set at a high rate relative to average earnings and/or from high employer social security contributions that add to wage costs. This section analyses the minimum wage and non-wage costs in Tunisia from an international comparative perspective, as well as the policies that have been put in place to reduce the cost of hiring youth. Although the Tunisian minimum wage does not appear to be particularly high in comparison to median wages and there is also a youth sub-minimum wage, sector bargaining agreements set wages considerably above the national minimum wage and might act as a barrier to youth employment. Employer social security contributions and payroll taxes are only marginally higher in Tunisia than they are in the average OECD country, and there exists a plethora of programmes waving social security contributions and/or providing direct wage subsidies to employers to take on young workers. However, many of these programmes are poorly targeted and/or implemented, benefit higher education graduates almost exclusively, and should be reformed to focus on those youth encountering the greatest employment difficulties only. Finally, public sector wages and benefits in Tunisia are set high in relation to what is on offer in the private sector and are likely to indirectly raise the cost of hiring for firms by increasing young people's reservation wages.

### *Minimum wages*

Minimum wages play an important role in addressing in-work poverty and inequality, but risks exist that they hinder (formal) employment if set too high. While the international evidence on the impact of minimum wages on employment is inconclusive and still the subject of a lively debate,[1] there is a certain consensus that minimum wages, if set too high, can have disemployment and informality effects on least-skilled workers as well as on the very young (Neumark and Wascher, 2007; Croucher and White, 2011).

Tunisia's national agricultural minimum wage (*Salaire Minimum Agricole Garanti* – SMAG) has been in place since 1966[2] and the non-agricultural minimum wage (*Salaire Minimum Interprofessionnel Garanti* – SMIG) since 1974.[3] Both are set by the *Ministère des Affaires Sociales* [Ministry of Social Affairs] through government decree, following consultations with the social partners.[4] The SMAG is calculated on a daily basis, while the SMIG is set both on an hourly and monthly basis, as well as for the two working hour regimes (40 and 48 hours) separately. Although the legislation does not specify how frequently the minimum wages should be reviewed, in practice they have been uprated approximately annually.

Figures 2.1 and 2.2 trace the real value of the SMIG and SMAG, respectively, since 1974.[5,6] Only the 48-hour monthly SMIG is shown in Figure 2.2, but the other SMIG rates are directly proportional to this rate. Both the SMIG and the SMAG initially experienced very sharp real increases up until the early 1980s. After that, workers witnessed a decade-long decline in the real minimum wage reflecting both higher inflation and lower annual increases in the nominal minimum wage. The value of the SMIG has changed very little since the early 1990s while the SMAG has seen larger increases,[7] particularly in the most recent period (i.e. in the aftermath of the revolution). The minimum wages were last increased in May 2014 to TND 319.904 (i.e. EUR 145) per month in the case of the SMIG (48-hour regime) and to TND 12.304 (i.e. EUR 5.6) per day in the case of the SMAG.

**Figure 2.1. Daily agricultural minimum wage (SMAG), Tunisia, January 1974 to May 2014**

Tunisian dinars (TND) at constant price,[a] May 2014

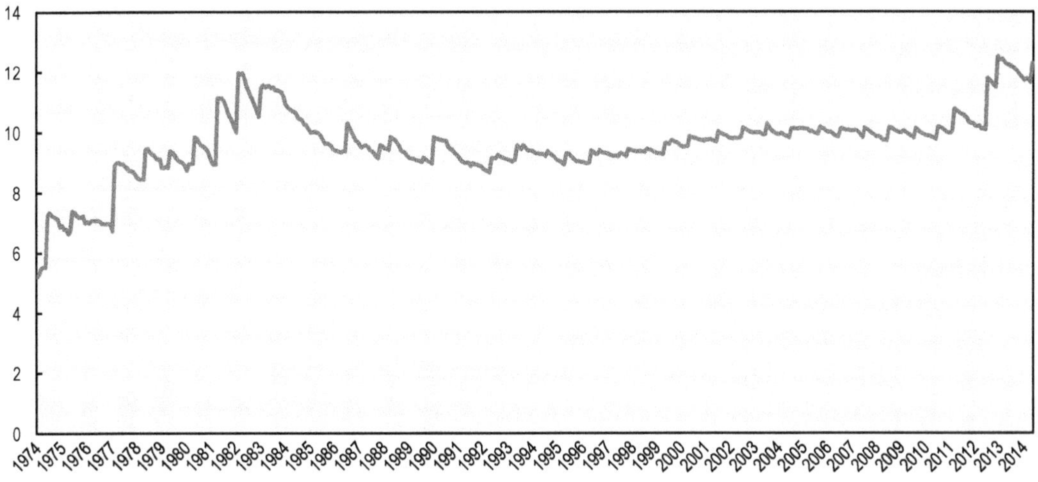


*a)* The deflator used is the consumer price index (CPI).

*Source*: OECD calculations based on Tunisian laws and decrees as published in the *Journal Officiel de la République Tunisienne* and *Institut National de la Statistique* for the CPI.

**Figure 2.2. Monthly[a] non-agricultural minimum wage (SMIG), Tunisia, January 1974 to May 2014**

Tunisian dinars (TND) at constant prices,[b] May 2014

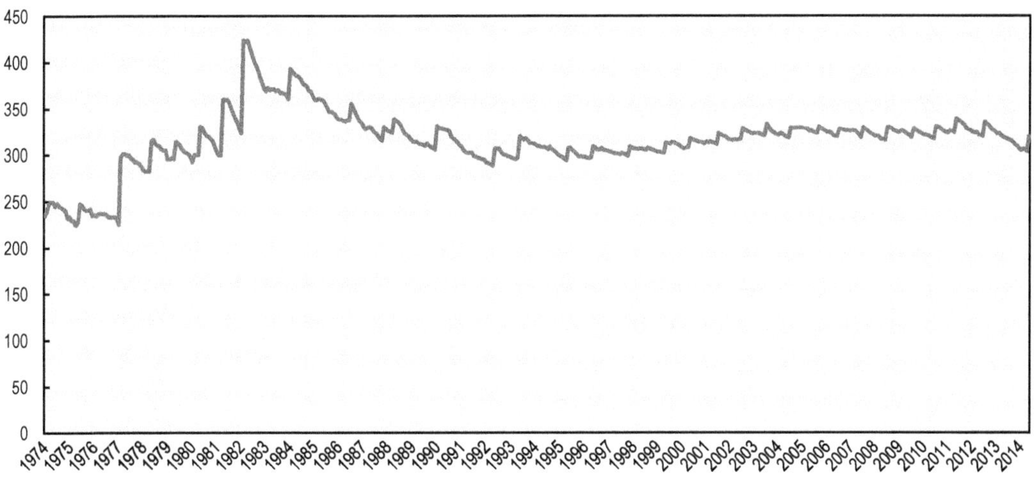


*a)* The nominal monthly SMIG from January 1974 to May 1975 is estimated based on the hourly minimum wage.

*b)* The deflator used is the consumer price index (CPI).

*Source*: OECD calculations based on Tunisian laws and decrees as published in the *Journal Officiel de la République Tunisienne* and *Institut National de la Statistique* for the CPI.

An international comparison suggests that the minimum wage in Tunisia does not appear to be set at a particularly high level in relation to median wages (Figure 2.3).[8] However, there is no robust evidence as to the effect of the minimum wage on inequality, poverty, employment or informality. This is to a large extent because data (and in particular salary data) are not made widely available to researchers.

**Figure 2.3. Minimum relative to median wages of full-time workers, Tunisia and OECD countries, 2012[a]**

Percentage

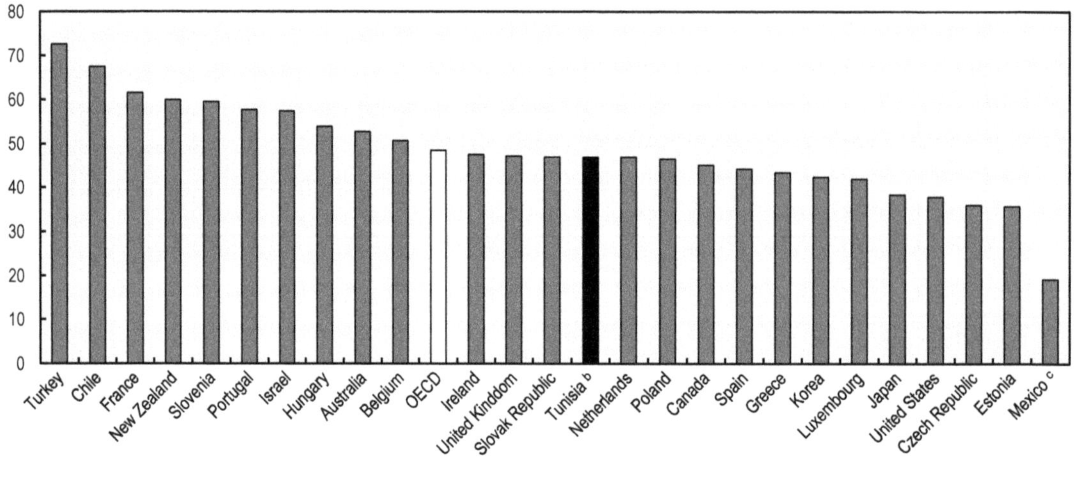


*a)* For Tunisia and Chile data refer to 2011.

*b)* For Tunisia the minimum wage refers to the May 2011 SMIG assuming a 48-hour regime. Gross median wages in Tunisia are calculated using net median wages of TND 422 for full-time private sector workers as calculated by CRES and ILO (2012) and estimating the social security contributions and income tax rate assuming a single person without children.

*c)* For Mexico the figure is calculated as a proportion of the average, not the median, wage.

*Source*: *OECD Database on Minimum Wages*; OECD calculations based on CRES and ILO (2012), *Enquête sur la Structure des Salaires, Tunisie 2011. Rapport Final* [Salary Survey], Centre de Recherches et d'Études Sociales, Tunis (for data on Tunisia).

Tunisia has a sub-minimum wage for youth aged under 18 set at 85% of the adult minimum wage. Sub-minimum wages for teenagers are a common strategy implemented across the OECD to counter the potentially negative impact of the minimum wage on youth employment. The application of lower wages on young workers may be particularly justified when the job offered includes a substantial training component. Examples of this include apprenticeship programmes in Germany and the United Kingdom, where starting salaries are lower in recognition of the lower productivity expected during the training period and subsequently increased as the training programme progresses. Table 2.1 shows that sub-minimum wages for youth exist in roughly half of the OECD countries that have a statutory minimum wage, and that this sub-minimum wage is set at around 72% of adult minimum wages – i.e. lower than the Tunisian youth sub-minimum wage.

### Table 2.1. Minimum wages (MW) for adults and youth, Tunisia and OECD countries, 2012 or latest year available

| Country | Adult MW | Adult MW/ Median wage (%) | Adult MW/ Mean wage (%) | MW at 17/ Adult MW (%) | Notes |
|---|---|---|---|---|---|
| Australia | Yes | 52.7 | 44.0 | – | |
| Austria | – | – | – | – | |
| Belgium | Yes | 50.7 | 43.0 | 73.0 | Youth sub-minima were fixed in 1991 as percentages of the MW for workers aged 21 and over: 94% for 20-year-olds; 88% for 19-year-olds; 82% for 18-year-olds; 76% for 17-year-olds; and 70% for 16-year-olds and younger workers. |
| Canada | Yes | 45.1 | 39.6 | – | |
| Chile | Yes | 67.4[a] | 43[a] | 75.0 | |
| Czech Republic | Yes | 36.0 | 30.6 | 80.0 | Reduced MW for workers under the age of 19 (80%) and for workers aged 19-21 with less than six months job tenure (90%). |
| Denmark | No | – | – | – | |
| Estonia | Yes | 35.7 | 30.0 | – | |
| Finland | No | – | – | – | |
| France | Yes | 61.5 | 49.8 | 90.0 | For younger workers with less than six months work experience in their activity of employment, the MW is reduced by 10% for workers aged 17 and by 20% for workers younger than 17. |
| Germany | No | – | – | – | |
| Greece | Yes | 43.4 | 29.5 | 87.0 | MW for blue-collar workers less than 25 years of age (introduced 14 February 2012). |
| Hungary | Yes | 53.9 | 39.6 | – | |
| Iceland | No | – | – | – | |
| Ireland | Yes | 47.6 | 43.7 | 70.0 | MW for workers aged under 18 (70% of adult minimum). |
| Israel | Yes | 57.4 | 42.5 | – | |
| Italy | No | – | – | – | |
| Japan | Yes | 38.3 | 33.3 | – | |
| Korea | Yes | 42.4 | 34.5 | – | Youth MW has been replaced by a MW based on experience. |
| Luxembourg | Yes | 42.0 | 34.5 | 80.0 | Single workers aged 17. Workers aged 15 and 16 are entitled to 75% of the adult MW. |
| Mexico | Yes | 19.2[b] | 19.2 | – | Mean wage instead of median wage. |
| Netherlands | Yes | 46.9 | 41.2 | 40.0 | Youth are entitled to a reduced MW, varying from 30% for 15-year-olds to 85% for 22-year-olds. |
| New Zealand | Yes | 59.9 | 51.3 | 60.0 | As of 1 April 2008, only paid to "new entrants" aged 16-17, i.e. with less than three months of job tenure, otherwise adult rate applies. |
| Norway | No | – | – | – | |
| Poland | Yes | 46.5 | 37.9 | – | |
| Portugal | Yes | 57.7 | 39.6 | 75.0 | Non-agricultural workers aged under 18. |
| Slovak Republic | Yes | 47.0 | 36.8 | 75.0 | Reduced MW for workers aged 16 and 17 (75%) and for those under the age of 16 (50%). |
| Slovenia | Yes | 59.5 | 48.3 | – | |
| Spain | Yes | 44.2 | 34.9 | – | |
| Sweden | No | – | – | – | |
| Switzerland | No | – | – | – | |
| Turkey | Yes | 72.5 | 38.4 | – | For under 16-year-olds, the MW is 85.6% of the adult MW. |
| United Kingdom | Yes | 47.2 | 38.8 | 60.0 | MW for workers aged 16 and 17. For workers aged 18-20, the MW is 81.5% of the adult MW. Median wage calculated from LFS. |
| United States | Yes | 37.8 | 27.2 | – | |
| OECD | 25/34 | 48.5 | 38.0 | 72.0 | |
| Latvia | Yes | 50.9 | 38.0 | – | |
| Lithuania | Yes | 47.8 | 35.7 | – | |
| Romania | Yes | 45.2 | 31.2 | – | |
| Non-OECD | 3/3 | 47.9 | 34.9 | – | |
| Tunisia | Yes | 46.9[a] | 34.7[a] | 85.0 | For workers aged under 18, the minimum wage equals 85% of the adult minimum wage. |

– Not applicable.

*Note*: For Tunisia, minimum wage refers to the SMIG assuming a 48-hour regime. Gross median and average wages are calculated using net median and average wages of TND 422 and TND 557 for full-time private sector workers as calculated by CRES and ILO (2012) and estimating the social security contributions and income tax rate assuming a single person without children.

*a)* Data refers to 2011. *b)* Calculated as a proportion of the average, not the median, wage.

*Source*: *OECD Database on Minimum Wages* and OECD calculations based on CRES and ILO (2012), *Enquête sur la Structure des Salaires. Rapport Final* [Salary Survey], Centre de Recherches et d'Études Sociales, Tunis (for data on Tunisia).

The evidence presented so far does not suggest that minimum wages in Tunisia present a major barrier to youth employment in Tunisia. They could still, however, encourage some employers to hire youth informally – particularly those that are low-skilled and/or have little experience. Indeed, the analysis presented in Chapter 1 indicates that one in eight employed youth in Tunisia earn below the minimum wage.[9] Additional analysis of the ILO's School-to-Work Transition Survey (SWTS) for Tunisia (2013) shows that those earning below the SMIG have much lower educational attainment than those earning above: two thirds of those earning below the minimum wage have no or only primary education, compared to only one-third of those earning above the SMIG.

This confirms the precarious situation of low-educated youth in Tunisia, and also that the cost of hiring may be more of a barrier to (formal) employment for these young people (and, therefore, that wage subsidies should be more targeted on unskilled youth, whose productivity is more likely to be below the going wage rate). That said, the proportion of youth earning below the minimum wage in Tunisia is not particularly high compared to what can be observed in some other countries. While in Chile, the fraction of workers (of all ages) paid below the minimum wage was estimated at 10% in 2009 (Wedenoja, 2013), the equivalent proportion was nearly 20% in Indonesia (Wage Indicator Foundation, 2011) and just under half in South Africa (Bhorat et al., 2012).

### *Sector wage agreements*

One possible concern in the case of Tunisia is the existence of sector wage agreements which set minimum wages above the SMIG, and sometimes considerably so. Tunisia has a tripartite system of collective bargaining operating at the sector level (for more detail, see Box 2.2).

Since 1973, and despite the lack of legal framework to guide negotiations, this system has resulted in a series of sector agreements which are renewed approximately every three years. Table 2.2 presents the collectively agreed minimum wage in 53 sectors of the Tunisian economy – most of which have been last revised in 2014. In many cases, these collective agreements resulted in minimum wages considerably above the SMIG. While it is true that qualification and skill requirements are likely to vary across sectors (and hence higher wages in some sectors might be justified), it is likely that sector minimum wages could present a barrier to entry for youth in some sectors of the economy.

Again, however, no research exists which evaluates the impact on (youth) employment of these sector wage agreements. While policy makers would greatly benefit from such research, it is also important that future collective wage bargaining carefully consider the situation of youth. Setting lower entry wages for youth might be one way of stimulating the hiring of youth in those sectors with collectively agreed pay considerably above the SMIG.

## Box 2.2. Trade unions and wage bargaining in Tunisia

Until recently, only one union was recognised in Tunisia: the *Union Générale Tunisienne du Travail* (UGTT). Other unions needed prior authorisation to operate and were not tolerated. After the revolution, however, a number of alternative unions have (re-)emerged, including: the *Confédération Générale des Travailleurs Tunisiens* (CGTT), the *Organisation Tunisienne du Travail* (OTT), and the *Union des Travailleurs Tunisiens* (UTT). An important challenge moving forward is to clarify how negotiations at company, sector and national level should proceed in the context of union pluralism.

It has been argued that, because the UGTT was not allowed to operate freely prior to the revolution, its power was relatively weak (Gouider, 2013). While estimates vary, the unionisation rate in Tunisia is not particularly high (16% according to Ferro, 2014), compared to 17% across OECD countries, on average, while the unionisation rate amongst youth is even lower: fewer than 5% according to estimates based on the ILO's School-to-Work Transition Survey 2013. Low unionisation rates may to a large extent be related to a lack of confidence in labour unions (see Figure A) and, according to ILO (2011), engaging in a new, post-revolutionary social dialogue will, in the first place, require broadening the membership base of unions to better reflect the working-age population.

**Figure A. Confidence in labour unions, Tunisia and selected OECD, emerging and MENA countries, 2010-14**

Percentage of respondents with a " great deal" or "quite a lot" of confidence in labour unions

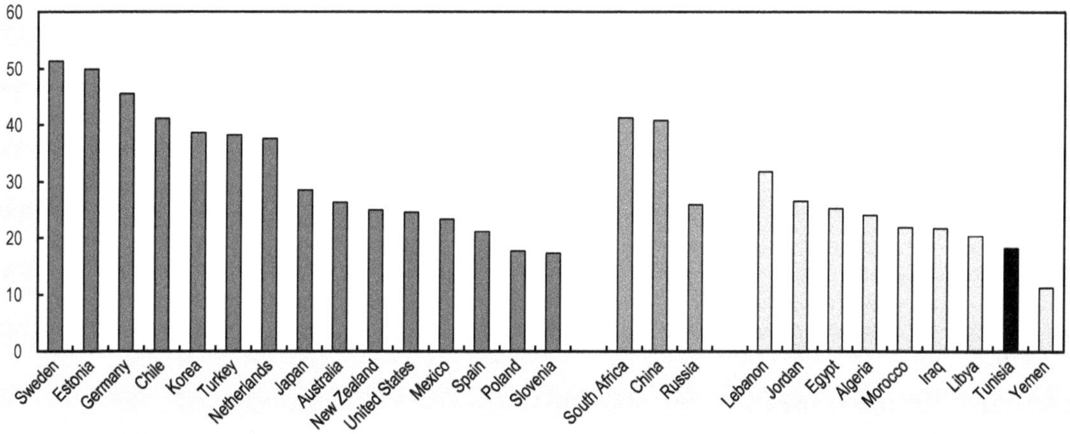


*Source*: World Values Survey (2010-2014).

Wage bargaining in Tunisia has been run along tripartite lines (government, UGTT and UTICA – *Union Tunisienne de l'Industrie, du Commerce et de l'Artisanat* – the main employer organisation). Bargaining takes place at the sector level and has resulted in collective agreements in most sectors of the formal economy. Extension of these agreements to non-union members is automatic upon approval of the agreement by government. With regard to the length of these agreements, they can either be indefinite or set for a period of maximum five years. In the former case, any party can discontinue the agreement as long as they give one month's notice. In practice, these agreements have been renewed approximately every three years. Since 2011, following an agreement between UGTT and UTICA, national collective agreements have focused on wages only, and have been renewed more frequently (2011, 2012 and 2014).

Although the Tunisian Labour Code allows for firm-level agreements (Book I, Title III, Chapter III), in practice these only play a minor role (Ennaccur, 2000; Kriaa, 2012) primarily because the remuneration and working conditions agreed as part of such firm-level negotiations cannot be less favourable than those stipulated in sector agreements (there is no possibility of opening closes). Individual firms therefore rarely take part in collective bargaining and resign themselves to applying remuneration and working conditions that have been agreed at the sector level. In some corners there have been calls for more decentralisation in the wage bargaining process and giving priority to firm-level wage agreements over sectoral ones (Kriaa, 2012).

### Table 2.2. Collectively agreed minimum wages by sector, Tunisia, 2014 or latest available year

| Sector | Collectively agreed minimum wage (MW) (TND per month) | Year |
|---|---|---|
| Trade and distribution of oil and its derivatives | 893.262 | 2014 |
| Banks and financial institutions | 832.106 | 2014 |
| Printing press | 618.293 | 2012 |
| Insurance | 605.617 | 2012 |
| Salt | 517.648 | 2014 |
| Bakeries | 475.361 | 2014 |
| Private education | 439.268 | 2014 |
| Management of solid and liquid waste | 418.385 | 2014 |
| Vehicle concessionnaires and manufacturers | 414.911 | 2014 |
| Wholesale, semi-wholesale and retail | 409.290 | 2014 |
| Dairy industry | 405.600 | 2012 |
| Coffee roasting | 403.936 | 2012 |
| Mills[a] | 403.685 | 2012 |
| Retail pharmacy | 402.276 | 2012 |
| Confectionary, and biscuit, chocolate and pastry manufacturers[b] | 398.736 | 2012 |
| Pasta and couscous | 396.925 | 2012 |
| Explosives | 393.560 | 2012 |
| Industry of shoes and footwear | 390.859 | 2014 |
| Agricultural equipment dealers and civil engineering | 389.775 | 2012 |
| Trade in building materials, wood and steel products | 386.047 | 2014 |
| Dry cleaning[b] | 384.384 | 2014 |
| General mechanics and fuel stations | 373.360 | 2012 |
| Plastic processing industry[b] | 371.904 | 2014 |
| Foundry, metallurgy and mechanical engineering[a] | 370.752 | 2012 |
| Surveillance and transfer of funds | 370.200 | 2012 |
| Travel agencies[b] | 367.987 | 2014 |
| Hotels and similar establishments | 365.308 | 2014 |
| Paint industry | 364.342 | 2014 |
| Construction and public works | 363.988 | 2014 |
| Wood, cork and furniture[a] | 363.646 | 2014 |
| Alcoholic beverages[a] | 362.953 | 2012 |
| Kindergartens and nurseries | 362.520 | 2012 |
| Soap and oil refineries | 359.659 | 2014 |
| Textile | 358.176 | 2014 |
| Hosiery and garments[b] | 358.176 | 2014 |
| Manufacturers of cleaning products and insecticides[a] | 355.499 | 2014 |
| Industry of building materials | 355.472 | 2012 |
| Canned food industry and oil packaging[b] | 355.056 | 2012 |
| Distribution of medicines | 351.255 | 2010 |
| Manufacturers of toiletries and perfumery | 351.176 | 2014 |
| Glass and mirror manufacturing | 349.506 | 2012 |
| Leather and hides[a] | 348.739 | 2014 |
| Printing industry, bookbinding, cardboard and paper processing, photography[a] | 347.699 | 2014 |
| Steel construction and building[c] | 344.708 | 2014 |
| Vehicle hire | 343.407 | 2011 |
| Soft drinks, syrups and mineral waters[a] | 340.940 | 2012 |
| Law clerks | 337.758 | 2014 |
| Private clinics | 319.299 | 2012 |
| Electricity and electronics[a] | 312.777 | 2012 |
| Cinemas | 301.587 | 2011 |
| Protection of persons with disabilities | 300.000 | 2013 |
| Road haulage | 297.327 | 2011 |
| Cafes, bars and restaurants[d] | 269.782 | 2010 |

*a)* The minimum wages are set on an hourly basis. These have been converted for the purposes of this table to a 40 hours regime assuming 208 hours per month. *b)* The minimum wages are set on an hourly basis. These have been converted for the purposes of this table to a 48 hours regime assuming 208 hours per month. *c)* The minimum wages are set on an hourly basis. These have been converted for the purposes of this table to a 42 hours regime assuming 182 hours per month. *d)* No new sector agreement has been reached in amendment to the collective agreement for the cafes, bars and restaurants sector has been signed since the three-year collective bargaining round of 2008, 2009 and 2010.

*Source:* OECD analysis based on sector bargaining agreements as published in the *Journal Officiel de la République Tunisienne*.

## *Non-wage costs and the tax wedge*

Non-wage costs that create an excessive gap between the total cost of labour and the net take-home pay (i.e. the tax wedge) can also have a deleterious effect on employment and formality (Lehmann and Muravyev, 2012). On the one hand, high additional costs on employers may dissuade them from hiring (formally) while, on the other hand, high income taxes and social security contributions for workers may reduce their incentives to work, or increase their likelihood of working informally. This section derives the tax wedge for Tunisia and puts it in an international comparative perspective. The focus here will be primarily on the demand side (i.e. the effect on employers and their hiring behaviour). The discussion of the possible impact of high income taxes and social security contributions on individuals' incentives to supply their labour (formally) will be left for Chapter 3, where other policies aimed at tackling informality in the Tunisian labour market will also be discussed.

In Tunisia, employer social security contributions on salaried non-agricultural workers in the private sector amount to 16.57% of gross wages, while workers themselves contribute 9.18% (see Box 2.3 for a brief description of the structure of the social security system in Tunisia). Personal income tax in Tunisia is progressive starting at 15% of earnings between TND 1 500 and TND 5 000 and gradually increasing to 35% of earnings above TND 50 000 (the first TND 1 500 are disregarded) – again, Box 2.3 provides further detail.

### Box 2.3. Personal income tax and social security in Tunisia

**Personal income tax**

The *Impôt sur le Revenu des Personnes Physiques* (IRPP) is an annual personal income tax payable by any individual ordinarily resident in Tunisia and working as a dependent employee in the public or private sector. The IRPP is progressive and calculated based on the rates and income brackets shown in the Table A below. These income brackets have not been uprated since 1983 (UGTT, 2006), meaning that Tunisian tax payers have been subject to considerable fiscal drag over the years. The impact of this on work incentives (or the likelihood of working informally) will be discussed in Chapter 3. The 2014 budget (*Loi des Finances 2014*) included a measure that exempts individuals earning up to TND 5 000 from income tax, which is a welcome development. However, this does not affect the personal income tax rates and brackets for any person earning more than TND 5 000, which are presented in Table A.

Taxable income is calculated as the gross wage minus an earnings disregard of 10%. Additional flat-rate deductions from the taxable income base are provided for: main earners, dependent children, children (aged 25 and below) attending tertiary education without a scholarship, disabled children (regardless of the age of the child), and dependent parents (see Table B). Again, most of these deductions have never been uprated since their introduction in 1990 and their real value has therefore been eroded by inflation (Limam, 2012; and UGTT, 2006). The small value of child benefits in particular will be discussed in further detail in Chapter 3, where the lack of government support towards meeting the costs of childcare will be argued to have a negative on parental (and in particular maternal) labour supply.

## Box 2.3. Personal income tax and social security in Tunisia *(cont.)*

### Table A. Personal income tax rates and brackets for individuals earning more than TND 5 000

| Income brackets (in TND) | Tax rate (in %) |
|---|---|
| 0 - 1 500 | 0.000 |
| 1 500.001 - 5 000 | 15.000 |
| 5 000.001 - 10 000 | 20.000 |
| 10 000.001 - 20 000 | 25.000 |
| 20 000.001 - 50 000 | 30.000 |
| More than 50 000 | 35.000 |

*Source*: Ministère de l'Économie et des Finances (2014), *Aperçu Général sur la Fiscalité*, www.finances.gov.tn/index.php?option=com_content&view=article&id=75&Itemid=258&lang=fr (accessed 13 February 2014).

### Table B. Deductions from the taxable income base

| Eligible workers | Deductions from taxable income (TND per year) | Source |
|---|---|---|
| Head of household (main earner) | 150 | Bulletin officiel des douanes et des impôts No. 2013/03/10 |
| Workers with a dependent child (20 years or younger) | 1st child: 90<br>2nd child: 75<br>3rd child: 60<br>4th child: 45 | Bulletin officiel des douanes et des impôts No. 2013/03/10 |
| Workers with a child (aged 25 and below) attending tertiary education without scholarship | 1 000 per child | Loi des Finances 2014 |
| Workers with a disabled child | 1 200 per child | Loi des Finances 2014 |
| Workers with a dependent parent | 5% of net income per dependent parent, up to a combined maximum of TND 150 | Ernst and Young (2013)[a], *The Worldwide Personal Tax Guide: Income Tax, Social Security and Immigration 2013-2014.* |

*a)* According to UGTT (2006) the deduction is TND 150 per dependent parent.

Alternative tax regimes exist for other categories of workers (e.g. the self-employed), and these will be discussed to some extent in Chapter 3 of this chapter.

### Social security contributions

Social security in Tunisia is managed by three state-run funds:

- The *Caisse Nationale de Retraite et de Prévoyance Sociale* (CNRPS) [National Pension and Social Contingency Fund], which manages pensions and other benefits for public sector workers;
- The *Caisse Nationale de Sécurité Sociale* (CNSS) [National Social Security Fund], which manages pensions and other benefits for private sector workers; and
- The *Caisse Nationale d'Assurance Maladie* (CNAM) [National Health Insurance Fund], which manages health insurance for both public and private sector workers.

Contributions to these funds vary by sector and type of worker. Table C below summarises the employer and employee social security contributions for public and private sector workers.

According to the Ministry of Social Affairs, statutory social security schemes cover the vast majority (85.6% in 2012) of the working population in (formal) employment (Ministère des Affaires Sociales, 2014). People who are not covered by any social insurance schemes are eligible for non-contributory social assistance programmes which will be discussed in further detail in Chapter 3.

**Box 2.3. Personal income tax and social security in Tunisia** *(cont.)*

**Table C. Social security contributions in the public and private sectors**

As a percentage of gross wages

| | Private sector[a] | | | | | Public sector[b] |
|---|---|---|---|---|---|---|
| | Salaried, non-agricultural | Salaried, agricultural | Salaried, agricultural (specialised/qualified) | Low-income workers[c] | Self-employed | |
| Employer | 16.57 | 7.72 | 12.48 | 5 | 14.71 | 20.5 |
| Employee | 9.18 | 4.57 | 6.99 | 2.5 | | 14.7 |
| Total | 25.75 | 12.29 | 19.47 | 7.5 | 14.71 | 35.2 |

*a)* Only certain regimes are shown in this table. Alternative regimes are available for: Tunisians working abroad; artists, creators and intellectuals; and students.

*b)* There are also special schemes for members of government, members of parliament and governors (not reported).

*c)* In addition, in the case of SMIG/SMAG earners, the basis on which the SSC's are calculated is two-thirds of the SMIG/SMAG rate.

*Source*: Ben Braham, M. (2012), "La protection sociale en Tunisie: État des lieux et perspectives" [Social protection in Tunisia: State of affairs and prospects], Notes de synthèse, Initiative pour le Développement Économique et Social (IDEES), Tunis; CNSS (n.d.), "Les régimes de couverture", www.cnss.nat.tn/fr/html/template3.asp?id=83 (accessed 17 February 2014).

The information on personal income tax and social security contributions can be used to calculate the tax wedge – the sum of personal income tax, employee plus employer social security contributions together with any payroll tax, minus benefits, expressed as a percentage of labour costs.

Figure 2.4 shows that the tax wedge in Tunisia is considerably higher than what is observed in the average OECD country (43.4% versus 35.6%)[10] – but this is primarily due to significantly higher income tax rates (19.4% versus 13.1%). Such high income tax rates could generate disincentives to work (formally) – an issue that will be addressed in more detail in the discussion on informality in Chapter 3.

On the other hand, social security contributions and payroll taxes in Tunisia, at 16.4% of total labour costs, are only marginally above the OECD average (14.4%) – suggesting that non-wage costs are unlikely to present a major impediment to hiring youth in Tunisia (or declaring them). A similar message emerges from the World Bank's Doing Business data: at 25.2% of company profits, the labour tax and contributions in Tunisia are only marginally higher than those typically observed in OECD countries (23.5%). In addition, much lower social security contributions are payable on workers earning the minimum wage (5% for employers) – a group which is likely to include many young workers.

**Figure 2.4. Income tax, employer and employee social security contributions, Tunisia and OECD countries, 2012[a]**

As a percentage of labour costs[b]

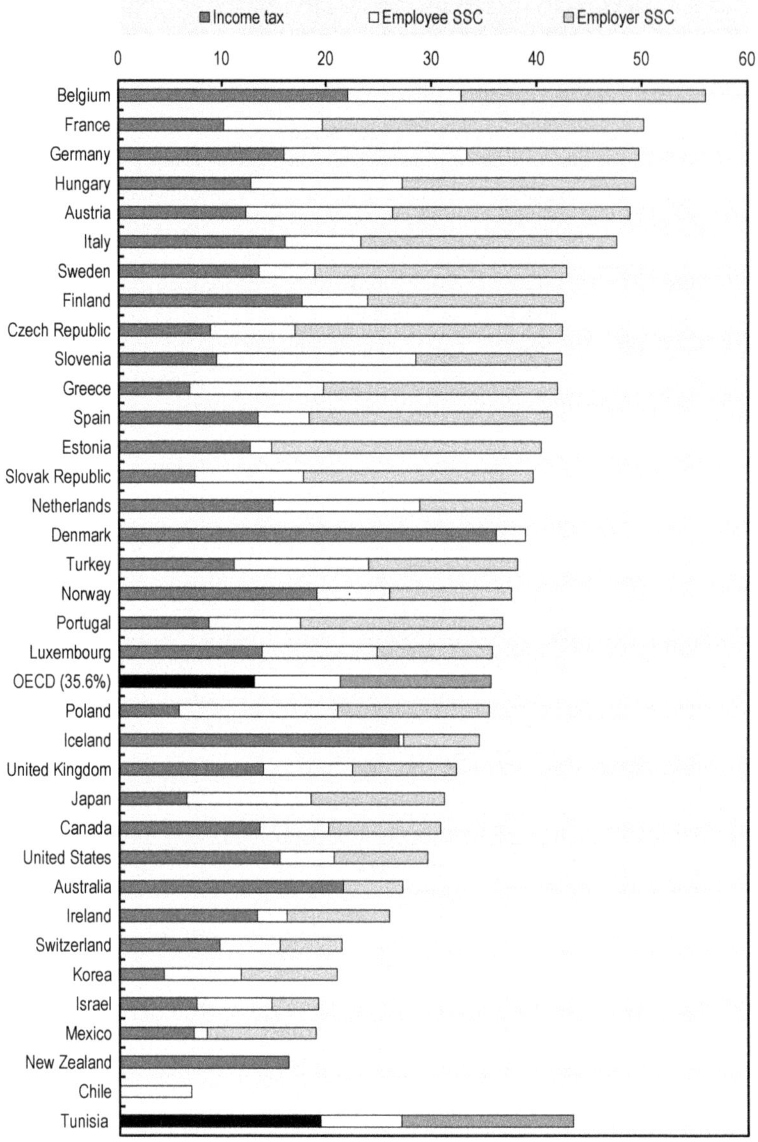


SSC: Social security contribution.

*a)* Data for Tunisia refers to 2011. Gross median wages in Tunisia are calculated using net median wages of TND 422 for full-time private sector workers as calculated by CRES and ILO (2012) and estimating the social security contributions and income tax rate assuming a single person without children.

*b)* The total cost of labour is the sum of gross average wage earnings, employer social security contributions and payroll taxes, where applicable.

*Source*: OECD (2013), *Taxing Wages 2013*, OECD Publishing, Paris, http://dx.doi.org/10.1787/tax_wages-2013-en; OECD calculations based on CRES and ILO (2012), *Enquête sur la Structure des Salaires, Tunisie 2011. Rapport Final* [Salary Survey], Centre de Recherches et d'Études Sociales, Tunis (for Tunisia).

### *Public sector employment, wages and benefits*

The cost of hiring in the private sector may also be affected indirectly by public sector employment and wage policies. In particular, higher rewards in the public sector (including state-owned enterprises) combined with the expectation that, eventually, a job in the public sector can be obtained, will raise reservation wages[11] and lead to public sector queuing. As a result, young people will be unwilling to accept private sector jobs at the going wage rate, raising the unemployment rate and making it more difficult for firms to recruit. If firms do raise their wages in response to higher public sector remuneration, this is likely to lead to a fall in competitiveness and in overall employment. In Tunisia, the public sector is oversized, public sector employment has been (and continues to be) used to address high levels of unemployment, and wages and benefits are significantly higher than in the private sector. All these elements combine to increase the likelihood of public sector queuing, and therefore unemployment.

In Tunisia, public sector jobs are generally much more desirable than private sector jobs (Ayadi, 2014). When asked who they would like to work for, over 65% of young people in Tunisia (aged 15-29) answered that they would like to work in the government/public sector, compared to only 22% who said they wanted to work in the private sector and 10% who expressed a desire to become self-employed.[12] To begin with, wages are on average significantly higher in the public sector than they are in the private sector. Although information on salary data is hard to come by, a graduate tracer study showed that, in 2007 and three years after graduation, the net wages of graduates employed in the public sector were about 35% higher than those of graduates working in the private sector (Ministère de l'Emploi et de l'Insertion Professionnelle des Jeunes and World Bank, 2009).[13] Angel-Urdinola et al. (2012) is one of the rare studies directly exploring wage information from the *Enquête Nationale sur la Population et l'Emploi* [National Population and Employment Survey] for 2010, and the authors show how the wage distribution for public sector workers shows a much higher concentration on the high end than the wage distribution for private sector workers.[14] However wages only tell part of the story. Benefits for public sector workers (e.g. maternity leave, pensions, etc.)[15] are also considerably more generous, as is job security (Gatti et al., 2013). It is not surprising, therefore, that a very high proportion of young people express a desire to work in the public sector.

Higher wages and benefits in the public sector are combined with a significant likelihood of obtaining a public sector job, so that the expected benefit of waiting is high. In Tunisia, the government sector's share of employment is relatively large – a labour market feature it shares with many other MENA countries (Assaad, 2013). 18.8% of total employment in Tunisia is in general government, compared to an OECD average of 16.5% (Figure 2.5) – however, this figure is much higher when including public enterprises, and it has also increased considerably in recent years. Assaad (2013) has argued that the creation of public sector jobs has frequently been used by Arab regimes as "a tool of political appeasement in the context of the "authoritarian bargain" social contract that they have struck with their citizens in the post-independence period." This policy appears to have been adhered to in Tunisia in the aftermath of the revolution: the public sector expanded to appease popular demands through the creation of 67 000 public sector jobs (ANETI, 2014). All out-sourcing in the public sector was abolished in 2011 and 31 000 cleaners and security staff were absorbed into regular jobs (Zribi and Bouktif, 2011). Similarly, all workers on public works programmes are in the process of being absorbed into the regular public workforce (see Chapter 3). This stands in countrast to the recent OECD experience, where many countries have put in place plans to reduce the size of their civil service, including in response to the financial and economic crisis (Box 2.4). While cutting public sector jobs may not be advisable in the current economic climate (particularly without adequate provisions for unemployment insurance and employability programmes), Tunisian policy-makers should nonetheless resist the urge to continue to use public sector job creation as a means to tackle the existing unemployment problem. In addition, the size of the public sector could be gradually and naturally reduced by reducing the turnover to replace the persons resigning or retiring – as has been done in a number of OECD countries (Box 2.4).

**Figure 2.5. Employment in general government, Tunisia, OECD and selected emerging economies, 2011[a]**

As a percentage of total employment

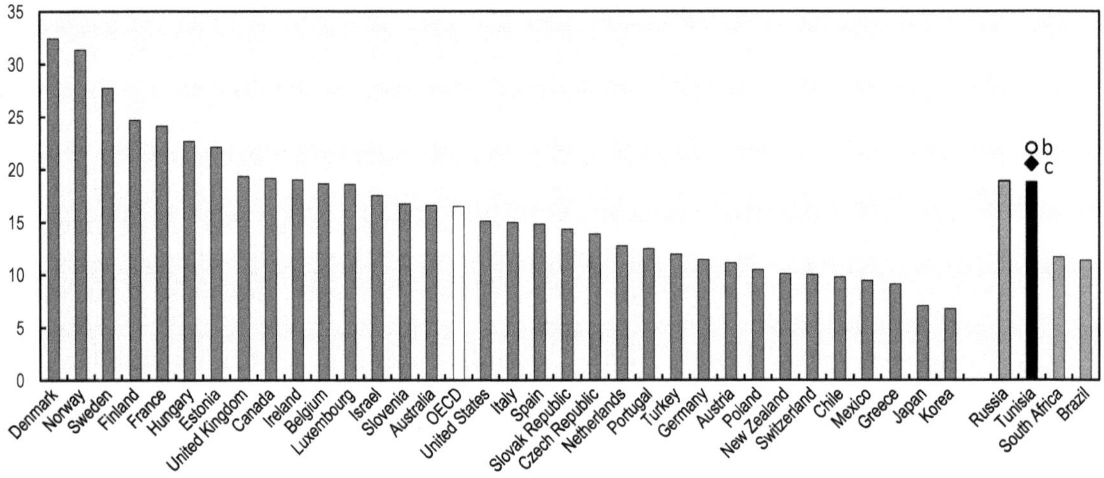


a) Data for Australia and Chile refer to the public sector (general government and public corporations). Data for Austria, Czech Republic, Italy, the Netherlands and New Zealand are expressed in full-time equivalents (FTEs). Germany, Ireland, Norway, Sweden, the United Kingdom and Ukraine: 2010 instead of 2011. Hungary, Japan, Mexico, Brazil and the Russian Federation: 2009 instead of 2011. Chile, Greece, Portugal and Switzerland: 2008 instead of 2011. France and South Africa: 2006 instead of 2011.

b) Tunisia 2011 with public enterprises (Boughzala, 2013).

c) Tunisia 2013 Ministère des Finances [Ministry of Finance] calculations based on the Enquête Nationale sur la Population et l'Emploi (ENPE) [National Population and Employment Survey] for Tunisia.

*Source:* International Labour Organization (ILO) LABORSTA database; *OECD Employment and Labour Market Statistics*, www.oecd-ilibrary.org/employment/data/oecd-employment-and-labour-market-statistics_lfs-data-en. Data for Korea were provided by government officials. OECD calculations based on the Enquête Nationale sur la Population et l'Emploi (ENPE) [National Population and Employment Survey] for Tunisia.Boughzala, M. (2013), "Youth Employment and Economic Transition in Tunisia", Global Economy and Development Working Papers, No. 57, Brookings Institute, Washington, DC, for Tunisia.

**Box 2.4. Reductions in public sector employment in OECD countries in response to the crisis**

Many OECD countries, in response to the economic and financial crisis and the pressure that this has put on public finances, have introduced plans to reduce the size of the civil service (Table A). In some countries, public sector employment will be scaled back considerably. The Czech Republic plans to remove 10% of the public workforce excluding teachers. By 2014, there should be 330 000 fewer public sector employees in the United Kingdom and around 25 000 fewer in Ireland. Other countries will only replace a certain number of vacant positions or retiring employees (France, Greece, Portugal and Spain).

**Table A. Staff reduction targets in OECD countries**

| Country | Reductions |
|---|---|
| Austria | 3 000 federal officials by 2014. |
| France | 97 000 public sector jobs by only replacing 1 out of 2 retiring state employees. |
| Germany | 10 000 federal public sector jobs by 2014. |
| Greece | 20% of retiring employees replaced, fewer public short-term contract employees. |
| Ireland | 24 750 public sector jobs by 2014. |
| Portugal | Recruitment freeze of civil servants (no replacements). |
| Slovenia | 1% of public sector employees from 2010-11. |
| Spain | 10% replacement of vacant positions between 2011-13. |
| United Kingdom | 330 000 public sector jobs by 2014. |

*Source:* OECD (2011), "Fiscal Consolidation: Targets, Plans and Measures", *OECD Journal on Budgeting,* Vol. 11/2.

In addition, public sector queuing in Tunisia has sometimes been encouraged by regulations concerning eligibility and selection criteria for public sector jobs. For example, during the 2011 public sector recruitment round (but also in the two subsequent years), strong preference was given to unemployed candidates registered with ANETI (the public employment service), as well as to older candidates and those who graduated longest ago (Decree No. 2011-544 of 14 May 2011). An incentive therefore existed either to remain unemployed or to work informally until a public sector job could be obtained. Such incentives are reinforced by age limits for entry into the public sector – currently set at 40 for non-graduates and 45 for graduates who have been registered unemployed for the past five years (i.e. beyond these age limits, individuals are no longer eligible for public sector recruitment rounds).[16] This provides additional incentives to try and obtain a public sector job while still young.

## *Hiring incentives*

### *Hiring incentives constitute the principal axis of Tunisia's active labour market programmes (ALMPs)*

Although the evidence presented thus far suggests that the cost of hiring may not present a major impediment to youth employment, Tunisia still has a large number of programmes in place to wave social security contributions for firms and/or subsidise a part of workers' wages. Some of these schemes affect all age groups and are primarily designed to stimulate investment.[17] These include, amongst others: total exemptions from social security contributions (SSC) for offshore companies (*exonération pour les entreprises totalement exportatrices*); SSC relief for a period of at least five years for investments in priority regional development zones (*prise en charge pour le développement régional*); SSC reductions for investments that promote the use of new technologies (*prise en charge pour la promotion de la technologie et de la recherche*); five year SSC exemptions for projects at least partially funded by the *Fond National de la Promotion de l'Artisanat et des Petits Métiers* (FONAPRAM) [National Fund for the Promotion of Crafts and Small Enterprises]; and SSC waivers for new promoters (*prise en charge pour les nouveaux promoteurs*). While these programmes aimed at attracting/promoting investment are also likely to encourage hiring, no evidence exists on their impact on employment.

The focus of this section, however, will be on active labour market programmes (i.e. programmes specifically designed to stimulate employment) that offer a mixture of social security reductions as well as direct wage subsidies to entice firms to take on workers. In Tunisia, such programmes are primarily focused on (highly educated) youth. They include: the *Stage d'Initiation à la Vie Professionnelle* (SIVP) [Initiation to the World of Work Internship], the *prise en charge par l'État de 50% des salaires versés* (PC50) [50% wage subsidy], the *Contrat d'Insertion des Diplômés de l'Enseignement Supérieur* (CIDES) [Higher Education Graduates Insertion Contract], the *Service Civil Volontaire* (SCV) [Voluntary Civil Service], the *Contrat d'Adaptation et d'Insertion Professionnelle* (CAIP) [Adaptability and Employability Contract], and the *Contrat de Réinsertion dans la Vie Active* (CRVA) [Contract for the Reintegration into Working Life].[18] Box 2.5 provides further detail on the target groups of these programmes, their length, the extent of the subsidy, as well as what is expected of employers and their size (in terms of number of beneficiaries).

### Box 2.5. Active labour market programmes that incentivise hiring

The bulk of active labour market programmes in Tunisia contain a significant hiring incentive component. The purpose of these programmes is to provide unemployed youth with work experience by incentivising firms (or non-governmental organisations) to take them on at a reduced cost for a fixed period of time. Many of these programmes also contain a training component. While a major reform of ALMPs has been announced (Decrees No. 2012-2369 of 16 October 2012 and No. 2013-3766 of 18 September 2013), the piloting of these new programmes will start from January 2015, during which time most of the programmes listed below will remain in place (with the exception of temporary programmes such as the PC50).

***Stage d'Initiation à la Vie Professionnelle (SIVP)***

The purpose of the *Stage d'Initiation à la Vie Professionnelle* (SIVP) [Initiation to the World of Work Internship] is to provide beneficiaries with relevant work experience in order to ease their school-to-work transition. It is aimed at first-time jobseekers with a higher education qualification.[1] The government pays the individual an allowance of TND 150 per month for a period of one year and provides health insurance coverage (exempting the firm from social security contributions). In addition, the government covers the cost of up to 200 hours of training (up to a ceiling of TND 900). In return, the firm pays the beneficiary an allowance of at least TND 150 per month, and commits to recruiting at least 50% of its interns received over the last three years (if not, the firm will not be eligible for any further subsidies for a period of two years starting from the end of the contract of its last intern). While the subsidy lasts for a period of one year it may, in exceptional circumstances, be extended by one more year.[2] In 2012, the SIVP had nearly 56 000 beneficiaries.

**Box 2.5. Active labour market programmes that incentivise hiring** *(cont.)*

***Service Civil Volontaire (SCV)***

The SIVP is less effective in areas where the private sector is less developed and therefore fewer internships are available. In order to provide unemployed university graduates with similar opportunities to undertake a subsidised internship in more rural areas, the government introduced the *Service Civil Volontaire (*SCV) [Voluntary Civil Service] in 2010 (Decree No. 2010-87 of 10 January 2010), which allows young people to gain experience in non-governmental organisations.[3] The target group is identical to that of the SIVP (first-time jobseekers with a higher education qualification) and also lasts one year (with a possible, but exceptional, renewal of one more year). The government pays the intern an allowance of TND 200,[4] provides health insurance coverage (exempting the organisation from social security contributions), as well as up to 60% of public transport costs. In 2012, the programme had just over 18 000 beneficiaries.

***Contrat d'Insertion des Diplômés de l'Enseignement Supérieur (CIDES)***

The *Contrat d'Insertion des Diplômés de l'Enseignement Supérieur* (CIDES) [Higher Education Graduates Insertion Contract] is a programme aimed at university graduates who have been unemployed for a period of at least two (consecutive) years[5] and is, essentially, a subsidised apprenticeship. While the programme initially contained significant subsidies for the host company,[6] in its current format it only pays a stipend of TND 150 to the apprentice (plus TND 50 for transport if he/she resides in a governorate other than where the firm is based), health insurance coverage (exempting the firm from social security contributions), and the cost of 300 hours of training.[7] In return, the firm pays the apprentice an allowance of at least TND 150 and commits to hiring him/her at the end of the CIDES contract (if not, the firm will not be eligible to receive any more subsidised apprentices for a period of two years). The number of beneficiaries of this programme fell significantly in 2012 as a result of the removal of the additional subsidies, and stood at fewer than 300 in 2012.

***Prise en charge par l'État de 50% des salaires versés (PC50)***

Firms based in priority regional development zones, or firms involved in high value-added and knowledge-intensive activities can, if they have been in operation for less than three years, benefit from a wage subsidy equivalent to 50% of the salary paid (up to a maximum of TND 250) for a period of one year for any first-time jobseeker with a higher education qualification that they recruit. In addition, firms involved in high value-added and knowledge-intensive activities are eligible for SSC exemptions for a period of seven years (the exemption gradually reducing from 100% of SSC in the first two years to 25% in the seventh). These programmes were announced as temporary measures and, unless renewed, will expire at the end of 2014. Only 300 graduates benefited from these programmes in 2012.

***Contrat de Réinsertion dans la Vie Active (CRVA)***

The purpose of the *Contrat de Réinsertion dans la Vie Active* (CRVA) [Contract for the Reintegration into Working Life] is to provide displaced workers with an opportunity to gain new skills through work experience in a private firm. It is aimed at workers on permanent contracts who were dismissed for economic/technical reasons and workers on temporary contracts who lost their job for similar reasons, but had been employed for a period of at least three consecutive years by the firm from which they were dismissed. While the CRVA is available to any worker, regardless of education (and age), the vast majority of its beneficiaries do not hold a tertiary qualification (Angel-Urdinola et al., 2013). The government pays beneficiaries a monthly allowance of TND 200 for a period of one year, provides health insurance coverage (exempting the firm from social security contributions), as well as the cost of 200 hours of training (up to a ceiling of TND 900) and up to 60% of the cost of public transport. In return, firms need to provide interns with a monthly allowance of at least TND 50 and commit to recruiting him/her at the end of the subsidy (otherwise, the firm will not be able to take on any further subsidised interns for a period of two years). In 2012, just over 350 individuals benefited from this programme.

## Box 2.5. Active labour market programmes that incentivise hiring *(cont.)*

***Contrat d'Adaptation et d'Insertion Professionnelle (CAIP)***

The *Contrat d'Adaptation et d'Insertion Professionnelle* (CAIP) [Adaptability and Employability Contract] is the equivalent of the SIVP for young people without a higher education qualification. For a period of one year, the government pays beneficiaries a monthly allowance of TND 100,[8] provides health insurance coverage (exempting the firm from social security contributions) and the cost of up to 400 hours of training (up to a maximum of TND 700). In return, firms pay an allowance of at least TND 50 per month, and commit to recruit the intern at the end of the subsidy (otherwise, the firm will not be allowed to receive any further subsidies for a period of two years). The total number of beneficiaries of this programme in 2012 was over 40 000.

***Contrat Emploi Solidarité Instrument 20***

Finally, through the *Contrat Emploi Solidarité* (CES) [Employment Solidarity Contract], some subsidies were managed at the local level to allow for a more tailored approach to tackling unemployment, the nature of which might vary from region to region. At some point, 41 instruments (or programmes) were delivered under the banner of the CES. However, following a national consultation in 2008 which sought to achieve coherence between these instruments and other ALMP programmes, most of the CES instruments were abolished, with the exception of instruments 16 (see Chapter 3) and instrument 20. Instrument 20 was essentially a subsidised internship in a non-governmental organisation (or in the public sector) for a period of one year (renewable up to three times) and benefiting higher education graduates who had been graduated for at least six months. The monthly stipend paid was TND 250 (i.e. more generous than what is provided by the programmes managed by ANETI). Since 2012, no new participants have been admitted to these CES programmes, and they are gradually being phased out. In April 2014, less than 500 individuals benefited from instrument 20.

1. Initially, the jobseeker needed to have graduated for at least six months before being eligible for the programme (Decree No. 2009-349 of 9 February 2009). However this condition was removed by Decree No. 2011-621 of 23 May 2011.

2. The renewal was initially only possible for six months (Decree No. 2009-349 of 9 February 2009), but was extended to one year by Decree No. 2011-98 of 11 January 2011.

3. While the original intention was to not make this programme available to graduates who had already participated in the SIVP, this condition was later removed by Decree No. 2011-98 of 11 January 2011. Similarly, the SCV was originally a part-time programme, but was changed to a full-time programme in 2011 (Decree No. 2011-621 of 23 May 2011).

4. Originally TND 150, but increased to TND 200 in 2011 (Decree No. 2011-621 of 23 May 2011).

5. Initially, this was three years (Decree No. 2009-349 of 9 February 2009), but it was lowered to two years in 2011 (Decree No. 2011-1 of 3 January 2011).

6. These subsidies included, originally, a TND 1 000 lump-sum upon hiring as well as a reduction in social security contributions for a period of seven years following the apprenticeship, with 100% waved in the first two years and gradually reducing to 25% by the seventh year (Decree No. 2009-349 of 9 February 2009).

7. Initially, this was 400 hours (Decree No. 2009-349 of 9 February 2009), but it was reduced to 300 hours in 2011 (Decree No. 2011-1 of 3 January 2011).

8. This value was set at TND 80 in 2009 (Decree No. 2009-349 of 9 February 2009), and increased to TND 100 in 2011 (Decree No. 2011-621 of 23 May 2011).

### *The international evidence suggests that hiring incentives have positive, albeit modest employment effects, and that much depends on their particular design*

Reductions in social security contributions and wage subsidies are (or have been) used in many countries as incentives for firms to take on new workers. In the case of low-skilled youth, they may be particularly useful since employers could be reluctant (or consider it risky) to take on young, inexperienced workers, particularly if minimum wages are set at a level above the expected productivity of such workers. A period of subsidised employment therefore offers firms the opportunity to observe the true productivity of young workers and/or raise this productivity (through on-the-job training) until it is commensurate with the unsubsidised wage paid. Similarly, in the case of the long-term unemployed, wage subsidies can be useful devices to give individuals work experience and keep their skills up to date, or enable them to acquire new ones.

The international evidence on the effectiveness of such programmes is mixed, however. While some reviews have concluded that "expenditures on subsidised jobs seem a waste of money from the perspective of the aggregate labour market outcomes" (Boone and van Ours, 2004), others have been more positive: "wage subsidies have generally had significant positive effects on improving employment outcomes for youth in transition and developed countries [...] with net employment effects from 12 to 15.6%" (Betcherman et al., 2004). On balance, most reviews conclude that the effect of wage subsidies is positive, albeit modest (Katz, 1996; OECD, 2005; Kluve, 2010; Neumark, 2013; Neumark and Grijalva, 2013).

Much of the effectiveness of wage subsidies depends on how they are designed. There are two key challenges in this respect: the first is to reduce deadweight loss (i.e. subsidising jobs that would have been created even in the absence of the subsidy); the second is to minimise substitution effects (i.e. the hiring of subsidised workers instead of non-subsidised ones, with no net employment effect). While neither of these are entirely avoidable, effective wage subsidies manage to mitigate these negative effects as much as possible by successfully targeting the individuals who need most help in finding work, as well as by putting measures in place that reward additional hiring only. However, while targeting and ensuring additional hiring may improve the effectiveness of wage subsidies, care needs to be taken not to introduce excessive administrative burdens on firms, which can reduce take-up (Neumark, 2013).

There is also evidence that wage subsidies are most effective when combined with other employability programmes. An evaluation of the New Deal in the United Kingdom (van Reenen, 2003) suggests that a combination with job search services and training can increase the effectiveness of wage subsidies. After six months of unemployment, 18-24 year-olds in the United Kingdom were required to enter a "Gateway" period where they were given extensive job search assistance. If they were unable to obtain an unsubsidised job, then they could enter one of four New Deal options. One of these was a job subsidy, the others involved full-time education and training, government-provided employment, or voluntary work. The evaluation showed that unemployed young men were about 20% more likely to get jobs as a result of the policy. Similarly, Katz (1996) attributes the success of some early wage subsidies in the United States to their combination with job development efforts and on-the-job training.

### *Wage subsidies in Tunisia are poorly targeted and/or implemented*

In Tunisia, wage subsidies (including social security wavers) lack some of these key design features or, where they possess them, they tend not to be implemented properly. First, targeting tends to be poor and access to such programmes is generally granted on a first-come-first-served basis (Broecke, 2013). In most cases, employers find a suitable candidate first, and then only proceed to apply for the subsidy. This means that young people who would have found employment anyway are most likely to participate in the programmes (Redjeb and Ghobentini, 2005; Haouas et al., 2012) – a phenomenon referred to as "creaming" by Subrahmanyam (2011) that results in large deadweight losses (Belghazi, 2012). While some programmes initially only accepted the long-term unemployed, such eligibility criteria have generally been removed over time. One example is the SIVP programme, which was initially restricted to graduates who had been unemployed for a period of at least six months – a condition that was later removed (see footnote 1 of Box 2.4).

A related issue is the disproportionate focus on higher education graduates.[19] The vast majority of programmes listed in Box 2.5 are aimed at university graduates, and only around a third of beneficiaries from these wage subsidy programmes are non-graduates, despite the fact that they represent 84.8% of the total young unemployed. While it is true that the majority of those registered with ANETI have a tertiary qualification, this is partly because they have the greatest incentives to register with the public employment service (due to a greater availability of programmes as well as access to civil service recruitment rounds). Also, while it is true that the CAIP (subsidy programme aimed at non-graduates) is less stringent in the sense that it is not restricted to first-time jobseekers (like, for instance, the SIVP), the CAIP is less generous to employers in at least two ways. First, the CAIP requires employers to premanently recruit every subsidised worker they take on, whereas the SIVP requires employers to recruit only 50% of their subsidised interns. Second, the CAIP represents a smaller subsidy, not only in absolute terms (TND 100 versus TND 200 for the SVIP), but also in relative terms when expressed as a percentage of the average wage of non-graduates and graduates, respectively. Indeed, the CAIP is equivalent to around 26% of average non-graduate wages, whereas the value of the SIVP is around 30% of average graduate wages.[20]

Wage subsidies have almost become a rite of passage into the world of work for university graduates in Tunisia, with a very large proportion of them benefiting from such programmes. Belghazi (2012) estimated that, between 2006 and 2010, around two fifths of the stock of unemployed university graduates had participated in such programmes, and nearly two thirds of the net flow of unemployed graduates over that same period. Not only do a large portion of university graduates benefit from such programmes, many often do so repeatedly[21] because of the lack of clear exit/graduation strategies (Belghazi, 2012; Angel-Urdinola and Leon-Solano, 2013). Given the lack of unemployment insurance in Tunisia, the widespread use of employment subsidies (and other employment programmes, as will be discussed later on) can, to some extent, be interpreted as a substitute for unemployment benefits. In comparison, much less support is available for non-graduates, displaced and/or vulnerable workers (Mathlouthi and Mezouaghi, 2006).

Another aspect of the poor targeting of employment subsidies in Tunisia is that most of these programmes rely on the existence of a relatively well-developed (formal) private sector. In rural areas, where fewer job opportunities exist, such programmes are less effective, yet it is exactly in those areas that unemployment rates are highest (Mathlouthi and Mezouaghi, 2006; Broecke, 2013). While the authorities have tried to address[22] this through the SCV programme, the insertion rate upon completion of this programme is extremely low (16.9%, of which only 5.8% in the private sector). The government's *Programme d'Encouragement à l'Emploi* (discussed in Box 3.3 of Chapter 3) holds more promise in helping unemployed youth in those areas – but was set to be discontinued at the end of 2014. One option worth exploring in less developed areas would be to combine wage subsidies with endeavours to get small enterprises to formalise and/or to allocate larger wage subsidies to firms located in those areas (Redjeb and Ghobentini, 2005).

In addition, there is evidence that, whatever targeting criteria do exist, these may not be applied in practice. ONEQ (2012) mentions irregularities in the allocation of SIVP subsidies and Belghazi (2012) cites further evidence (collected by ANETI) that the rate of absenteeism from (and, by implication, misuse of) employment programmes is high – both of which indicate a need for increased monitoring (see also Angel-Urdinola and Leon-Solano, 2013 on this topic). Similarly, while there are expectations placed on firms to absorb a certain proportion of subsidised interns into their regular workforce, in practice this rarely happens.

Finally, while most of the programmes listed in Box 2.5 are meant to contain a (sometimes substantial and compulsory) training component, in practice this rarely materialises. According to Belghazi (2012) only 513 of the 49 000 SIVP and CIDES beneficiaries in 2010 participated in training of some sort – which is extremely low, given in particular that the CIDES programme is meant to be a subsidised apprenticeship. While making training a compulsory part of some of these programmes might help, there are also issues to resolve around: i) how such training is procured; ii) how to incentivise employers who are often only interested in using such programmes to reduce the cost of labour; and iii) the certification of such training programmes (or the lack thereof), which reduces the incentives of individuals to participate in them (for further detail, see Belghazi, 2012). In addition, it has been argued that, because ALMP programmes place participants on a non-standard contract, employers are less keen to invest in their training.[23] Finally, when training does occur, it has tended to be primarily supply-driven and provided in-class, so that its added value is questionable.

The discussion in this section has highlighted important deficiencies in the design of wage subsidies in Tunisia. This is not to say that these programmes are entirely ineffective – only that they could be improved significantly. Given limited resources, as well as the evidence presented which suggests that the cost of hiring may not be a major impediment to the hiring of youth in Tunisia, smaller programmes more targeted at youth encountering the greatest difficulty in finding work might be considerably more cost-effective than the set of programmes currently in place. The effectiveness of these programmes might also be improved by more robust and regular evaluations. In the case of wage subsidies in Tunisia, the only semi-rigorous evaluation is Broecke (2013), who estimated the impact of the SIVP programme on the labour market outcomes of university graduates. Although this evaluation finds that graduates who benefited from the programme appear less likely to be unemployed and considerably more likely to have found a job in the private sector – this will partly reflect selection into the programme, which is not random. The evaluation also presents evidence suggestive of poor targeting and therefore large deadweight losses.

### *The announced ALMP reform is unlikely to improve matters significantly*

A reform of all ALMPs in Tunisia has been approved by Decree No. 2012-2369 of 16 October 2012 (subsequently modified and supplemented by Decree No. 2013-3766 of 18 September 2013) and was set to be introduced (on a pilot basis) from January 2015 onwards. With regards to wage subsidies, the reform fuses all wage subsidy programmes into one *Chèque d'Appui à l'Emploi* [Employment Support Cheque] available to all first-time jobseekers, regardless of educational attainment. The cheque would consist in a 50% wage subsidy (up to a ceiling which is still to be announced) as well as exemptions from social security contributions for a period of one year (renewable only once under exceptional circumstances, and only in high-value-added or knowledge-intensive firms). While the streamlining of wage subsidy programmes and making them equally available to graduates and non-graduates are welcome developments, attention will need to be paid to ensure an adequate balance between the two types of beneficiaries and it is not clear at this stage how, in practice, this will be achieved. To a large extent, the success of this programme for non-graduates will depend on whether the PES can be made more attractive to these jobseekers, and more may need to be done in that respect. In addition, while the cheque normalises the contract situation of beneficiaries (they will now be hired on standard fixed-term or open-ended contracts) and the government will now pay social security contributions on behalf of the employer,[24] its targeting will be no better than that of the existing programmes. The reform is therefore unlikely to significantly improve the use of wage subsidies to encourage youth employment in Tunisia.

## Giving flexibility to employers while protecting workers (not jobs)

Employment protection legislation plays a critical role in shielding workers from the negative consequences of arbitrary actions by employers (e.g. loss of income and depreciation of human capital) and makes firms internalise at least some of the costs of labour turnover (e.g. the public provision of job-search assistance and active labour market programmes). It may also encourage longer working relationships with workers, thereby facilitating industrial stability, the build-up of firm-specific human capital and innovation. When employment protection is too rigid, however, it undermines firms' ability to respond quickly to changes in technology or consumer demand.[25] Overly strict regulations reduce job flows, have a negative impact on employment of some groups of workers (notably youth), encourage labour market duality and hinder productivity and economic growth (OECD, 2013b).

This section analyses employment protection legislation in Tunisia from an international comparative perspective. The *Code du Travail* [Labour Code] (last revised in 2011) and the *Convention Collective Cadre* (in the case of graduates) contain the rules and regulations regarding hiring and firing, although provisions on these can also be included in sector collective agreements as long as they are more generous towards the employee. In practice, however, deviations from the Labour Code are minimal – with the exception of provisions for severance pay, which can be significantly higher (see Annex 2.A2). Tunisia combines high levels of protection on regular employment with very light legislation on temporary work, resulting in a "dual" labour market where youth may end up getting stuck in precarious employment without ever making the conversion to more stable jobs.

Moving forward, while the flexibility provided by non-regular employment contracts provides an important mechanism for firms to adapt to changing circumstances, steps should be taken to narrow the gap in employment protection between open-ended and temporary contracts. Also, while flexibility is crucial for efficient job reallocation, greater job creation and economic growth, it is important that workers who are displaced receive the necessary social protection as well as assistance to find new work. Policies to achieve this will be discussed in further detail in Chapter 3.

### *Employees on regular contracts benefit from high levels of protection against individual dismissal*

In Tunisia, workers on regular employment contracts benefit from a high level of protection against individual dismissal.[26] First, dismissal on grounds other than economic or serious misconduct is virtually impossible. Second, in order to terminate a regular employment contract for economic reasons, employers need to first file a request with the local labour inspectorate, presenting evidence of the firm's economic difficulties. The *Commission de Contrôle des Licenciements* [Termination Commission] then expresses its opinion as to whether it accepts termination of employment on economic grounds or not – although this commission primarily plays a consultative role and the employer, if in disagreement, does not need to abide by its judgment.

The problem arises if the case is taken to court, however, as judges can call into question whether or not the dismissal was needed or not – effectively taking on a "managerial" role – rather than sticking to assessing whether the dismissal was truly for economic reasons or not.

This uncertainty in jurisprudence, combined with relatively high compensation required in the case of unfair dismissal (between one and two months for every year of service, up to a maximum of 36 months of pay)[27] and the ability to make an unfair dismissal claim for up to a year after dismissal, severely hamper the ability of employers to rapidly adjust to changing economic circumstances.

Finally, although ordinary severance pay as stipulated in the Labour Code is not excessive, collective sector agreements frequently raise the level of severance pay considerably above what is required by Labour Code (see Annex 2.A2).

These costs and uncertainties may be particularly burdensome for small businesses (Haouas et al., 2012). That said, there is no possibility of reinstatement if a dismissal is found to be unfair and the length of the trial period in Tunisia is exceptionally long (six months for *agents exécutifs* [executive agents], nine months for *agents de maîtrise* [supervisors], and one year for *cadres* [higher education graduates]) – allowing firms plenty of time to test new workers.

Finally, there are no additional layers of protection in the case of collective dismissals in Tunisia: the rules for dismissing one or more workers for economic reasons are identical. By OECD standards, these rules and regulations rank Tunisia among the countries with the most rigid EPL against individual dismissal (Figure 2.6) – although many of the large emerging economies have even stricter rules (e.g. the Russian Federation, India, Indonesia and China).

**Figure 2.6. Employment protection legislation on regular employment (individual dismissal), Tunisia, OECD and selected other countries, 2013[a]**

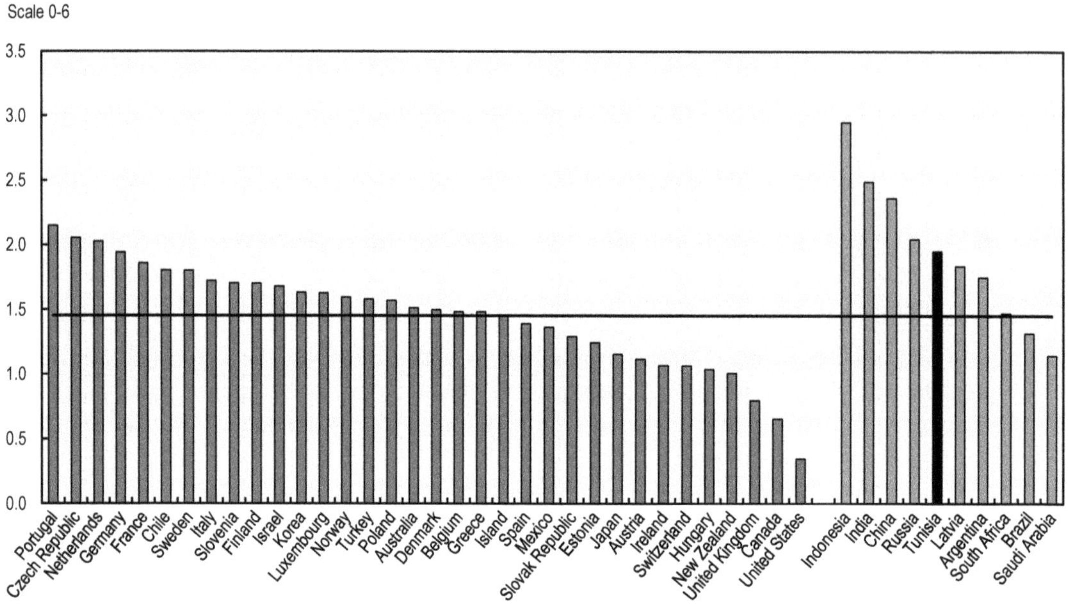


*a)* Data correspond to 2012 for Argentina, Brazil, China, India, Indonesia, Russian Federation, Saudi Arabia and South Africa.

*Source*: *OECD Employment Protection Database*, 2013 update, http://dx.doi.org/10.1787/lfs-epl-data-en.

## *Employment protection legislation on temporary employment is very lax*

By contrast, employment protection legislation on temporary contracts in Tunisia is very lax (Figure 2.7). First, while fixed-term contracts can be used under specific conditions where the nature of the work is temporary, the Labour Code also allows their use upon mutual agreement between the firm and the worker, even where the activity to be undertaken is of a permanent nature. In addition, there are no restrictions on the number of renewals or successive temporary contracts under which a worker can be employed by the same firm without interruption – as long as the maximum cumulative duration of four years is respected. This maximum duration for which temporary contracts may be used is also relatively long by OECD standards. Even if the same employee continued working at the firm, however, it is not clear that, if the employer were to be challenged, judges would order the conversion of the temporary contract into a permanent one – thereby severely discouraging employees from taking legal action (as they are likely to prefer a precarious job to no job at all).[28] Moreover, once an employee has reached the four-year limit, the employer can simply draw up a new fixed-term contract with a different employee and for another four years – in essence allowing companies to indefinitely carry out permanent activities by means of fixed-term contracts.[29]

Temporary work agency (TWA) employment, while authorised, is only very loosely regulated in Tunisia. The labour code (articles 28, 29 and 30) only contains some limited regulations regarding outsourcing,. As such, there are virtually no restrictions on the types of work for which TWA employment is allowed and no limits on the number of renewals or on the maximum cumulative duration of TWA assignments.[30] Starting up a TWA does not require any authorisation and reporting obligations other than those required when opening any other business. Finally, the Labour Code makes no provisions regarding equal pay or working conditions between TWA workers and workers on regular contracts. The lack of legislation around TWA employment leaves this form of employment open to abuse, and legislation surrounding the circumstances under which it may be used as well as the rights and obligations of the various actors involved is highly needed.

**Figure 2.7. Employment protection legislation on temporary employment, Tunisia, OECD and selected other countries, 2013[a]**

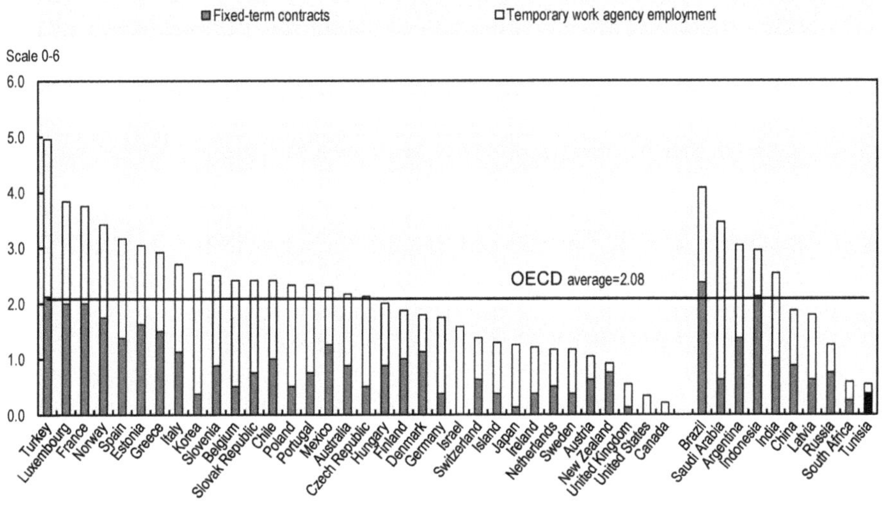


*a)* Data correspond to 2012 for Argentina, Brazil, China, India, Indonesia, Russian Federation, Saudi Arabia and South Africa.

*Source*: *OECD Employment Protection Database*, 2013 update, http://dx.doi.org/10.1787/lfs-epl-data-en.

## *Labour market duality reduces job quality and productivity*

In Tunisia, the Labour Code revisions of 1994 and 1996 sought to increase flexibility in the labour market (Belghazi, 2012; Haouas et al., 2012). According to many, this has led to an increase in the precariousness of employment relationships as employers tried to avoid stricter employment regulations on regular contracts by substituting temporary (fixed-term and TWA) workers for permanent ones (UGTT, 2008; Gouider, 2013), as well as increasingly relying on dependent-self-employed[31] and/or casual workers (Charmes et al., 2004; Meddeb, 2010). Indeed, as shown in Chapter 1, a very high proportion of employed youth in Tunisia are on temporary contracts. This pattern is typical of countries that have liberalised the use of non-regular contracts while maintaining strict employment protection legislation on open-ended contracts, resulting in a "dual" labour market with protected groups on the one hand and marginalised, excluded ones on the other – yet with little or no long-run impact on overall employment levels (OECD, 2014b). Moreover, when the gap between the two types of contracts is large, conversion opportunities are likely to be reduced, thereby transforming temporary work into a trap rather than a stepping stone into more stable employment (Boeri, 2011). This reflects the fact that outsiders end up moving from one temporary contract to another while insiders enjoy high protection and protracted stability. Those under fixed-term or non-regular contracts (often youth and other disadvantaged groups) tend to bear the main burden of employment adjustments when they occur. Such labour market dualism, by reducing the career opportunities for young workers in particular, tends to undermine their skills and is an important source of inequality.

These types of reforms have therefore led to "bad flexibility" (Fornero, 2013) with adverse effects on employment quality (see Box 2.6) which may have consequences that go well beyond the well-being of individual workers. By reducing workers' motivation, flexibility, willingness to take up new duties, their incentives to invest in firm-specific skills, as well as increasing work-related stress and worker turnover, concerns over job insecurity could reduce productivity and increase recruitment costs for firms (OECD, 2014a). Firms, in turn, are less likely to invest into workers who are unlikely to keep their job (OECD, 2014b) – further contributing to lower productivity. In conclusion, therefore, while temporary contracts can perform a useful function by giving employers the necessary flexibility to adapt their workforces to changing business conditions as a result of technological change, globalisation and the macro-economic situation, it is important to limit their improper use. In particular, they should not be seen as a way to systematically transfer risks from employers to employees.

The gap in employment protection legislation on permanent and temporary contracts in Tunisia therefore needs to be reduced. On the one hand, this will require reductions in the level of protection granted to regular workers. In particular, firing regulations should be eased and the definition of fair dismissal should be extended to cover dismissal on capability grounds (other than just serious misconduct). The judicial review process of the reasons for dismissal should be limited to the issue of whether dismissal for economic reasons masks any other motive or not, and should not focus on whether economic dismissal was needed in the first place or not. The level of compensation following unfair dismissal should be reduced. This could be particularly important for small firms. While perhaps more difficult to influence, excessive severance payments as stipulated in collective sector agreements should be kept in check.

In addition to easing EPL on permanent contracts, the use of temporary work should be regulated more carefully. One option in the case of Tunisia would be to place more restrictions on what temporary and TWA work may be used for, as well as for how long – although the danger is that increasing such restrictions may induce perverse effects on temporary workers by increasing their job insecurity, particularly for workers who have limited perspectives of conversion. An alternative solution would be to attempt to make firms internalise the cost of using non-temporary contracts. This could be achieved through the use of fiscal measures which make it more expensive for firms to hire workers on non-regular contracts. Although no evaluations exist as yet, such measures have been introduced recently by a number of countries. In Italy, for example, the 2012 labour market reform made fixed-term contracts more costly than standard open-ended contracts by introducing an additional payroll tax of 1.4% which is reimbursed in case the contract is transformed into a permanent one (Fornero, 2013). Similarly, in France, employers must pay an additional contribution comprised between 4.5% and 7.0% of the gross wage in the case of fixed-term contracts lasting less than three months (OECD, 2014b) and, in Slovenia, a higher rate of social security contributions for fixed-term contracts has been established by the 2013 labour market reform. However, as in the case of Italy, if a fixed-term contract is converted into an open-ended one, then the employer is exempted from social security contributions for up to two years (OECD, 2014b). Another way of reducing the gap in employment protection between temporary and regular contracts would be to achieve greater convergence of termination costs between the two types of contract (i.e. moving towards a "unified contract" as in Ireland, New Zealand and the United Kingdom – see OECD, 2014b). Indeed, for employers in Tunisia, one of the greatest attractions of temporary contracts is the lack termination costs. Introducing the same rules for severance pay on temporary contracts would make the latter less attractive to employers and reduce their use. That said, while Tunisia should consider introducing measures to narrow the difference in cost and difficulty of using temporary and fixed-term contracts, care needs to be taken that such interventions do not backfire by making hiring regulations overly restrictive. Any reforms in this area will therefore require a careful balancing act.

### Box 2.6. Non-regular employment and job quality

Recent and ongoing OECD work is aiming to bring job quality to the forefront of the policy debate, by arguing that labour market performance should be assessed in terms of the increase in both the number and quality of job opportunities. Indeed, the jobs people hold are one of the most powerful determinants of well-being, given that most people spend a substantial part of their time at work. Job quality inherently represents a multi-dimensional construct. Three key dimensions that are particularly relevant for workers' well-being include:

- ***Earnings inequality***. Average earnings and subjective well-being are positively correlated across countries, as well as between individuals within countries. In addition, however, for a given level of average income, overall well-being will be higher the more equal its distribution. This aspect of job-quality therefore attempts to measure both the average level of earnings and its distribution across the workforce.
- ***Labour market security***. Job security is a major determinant of individual well-being: when workers are asked to state their preferences with regards to different aspects of work, the results rank job security consistently as the most important item. The adverse consequences of the risk of unemployment on well-being are partially offset, however, by unemployment insurance programmes. This aspect of job quality therefore measures both the unemployment risk and unemployment insurance.
- ***Quality of the working environment***. The final key component of job quality refers to the balance of job demands and job resources required in order to sustain a health working life. In particular, excessive demands combined with insufficient resources create job strain, which is a crucial risk factor for workers' physical and mental well-being. Job demands refer to the overall time pressure faced by employees, the existence of conflicts between job requirements and personal ways of thinking or behaving, the exposure to physical health risk factors at work and intimidation in the workplace. Job resources include work autonomy and opportunities to learn at work.

Research has shown that temporary work is negatively and significantly associated with job quality in all three dimensions: they face lower earnings, higher levels of labour market insecurity and higher job strain. Chapter 4 in *OECD Employment Outlook* (OECD, 2014b) shows that non-regular workers, notably fixed-term and temporary-work-agency workers, appear to feel much more insecure than permanent employees with regards to the risk of job loss and the probability of re-employment after job loss. Moreover, there is no evidence that non-regular workers are compensated for their lower job security through higher wages. On the contrary, the majority experience worse outcomes in terms of job security and wages, even though the situation differs across countries and contracts. Finally, the higher incidence of job strain among temporary workers tends to be driven both by higher job demands and lower job resources. Again, OECD (2014b) shows that temporary workers face a reduced probability of receiving employer-sponsored training: evidence based on the Survey of Adult Skills shows that, on average, being on temporary contracts reduces the probability of receiving employer-sponsored training by 14% in OECD countries.

*Source*: See OECD (2014), *OECD Employment Outlook 2014*, OECD Publishing, Paris, http://dx.doi.org/10.1787/empl_outlook-2014-en, Chapter 4 "Non-regular Employment, Job Security and the Labour Market Divide".

### *The focus should be on protecting workers, not jobs*

The apparent trade-off between the need for flexibility, on the one hand, and for adequate protection, on the other, can somewhat be resolved by shifting the focus of protection away from jobs and onto workers – so-called "flexicurity". The idea is that while the reallocation of workers from low-productivity firms to high-productivity ones through job destruction and creation is facilitated by flexible labour markets, the workers who might be displaced as a result of such activity are given adequate social protection and assistance to help them maintain their incomes and find a new job. This will involve the provision of efficient (re-)employment services as well as income support to workers in the event of lay-off. Both of these exist in Tunisia but, as the next chapter will demonstrate, do not yet provide sufficient protection and support for workers in the event of job loss. The next chapter will explore how Tunisia can improve social protection mechanisms in Tunisia, as well as how better employment services for youth can be delivered.

# Notes

1. See, for instance, Card and Krueger (1995) versus Neumark and Wascher (1995) and, more recently, Dube et al. (2010) and Allegretto et al. (2011) versus Neumark et al. (2013).
2. Decree No. 1965-66 of 31 December 1965. Minimum wages for the agricultural sector already existed before 1966, but differed by geographical region (North, Centre and South) and professional category (see the Decree of 30 April 1956). Only in 1966 a unique national SMAG that applies to all geographical regions and professional categories was introduced.
3. Decree No. 1973-247 of 26 May 1973 announced the SMIG, while it was first set by Decree No. 1974-63 of 31 January 1974.
4. Tunisia has recently set up two new commissions: one looking at living costs and the other concerned with productivity issues. Both are made up of 15 members each (with five members from UTICA, the UGTT and the Government, respectively). While these commissions are not expected to directly influence the minimum wage negotiations, it is hoped that the latter will be informed by the work of the commissions.
5. The first decree setting the SMIG was Decree No. 1974-63 du 31 janvier 1974 fixant le salaire minimum interprofessionnel garanti dans le secteur non-agricole. While the SMAG had been set prior to 1974, a common starting point was chosen for the charts.
6. The full set of data for these figures is provided in Annex 2.A1.
7. Higher minimum wages are set for certain categories of "specialised" and "qualified" agricultural workers (so-called *primes de technicité*). A single *prime de technicité* [technical premium] was introduced in 2001 for qualified and specialised workers – although higher minimum wages for these categories (and other sub-categories) of workers already existed prior to that. The reason these are not included in the Figure 2.1 is that a uniform minimum wage for specialised and qualified workers was introduced only in 2001.
8. From the worker's perspective, it is important to stress that comparisons based on gross minimum wages do not take into account differences in taxes and benefits, and can therefore only give a partial indication of the true value of wage floors.
9. One potential issue is that many of Tunisia's ALMPs pay stipends considerably below the national minimum wage, which may be argued to institutionalise low-pay work (see Hibou et al., 2011).
10. The World Bank (Belghazi, 2012) has estimated the tax wedge for Tunisia to be 40.5% for minimum wage (SMIG) earners and 51.6% for someone with a three-year degree. The OECD's estimate differs from this for a number of reasons. First, The OECD uses a different definition of the tax wedge as the sum of personal income tax, employee and employer social security contributions plus any payroll tax less cash transfers, expressed as a percentage of labour costs for employers.

The World Bank defines it as the difference between the total cost of labour and the net take-home pay, expressed as a percentage of the net take-home pay. Second, whilst the OECD uses an average wage, the World Bank estimates the tax wedge for a range of different salaries (mostly for highly educated individuals). Third, the World Bank model ignores the earnings disregard of 10%.

11. There is some evidence that reservation wages in Tunisia may be relatively high. OECD analysis based on the ILO's School-to-Work Transition Survey for Tunisia (2013) indicates that the net reservation wage for unemployed youth with a tertiary qualification is TND 563. This compares to a median wage for full-time workers (all education level) in the private sector of TND 422 (CRES and ILO, 2012).

12. OECD calculations based on the ILO's School-to-Work Transition Survey for Tunisia (2013).

13. In 2007 prices, these net wages were estimated at TND 625 and TND 461 for the public and private sectors, respectively.

14. Of course, salaries in certain private sector jobs may exceed those paid in the public sector. On average, however, public sector workers earn significantly more than private sector workers.

15. For a discussion of maternity leave and benefits, see Chapter 3. With regards to old age pension schemes, pensions in the private sector are calculated based on 80% of the average salary of the last ten years, and capped at six times the national minimum wage (SMIG). In comparison, public sector pensions are calculated as 90% the last/best salary (provided it was granted for two consecutive years), with no upper ceiling.

16. Decree No. 2006-32 of 21 April 2006.

17. These were originally set out in the *Code d'Incitations aux Investissements* [Investment Promotion Code] (Law No. 93-120 of 27 December 1993) and revised on numerous occasions since through a series of laws and decrees. He latest version of the code dates from June 2011.

18. Only active labour market programmes (ALPMs) with a compulsory internship/employment element combined with a subsidy towards the receiving firm/NGO will be discussed in this section. Other programmes, like the *Programme d'Encouragement à l'Emploi* (PEE) [Employment Promotion Programme], which does not have a compulsory internship component, will be discussed later on in this chapter.

19. Bouzaiene (2007) argues that the disproportionate focus of employment programmes on higher education graduates under Ben Ali (but which continued after the revolution) stems from a fear of a repeat of the 1984 uprisings. Bouzaiene argues that Tunisia, along with other Arab states, sought to guarantee employment for those sub-sections of the population that were most likely to vocalise any discontent.

20. Average salaries for university graduates (TND 675.372) and those with only primary or secondary education (TND 391.408) were obtained from the ILO's School-to-Work Transition Survey for Tunisia (2013). The subsidies applied were TND 100 for non-graduates and TND 200 for graduates.

21. Nothing precludes an individual from benefiting from all ALMP programmes. A simple calculation therefore shows that university graduates could benefit from

eight different ALMP programmes and for a period of 108 months (i.e. nine years). In the case of non-university graduates, there are only three programmes, and the cumulative time that an individual can spend in them is 24 months.

22. Other programmes aimed at increasing employment opportunities in more deprived regions include the *Contrat Emploi Solidarité* [Employment Solidarity Contract – see Chapter 3] as well as regional development programmes.

23. The impending labour market reform proposes to standardise the contracts of ALMP participants (into regular temporary or open-ended contracts). However, it is not clear that moving simply to a standard temporary contract will improve this situation, since employers tend to invest less in training for temporary workers (OECD, 2014a).

24. Previously, social security contributions were simply waved, so that the young person did not build up any contributions towards his/her pension while completing their internship.

25. It is important to note that employment protection is only one of the policies and institutions affecting labour market flexibility. Other important aspects include regulations affecting working hours and part-time contracts, as well as policies affecting wage setting and safety nets (Venn, 2009), and these are discussed elsewhere in the report.

26. This assessment of the strictness of employment protection on regular contracts is broadly in line with those made by the World Bank's Doing Business Employing Workers Index (see Angel-Urdinola and Kuddo, 2010).

27. Although this is lower in case the termination of contract was for a real and serious cause, but without following the legal or conventional procedures, in which case compensation is between one and four months of pay.

28. This uncertainty is particularly great in the case of out-sourced workers, given that jurisprudence has been mixed on the issue of TWA agencies using ex-workers from the client firm.

29. Although some collective agreements have sought to put limits on these practices (Mzid, 2009).

30. While there is no limit on the duration of TWA assignments, the length of time for which the worker can be employed by the TWA is fixed by the standard regulations on fixed-term and open-ended contracts.

31. Own-account self-employed workers are independent contractors who either autonomously produce and sell goods or engage with their clients in contracts for services, regulated by commercial law. In practice, however, the conditions of work are often similar to those of employees, in the sense that they work mainly or exclusively for a specific client-firm with limited autonomy and often closely integrated into its organisational structure. When these conditions are met, these contracts represent *de facto* another substitute for regular, open-ended employment relationships, typically entailing lower social security contributions, hiring and termination costs for the employer and different social protection rights for the worker (OECD, 2014a).

## *References*


Allegretto, S.A., A. Dube and M. Riech (2011), "Do Minimum Wages Really Reduce Teen Employment? Accounting for Heterogeneity and Selectivity in State Panel Data", *Industrial Relations*, Vol. 50, No. 2, pp. 205-240.

ANETI – Agence Nationale pour l'Emploi et le Travail Indépendant (2014), "Près de 67 mille recrutés dans la Fonction publique au cours des trois dernières années" [Nearly 67 000 public sector recruitments over the past three years], Agence Nationale pour l'Emploi et le Travail Indépendant, Tunis, http://emploi.nat.tn/fo/Fr/global.php?page=2&id=2861 (accessed 30 April 2014).

Angel-Urdinola, D.F. and A. Kuddo (2010), "Key Characteristics of Employment Regulation in the Middle East and North Africa", *World Bank Social Protection and Labour Discussion Papers*, No. 1006, World Bank, Washington.

Angel-Urdinola, D.F. and R. Leon-Solano (2013), "A Reform Agenda for Improving the Delivery of ALMPs in the MENA Region", *IZA Journal of Labor Policy*, Vol. 2, No. 13, Springer Open, pp. 1-25.

Angel-Urdinola, D.F., A. Hilger and R. Leon-Solano (2013), "Public Employment Programs in Tunisia", in D.F. Angel-Urdinola, A. Kuddo and A. Semlali (eds.), *Building Effective Employment Programs for Unemployed Youth in the Middle East and North Africa*, World Bank, Washington, DC.

Angel-Urdinola, D.F., A. Kuddo and A. Semlali (2012), "Public Employment Services in the Middle East and North Africa", Draft dated May 2012, World Bank, Washington, DC.

Apps, P. and R. Rees (2005), "Gender, Time Use and Public Policy Over the Life Cycle", *Discussion Papers*, No. 500, Centre for Economic Policy Research, Australian National University.

Assaad, R. (2013), "Making Sense of Arab Labor Markets: The Enduring Legacy of Dualism", *IZA Discussion Papers*, No. 7573, Bonn.

Ayadi, M. (2014), *Les Régimes de Salaires Publics-Privés en Tunisie*, Institut Arabe des Chefs d'Entreprises.

Belghazi, S. (2012), *Évaluation stratégique du Fonds National pour l'Emploi* [Strategic Evaluation of the National Employment Fund], Report commissioned by the World Bank, Washington, DC.

Ben Braham, M. (2012), "La protection sociale en Tunisie: État des lieux et perspectives" [Social protection in Tunisia: State of affairs and prospects], *Notes de synthèse*, Initiative pour le Développement Économique et Social (IDEES), Tunis.

Betcherman, G., K. Olivas and A. Dar (2004), "Impacts of Active Labor Market Programs: New Evidence from Evaluations with Particular Attention to Developing and Transition Countries", *World Bank Social Protection Discussion Papers*, No. 0402, World Bank, Washington DC.

Bhorat, H., R. Kanbur and N. Mayet (2012), "Minimum Wage Violation in South Africa", *International Labour Review*, Vol. 151, No. 3, pp. 277-287.

Boeri, T. (2011), "Institutional Reforms and Dualism in European Labor Markets", in O. Ashenfelter and D. Card (eds.), *Handbook of Labor Economics*, Vol. 4b, North Holland, Amsterdam.

Boone, J. and J.C. van Ours (2004), "Effective Active Labor Market Policies", *IZA Discussion Papers*, Bonn.

Bouzaiene, S. (2007), "Les problèmes d'insertion professionnelle des diplômés tunisiens de l'enseignement supérieur: Diagnostics d'une exclusion" [Difficult school-to-work transitions of Tunisian higher education graduates: Analysis of an exclusion], Masters Thesis, Institut d'Études Politiques de Lyon, Université Lyon 2.

Broecke, S. (2013), "Tackling Graduate Unemployment in North Africa through Employment Subsidies: A Look at the SIVP Programme in Tunisia", *IZA Journal of Labor Policy*, Vol. 2, No. 9, pp. 1-19, Bonn.

Card, D. and A.B. Krueger (1995), "Time-series Minimum-wage Studies: A Meta-analysis", *American Economic Review*, Vol. 85, No. 2, pp. 238-243.

Charmes, J., M. Lakehal and N. Ziadi (2004), "Industrialisation and New Forms of Employment in Tunisia", in G. Standing and M. Chen (eds.), *Reconceptualising Work*, ILO, Geneva.

CNSS – Caisse Nationale de Sécurité Sociale (n.d.), "Les Régimes de Couverture" [Social Security Regimes], CNSS, Tunis, www.cnss.nat.tn/fr/html/template3.asp?id=83 (accessed 17 February 2014).

CRES – Centre des Recherches et des Études Sociales, and ILO – International Labour Organization (2012), *Enquête sur la Structure des Salaires, Tunisie 2011. Rapport Final* [Salary Survey, Tunisia 2011, Final Report], Centre des Recherches et des Études Sociales, Tunis.

Croucher, R. and G. White (2011), *The Impact of Minimum Wages on the Youth Labour Market: An International Literature Review for the Low Pay Commission*, Technical Report, Low Pay Commission, London.

Dube, A., T.W. Lester and M. Reich (2010), "Minimum Wage Effects Across State Borders: Estimates Using Contiguous Counties", *Review of Economics and Statistics*, Vol. 92, No. 4, pp. 945-964.

Ennaceur, M. (2000), "Les syndicats et la mondialisation: Le cas de la Tunisie" [Trade unions and globalisation : The case of Tunisia], *Working Papers*, No. DP/120/2000, ILO, Geneva.

Ernst and Young (2013), *The Worldwide Personal Tax Guide: Income Tax, Social Security and Immigration 2013-2014*, Ernst and Young.

Ferro, J. (2014), "Le modèle scandinave de Rached Ghannouchi est-il applicable en Tunisie?" [Can Rached Ghannouchi's Scandinavian model be applied to Tunisia?], *MENA Post*, 2 January.

Fornero, E. (2013), "Reforming Labor Markets: Reflections of an Economist Who (unexpectedly) Became the Italian Minister of Labor", *IZA Journal of European Labor Studies*, Vol. 2, No. 20, Bonn.

Gatti, R., M. Morgandi, R. Grun, S. Brodmann, D. Angel-Urdinola, J.M. Moreno, D. Marotta, M. Schiffbauer and E.M. Lorenzo (2013), *Jobs for Shared Prosperity: Time for Action in the Middle East and North Africa*, World Bank, Washington, DC.

Gouider, A. (2013), "The Tunisian Labour Market After the Arab Spring: Trends, Prospects and New Policies", *International Journal of Management Concepts and Philosophy*, Vol. 7, No. 1, Inderscience, Olney, pp. 31-46.

Haouas, I., E. Sayre and M. Yagoubi (2012), "Youth Unemployment in Tunisia: Characteristics and Policy Responses", *Topics in Middle Eastern and African Economies*, Vol. 14, Middle East Economic Association and Loyola University Chicago, pp. 395-415, September.

Hibou, B., H. Meddeb and M. Hamdi (2011), *Tunisia After 14 January and its Social and Political Economy: The Issues at Stage in a Reconfiguration of European Policy*, Euro-Mediterranean Human Rights Network, Copenhagen.

ILO – International Labour Organization (2011), *Tunisia – A New Social Contract for Fair and Equitable Growth Studies on Growth with Equity*, ILO, Geneva.

Katz, L.F. (1996), "Wage Subsidies for the Disadvantaged", *NBER Working Papers*, No. 5679, NBER, Cambridge, United States.

Kluve, J. (2010), "The Effectiveness of European Active Labor Market Programs", *Labour Economics*, Vol. 17/6, pp. 904-918.

Kriaa, M. (2012), "Le marché de l'emploi: État des lieux et perspectives" [The labour market: State of affairs and prospects], *Notes de Synthèse*, Initiative pour le Développement Économique et Social (IDEES), Tunis.

Lehmann, H. and A. Muravyev (2012), "Labor Market Institutions and Informality in Transition and Latin American Countries", *IZA Discussion Papers*, No. 7035, Bonn.

Limam, R. (2012), *La redistribution des revenus* [The redistribution of income], Institut Tunisien de la Compétitivité et des Études Quantitative, Tunis.

Mathlouthi, Y. and M. Mezouaghi (2006), *L'impact des politiques actives d'emploi sur les diplômés de l'enseignement supérieur: Les enseignements de l'expérience tunisienne* [The Impact of Active Labour Market Policies on Higher Education Graduates: Lessons from the Tunisian Experience], Fondation Friedrich Ebert and European Commission, Tunis.

Meddeb, H. (2010), "La Tunisie, pays émergent?" [Tunisia: An emerging economy ?], *Sociétés Politiques Comparées*, No. 29, Fonds d'Analyse des Sociétés Politiques, Paris.

Ministère des Affaires Sociales (2014), "Social Statistics Yearbook 2012" [available in Arabic] www.social.gov.tn/fileadmin/user1/doc/annuairestatsocial2012.pdf (accessed 11 February 2014).

Ministère de l'Économie et des Finances (2014), *Aperçu Général sur la Fiscalité* [General Overview of the Tax System], www.finances.gov.tn/index.php?option=com_content&view=article&id=75&Itemid=258&lang=fr (accessed 13 February 2014).

Ministère de l'Emploi et de l'Insertion Professionnelle des Jeunes and World Bank (2009), *L'insertion des jeunes diplômés de l'enseignement supérieur – Promotion 2004 : Analyse comparative des résultats de deux enquêtes (2005 et 2007)* [The School-to-Work Transition of Young Higher Education Graduates – the Class of 2004 : Comparative Analysis of the Results of two Surveys (2005 and 2007)], République Tunisienne, Tunis.

Mzid, N. (2009), "Droit du travail, entreprise et flexibilité de l'emploi" [Labour law, companies and labour market flexibility], Mimeo, University of Sfax, Tunisia.

Neumark, D. (2013), "Spurring Job Creation in Response to Severe Recessions: Reconsidering Hiring Credits", *Journal of Policy Analysis and Management*, Vol. 32, No. 1, pp. 142-171.

Neumark, D. and D. Grijalva (2013), "The Employment Effects of State Hiring Credits During and After the Great Recession", *NBER Working Papers*, No. 18928, NBER, Cambridge, United States.

Neumark, D. and W.L. Wascher (2007), "Minimum Wages and Employment", *Foundations and Trends in Microeconomics*, Vol. 3, No. 1-2, pp. 1-182.

Neumark, D. and W. Wascher (1995), "Minimum-wage Effects on School and Work Transitions of Teenagers", *American Economic Review*, Vol. 85, No. 2, pp. 244-249.

Neumark, D., J.M.I. Salas and W. Wascher (2013), "Revisiting the Minimum Wage-employment Debate: Throwing Out the Baby with the Bathwater?", *NBER Working Papers*, No. 18681, Cambridge, United States.

OECD (2014a), "How Good Is Your Job? A Framework for Measuring and Assessing Job Quality", Chapter 3 in *OECD Employment Outlook 2014*, OECD Publishing, Paris, http://dx.doi.org/10.1787/empl_outlook-2014-en.

OECD (2014b), "Non-regular Employment, Job Security and the Labour Market Divide", Chapter 4 in *OECD Employment Outlook 2014*, OECD Publishing, Paris, http://dx.doi.org/10.1787/empl_outlook-2014-en.

OECD (2013a), *Taxing Wages 2013*, OECD Publishing, Paris, http://dx.doi.org/10.1787/tax_wages-2013-en.

OECD (2013b), "Protecting Jobs, Enhancing Flexibility: A New Look at Employment Protection", Chapter 2 in *OECD Employment Outlook 2013*, OECD Publishing, Paris, http://dx.doi.org/10.1787/empl_outlook-2013-en.

OECD (2011), "Fiscal Consolidation: Targets, Plans and Measures", *OECD Journal on Budgeting*, Vol. 11/2, OECD Publishing, Paris, http://dx.doi.org/10.1787/16812336.

OECD (2005), "Labour Market Programmes and Activation Strategies: Evaluating the Impacts", Chapter 4 in *OECD Employment Outlook 2005*, OECD Publishing, Paris, http://dx.doi.org/10.1787/empl_outlook-2005-en.

ONEQ – Observatoire National de l'Emploi et des Qualifications (2012), *Rapport de suivi des programmes actifs d'emploi: Réalisations de l'année 2012* [Monitoring Report of Active Labour Market Programmes: 2012 Achievements], Observatoire National de l'Emploi et des Qualifications, Tunis.

Redjeb, M.S. and M. Ghobentini (2005), "L'intermédiation sur le marché du travail en Tunisie" [Intermediation in the Tunisian labour market], *Cahiers de la stratégie de l'emploi* (Employment Strategy Papers), No. 2005/19, ILO, Geneva.

Subrahmanyam, G. (2011), "Tackling Youth Unemployment in the Maghreb", *African Development Bank Economic Briefs*, AfDB, Tunis.

UGTT – Union Générale Tunisienne du Travail (2008), *Mutations du marché du travail, la précarité et ses impacts en Tunisie – Résultats d'une enquête quantitative et qualitative dans le Grand Tunis* [Labour Market Transformations, Precarity and their Impact in Tunisia – Results from a Quantitative and Qualitative Survey in Greater Tunis], UGTT, Tunis.

UGTT (2006), *La Fiscalité en Tunisie et la question de la cohésion sociale* [The Tunisian Tax System and the Question of Social Cohesion], UGTT, Tunis.

Van Reenen, J. (2003), "Active Labour Market Policies and the British New Deal for the Young Unemployed in Context", *NBER Working Papers*, No. 9576, NBER, Cambridge, United States.

Venn, D. (2009), "Legislation, Collective Bargaining and Enforcement: Updating the OECD Employment Protection Indicators", *OECD Social, Employment and Migration Working Papers*, No. 89, OECD Publishing Paris, http://dx.doi.org/10.1787/223334316804.

Wage Indicator Foundation (2011), "Minimum Wage Non-compliance in Indonesia", Wage Indicator Foundation, Amsterdam.

Wedenoja, L. (2013), "The Employment and Wage Effects of Minimum Wages in a Context of Informality and Non-compliance: Evidence from Chile", Mimeo, Cornell University, New York.

Zribi, M. and H. Bouktif (2011), "L'approche tunisienne en matière de justice sociale et lutte contre la pauvreté et l'exclusion" [The Tunisian approach to social justice and the fight against poverty and exclusion], Séminaire international justice sociale et lutte contre l'exclusion dans un contexte de transition démocratique [International seminar on social justice and the fight against social exclusion in the context of a democratic transition], Ministère des Affaires Sociales, 21/22 September 2011, Tunis.

# *Annex 2.A1*
# *Historical values of the minimum wage in Tunisia*

**Table 2.A1.1. Nominal values of the non-agricultural minimum wage (SMIG), 1974-2014[a,b]**

| Date of implementation | Monthly SMIG (in TND) | | Hourly SMIG (in TND) | |
|---|---|---|---|---|
| | 48 hours | 40 hours | 48 hours | 40 hours |
| 1st May 2014 | 319.904 | 274.559 | 1.538 | 1.584 |
| 1st July 2012 | 301.808 | 259.479 | 1.451 | 1.497 |
| 1st May 2011 | 286.000 | 246.306 | 1.375 | 1.421 |
| 1st July 2010 | 272.480 | 235.040 | 1.310 | 1.356 |
| 1st August 2009 | 260.624 | 225.160 | 1.253 | 1.299 |
| 1st July 2008 | 251.888 | 217.880 | 1.211 | 1.257 |
| 1st July 2007 | 239.824 | 207.828 | 1.153 | 1.199 |
| 1st July 2006 | 231.296 | 200.721 | 1.112 | 1.158 |
| 1st September 2005 | 224.224 | 194.827 | 1.078 | 1.124 |
| 1st July 2004 | 218.192 | 189.800 | 1.049 | 1.095 |
| 1st July 2003 | 211.120 | 183.906 | 1.015 | 1.061 |
| 1st July 2002 | 202.592 | 176.799 | 0.974 | 1.020 |
| 1st July 2001 | 195.520 | 170.905 | 0.940 | 0.986 |
| 1st May 2000 | 186.992 | 163.798 | 0.899 | 0.945 |
| 19th August 1999 | 180.960 | 158.771 | 0.870 | 0.916 |
| 1st May 1999 | 178.880 | 156.691 | 0.860 | 0.904 |
| 20th August 1998 | 172.848 | 151.664 | 0.831 | 0.875 |
| 7th November 1997 | 170.352 | 149.237 | 0.819 | 0.861 |
| 20th July 1997 | 164.320 | 144.211 | 0.790 | 0.832 |
| 9th September 1996 | 162.240 | 142.131 | 0.780 | 0.820 |
| 1st May 1996 | 160.160 | 140.051 | 0.770 | 0.808 |
| 1st May 1995 | 154.128 | 135.024 | 0.741 | 0.779 |
| 1st August 1994 | 147.056 | 129.131 | 0.707 | 0.745 |
| 1st August 1993 | 144.976 | 127.051 | 0.697 | 0.733 |
| 1st May 1993 | 142.896 | 124.971 | 0.687 | 0.721 |
| 1st August 1992 | 134.992 | 118.398 | 0.649 | 0.683 |
| 1st May 1992 | 132.912 | 116.318 | 0.639 | 0.671 |
| 1st August 1991 | 125.016 | 109.706 | 0.867 | 0.633 |
| 1st January 1990 | 123.016 | 107.706 | 0.591 | 0.621 |
| 1st August 1989 | 113.032 | 99.386 | 0.546 | 0.570 |
| 1st April 1988 | 110.032 | 96.386 | 0.529 | 0.556 |
| 1st November 1987 | 105.040 | 92.226 | 0.505 | 0.532 |
| 1st July 1986 | 100.048 | 88.066 | 0.481 | 0.508 |
| 1st January 1984 | 95.056 | 83.906 | 0.457 | 0.484 |
| 1st February 1982 | 85.072 | 75.586 | 0.409 | 0.436 |
| 1st April 1981 | 64.704 | 55.586 | 0.743 | 0.843 |
| 1st May 1980 | 54.704 | 45.586 | 0.263 | 0.263 |
| 1st February 1980 | 49.703 | 41.418 | 0.239 | 0.239 |
| 1st May 1979 | 48.256 | 40.212 | 0.232 | 0.232 |
| 1st May 1978 | 44.564 | 37.136 | 0.214 | 0.214 |
| 1st February 1977 | 40.144 | 33.453 | 0.193 | 0.193 |
| 1st June 1975 | 30.160 | 25.133 | 0.145 | 0.145 |
| 1st January 1974 | 27.040 | 22.533 | 0.130 | 0.130 |

*a)* The nominal monthly SMIG for January 1974 is estimated based on the hourly minimum wage.

*b)* Minimum wages for people younger than 18 equals 85% of the adult minimum wage.

*Source*: *Journal Officiel de la République Tunisienne.*

**Table 2.A1.2. Nominal values of the agricultural minimum wage (SMAG), 1965-2014**

| Date of implementation | SMAG per day of work (in TND) |
|---|---|
| 1st May 2014 | 12.304 |
| 1st December 2012 | 11.608 |
| 1st July 2012 | 10.608 |
| 1st March 2011 | 9.000 |
| 1st July 2010 | 8.380 |
| 1st August 2009 | 8.019 |
| 1st July 2008 | 7.749 |
| 1st July 2007 | 7.379 |
| 1st July 2006 | 7.129 |
| 1st September 2005 | 6.909 |
| 1st July 2004 | 6.709 |
| 1st July 2003 | 6.509 |
| 1st July 2002 | 6.259 |
| 1st July 2001 | 6.059 |
| 1st May 2000 | 5.809 |
| 19th August 1999 | 5.609 |
| 1st May 1999 | 5.509 |
| 20th August 1998 | 5.309 |
| 7th November 1997 | 5.209 |
| 20th July 1997 | 5.061 |
| 9th September 1996 | 4.961 |
| 1st May 1996 | 4.861 |
| 1st May 1995 | 4.661 |
| 1st August 1994 | 4.461 |
| 1st August 1993 | 4.361 |
| 1st May 1993 | 4.261 |
| 1st August 1992 | 4.061 |
| 1st May 1992 | 3.961 |
| 1st August 1991 | 3.761 |
| 1st January 1990 | 3.661 |
| 1st August 1989 | 3.315 |
| 1st April 1988 | 3.200 |
| 1st November 1987 | 3.050 |
| 1st July 1986 | 2.900 |
| 1st January 1983 | 2.640 |
| 1st February 1982 | 2.400 |
| 1st April 1981 | 2.000 |
| 1st May 1980 | 1.631 |
| 1st February 1980 | 1.483 |
| 1st May 1979 | 1.440 |
| 1st May 1978 | 1.332 |
| 1st February 1977 | 1.200 |
| 1st June 1975 | 0.900 |
| 1st June 1974 | 0.800 |
| 1st May 1971 | 0.600 |
| 1st October 1969 | 0.550 |
| 1st May 1968 | 0.500 |
| 1st January 1965 | 0.385 |

*Source*: *Journal Officiel de la République Tunisienne.*

# *Annex 2.A2*
# *Additional provisions made in collective sector agreements for trial periods, notice periods and severance pay*

### Table 2.A2.1. Collectively agreed: Employment protection indicators by sector

| Sector | Notice periods | Trial period | Severance pay |
|---|---|---|---|
| Construction and public works | 1 month | 1 year: managers<br>9 months: supervisors<br>6 months: operatives<br>With possibility of renewal for one further period of the same duration | 18 days' wages/year of actual service, up to a maximum of 6 months' wages |
| Travel agencies | 1 month | 1 year: managers<br>9 months: supervisors<br>6 months: operatives<br>With possibility of renewal for one further period of the same duration | 1 month's wages/year of actual service, up to a maximum of 6 months' wages |
| Insurance | 1 month | 1 year, renewable once for the same period for senior managers and administrative staff only | 1/24 of annual wages per 6 months of actual service, up to a maximum of 14 months' wages |
| Banking | 1 month | 1 year, renewable once for the same period | 2/24 of average annual wages per 6 months of actual service, up to a maximum of 28 months' wages |
| Bakeries | 1 month | 6 months: operatives<br>9 months: supervisors<br>12 months: managers<br><br>with possibility of renewal for one further period of the same duration | 1 month's wages/year of actual service (based on final wages earned) up to a maximum of 6 months' wages, provided that the sum of the severance, service gratuity and notice period payments does not exceed 12 months' wages for those with less than 15 years' service, 13 months for those with more than 15 years' service and 14 months for those with more than 20 years' service |
| Cafés, bars, restaurants and similar establishments | 1.5 months | 6 months, renewable once for the same period | – 2 days' wages/month of service up to a maximum of 3 months' wages in small businesses<br>– 2.5 days' wages/month of service up to a maximum of 5 months' wages in medium-sized businesses<br>– 3 days' wages/month of service up to a maximum of 6 months' wages in large businesses |
| Private clinics | 1 month | 6 months: operatives<br>9 months: supervisors<br>1 year: managers<br>renewable for one further period of the same duration | 1 day's wages/month of service up to a maximum of 3 months' wages |
| Wholesale, semi-wholesale and retail trading | 1 month for operatives and 2 months for others | 6 months: operatives<br>9 months: supervisors<br>1 year: managers<br>renewable for one further period of the same duration | 1 month's wages/year of service for administrative staff and 15 days' wages/year of service for workers, up to a maximum of 6 months' wages |
| Trade in building materials, timber and steel products | 1 month | 6 months: operatives<br>9 months: supervisors<br>1 year: managers<br>renewable for one further period of the same duration | 1 month's wages/year of service for managers and supervisors and 15 days' wages/year of service for operatives (final wages basis), up to a maximum of 6 months' wages |
| Agricultural and civil engineering equipment | 1 month | 6 months: operatives<br>9 months: supervisors<br>1 year: managers<br>renewable for one further period of the same duration | 1 month's wages per year of service, up to a maximum of 12 months' wages |

## Table 2.A2.1. Collectively agreed: Employment protection indicators by sector *(cont.)*

| Sector | Notice periods | Trial period | Severance pay |
|---|---|---|---|
| Confectionary, and biscuit, chocolate and pastry manufacturers | 1 month | 6 months: operatives<br>9 months: supervisors<br>1 year: managers<br>renewable for one further period of the same duration | 1 day's wages/month of service, up to a maximum of 6 months' wages |
| Automotive vehicle manufacturers and distributors | 1 month | 6 months: operatives<br>9 months: supervisors<br>1 year: managers<br>renewable for one further period of the same duration | 18 days' wages/year of service (those with between 1 and 10 years of service), 20 days' wages/year of service (those with between 11 and 15 years of service), 22 days' wages/year of service (those with between 16 and 22 years of service) and 24 days' wages/year of service (those with 23 or more years of service), up to a |
| Steel construction and building | 1 month | 6 months: operatives<br>9 months: supervisors<br>1 year: managers<br>renewable for one further period of the same duration | 15 days' wages/year of service (final wages basis), up to a maximum of 6 months' wages |
| Kindergartens and nurseries | 1 month (for those with less than 5 years' service) and 2 months (for those with more than 5 years' service) | 1.5 years for managers and 1 year for operatives or supervisors | 26 days' wages/year of service, up to a maximum of 6 months' wages |
| Leather and hides | 2 months | 1 year | 1 month's wages/year of service, up to a maximum of 7 months' wages |
| Electricity and electronics | 1 month: operatives<br>2 months: supervisors<br>3 months: managers | 6 months: operatives<br>9 months: supervisors<br>1 year: managers<br>renewable for one further period of the same duration | 1 day's wages/month of service, up to a maximum of 6 months' wages |
| Private education | 2 months | 6 months: operatives<br>9 months: supervisors<br>1 year for teaching staff and managers, renewable for one further period of the same duration | 26 days' wages/year of service, up to a maximum of 6 months' wages |
| Firms providing surveillance, security services and cash transportation services | 1 month | 6 months: operatives<br>9 months: supervisors<br>1 year: managers<br>renewable for one further period of the same duration | 1 day's wages/month of service (final wages basis), up to a maximum of 4 months' wages |
| Print media businesses | 1 month for administrative staff and 18 days for technical and blue-collar staff | 3 months: operatives<br>6 months: supervisors<br>1 year: managers renewable for one further period of the same duration | 1 month's wages/year of service, up to a maximum of 15 months' wages for journalists who are managers and 18 days' wages/year of service, up to a maximum of 6 months' wages for other categories of staff |
| Manufacturers of toiletry products and perfumery | 1 month | 6 months: operatives<br>9 months: supervisors<br>1 year: managers<br>renewable for one further period of the same duration | 15 days' wages/year of service (final wages basis), up to a maximum of 6 months' wages |
| Manufacturers of cleaning products and insecticides | 1 month | 6 months: operatives<br>9 months: supervisors<br>1 year: managers<br>renewable for one further period of the same duration | Businesses with fewer than 120 workers: 15 days' wages/year of service for workers (on an hourly rate) and 1 month's wages/year of service for employees (paid monthly), up to a maximum of 6 months' wages<br>Businesses with more than 120 workers: 20 days' wages/year of service for workers (on an hourly rate) and 1 month's wages/year of service for employees (paid monthly), up to a maximum of 9 months' wages |
| Paint manufacture | 15 days for workers on an hourly rate and 1 month for those paid monthly | 6 months: operatives<br>9 months: supervisors<br>1 year: managers<br>renewable for one further period of the same duration | 1 day's wages/month of service, up to a maximum of 6 months' wages |

**Table 2.A2.1. Collectively agreed: Employment protection indicators by sector** *(cont.)*

| Sector | Notice periods | Trial period | Severance pay |
|---|---|---|---|
| Foundry work, metallurgy and mechanical engineering | 1 month | 1 year, renewable for one further period of the same duration | 15 days' wages/year of service, up to a maximum of 6 months' wages |
| Classified tourist hotels and similar establishments | 1.5 months | 6 months for operatives and supervisors and 1 year for managers, renewable for one further period of 3 months for operatives and supervisors and 6 months for managers | 1 month's wages/year of service (gross final wages basis), up to a maximum of 9 months' wages |
| Printing industry, bookbinding, cardboard and paper processing, photography | 1 month | 6 months: operatives<br>9 months: supervisors<br>1 year: managers<br>renewable for one further period of the same duration | 15 days' wages/year of service for workers and 1 month's wages/year of service for administrative staff, up to a maximum of 6 months' wages |
| Hosiery and garment-making | 1 month | 6 months: operatives<br>9 months: supervisors<br>1 year: managers<br>renewable for one further period of the same duration | 1.5 day's wages/month of service, up to a maximum of 9 months' wages |
| Shoes and footwear | 15 days for hourly paid workers and 1 month for monthly paid workers, except for supervisors (2 months) and managers (3 months) | 6 months: operatives<br>9 months: supervisors<br>1 year: managers<br>renewable for one further period of the same duration | 15 days' wages/year of service, up to a maximum of 6 months' wages for fair dismissal and 21 days' wages/year of service, up to a maximum of 8 months' wages for unfair dismissal |
| Plastics processing | 1 month | 6 months: operatives<br>9 months: supervisors<br>1 year: managers<br>renewable for one further period of the same duration | 15 days' wages/year of service, up to a maximum of 6 months' wages |
| Building materials | 15 days (operatives), 30 days (supervisors) and 45 days (managers) | 6 months: operatives<br>9 months: supervisors<br>1 year: managers<br>renewable for one further period of the same duration | 15 days' wages/year of service for operatives and 1 month's wages/year of service for supervisors and managers, up to a maximum of 6 months' wages |
| Wood, cork and furniture | 1 month (operatives and supervisors) and 2 months (managers) | 6 months: operatives<br>9 months: supervisors<br>1 year: managers<br>renewable for one further period of the same duration | 18 days' wages/year of service, up to a maximum of 9 months' wages |
| Manufacture of and trade in alcoholic beverages | 1 month | 3 months: operatives<br>9 months: supervisors<br>1 year: managers<br>renewable for one further period of the same duration | 21 days' wages/year of service, up to a maximum of 9 months' wages |
| Dairy | 45 days | 3 months: operatives<br>9 months: supervisors<br>1 year: managers<br>renewable for one further period of the same duration | 45 days' wages/year of service, up to a maximum of 12 months' wages |
| Canned and semi-canned foods, and canned oils | 1 month | 6 months for workers in categories 1, 2 and 3 and 1 year for the rest | 1 month's wages/year of service, up to a maximum of 9 months' wages |
| Vehicle hire | 1 month: operatives and supervisors<br>3 months: managers | 1 year, not renewable for operatives, and renewable for one further period of the same duration for supervisors and | 1 day's wages/month of service, up to a maximum of 6 months' wages |
| General mechanics and fuel stations | 2 months | 6 months: operatives<br>9 months: supervisors<br>1 year: managers<br>renewable for one further period of the same duration | 1 day's wages/month of service, up to a maximum of 6 months' wages |

## Table 2.A2.1. Collectively agreed: Employment protection indicators by sector *(cont.)*

| Sector | Notice periods | Trial period | Severance pay |
|---|---|---|---|
| Mills | 1 month | 6 months (supervisors), renewable for one further period of 3 months<br>6 months (supervisors) and 9 months (managers), renewable for one further period of the same duration | 1 month's wages/year of service, up to a maximum of 8 months' wages |
| Pasta and couscous | 1 month: operatives<br>2 months: supervisors<br>3 months: managers | 6 months (operatives), renewable for one further period of 3 months,<br>6 months (supervisors) and 9 months (managers), renewable for one further period of the same duration | 18 days' wages/year of service for operatives and 1 month's wages/year of service for administrative staff, up to a maximum of 9 months' wages |
| Oil and its derivatives | 1 month | 1 month for unskilled workers, 3 months for semi-skilled workers and 6 months for the rest, renewable for one further period of the same duration | 1¼ month's wages (125%)/year of service, up to a maximum of 24 months' wages |
| Retail pharmacy | 1 month | 6 months: operatives<br>9 months: supervisors<br>1 year: managers<br>renewable for one further period of the same duration | 1 month's wages/year of service (final wage basis), up to a maximum of 12 months' wages |
| Ports and docks | 1 month | 1 year, renewable for two further periods of 6 months for managers and for one further period of 6 months for others | 1 month's wages/year of service, up to a maximum of 6 months' wages |
| Wholesale and semi-wholesale distribution of medicinal products | 1 month | 6 months: operatives<br>9 months: supervisors<br>1 year: managers<br>renewable for one further period of the same duration | 1 month's wages/year of service, up to a maximum of 6 months' wages |
| Tunisian salt | 18 days for hourly paid workers, 1 month for monthly paid workers, 3 months for supervisors and 6 months for managers | 6 months: operatives<br>9 months: supervisors<br>1 year: managers<br>renewable for one further period of the same duration | 1.5 month's wages/year of service, up to a maximum of 15 months' wages |
| Cinemas | 1 month | 3 months, renewable for one further period of the same duration | 1 day's wages/month of service (final wage basis), up to a maximum of 6 months' wages |
| Soap and oil refineries and secondary extraction factories | 1 month (operatives),<br>3 months (supervisors and managers) | 6 months: operatives<br>9 months: supervisors<br>1 year: managers<br>renewable for one further period of the same duration | 1 day's wages/month of service, up to a maximum of 6 months' wages |
| Explosives | 1 month | 6 months: operatives<br>9 months: supervisors<br>1 year: managers<br>renewable for one further period of the same duration | 1 day's wages/month of service, up to a maximum of 6 months' wages |
| Dry cleaning establishments and laundries | 15 days for hourly paid workers, 1 month for monthly paid workers | 6 months: operatives<br>9 months: supervisors<br>1 year: managers<br>renewable for one further period of the same duration | 15 days' wages/year of service, up to a maximum of 6 months' wages |
| Textiles | 1 month | 6 months: operatives<br>9 months: supervisors<br>1 year: managers<br>renewable for one further period of the same duration | 1 day's wages/month of service, up to a maximum of 6 months' wages |
| Coffee-roasting | 30 days for hourly paid workers, 45 days for those paid monthly | 6 months: operatives<br>9 months: supervisors<br>1 year: managers<br>renewable for one further period of the same duration | 15 days' wages/year of service, up to a maximum of 10 months' wages |
| Glass and mirror manufacturing | 1 month | 6 months: operatives<br>9 months: supervisors<br>1 year: managers<br>renewable for one further period of the same duration | 1 month's wages/year of service, up to a maximum of 12 months' wages |
| Haulage of goods by road | 1 month | 6 months: operatives<br>9 months: supervisors<br>1 year: managers<br>renewable for one further period of the same duration | 1 day's wages/month of service, up to a maximum of 4 months' wages |
| Factories producing soft drinks, syrups and mineral waters | 1 month | 3 months (operatives), 8 months (supervisors) and 1 year (managers), renewable for one further period of the same duration | 18 days' wages/year of service for operatives and 1 month's wages/year of service for administrative staff, up to a maximum of 7 months' wages |

*Source:* Sector bargaining agreements as published on www.iort.gov.tn.

# *Chapter 3*

# Improving the employability of Tunisian youth through labour market and social policies

*This chapter analyses the extent to which labour market and social policies support the employability of youth in Tunisia. In particular, the chapter discusses: social protection mechanisms to mitigate the negative consequences of being out of work; public employment services to help young people (back) into work; entrepreneurship training and support programmes to assist youth in setting up their own businesses; as well as social policies to help youth (and young women in particular) overcome barriers to employment related to family responsibilities. The chapter finds that, despite Tunisia's relatively developed social protection system, many youth are likely to fall between the cracks because of high levels of unemployment and informality. This lack of protection presents a significant barrier to the ability of youth to look for and find productive employment. In addition, public employment services generally lack the capacity to provide unemployed youth with the tailored support they require. Finally, Tunisia could do significantly more to help young parents juggle work and caring responsibilities, particularly with regards to parental leave and support for parents in meeting the costs of childcare.*

The statistical data for Israel are supplied by and under the responsibility of the relevant Israeli authorities. The use of such data by the OECD is without prejudice to the status of the Golan Heights, East Jerusalem and Israeli settlements in the West Bank under the terms of international law.

## Introduction

Chapter 2 discussed potential demand-side barriers to youth employment in Tunisia, including the cost of hiring and employment protection legislation. This chapter takes a look at the supply-side of the equation and asks how labour market and social policies can best promote the employability of youth. In this respect, social protection systems can play a key role in providing an adequate safety net for youth who are out of work, not only in shielding them from poverty but also in giving them the means to look for new and productive employment – a process which can further be reinforced by effective public employment services (PES) as well as entrepreneurship programmes for those youth willing and able to set up their own business. Again, while important on their own, these policy challenges should also be seen from the perspective of the significant economic restructuring that is likely to result from green growth: workers displaced from declining "brown" jobs need to be able to move quickly into new green jobs that make good use of their skills. Adequate protection in case of employment loss, as well as high-quality public employment services and active labour market policies to help people back into work will be critical to ensure that high worker mobility is reconciled with income security and high rates of employment. The final section of this chapter pays particular attention to the employability of young women, and on how social policies could be mobilised to help young families better balance work and caring responsibilities, thereby boosting female labour force participation.

The chapter's main findings are:

- ***Social protection.*** Even though Tunisia has a comprehensive social insurance system in place, high unemployment and informality rates mean that up to two thirds of youths will not be contributing, and therefore benefiting, from such protection.[1] Even youth who are covered by social insurance are unlikely to receive unemployment benefits in the case of job loss, as eligibility criteria for the current scheme are very strict and therefore very few youth (or even adults) are likely to be entitled. Unconditional cash transfers and free/subsidised health care for the poor exist, but are aimed predominantly at families (and, even then, are poorly targeted). In this context, public works programmes could serve as a useful safety net for the young – however some of these programmes have become defunct or are poorly targeted and/or implemented.
- ***Employment services.*** Very few youth say they found work through ANETI (A*gence Nationale pour l'Emploi et le Travail Indépendant*), Tunisia's public employment service (PES). The vast majority of active labour market programmes (ALMPs) provided are aimed at university graduates, which lowers ANETI's attractiveness to non-university graduates. Lower-skilled youth are therefore much less likely to register with the PES. ANETI also lacks the capacity to provide high quality counselling, job search assistance, and matching and placement support. The geographical reach of the service is limited and most staff are submerged in administrative tasks. While efforts have been made after the revolution to increasingly involve non-governmental organisations in the delivery of ALMPs, private employment agencies in Tunisia are prohibited by law (although, in practice, they do exist).
- ***Entrepreneurship support.*** Tunisia has a relatively well-developed start-up support system, with the provision of information, training, finance and follow-up services in the first two years of operation. That said, considerable duplication exists in the provision of such services, and more could be done also to provide medium- to long-term assistance, as well as additional support for potential female entrepreneurs who

face multiple obstacles in setting up a business. Early stage entrepreneurial activity is relatively uncommon in Tunisia, and young people in Tunisia say they receive less access to training and finance than their peers in OECD countries.

- ***Family policies.*** Tunisia could also do much more to support young parents juggle work and caring responsibilities. This is particularly important for women, who often bear the brunt of caring responsibilities, which partly explains their lower labour force attachment. Given their higher educational attainment, low female labour force participation represents a significant waste of human capital. Both maternity and paternity leave are extremely low in Tunisia, meaning that childbearing is likely to force discontinuities in women's working careers and could lead to their permanent exit from the labour market. In addition, little support exists to help parents meet the costs of childcare and, as a result, a relatively low proportion of young children are enrolled in early childhood education and care (ECEC). Part-time employment is available, but few youths work part-time. Finally, a tax-benefit system that has a tendency to cast women in the role of second earners or carers also does not help in promoting female labour force participation.

**Box 3.1. Key recommendations**

Given these outstanding challenges, the OECD suggests that:

- The government should ensure that youth, regardless of whether they are in work or not, receive the necessary social protection to enable them to seek, or engage in, productive employment, while at the same time making sure that incentives to work (formally) are not harmed.
  - Free basic health care should be provided to all citizens, including the unemployed and those active in the informal sector, and regardless of previous work history and/or social security contributions.
  - An unemployment insurance system to help individuals and households smooth consumption when they become unemployed through no fault of their own should be introduced. Initially, when the ability to administer benefits effectively and the capacity to monitor work in the informal sector while claiming benefits are still limited, replacements rates should be relatively low and benefit durations short. This will help to prevent abuses, while at the same time ensuring that work incentives are not harmed. With time, the generosity of unemployment benefits could be gradually increased, conditional on greater job search requirements. To ensure that recipients are also given the necessary assistance to get back into work as soon as possible, the administration of the benefit should be done by (or in close collaboration with) ANETI, the public employment service.
  - In addition, in the case of youth (who are less likely to be covered by traditional unemployment insurance systems due to a lack of necessary contributions or sufficiently long employment history), special financial support to assist them in the job-seeking process (a jobseeker's allowance) could be introduced – similar, for example, to Instrument E of the *Fonds d'Insertion et d'Adaptation Professionnelle* (FIAP) in place from 1990 to 2009, and which covered transport and accommodation costs to allow jobseekers to attend interviews.
  - The *Programme National d'Aide aux Familles Nécessiteuses* (PNAFN) – an unconditional cash transfer programme, eligibility for which is not based on work history but instead on income and assets – could play a critical role in offering a basic social safety net of last resort for the poorest in society. However, to in order to fulfil this function adequately, the PNAFN would need to be much better targeted than it currently is (with more transparent eligibility criteria), as well as aimed at poor individuals regardless of whether they have a family or not. A better administration of the programme would also require additional capacity in the form of social workers, as well as continued efforts to improve the poverty register.

### Box 3.1. Key recommendations *(cont.)*

- Public works programmes (or even employment guarantees) could be used to provide an essential insurance function to the unemployed, while also providing work experience and training. While such programmes exist in Tunisia, they need to be revised to ensure that they are targeted on those who need them most and that selection of participants happens in a more transparent manner. Such programmes appear particularly promising where they closely involve the community, focus on works other than just infrastructure (e.g. social work), and offer participants training to help them find a longer-term and sustainable route out of poverty. In the case of Tunisia (given the demands of public sector job creation), the delivery of such programmes through NGO's is particularly encouraged.

• The government should put in place a comprehensive and evidence-based strategy to tackle informality. As part of this strategy:

- Better monitoring of compliance with the law is needed, while ensuring that vulnerable workers do not have their livelihoods put at risk by overly vigorous enforcement activities. The focus should not merely be on inspecting and sanctioning, but also on trying to find durable solutions in partnership with the firms/individuals concerned.
- Income tax bands and rates should be revised so that formal work pays and individuals do not seek to remain undeclared because of high marginal tax rates.
- At the same time, the tax regime for the self-employed needs to become less generous and brought more in line with that of dependent workers, in order to reduce the incidence of false self-employment as well as avoid resentment on the part of wage earners who pay much higher taxes.
- The link between taxes/social security contributions and benefits needs to be improved, alongside a more general effort to improve trust in government as well as the quality of public services.
- Public sector recruitment rules need to be revised and/or work activity monitored more closely so that individuals are not encouraged to work informally while queuing for a public sector job.

• The capacity of the public employment service needs to be boosted to allow it to fulfill its key role in supporting youth to find work. This will include:

- Additional investments in ANETI as well as a geographic expansion of its network, but also a better use of its existing resources (e.g. delegating administrative tasks away from counsellors to appropriately qualified staff; virtual access to employment services in more remote areas; and merging the specialised PES offices dedicated to higher education graduates with the standard PES offices).
- Efforts made to work closer with NGOs in the delivery of ALMPs should be stepped up.
- In addition, Tunisia should legalise and regulate private employment services. On the one hand, this would clarify the rights and obligations of all parties involved and thereby reduce abuse. On the other, it would allow ANETI to exploit possible complementarities by entering into public-private partnerships and outsource some of its activities to firms that have the skills and expertise to deliver such services more effectively.
- In both cases, the outsourcing of activities should be accompanied by careful performance management arrangements. Tunisia should draw on its comparatively strong social security information systems to track labour market outcomes of ALMP participants and reward NGO's/firms on the basis of: i) the quality of employment outcomes achieved (i.e. more durable employment outcomes should be rewarded more highly); and ii) the relative labour market disadvantage of the unemployed person helped into a job (i.e. positive employment outcomes for the harder-to-help, like the long-term unemployed, should be rewarded more highly).

**Box 3.1. Key recommendations** *(cont.)*

- Tunisia should maintain and fine-tune its efforts to support young entrepreneurs as an important tool for tackling youth unemployment. In particular:
  - The various structures (*Espaces Entreprendre*, business centres, *Espaces Tremplin*, incubators) providing entrepreneurship support services should be rationalised in an effort to reduce duplication and get the most out of the scarce resources available.
  - More support should be available to entrepreneurs in the medium- to long-term (e.g. continued coaching) so as to raise the survival rates of start-ups.
  - The amount of start-up finance should be decided on the basis of the merits and needs of the business idea, and not on the basis of the individual's qualifications.
  - Given the additional barriers they face as well as their low labour force participation rates, potential female entrepreneurs should be given additional and targeted support. Setting up a single body responsible for co-ordinating the promotion of women's enterprise development could help in this respect. Better family policies, as outlined in the next recommendation, would also help in promoting female entrepreneurship in Tunisia.
- Finally, young families should be given more support to help them juggle work and family responsibilities. In particular: i) maternity and paternity leave entitlements should be increased. Paid leave is too short in Tunisia, while unpaid leave is inexistent and should be introduced; ii) the government should do more to help parents (in particular the poorest) to meet the relatively high costs of childcare, as well as to extend provision; and iii) men and women should be given the same incentives to take up paid employment by the tax-benefit system.

## Social protection systems to tackle poverty and help youth realise their potential

Adequate social protection systems are needed not just in a pursuit of social justice and equity, or to provide all citizens with a minimum acceptable livelihood and protection against risk; but also because they can support the emergence of a dynamic and inclusive labour market, where individuals are empowered and encouraged to pursue productive opportunities when they arise. However, while such programmes can have positive employment effects by alleviating liquidity constraints of the unemployed and allowing them to make better employment choices, one key challenge is to mitigate the possible negative effects they can have on work incentives and on the expansion of formal employment.

Tunisia has a comprehensive social insurance system in place covering most of the contingencies listed in the ILO's Social Security (Minimum Standards) Convention No. 102 (Ben Cheikh, 2013) with a legal coverage rate of 85.6% (Ministère des Affaires Sociales, 2014). However, many youth fall between the cracks of these contributory schemes, either because they are unemployed or, if employed, work in the informal sector. Tunisia also has non-contributory social assistance programmes in place for those out of work and workers ineligible for social insurance schemes. However, while estimates of coverage rates for youth are not available, poor targeting and vague eligibility criteria are likely to mean that many young people do not benefit from these programmes either. Such low coverage means that youth are particularly vulnerable and exposed to the risk of poverty.[2] Active labour market policies, particularly after the revolution (with *Amal* – see Box 3.4 in this chapter), have to some extent tried to fill this void – but at great financial cost and with little gain in employment. In this context, public works programmes (or employment guarantees) could serve as a useful safety net for the young – however some of these programmes have become defunct or, as in the case of wage subsidies, are poorly targeted and/or implemented.

## *Social insurance coverage for youth is low*

Tunisia has a comprehensive social insurance system, providing medical care as well as benefits for sickness, invalidity and employment injury, old-age, survivors, and family and maternity. These are managed by three state-run funds: the *Caisse Nationale de Retraite et de Prévoyance Sociale* (CNRPS) [National Pension and Social Contingency Fund] for public sector workers; the *Caisse Nationale de Securité Sociale* (CNSS) [National Social Security Fund] for private sector workers; and a health insurance fund, the *Caisse Nationale d'Assurance Maladie* (CNAM) [National Health Insurance Fund], for both the public and private sectors (see Box 2.3). Significant efforts have been made over time to extend social security coverage to increasingly larger parts of the population, including students (1965), salaried workers in the agricultural sector (1981), the self-employed (1982), and certain categories of low-income workers (domestic employees, workfare participants, small-scale fishermen, farmers and artisans – since 2002). As a result, the legal coverage rate of Tunisia's social security system is now 85.6% (100% in the public sector and 81.5% in the private sector – Ministère des Affaires Sociales, 2014).

Two categories of individuals are not covered by social insurance, however: those without a job and, by definition, those who work in the informal sector. Given the high rates of unemployment and informality amongst youth in Tunisia, many young people will therefore not be covered by such contributory schemes (including health insurance, unless they are so by virtue of being a dependent child[3] or through their partner).[4] While some non-contributory schemes are in place to act as a safety net of last-resort (including cash transfers and free or subsidised health care), these are often poorly targeted (see discussion below). The next section will focus on the problem of informality in Tunisia, as well as on possible solutions for tackling it. There are at least two important questions here: the first concerns the size/importance of informality in the economy; the second relates to the reasons behind informality and, in particular, the extent to which informal work is a choice or not. Answers to the latter question have significant implications for policy as the interventions most appropriate to deal with informality will depend on them.

## *Informal employment is high among Tunisian youth*

This section will argue that, while informality is a complex phenomenon, the high levels of informal employment observed in Tunisia are likely to reflect the poor job creation record of the economy in recent years, forcing individuals to accept poor quality, low productivity jobs as a means of survival. Given high unemployment levels, the bargaining power of workers vis-à-vis employers is greatly reduced and undeclared work may therefore be forced onto them. Better inspection that aims to find solutions to informal work practices (without putting at risk individuals' livelihoods) is therefore needed. However, some informality is likely to reflect a choice as well, and some key factors identified in this respect are: i) high individual income taxes – particularly where these are combined with poor (perceived) quality of public services received in return for those taxes and social security contributions and/or (perceived) inequalities in taxes paid and benefits received between different groups (as is the case between wage earners and the self-employed in Tunisia); and ii) incentives introduced by public sector recruitment rules that encourage informal employment while queuing. The discussion that follows also highlights the fact that tackling informality goes beyond mere labour market and social policies, and therefore requires a comprehensive strategy – a discussion of which is unfortunately beyond the scope of the present report.

### *Measuring informality*

With regards to the measurement of informality, no universally accepted definition exists (see Chapter 1). As a result, estimates vary widely. In the case of Tunisia, the latest, and probably most reliable, estimates (Ben Cheikh, 2013) suggest that informality is significant, with 37% of those working in the private sector working informally (i.e. with no social security coverage).[5] This figure is much higher in the agricultural sector (52%) than in the non-agricultural sector (33%), but the largest group of informal workers (between 38%-50%) can be found in the construction sector (Ben Cheikh, 2013; Rijkers et al., 2013). No separate estimates exist for youth. However, using the ILO's 2013 School-to-Work Transition Survey (SWTS) for Tunisia, it is estimated that the problem is significantly worse for youth, with just over half (53%) of all employed youth not contributing to social security. While this is likely to be an overestimate (primarily because it relies on self-reported status in the job),[6] it is still possible to make relative comparisons with some other MENA and developing/emerging countries (Figure 3.1). This suggests that informality amongst youth in Tunisia is higher than what is encountered in Jordan, but lower than the levels observed in Egypt.

**Figure 3.1. Informality in Tunisia and selected other countries**

Proportion of youth employed without social security contributions

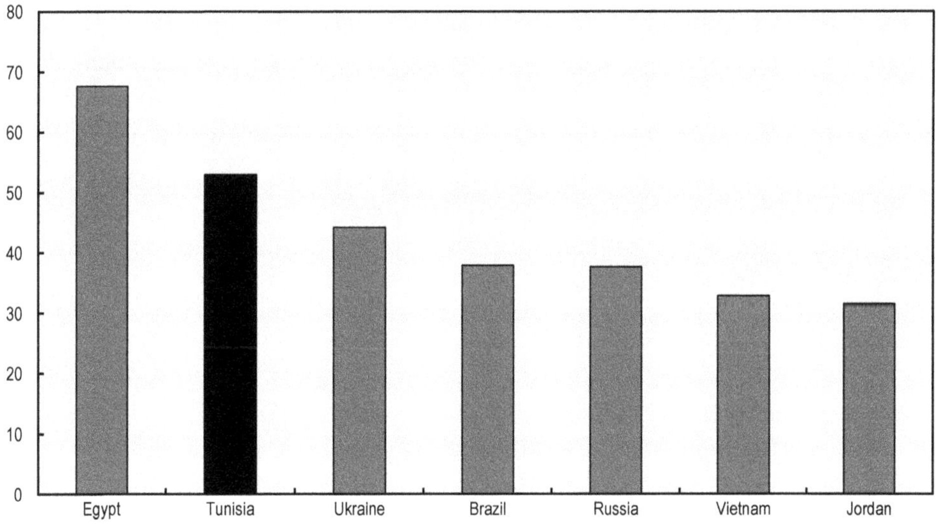


*Source*: OECD calculations based on the ILO School-to-Work Transition Surveys.

### *The causes of informality, and how to tackle it*

The second issue relates to the causes of informality. An important aspect of this is whether informality reflects a choice on the part of the worker or not. While in practice this is difficult to verify, at least one indication can be obtained from the analysis of wages in the formal and informal sectors. Indeed, if informality were a choice, then we would expect individuals in the informal sector to earn more than those in the formal sector, as compensation for the foregone benefits. However, analysis of the ILO's 2013 SWTS for Tunisia shows that youth working in the informal sector earn only just over half as much as youth working in the formal sector (TND 345 versus TND 609) – i.e. significantly less.[7] In other words: young people working in the informal sector not only have less protection and fewer benefits than those working in the formal sector, they also earn much less.

This evidence suggests that, to a large extent, informality in Tunisia does not reflect a choice and is more likely to be related to a scarcity of formal jobs, with employers reluctant to declare their employees. Given high levels of unemployment, the bargaining power of employees is weak, and they accept whatever job is offered to them. Evidence presented earlier in this report suggested that neither minimum wages nor employer social security contributions appear to be set at particularly high levels in Tunisia from an international perspective, and so they are unlikely to be a major explanation behind high informality in Tunisia. Nevertheless, it was argued that considerably higher sector minimum wages could present a potential barrier to youth accessing formal jobs, and that future sector wage agreements should carefully consider the situation of youth. In addition, while targeted reductions in social security contributions and/or wage subsidies were advocated in the case of low-skilled youth and those encountering significant difficulties in the labour market, the majority of such programmes in Tunisia were found to be creaming the best candidates and likely to entail very large deadweight losses. Re-focusing those programmes on those most in need might help reduce informality.

Employment protection legislation could be another reason why employers may be reluctant to take on youth formally – particularly if dismissal is difficult and costs are high, as is the case in Tunisia. However, given the flexibility around fixed-term contracts and the lack of legislation around temporary agency work in Tunisia, it is unlikely that strict employment protection on regular contracts would push employers to hire youth informally. In addition, even on open-ended contracts, trial periods in Tunisia are unusually long, thereby reducing the risks of employers to hire youth formally. It is unlikely therefore that employment protection legislation is a key barrier to formality in Tunisia (although, as was argued in Chapter 2, it is likely to be a major source of poor job quality for youth).

Given high unemployment rates and, therefore, the relative weak bargaining position of workers, it is important that the existing law be better enforced to minimise abuse by employers. Indeed, in the case of Tunisia, labour market flexibility has to a large extent been achieved simply by not enforcing the laws (Angel-Urdinola and Kuddo, 2010). This is not an optimal choice, because it undermines the rule of law, exposes firms to costly uncertainty, impedes decent formal employment growth and leaves workers without adequate protection (Nicoletti and Scarpetta, 2005). Compliance with the law will therefore need to be better monitored and non-compliance appropriately punished. Evidence suggests that employers' perception of the probability of being audited as well as the level of the penalty if caught matter (OECD, 2008). Tunisia has the capacity to carry out such inspections: while the ILO (2006) recommends that advanced countries should have at least one labour inspector per 10 000 employed persons and transition countries one per 20 000, Tunisia has approximately one inspector per 10 000 employed persons (i.e. in line with developed country standards). However, while better and more frequent monitoring will be required, it is also important to make sure that vulnerable workers do not have their livelihoods put at risk by overly vigorous enforcement activities. The focus should not merely be on inspecting and sanctioning, but also on trying to find durable solutions in partnership with the firms concerned.

While the previous discussion has suggested that for many workers in Tunisia informality does not appear to be a choice, it is evident that for some it is. On the one hand, income tax rates are high (see Chapter 2) and so some wage earners might choose to remain undeclared. As argued in the previous section, the income tax bands in Tunisia have not been uprated since 1983 which has led to considerable fiscal drag over the years. While a recent decision to exempt those earning below TND 5 000 (net) from income tax is a welcome development, the tax bands themselves should also be revised, and uprated regularly. It has also been argued that rules to allocate public sector jobs (often based on the length of time spent unemployed)[8] increase incentives for informal work while queuing (Angel-Urdinola and Tanabe, 2012; Gatti et al., 2011).[9]

Informality is also high among the self-employed and family workers. One reason for this could be the relatively high social security contributions expected from the self-employed. In economies with low social security coverage, subsidising the contributions of the self-employed, who are generally much more difficult to reach than wage earners, might be a good way to extend social protection coverage. This was the case in Korea in 1989, when health insurance coverage was extended to the self-employed (OECD, 2008). On the other hand, the income tax regime for the self-employed in Tunisia already provides significant (and arguably disproportionate) advantages (the so-called *régime forfaitaire* [flat-rate scheme]),[10] so that under-reporting of income and false self-employment are rife (Limam, 2012; El Elj, 2014). This also breeds resentment among wage earners who pay significantly higher taxes, and may further encourage them to ask their employers not to be declared. The tax treatment for the self-employed is too preferential in Tunisia and the gap with wage earners should be reduced. In addition, the provision of free or subsidised health care to poor families with no standard social security coverage (see discussion below) – or at least the poor targeting of it – has been argued to further reduce the incentive of the self-employed to formalise (Ben Cheikh, 2013). While no robust evidence exists to either prove or disprove this argument, from a theoretical point of view, the strength of this argument will depend on: i) the difference in the value of benefits provided for the workers; and ii) the difference in the costs of those benefits or, more synthetically, on the difference between net benefits (or net costs) in the contributory and the non-contributory programmes. Most of the empirical literature on this issue suggests that non-contributory health programmes do not appear to be key drivers of informality (OECD, 2011a).

Finally, international evidence indicates that reductions in informality are also achieved through economic growth (Perry et al., 2007) – so it is likely that a continued emphasis on creating the right conditions for economic growth will lead to gains in formal employment in Tunisia (although policies that promote economic growth alone will not solve the problem of informal employment: a more articulated policy solution is necessary – OECD, 2008). There is also a strong link between educational attainment and informality. While 37% of youth working in the formal sector have a tertiary qualification, only 12% of youth active in the informal sector do. A continued focus on improving educational attainment could therefore also be expected to lead to higher rates of formal employment. Last, but not least, international evidence shows that successful policies to tackle informality often go beyond labour market policies and into the realm of tax policy and public service provision. Box 3.2 provides a short check-list of such policies.

### Box 3.2. Tackling informality: Going beyond labour market policies

There is no simple solution for tackling informality, and the right approach will vary from country to country, or even within countries depending on the causes, which can be multiple and complex. In a very general sense, combating informal employment requires a comprehensive approach to reduce the costs and increase the benefits to businesses and workers of operating formally and ensure that regulations are adequately enforced. While this report has discussed the possible role played by labour costs and employment protection legislation in generating informality in Tunisia, neither of them were believed to be major sources of concern (with the exception, perhaps, of sector wage agreements). However, the size of the informal sector may also be related to a wider set of policies that go beyond labour market policies as such and, therefore, beyond the scope of the present report. While not all of the policies listed below may be directly relevant to the case of Tunisia, they nonetheless provide a useful checklist for policy makers concerned about reducing the size of the informal economy:

- ***Detection and enforcement***. Measures in this area include: information exchange (linking computer files); co-operation between labour, social security and tax inspectorates; [1] administrative requirements for the immediate declaration of new hires; making chief contractors responsible for compliance by sub-contractors; requiring accuracy of accounts and record-keeping among small businesses; etc. On the downside, there is a risk that such measures increase the administrative burden and red tape, in itself a major reason for non-declaration and informality. Indeed, red tape (e.g. requirements to obtain various licences before starting a business) is often thought to be the most important single cause of undeclared work.
- ***Improved tax administration***. While high tax rates per se do not appear to influence levels of undeclared work in international (or time-series) comparisons, complex tax systems can increase compliance costs for taxpayers and therefore encourage under-declaration. Simplification and/or training in how to comply with the requirements could help in this respect. At the same time, methods of tax administration influence incentives for concealment of dependent employment. For example, if assessed liability to tax is based on the observed volume of labour input (e.g. as detected by inspection visits which determine the number of employees working at a given work site) there are still incentives for under-declaring earnings per employee. To counter this, the tax authorities may appeal to employment regulations such as the minimum wage and restrictions on part-time and temporary work. This issue helps explain why countries with a large informal economy maintain *de facto* strict employment regulations, even though these regulations are seen by many analysts as a prime cause of informality.
- ***The tax treatment of business profits***. Labour costs (which include employer social security contributions as well as wages and salaries) are deducted from business value added in determining taxable profits, so if taxation is based on assessments of value added (i.e. sales less non-labour input costs) rather than assessment of labour inputs, there is usually little incentive to conceal dependent employment. In cases where effective marginal tax rates on profits (i.e. earnings from self-employment, in the case of unincorporated businesses) exceed tax rates on labour incomes, there is a positive tax incentive to declare wages and salaries. But factors such as partial exemption from social security contributions and simplified tax regimes for self-employment incomes, or dividend tax reliefs and low corporate tax rates when combined with high social security contributions on wages and salaries, may to varying degrees reverse this incentive.
- ***Tax concessions in sectors where the incidence of undeclared work is high***. Income tax credits and reductions in consumption taxes are costly, but can increase incentives to declare work in certain sectors where undeclared work is high. Service employment cheques in France have also achieved administrative simplification.
- ***Trust in government***. The informal economy involves broad issues of the legitimacy of central government and its taxation and regulatory powers. If central government is viewed as corrupt, unresponsive and wasteful with money, or if local actors view central government as a foreign power, tax evasion may be socially valued. But in informal arrangements and verbal contracts, the risk of being cheated is considerable: if the government enforces contracts and protects property rights, economic actors often prefer to conduct arms-length business on a formal basis in spite of tax costs.

**Box 3.2. Tackling informality: Going beyond labour market policies** *(cont.)*

- ***Improving the quality of public services.*** One key aspect of trust in government is the quality of the services that it provides in return for tax and social security contributions. Indeed, workers' perceptions of the value of the benefits they are likely to receive from social protection schemes may be a factor encouraging formal work or the full declaration of earnings if workers have some say in whether or not they are employed formally. One aspect of this may be establishing a closer link between contributions and benefits in the design of pension systems: the closer this link, the less workers will perceive pension contributions as a tax, and thus the lower the negative effect of contributions on formal sector participation. Easing somewhat access conditions for unemployment benefits, increasing the link between benefits and contributions (while being careful to preserve work incentives) and/or reducing contribution rates could also improve incentives for formalisation.
- ***Taxpayer education to foster a culture of compliance.*** Taxpayer education covers a wide range of activities and actors – from government programmes to encourage tax-compliant behaviour, to efforts by business organisations to mobilise and represent the interests of their members on tax issues, to civil society initiatives to bring citizens into policy debates on tax collection and redistribution. Engaging and educating potential taxpayers can help to strengthen feelings of responsibility and identity to the state. This often needs to start from an early age. Investments therefore need to be school-based and foster ethnical values based on justice, solidarity and the "common good".

1. An interesting and recent example of this is Korea's attempt at moving towards a more integrated social insurance system where the different insurers can share information with each other, as well as with the tax inspectors (OECD, 2013, *Strengthening Social Cohesion in Korea*, OECD Publishing, Paris).

*Source*: OECD (2004), "Informal Employment and Promoting the Transition to a Salaried Economy", Chapter 5 in *OECD Employment Outlook 2004*, OECD Publishing, Paris, http://dx.doi.org/10.1787/empl_outlook-2004-en; OECD (2008), "Declaring Work or Staying Underground: Informal Employment in Seven OECD Countries", Chapter 3 in *OECD Employment Outlook 2008*, OECD Publishing, Paris, http://dx.doi.org/10.1787/empl_outlook-2008-en; OECD (2013), "Building Tax Culture, Compliance and Citizenship: A Global Source Book on Taxpayer Education – Draft for Consultation", OECD Publishing, Paris, www.oecd.org/ctp/tax-global/sourebook-taxpayer-education.pdf.

## *Unemployment benefits are rare, and youth are unlikely to benefit*

Unemployment benefits help individuals and households to smooth consumption when faced with job loss. They also give the unemployed time to find a new, well-matched job and can help prevent workers from falling into informality (OECD, 2008). Indeed, the role of unemployment benefits in overcoming such liquidity constraints might be particularly important in emerging economies given financial market imperfections and relatively low levels of wealth (OECD, 2011a).

An unemployment benefit was introduced in Tunisia in 1997 (Decree No. 97-1925 of 29 September 1997), and later modified by Decrees No. 2002-886 of 22 April 2002 and No. 2006-1025 of 13 Avril 2006.[11] The benefit consists of 12 monthly instalments set at the level of the national non-agricultural minimum wage (SMIG), as well as health insurance and family allowances for one year. Eligibility criteria for the benefit are, however, very strict and very few youth are therefore likely to be entitled. The benefit is only available to higher education graduates who were on a permanent contract in the non-agricultural sector and had been in their last job for an uninterrupted period of at least three years prior to redundancy. In addition, the benefit is only paid to those workers who lose their job involuntarily as a result of firm closure for economic or technological reasons, or as a result of unexpected firm closure without paying heed to the procedures laid out in the Labour Code. In practice, very few of the unemployed receive unemployment benefits (5% of dismissed workers according to Subrahmanyam and Castel, 2014) and, because of the requirement of three years uninterrupted work for the same employer (on a permanent contract), it is unlikely to benefit many young people in particular.

As part of the Social Contract (signed on 14 January 2013, two years after the revolution) the government and the main social partners (UGTT and ANETI) committed to setting up an unemployment insurance system through the means of an independent fund financed by employee, employer as well as government contributions. The text of the Social Contract suggests that this unemployment insurance will remain limited to individuals who are unemployed through no fault of their own as a result of economic or technical difficulties encountered by the firm, or its sudden closure. Details of the scheme are still to be worked out, in particular how it will be financed and managed, as well as the generosity and duration of benefits, the conditions, and the support that workers will receive in searching for a new job.

In setting up an unemployment insurance system, some important decisions will need to be taken and policy makers will face some key trade-offs. While more generous benefits (both in terms of duration and income replacement, but also in terms of eligibility conditions) provide better insurance and can incentivise workers to be declared (or declare earnings fully), there is widespread consensus that more generous unemployment benefits are also associated with longer unemployment duration and higher aggregate unemployment (Venn, 2012). To counter such negative effects, countries have introduced various job-search and availability requirements, as well as better monitoring and, in some cases, sanctions for refusing a job offer or participation in an active labour market programme. Box 3.3 provides further detail on how OECD and EU countries have chosen to design their unemployment benefit systems.

In the case of Tunisia, it may be a good idea to start with relatively low replacement rates and short benefit durations. With time, as the ability to administer benefits effectively improves (as well as the capacity to monitor) the generosity of unemployment benefits could be gradually increased. It might also be a good idea to target benefits as much as possible towards job losers who face the greatest liquidity constraints and therefore are most likely to make sub-optimal employment choices. Flat benefit schedules, as in China, or means-tested ones, as in Brazil, are two options worth considering.[12] Efforts to build an unemployment insurance mechanism should be accompanied by investments in activation policies to avoid the risk of unemployment traps and benefit dependency. Such policies may be relatively light if benefits are not over-generous, which might be another reason to start with relatively short maximum duration of benefits and low replacement rates. Finally, measures should also be taken to make work pay: given the relatively high personal income tax rate in Tunisia there is a risk that, if unemployment benefits are too generous to start with, they will harm incentives to look for a job.

Developing a successful activation strategy for recipients of unemployment benefits will, of course, be made much easier if the administration of benefits and ALMP programmes are co-ordinated. Many OECD countries have moved towards "one-stop shop" or service centres for benefit recipients and jobseekers, with the aim of simplifying access to support services and, possibly, exploit synergies between institutions. Having all the clients enter through a single "gateway" also makes it easier to target services and interventions to suit the particular needs and circumstances of clients. For example, after a public employment service reform implemented in France in 2009, benefit administration as well as support and guidance for the unemployed are now delivered through one single institution, the *Pôle Emploi*. Similarly, in the case of Tunisia, it would make sense to merge ANETI with the administration of unemployment benefits.

## Box 3.3. Generosity and eligibility criteria for unemployment benefits across the OECD

### Generosity

The generosity of unemployment benefits varies widely across the OECD, both in terms of the replacement rate and the maximum duration of benefits. The average net replacement rate (NRR) of unemployment benefits in OECD countries was 34% in 2012, ranging from a low 17% in Hungary to a maximum of 64% in Belgium (Figure A). The average maximum duration of benefits was 15 months in 2010, ranging from a low five months in the Czech Republic, to 36 months in Iceland. In one country (Belgium) benefit duration is unlimited.

**Figure A. NRR[a] summary measure of benefit entitlements, OECD, 2012**

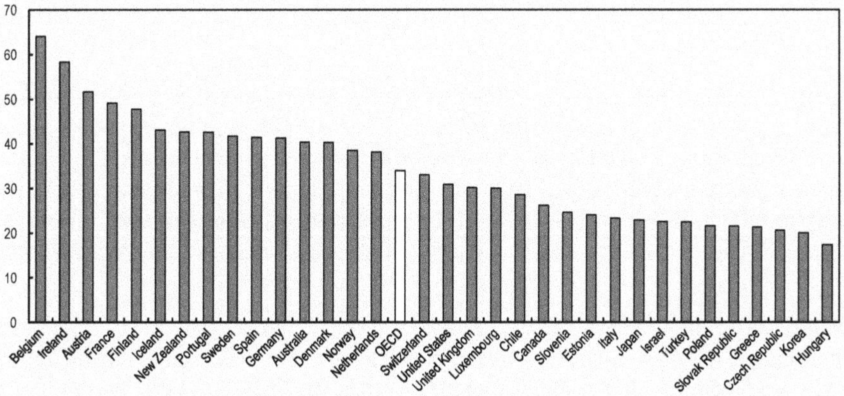


*a)* The NRR expresses net unemployment benefit levels as a percentage of previous net earnings. The summary measure presented here includes both unemployment insurance and unemployment assistance benefits, and is defined as the average of the net unemployment benefit (excluding social assistance and housing benefit) replacement rates for two earnings levels, three family situations and 60 months of unemployment.

*Source*: OECD (2012), "Net Replacement Rates for Six Family Types: Initial Phase of Unemployment", *Benefits and Wages: Statistics*, www.oecd.org/els/benefitsandwagesstatistics.htm (accessed 2 June 2014).

### Entitlement conditions

Entitlement conditions describe the employment and contribution conditions necessary to be eligible for unemployment benefits. In some countries (Australia and New Zealand) unemployment benefits are non-contributory (financed out of general taxation revenue) and therefore do not depend on previous employment history. Among those countries with contributory schemes, most countries require a year or less of employment and/or contributions. More than one year is required in Belgium, Ireland, Italy, Portugal and Turkey, and three years in the Slovak Republic. While workers who are voluntarily unemployed are not eligible for unemployment benefits in many countries (Canada, Estonia, Greece, Italy, Korea, Luxembourg, the Netherlands, Portugal, Spain, Turkey and the United States), sanctions are introduced in others. For example, in the Czech Republic, benefits are reduced, while in other countries benefits are delayed or suspended for a period ranging from three weeks (Denmark) to around six months (Poland).

### Job search and availability criteria

Job search and availability criteria relate to the benefit recipients' availability for work while participating in ALMPs and the type of job offers that they are obliged to take up. These are stricter in some countries than in others. For instance, while ALMP participants are not required to be available for work in Canada, Greece, Hungary, Israel, Korea, Portugal and the United States, they must remain available and actively looking for work in Australia, Denmark, Estonia, Germany, New Zealand, Sweden and Switzerland. In other countries, work availability is required, but not necessarily job search (Austria, the Czech Republic, Italy, Japan, Norway, Poland, Spain and Turkey), while in the Slovak Republic job search is only required during the last two months of participation in programmes lasting longer than two months. Finally, some countries (including Belgium, Finland, Luxembourg, Slovenia and the United Kingdom) exempt participants in some ALMPs (most commonly training programmes) from being available for work.

## Box 3.3. Generosity and eligibility criteria for unemployment benefits across the OECD *(cont.)*

Demands also vary across countries in terms of the occupation and geographical mobility required from unemployment beneficiaries. In Australia, Denmark, Germany, Hungary, Ireland, Japan, New Zealand, Norway and Poland, unemployment benefit recipients are required to accept any job that they are capable of doing, regardless of their previous occupation. Canada, the Czech Republic, Italy, Luxembourg, Portugal, the Slovak Republic and Sweden do not have explicit occupational mobility requirements, but the unemployment benefit recipient's previous occupation, skills and/or education are taken into account. At the other end of the spectrum, jobseekers in Greece and those aged over 50 in Belgium can refuse job offers in other occupational areas indefinitely without sanction. In Turkey, jobseekers specify up to ten occupations in which they will accept work and can refuse job offers outside these occupations indefinitely. In the remaining countries, unemployment benefit recipients can refuse job offers outside their previous occupation for a limited period at the beginning of the unemployment spell, with requirements becoming stricter as the duration of unemployment lengthens.

With regards to geographical mobility, most countries set a time or distance limit, above which benefit recipients are justified in refusing a job offer. When geographical mobility is required, relocation or commuting subsidies can be offered (e.g. Slovak Republic), while in other countries valid reasons for refusing a job offer that requires relocation include family responsibilities (e.g. Norway). Similarly, required commuting times can be shorter for jobseekers with significant family responsibilities (e.g. Australia, Hungary, Portugal and Slovenia) or due to health or age considerations (Belgium and Luxembourg). On the other hand, longer commuting times may be required after prolonged spells of unemployment (the Netherlands and the United Kingdom).

Finally, many countries also allow jobseekers to refuse job offers if the wage is lower than the unemployment benefit (Belgium, Finland, Hungary, Israel, Luxembourg, Portugal), lower than the unemployment benefit recipient's previous wage or a specific fraction thereof (Austria, Estonia, Sweden, Turkey), or lower than the usual wage for that job (Canada, Denmark, Japan, United States). In France and Germany, the required salary for a suitable job falls with the duration of unemployment.

### Monitoring

Countries vary also in the extent to which, as well as in the systems they use for monitoring job-search effort. Unemployment benefit recipients are required to prove job-search activity fortnightly or more often in Australia, Portugal, the Slovak Republic (for most unemployed) and the United Kingdom, and monthly in Austria, Estonia, France, Japan, Korea and Switzerland. At the other end of the scale, jobseekers in Greece, Hungary, Israel, Italy, Poland, Spain, Sweden and Turkey are not required to prove job search (although in some of them jobseekers must prove they have followed up on referrals to job vacancies from the PES). In Canada, jobseekers are required to confirm their availability for work each fortnight, but evidence of job-search activity is only needed if requested. Likewise, the unemployed in most states of the United States are required to keep records of job-search activities, which must be produced upon request.

### Sanctions

Sanctions for refusing a job offer or ALMP placement exist in a number of countries. Greece, Ireland, Italy, Luxembourg, Portugal, Slovak Republic, Slovenia, Turkey and the United States suspend benefits completely for an initial refusal of a job offer or ALMP placement. Suspensions are relatively short (one month or less) in Denmark, Estonia, Germany, Japan and Korea. In several countries, benefits are reduced for a fixed period (France, the Netherlands, Sweden) or until the jobseeker complies with the requirement (New Zealand), rather than suspended. By contrast, relatively long benefit suspensions apply in Israel and Poland.

Many countries have escalating sanctions for unemployment benefit recipients who repeatedly refuse suitable job offers or participation in ALMPs without good reasons. Aside from those countries that suspend benefits completely following the first refusal, Belgium, Denmark, Estonia and Finland suspend benefits completely following a second refusal and Sweden and Spain following a third refusal.

*Source*: Venn, D. (2009), "Legislation, Collective Bargaining and Enforcement: Updating the OECD Employment Protection Indicators", *OECD Social, Employment and Migration Working Papers*, No. 89, OECD Publishing, Paris, http://dx.doi.org/10.1787/223334316804; OECD (2012), "Net Replacement Rates for Six Family Types: Initial Phase of Unemployment", *Benefits and Wages: Statistics*, www.oecd.org/els/benefitsandwagesstatistics.htm (accessed 2 June 2014).

Another reason why Tunisia, if it decides to introduce an unemployment insurance scheme, may initially wish to keep its generosity limited is the presence of a large informal sector. Indeed, in countries where the informal sector is large, setting up an unemployment insurance scheme brings particular challenges because of the difficulty of monitoring employment in the informal sector: benefit recipients can draw their maximum entitlement to unemployment benefits while continuing to work informally. On the other hand, the more generous the benefit and the stronger the link between contributions and benefits, the higher the incentives will be for people to contribute and declare their work.

An alternative way of dealing with the problem of monitoring informal work while drawing unemployment benefits is to introduce a system of mandatory self-insurance based on individual savings accounts, as was done in Chile. Such systems impose mandatory savings that may be accessed when a worker is dismissed or during a specified period of unemployment. Any savings that are left upon retirement can be converted into a pension or may be withdrawn in their entirety. Because the unemployed individual is drawing on his/her own savings, self-insurance provides good incentive to stay employed or return to work when unemployed.

Either way, on top of the unemployment insurance scheme (or the individual savings account), there may be a need for some additional support for those who do not meet the eligibility criteria for unemployment insurance, have exhausted their eligibility for unemployment insurance benefits, or have run down the savings from their mandatory savings account. This was done in Chile with the *Fondo de Cesantía Solidario* [Unemployment Solidarity Fund]. Such additional unemployment assistance is frequently means-tested to improve its targeting (Stovicek and Turrini, 2012). In many OECD countries, those who do not qualify for any unemployment benefit receive social assistance benefits, eligibility for which is based on income and assets, not work history. However, in the case of Tunisia, a greater priority may be to extend general social assistance, such as the *Programme National d'Aide aux Familles Nécessiteuses* (PNAFN) [National Support Programme for Disadvantaged Families] – discussed in the next section – to guarantee a basic income for individuals regardless of their current and previous work status.

The setting up of an unemployment insurance system cannot be seen in isolation and may require simultaneous changes in other policy areas. One of these is severance pay. Many emerging economies (including Tunisia) rely on severance pay (which imposes a penalty on employers in the case of unfair dismissal) to provide income support for job losers. This is primarily because the public provision of unemployment insurance is costly and because many countries lack (or have lacked) the institutional capacity to successfully run such systems. The downside of severance pay, however, is that it slows down firm dynamics by protecting jobs (rather than workers) and therefore inhibits the reallocation of resources between expanding and declining firms. The introduction of unemployment insurance in Tunisia should, therefore, go hand in hand with a reduction in severance pay until an optimal balance between the two is found.

Finally, in the case of youth (and depending on the exact eligibility criteria that will be settled on for the Tunisian unemployment insurance system), it is worth pointing that many are still likely to miss out on unemployment benefits due to a lack of necessary contributions or sufficiently long employment history to qualify. This is a common problem encountered in other countries as well, which is why some of them provide special financial support to assist young people in the job-seeking process. In Australia, for example, Youth Allowance supports young people with financial assistance if they are 16-21 years old and looking for full-time work or undertaking approved activities and, in the United Kingdom, there is a special Jobseeker's Allowance for 16-24 year-olds. In the case of Tunisia, however, some of the ALMPs (and particularly those introduced after the revolution) have operated as *de facto* unemployment benefits (see Box 3.4) – albeit very expensive ones, as well as badly targeted (only higher education graduates were eligible). Moving forward, it might make more sense to introduce a small jobseekers' allowance (e.g. to cover transport costs) which is targeted on poor youth only and/or those living in more remote areas – similar to Instrument E of the *Fonds d'Insertion et d'Adaptation Professionnelle* (FIAP) [Insertion and Professional Adaptation Fund] in place from 1990 to 2009, and which covered transport costs (and sometimes accommodation) to allow jobseekers to travel to another locality for an interview.

**Box 3.4. ALMPs as unemployment benefits in disguise**

**Amal**

Shortly after the revolution, the interim government introduced a new programme called *Amal*[1](meaning "hope" in Arabic) to try and address the high unemployment rates amongst university graduates (Decree No. 2011-621 of 23 May 2011). The programme was meant to provide first-time jobseekers with a monthly stipend of TND 200 for a period of one year, conditioned on their participation in training, counselling, and/or an internship. As part of the programme, the government would cover the cost of up to 400 hours of training. The authorities were taken by surprise as 155 000 unemployed university graduates claimed the benefit, compared to the 30 000 they had expected (Angel-Urdinola and Leon-Solano, 2013).[2] This put considerable pressure on ANETI, the public employment service, which did not have the capacity to deal with such a high workload. As a result, out of those who enrolled, fewer than 20 000 received any type of services (Angel-Urdinola and Leon-Solano, 2011). In practice, therefore, *Amal* turned out to be not much more than an unemployment benefit paid for a period of one year, with little effect on employment outcomes. Being hugely expensive, it was quickly abandoned and replaced in 2012 by the *Programme d'Encouragement à l'Emploi* [Employment Incentive Programme].

**Programme d'Encouragement à l'Emploi**

Following the debacle that was *Amal* and, in particular, the pressure it put on the country's budget, it was temporarily replaced by the *Programme d'Encouragement à l'Emploi* (PEE) in 2012 (Decree No. 2012-953 of 2 August 2012, later amended and extended until the end of 2014 by Decree No. 2013-3766 of 18 September 2013). In many ways, the PEE is similar to *Amal*, except that it is better targeted in order to contain costs. Also aimed at university graduates, it pays those aged 26 and over (originally 28 years and over) a monthly stipend of TND 200 in the first semester of participation and TND 150 during the second semester[3], as well as social security coverage, conditional on the individual's participation in training, doing an internship, or setting up a micro-project. In addition, when participating in an internship, the recipient receives a bonus of TND 600 paid in two instalments (one after three months of work, and the other after six months) conditional on providing evidence (payment slips) that he/she has been attending work.[4] Apart from the age condition, the additional targeting requires the individual: i) to have graduated at least two years ago; ii) to be registered with ANETI;[5] iii) to come from a family whose income does not exceed three times the minimum wage (SMIG); iv) not to have graduated from either medicine, dentistry, pharmacy, veterinary sciences, engineering (with the exception of agronomy) and architecture; v) not to be repaying a loan received for setting up a project; and vi) not to have benefited from another employment programme in the past six months. Despite the fact that the PEE remains a programme exclusively for higher education graduates, its targeting is one of its most attractive features and should be extended to other ALMPs. As in the case of *Amal*, anecdotal evidence suggests that, in practice, few PEE participants benefit from any of the employment services it claims to provide. The programme is set to be closed down at the end of 2014, when it will be replaced by the new *Chèque d'Amélioration de l'Employabilité* [Employability Improvement Cheque] – see Box 3.5.

1. The official name of the programme (as introduced by the Decree) is the *Programme de Recherche Active d'Emploi.*

2. According to Angel-Urdinola and Leon-Solano (2011), many youth quit the SIVP programme in order to benefit from Amal, which offered a more generous stipend.

3. These are reduced to TND 150 and TND 100, respectively, for individuals who have previously benefited from the SIVP.

4. Individuals wishing to set up their own business receive help with the identification and development of the project. In addition, and conditional on obtaining a financing agreement, they can receive a sum of up to 10% of the cost of the project (and not exceeding TND 5 000) as start-up finance. This is in addition to the monthly instalment of TND 200 paid for a period of one year.

5. Initially, the decree specified that the individual needed to have been registered with ANETI for a period of at least three months, but this requirement was later removed.

## *Social transfers could provide a safety net, but are poorly targeted*

The problem of informality has prompted many countries to introduce non-contributory schemes (Pagés et al., 2013). Tunisia also has a number of non-contributory safety nets in place for disadvantaged individuals, including: the *Programme National d'Aide aux Familles Nécessiteuses* (PNAFN) [National Support Programme for Disadvantaged Families] and free (*carte de soins gratuits* – AMG1) or subsidised (*carte de soins à tarifs réduits* – AMG2) health care provided in public hospitals. While in theory such programmes provide the opportunity to provide safety nets for many youth who are either unemployed or work in the informal sector, their poor targeting implies that few are likely to benefit in practice. Improving the administration and targeting of these programmes could make a significant contribution to poverty, both in and out of work, and help youth overcome the barriers of deprivation in finding quality employment.

The PNAFN is an unconditional cash transfer provided to disadvantaged families whose self-declared incomes do not exceed the national poverty line.[13] In addition, some other criteria are taken into account, including: living conditions (the state of housing and the presence of household goods), family size, the presence of family members with disabilities or chronic illnesses. The value of the subsidy is TND 100 per month, plus TND 10 per child (capped at TND 30). The benefit is paid for an undefined period of time, as long as the participants fulfil the eligibility conditions. Targeting is largely based on self-selection (the family needs to file a written application) while the income and living conditions of the household are subsequently assessed by social workers from the *Direction Régionale des Affaires Sociales, de la Solidarité et des Tunisiens à l'Étranger* [Regional Directorate for Social Affairs, Solidarity and Tunisians Abroad]. Such targeting is assisted by the *Fichier de la Pauvreté* [Poverty Register] (Zribi and Bouktif, 2011). In 2012, 200 000 families were in receipt of the PNAFN (Ministère des Affaires Sociales, 2014).

In addition to the cash transfer, PNAFN beneficiaries are eligible for free medical care. For non-PNAFN beneficiaries, subsidised health care is provided if family income does not exceed the SMIG (two-member families), 1.5 times the SMIG (3-5 members), two times the SMIG (more than five members) – and if they do not, and cannot, contribute to social security. Once again, the family needs to submit a written application and the benefits, if awarded, are valid for a period of five years, after which an application for renewal needs to be filed. 230 000 free and 578 000 subsidised health insurance cards were awarded in 2012 (Ministère des Affaires Sociales, 2014).

While few evaluations of these programmes exist, the available evidence suggests that they are poorly targeted and lack the necessary means and support systems to be properly implemented. Joint work by the INS, CRES and AfDB (2013) estimates that nearly half of Tunisia's families living in poverty do not benefit from any of these programmes. 37.2% of PNAFN beneficiaries belong to the bottom income quintile, while 6.1% to top income quintile. While such targeting compares relatively favourably to other social transfer programmes in the MENA region, programmes in Latin America and the Caribbean and in Eastern Europe and Central Asia tend to do better (Silva et al., 2012) – although this is not universally so (see OECD, 2013c for Colombia). In the case of Brazil's *Bolsa Família*, for example, it has been estimated that nearly three quarters of the cash transfer go to the poorest quintile (Fiszbein and Schady, 2009). As a result, social transfer programmes in Tunisia have only little impact on poverty: INS, CRES and AfDB (2013) have estimated that the poverty rate would be 16.5% instead of 15.7% in the absence of the PNAFN (and the extreme poverty rate 5.3% compared to 4.6%). In comparison, *Bolsa Família* has been estimated to nearly halve extreme poverty from 8.0% to 4.7% (IPEA, 2013).

Such poor targeting results, in the first instance, from the self-targeting on which the PNAFN and the AMG programmes rely. Many of the poorest families are unable to travel the distance and/or put together the necessary application files required, meaning they end up being excluded from the programme (INS, CRES and AfDB, 2013). In addition, the eligibility criteria lack transparency (Handoussa and Tzannatos, 2002) opening the door to clientelism. While the national poverty line may be seen as one objective criterion, in practice even this figure has been hotly debated amongst public institutions in the past (Ben Mahmoud, 2011). Moreover, allocation of the budget will depend on regional budgets and is therefore rationed. This results in some families in one governorate receiving the benefit while others, perhaps more deprived but living in a different governorate, do not. Ben Braham (2012) further highlights the lack of capacity (only one social worker per 70 000 inhabitants and only one visit per quarter to remote areas)[14] to adequately manage the programme, as well as the lack of exit strategy and criteria meaning that families can benefit from the PNAFN indefinitely (even if their circumstances change). Finally, because the benefit is targeted at families, youth will not be able to benefit unless they are counted as dependent children, or they have a young family themselves.

The safety net provided by PNAFN and AMG in Tunisia could be improved to better help individuals, including youth, overcome poverty-related barriers to finding employment. By providing a basic income floor for the poor, regardless of whether they are in work or not, the PNAFN could also fulfil the role of unemployment assistance to those not (or no longer) eligible for unemployment insurance (see previous sub-section). To achieve these goals, however, the programme's eligibility criteria will need to be made more transparent and less dependent on subjective assessments by social workers and/or the decision of the regional directorate of social affairs. Most cash transfers in Latin America, for example, base eligibility on easily observable and clearly defined household characteristics (OECD, 2011a; Azevedo and Robles, 2013). The ongoing work on improving the poverty register in Tunisia is welcome (AfDB, 2012) and closer links should be made between this database and those held by social security so that past (and future) income can be better monitored. Related to this, families' eligibility should also be re-assessed routinely and, in order to promote graduation/exit from the cash transfer, recipients should be connected with income-generation and labour-market participation programmes (so-called "activation" measures). Finally, revising eligibility criteria, but also how the benefit is administered, should be based on a detailed analysis of the poor population that is currently not in receipt of the benefit – little is currently known about this group and the reasons why they are excluded.

Cash transfers may raise the concern that, through their effect on the incomes of families, they reduce work incentives and therefore labour supply. The evidence, however, suggests that these types of programmes have little adverse impact on employment because: i) they are usually not conditioned on labour force status; ii) the means-tests are frequently only loosely applied; and iii) the level of transfer is usually low relative to household income (OECD, 2011a). Social transfers have also raised concerns that they increase the likelihood of informal employment, or the time that people spend on informal work, because eligibility for the programme might be lost if earnings exceed a certain threshold (Pagés et al., 2013). In the case of Tunisia's AMG2, Ben Cheikh (2013) has argued that the poor targeting of the programme allows a large number of individuals to benefit from low-cost healthcare which reduces their incentive to contribute to social security. While the previous discussion has suggested that non-contributory health programmes in and of themselves do not appear to be key drivers of informality, better targeting and monitoring might still reduce the risk of informality in response to social transfers. In addition, improving the (perceived) benefits of social security would encourage individuals to leave the free/subsidised scheme in favour of the paying scheme.

Finally, Tunisia should reduce its reliance on energy and food subsidies as social transfers, re-directing these resources into the improved PNAFN and AMG. Various studies have shown that price subsidies in Tunisia (and elsewhere) tend to be extremely poorly targeted, often even regressive. In the case of food subsidies, INS, CRES and AfDB (2013) have estimated that the average subsidy going to individuals in the richest quintile is 30% higher than the average subsidy received by individuals in the poorest quintile. In the case of petrol and diesel, the World Bank (2013) has calculated that the poorest quintile receive only 2% of these subsidies, compared to 67% and 60% respectively for the richest quintile. While it has to be acknowledged that the phasing out of such subsidies is difficult politically,[15] it can be achieved by carefully managed awareness campaigns as well as ensuring that the transition from price subsidies to cash transfers is gradual and ensures that the poorest groups do not experience significant falls in their purchasing power. In the Latin American context, conditional cash transfers generally emerged as replacements for less effective price subsidies (Azevedo and Robles, 2013).

### *Public works programmes can boost incomes and work experience*

In some developing and emerging economies, public works programmes arebeing used to reduce individuals' vulnerability to shocks and provide a basic safety net. While public works programmes can be purely infrastructure-oriented, the focus in this section is on those programmes the primary aim of which is social protection. In this case, they have also sometimes been referred to as "workfare" programmes or, where the unemployed are guaranteed a certain amount of work per year, as "employment guarantees". Well-known examples of public works programmes include the Mahatma Gandhi National Rural Employment Guarantee Scheme (MGNREGS) in India, Ethiopia's Productive Safety Net Programme (PSNP) and Argentina's *Jefes de Hogar* (Heads of Household) programme. In countries with no formal unemployment insurance, such programmes (particularly where they guarantee employment) can perform an essential insurance function.

Besides providing income support, public works programmes have been argued to bring a number of other benefits (Subbarao et al., 2013). Because they provide individuals with work experience, they help maintain and/or improve skills and therefore promote labour force participation and more permanent pathways out of poverty than simple cash transfer programmes. They can be particularly helpful for groups on the margins of the labour market, such as women, youth and the low-skilled, and help them raise their bargaining power by guaranteeing work at the minimum wage rate and, therefore, enforcing a minimum wage rate on all casual work. Such bargaining power extends to non-participants as well (Butta et al., 2012). They are also largely self-targeting (as discussed below). In addition, public works programmes have a number of secondary benefits, including the creation of public goods and the promotion of social cohesion. In some countries, they have also been used for environmental (e.g. generation of water storage, afforestation, compost generation, etc.) and social purposes (running child care centres, nursing homes, school kitchens, etc.) – Lieuw-Kie-Song et al. (2010). More recently, some programmes have also been moving beyond the mere provision of temporary work by providing training opportunities to prepare participants for possible longer-term employment, self-employment, or further education and training. The basic motivation behind this is to provide individuals with a more permanent pathway out of workfare and poverty. The type of training provided can include vocational training, basic skills training (literacy and numeracy) as well as entrepreneurship training.

Public works programmes can differ in a number of important respects, including their exact purpose, the length for which they are provided, their targeting methods, as well as the extent to which communities are involved. Some programmes provide only short-term safety nets and are designed primarily to provide a basic income to vulnerable individuals in times of need. Other programmes, however, run all year round. They offer longer-term work opportunities and, as a result, a more reliable source of income, typically providing individuals with the equivalent of around 100 days of work per year. Some programmes guarantee each eligible individual a certain amount of work each year ("employment guarantee") while others still aim to fit in with seasonable labour requirements for other activities.

Public works programmes have often been targeted specifically at geographical areas containing a disproportionate share of the poor and/or unemployed. A number of additional targeting mechanisms can be used (Subbarao et al., 2013) including the use of means-tests based on actual or proxy income (e.g. easily observable household characteristics, such as the location and quality of housing, the presence of certain durable goods, education, etc.) Most of the time, however, public works programmes rely on self-selection as the primary targeting mechanism, and the central parameter here is the wage at which such work is rewarded. They key is to set the wage for such programmes at a level low enough to attract only those in need of temporary work, but high enough to provide an adequate source of income. As pointed out by Murgai et al. (2013), it is important also to consider the wage foregone in setting compensation levels, as individuals will frequently give up some other source of income in order to participate in the programme. The net effect of the wage paid on participants' household income needs to take into account this opportunity cost. In general, the higher the wage rate, the fewer jobs that will be created, the less effective targeting of the poor will be, and the higher the risk of adverse effects on other sectors (Vaidya, 2013).

Finally, some programmes have involved the community in selecting programme participants since they can be argued to have a better sense of who is truly in need. The role of communities can extend beyond the selection of participants, however (Subbarao et al., 2013). In particular, involving the community in the choice of projects has been argued to promote participants' ownership of the programme, which can lead to better quality work as well as maintenance upon completion of the project. On the downside, it can increase corruption since it opens up the possibility of political capture by local elites. Such corruption can be mitigated by having clear and transparent selection criteria for programme participants, as well as for the types of projects carried out.[16]

Tunisia has (or had) a number of public works programmes in place, which are managed by a range of different actors. The main ones are: i) those funded by the *Fonds National de l'Emploi* [National Employment Fund][17] and managed by the Regional Councils (Instrument 16 of the *Contrat Emploi Solidarité* [Employment Solidarity Contract][18]) – but which are currently being phased out; and ii) the regional development programmes managed by the *Ministère du Développement Régional* [Ministry of Regional Development], including the *Programme de Développement Intégré* (PDI) [Integrated Development Programme] and the *Programme des Chantiers Régionaux de Développement* (PCRD) [Regional Public Works Development Programme]. In addition, Tunisia (with the assistance of the World Bank) is experimenting with new models of delivering workfare programmes (discussed at the end of this section).

CES Instrument 16 has traditionally provided labour-intensive public works (e.g. maintenance works of roads and public buildings and spaces) combined with apprenticeship-style training. Participation is restricted to those aged under 35, limited in time (nine months) and pays a stipend to participants of TND 200 per month (Decree No. 2013-3766 of 18 September 2013 – it was TND 120 prior to that). Little (if any) evaluation of these programmes exists, but anecdotal evidence suggests that the distribution of funds has often been hi-jacked by local interest groups (Belghazi, 2012). One key reason for this political capture has been the targeting mechanism adopted by these programmes, which relies primarily on the *Chefs de Délégation* for drawing up the list of participants with final approval granted by the Governor. There are cases of public works projects that are never completed and/or that pay wages workers who do not show up for work (Angel-Urdinola et al., 2013). Although these programmes were expected to be run in close collaboration with ANETI (the public employment service), there was in fact very little communication and collaboration. In practice, many of these programmes appeared to have become dysfunctional and operated primarily as cash transfer programmes with little targeting on those who needed them most. Instrument 16 is now in the process of being phased out. Nearly 21 000 participants in the programme at the end of 2013 will gradually be absorbed as permanent workers into the public sector.[19] No new participants are being admitted into the programme.

As mentioned above, in addition to CES Instrument 16 (which was designed as an active labour market programme), there are two other public works programmes in Tunisia, both managed by the Ministry of Regional Development: the PDI and the PCRD. Although these are primarily focused on narrowing the infrastructure gap between Tunisia's least and most disadvantaged regions, both these programmes also have an important employment generation objective. In the case of the PDI, workers are employed full-time and receive a salary of around TND 320 per month, with no limit on the duration for which they can remain in the programme. In the case of the PDCR, only a few days of work per month are provided, and a salary of TND 120 is paid. While the PCRD is implemented nation-wide, the PDI operates only in 90 of the 264 delegations, selected on the basis of certain social, economic and environmental criteria. In 2012, over 78 000 people participated in these programmes, however eligibility criteria for participation are not clear.

Going forward, there appears to be a role for public works programmes as safety net/ALMP in Tunisia, but in order to be more effective they will need to be reformed, or at least brought back in line with their original objectives. First, these programmes should be targeted on the regions with the highest unemployment rates. Second, they should be targeted at individuals who need them most. Wages paid can be the key self-selection criterion, but at the same time they need to provide a minimum level of income. Third, additional criteria (like months spent unemployed and/or means tests) could be introduced where demand exceeds supply, but selection needs to remain transparent. One way of avoiding the need for selection is to simply guarantee each participant/household a certain number of days of work per year (i.e. an employment guarantee) – although this would, of course, depend on available budgets. Fourth, offering work on a part-time basis will give the participants the time, as well as the incentives, for seeking other income-generating activities. Fifth, participants should be given the opportunity to participate in training and/or receive the necessary support to set up their own business, so that graduation from the programme and a more permanent and sustainable path out of poverty can be achieved. Sixth, the local community should be involved in the selection of projects, so that ownership is increased and therefore the likelihood of success. Seventh, such programmes should not only provide unskilled work, but can also offer skilled work for graduates, particularly if combined with the provision of social services (e.g. caring or education services). Finally, a much closer collaboration with ANETI and monitoring of programme participants is recommended. South Africa's Community Work Programme (Box 3.5) is an interesting example that policy makers in Tunisia may wish to pay attention to.

### Box 3.5. South Africa's Community Work Programme

Despite relatively strong economic performance, poverty levels in South Africa remain high and income inequality has even increased slightly in recent years. While South Africa has a number of cash transfer programmes in place to support the incomes of those at the bottom (the Disability Grant, the Old Age Pension and the Child Support Grant), a chief concern remains that approximately one in four working age South Africans are unable to find work and the majority of the jobless have no access to any income support, apart from those with benefiting from the Unemployment Insurance Fund for a limited period of time. This situation highlighted the need for a meaningful safety net for the unemployed, that provides both work and income, and was a key motivation behind the creation of the Community Work Programme.[1]

The CWP began as a pilot in 2007 and was partially modelled on India's National Rural Employment Guarantee Scheme (NREGA). Similar to the Indian model, the CWP offers (but does not guarantee) unemployed adults up to 100 days of paid labour per year. Contrary to the NREGA (and to South Africa's other public works programmes), however, the work is spread across the year and is part-time (usually two days per week), in order to provide participants with a regular, predictable income floor (instead of one or two intensive periods of employment per year). Participants are offered a wage roughly equal to the sectoral minimum wage for farm workers. The scheme is run at the local municipality level, and has a strong participatory element to identify key needs within each community. Activities are labour intensive (all projects are required to have a 65:35 ratio of wage to non-wage costs) and extend beyond the creation of basic infrastructure. There is a strong focus on social services and food security, and work includes the training of community carers, teaching assistants, the creation of food gardens, and the provision of health and hygiene education.

The CWP is designed as an employment safety net, not an employment solution for participants. It is therefore meant to complement, not replace, existing livelihood strategies of unemployed and underemployed people. The programme had just over 200 000 participants in 148 different sites at the end of March 2014. Beyond job creation, the programme has been reported to contribute to lower crime rates, increased attendance at school as well as greater social cohesion – although such outcomes are, of course, difficult to measure. More generally, while the effectiveness of public works programmes as a safety net has been well established, the international evidence on public works programmes as an effective active labour market programme is still quite limited.

1. The South African Government has had a strong commitment to public employment prior to CWP – called the Expanded Public Works Programme.

*Source*: Stanwix, B. and C. Van Der Westhuizen (2012), "Predicted Poverty Impacts of Expanding the Community Work Programme in South Africa: An Analysis of Income Poverty and Inequality", Development Policy Research Unit, Cape Town; Vawda, S., M. Prinsloo, A. Mostert and N. Mazibuko (2013), "The Community Work Programme, Trade and Industrial Policy Strategies", Pretoria; Subbarao, K., C. del Ninno, C. Andrews and C. Rodríguez-Alas (2013), "Public Works as Safety Net: Design, Evidence, and Implementation", World Bank, Washington, DC.

In this vein, it is worth mentioning some recent initiatives of the Tunisian Government, in partnership with the World Bank, to experiment with new models of delivering workfare programmes, such as the public works and local participation programme in Jendouba (Angel-Urdinola, 2013). This programme is based on a partnership with local NGO's and aims to temporarily employ (4-6 months) around 3 000 lowly skilled and unemployed individuals in 100 projects, while also improving the local infrastructure base. The projects will be identified by the NGO's in collaboration with the local population. NGO's are also expected to monitor the presence of participants as well as ensure they receive the necessary training. NGO's are held accountable not only for the completion of the project, but also for the quality of the works. Such partnerships with the NGO sector are a promising way forward as they allow the Tunisian Government to rapidly compensate capacity constraints it may face in its own administration.

## Delivering employment services that work for youth

Public employment services (PES) can play a central role in matching the supply of labour to demand through the provision of information, placement and active support services. They are usually the primary government institution responsible for implementing active labour market programmes. Tunisia's PES, the *Agence Nationale pour l'Emploi et le Travail Indépendant* (ANETI) [National Employment and Self-Employment Agency] was established in 1973. It currently counts 78 general offices as well as ten specialised offices for *cadres* [in this case best translated as higher education graduates] and 12 *Espaces Entreprendre* [Entrepreneurship Spaces] – all staffed by approximately 1 000 jobs counsellors in total.[20] These counsellors are specialised either in information and guidance; or in recruitment and placement; or in self-employment promotion.

### *Few youth find jobs through the public employment service*

In practice, few youth in Tunisia find work through ANETI. According to the ILO's 2013 School-to-Work Transition Survey for Tunisia, only 4.9% of youth (aged 15-29) currently employed found work through the public employment service. The vast majority said they found work either through friends or relatives, or by direct contact with employers. While a much larger proportion of those currently unemployed and looking for work use the public employment service (nearly two out of five young men, and two thirds of young women), direct contact with employers remains the number one approach for young men to try and find work (Figure 3.2).

**Figure 3.2. How youth look for and find work in Tunisia, 2013**

As a percentage of working and non-working youth, respectively

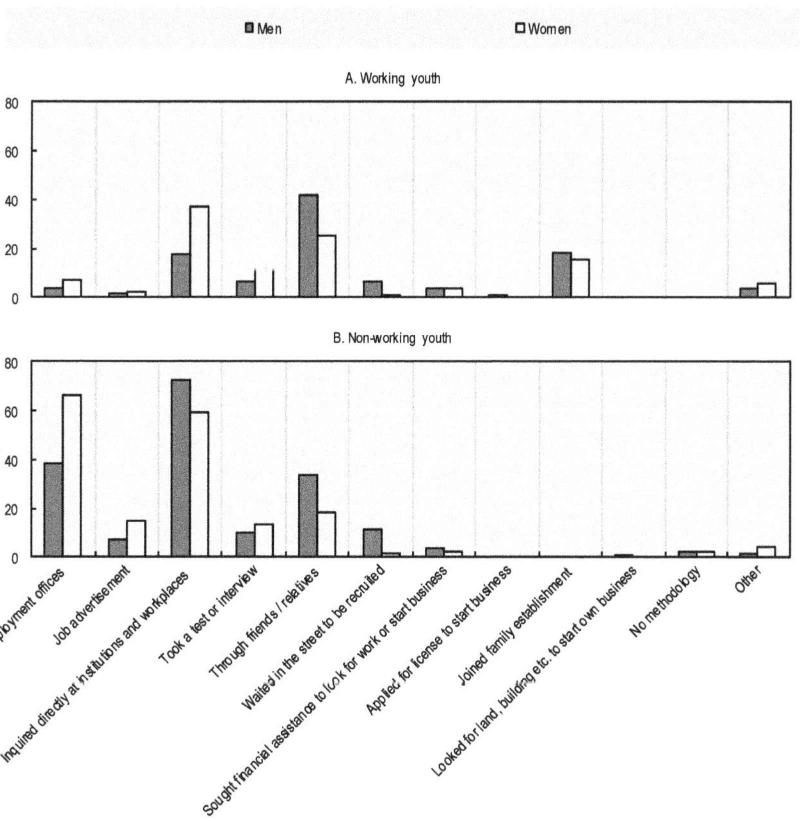


*Source*: OECD calculations based on the ILO School-to-Work Transition Survey for Tunisia (2013).

Higher education graduates are more likely to use the public employment service than non-graduates. Indeed, ANETI's coverage rate for unemployed higher education graduates is approximately double its coverage rate for non-graduates.[21] This difference can to a large extent be attributed to the fact that non-graduates face far fewer incentives to register with ANETI. As mentioned previously, the vast majority of ALMP programmes in Tunisia are aimed at university graduates, and registration with the public employment service is also a prerequisite for public employment recruitment rounds (which target university graduates primarily).

### *Greater capacity will be critical to the delivery of effective employment services*

The discrepancy between the proportion of youth who say they use the public employment service, on the one hand, and the proportion who find work through it, on the other, could also be explained by the limited capacity of ANETI to adequately help jobseekers. The ANETI network translates into just over three PES offices per governorate and a staff caseload of 1:267, which compares unfavourably with the ILO's recommended 1:100 (Angel-Urdinola and Leon-Solano, 2013).[22] Counsellors often lack specialised training and continued professional development is unstructured (UGTT, 2008). In addition, these limited resources are used inefficiently, with PES staff spending a large amount of their time on administrative tasks, at the expense of providing core services like counselling, job search assistance, and matching and placement support. Guidance services frequently consist in no more than the provision of a simple information desk and jobseekers rarely benefit from a skills appraisal or a personal development plan (UGTT, 2008). The PES came under particular pressure with the introduction of *Amal* after the revolution, which led to a large increase in the number of unemployed graduates registering with ANETI and a surge in administrative work for PES staff. As a result, very few of the *Amal* beneficiaries received anything more than a cash benefit. Even when *Amal* was replaced by the far more targeted *Programme d'Encouragement à l'Emploi*, most participants continued to not receive any of the employment services the programme claimed to provide. Indeed, ILO and ONEQ (2014) show that only 4.4% of youth who entered in contact with the PES say they benefited from job search advice; 9.4% were informed about vacancies; and 2.3% were alerted about possible education and training possibilities.

Looking forward, the capacity of the PES will need to be improved significantly if it is to be able to provide employment services effectively. Greater investments will need to be made to increase the number of offices as well as staffing levels. Existing resources could also be used more efficiently. For instance, administrative tasks could be delegated away from counsellors to less-qualified staff, which would free up counsellors' time to do what they have been trained for (Belghazi, 2012);[23] virtual access to employment services (e.g. to vacancies, advice, etc.) could be installed in more remote areas (e.g. in youth associations, public spaces, universities, schools, etc. – Redjeb and Ghobentini, 2005); and the specialised PES offices dedicated to higher education graduates only should be abolished and merged with the standard PES offices (which they are often co-located with anyway) – Belghazi (2012). While on paper, the comprehensive set of services to be provided as part of the *Chèque d'Amélioration de l'Employabilité* [Employability Improvement Cheque] proposed as part of the ALMP reform (see Box 3.6) looks promising, the experiences of both *Amal* and the PEE show that the capacity of ANETI to deliver this programme will be absolutely critical to its success.

**Box 3.6. The *Chèque d'Amélioration de l'Employabilité***

The *Chèque d'Amélioration de l'Employabilité* [Employability Improvement Cheque] is one of four programmes of the ALMP reform introduced by Decree No. 2012-2369 of 16 October 2012 and which is meant to be launched (most likely on a pilot basis) from 1 January 2015 onwards. To some extent it is a catch-all programme, providing participants with job search assistance (supplemented by other activities to strengthen the person's labour market readiness if needed), a competency and needs assessment, work experience, training and/or business start-up assistance. During their participation in the programme beneficiaries will receive a stipend of TND 200 if they have at least a higher technician diploma (*brevet de technicien supérieur*) or university degree, while those with lower level qualifications will receive TND 100. The maximum participation period is set at 24 months.

It is a welcome development that the programme has been opened up to non-graduates, although how resources will be prioritised between different participants is still unclear at this stage. In line with previous ALMPs in Tunisia, the stipend increases with educational qualification, but it is not clear what the reasoning behind this is. If anything, it could be argued that the least educated (who are often the least advantaged) would need more help. Finally, as shown by the experiences of both *Amal* and the PEE, the programme's success will be critically dependent on ANETI's capacity to provide participants with the necessary employability services. This will require significant additional resources for, as well as a restructuring of, employment services in Tunisia.

### *Private employment services are prohibited in Tunisia, but partnerships with the private sector could help ease pressure on the PES*

The ILO, through Convention No. 181, acknowledges the "role private employment agencies may play in a well-functioning labour market". While they "have long complemented the traditional employment market" the ILO now considers private employment agencies as "a catalyst of new forms of human resource management services" and recognises that they "can be contributors to better working conditions" (ILO, 2007). At the same time, through Convention No. 96, the ILO encourages countries to either abolish fee-charging employment agencies conducted with a view to profit, or to regulate them.

Tunisia has not ratified ILO Convention 181 (concerning private employment agencies) and, in fact, article 285 of its Labour Code prohibits the operation of private employment agencies, whether fee-paying or not, giving ANETI a *de facto* monopoly status. Tunisia should consider revising this article and allow (and regulate) the operation of private employment agencies because, as evidenced above, capacity constraints signify that ANETI cannot do everything on its own, and that it would greatly benefit from contracting out some of its services to other providers. Such outsourcing can bring a number of advantages (OECD, 2013d), including: bringing in specialist skills unavailable in the public sector; fostering competition between employment services which can potentially reduce delivery costs and stimulate innovation; spurring improved performance in the public employment service; as well as the expansion of service delivery capacity without the long-term commitments involved in public sector employment (although some stability of the contracting framework is desirable to build up private sector capacity). In many OECD countries, the PES outsources at least some specific functions (OECD, 2013d) – e.g. job-search training activities in Finland, job clubs in Norway – while some countries (e.g. Australia and the United Kingdom) rely on large-scale contracting out (see Box 3.7). In Tunisia, ANETI could fulfil the function of "gateway" and decide which jobseekers need to be referred to employment agencies for specific services.

## Box 3.7. Australia's fully outsourced employment service

While in many OECD countries public employment services outsource at least some of their activity to private employment agencies, Australia's approach is unique in that its mainstream employment service is entirely outsourced to over a hundred for-profit and non-profit provider organisations competing in a "quasi-market", with their operations financed by service fees, placement and employment outcome payments, and a special fund for measures that tackle jobseekers' barriers to employment. The first version of this system was set up in 1998 as the Job Network (JN). The system operating since 2009, Job Services Australia (JSA) integrated JN provision with previously separate programmes targeted at highly disadvantaged youths and adults and with the management of the Work for the Dole programme.

Australia's approach has been judged to be successful. In a recent country review of Australia, the OECD concluded that, despite possible refinements of the design and management of its employment services, the interlocking elements in place in this quasi-market are highly effective and, together with the strategy of activating inactive benefits, have contributed to the strong performance of the Australian labour market.

Three key elements in particular help explain the success of Australia's employment service:

- First, outcome-based contracts give providers flexibility to personalise service provision and allow case managers to tailor services to different participants. There is no requirement on providers to spend fee income on any particular client. While individual clients attract funding for intensive services based on their level of disadvantage – which is assessed mainly based on administrative records and client responses to a series of questions asked as part of the Job Seeker Classification Instrument (JSCI) – providers are then free to allocate services across individuals to maximise their effectiveness in terms of generating paid employment outcomes. This arrangement assumes that providers have the best knowledge of their clients' needs, which is more efficient than if the government decided which services were needed by individual clients, and purchased those.
- A second strength of the system is that it focuses providers and their case managers on achieving not just any job outcome, but on achieving entry into sustained employment. Outcome Payments are made when clients reach 13 weeks in employment and again when they reach 26 weeks.
- Third, from 2000, the government began to regularly publish Star Ratings of provider performance which are currently available for over 2 000 individual sites, based on how many paid placements and paid outcomes were achieved, with regression adjustments taking client characteristics and the state of the local labour market into account. In subsequent tender rounds, providers with low Star Ratings lost business, which was reallocated to higher performing providers and to some new entrants to the market.

Although the Australian experience demonstrates that a quasi-market for employment services can operate effectively, it does require an active national management framework. The benefit administration organisation, Centrelink maintains a national database of jobseekers characteristics and assesses which benefit claimants are required to search for work, or have failed to comply with requirements. The Australian Department of Employment defines complex contracts with employment service providers, maintains a national database of jobseeker characteristics and estimates comparative measures of employment service provider performance as the basis for renewing or terminating contracts. It also audits provider activity on an ongoing basis for contract compliance, assuring the validity of expense claims, service quality, general organisational health and other factors. Although this management framework has a cost, it does tend to ensure that the quasi-market rewards the right outcomes and that only high-performing providers can remain in the market.

*Source*: OECD (2012), "Net Replacement Rates for Six Family Types: Initial Phase of Unemployment", *Benefits and Wages: Statistics*, www.oecd.org/els/benefitsandwagesstatistics.htm (accessed 2 June 2014); OECD (2013), "Activating Jobseekers: Lessons from Seven OECD Countries", Chapter 3 in *OECD Employment Outlook 2013*, OECD Publishing, Paris, http://dx.doi.org/10.1787/empl_outlook-2013-en.

The monitoring of employment outcomes (performance management) is critical to the success of public/private partnerships in the delivery of employment services. Such performance is often measured in terms of job placements and, especially for harder-to-help groups, longer-term employment outcomes. Australia and Switzerland operate a more complex performance management system and use regression analysis techniques to adjust employment office performance for jobseeker as well as local labour market characteristics (OECD, 2013d). This approach effectively benchmarks performance and acknowledges that factors other than the effectiveness of employment services may affect the labour market outcomes of individuals, and helps to ensure that harder-to-help groups are not discriminated against. Another example is Austria, where the effect of a set of exogenous variables on labour market outcomes is estimated using econometric analysis. The variables considered are: the relative share of the working age population born in other EU15 countries; the relative unemployment rate; the share of part-time workers; the labour force participation rate; the gender wage gap; and median income. Based on these factors, each district is assigned to a specific cluster using cluster analysis, and performance of employment services are then compared within such clusters (Adamecz, 2013). In the case of Tunisia, the social security records database could be matched to data on participation in employment programmes to provide a relatively accurate picture of the labour market outcomes of clients referred to private employment agencies.[24] As in the case of Australia and Switzerland, such data could be adjusted for the characteristics of the individual and/or local labour markets. Private employment agencies could then be rewarded based on their success in obtaining quality and long-term labour market outcomes for their clients. Such rewards could, for instance, be proportional to the length of the job match achieved.

A second reason why Tunisia should consider legalising and regulating private employment agencies is that, while private employment agencies are, in theory, banned by the Labour Code, in practice many private employment agencies operate in the country, including some of the leading international firms (UGTT, 2008). This is partially because the Labour Code permits temporary work agencies and also states that "*les annonces des offres et des demandes d'emploi par la voie des moyens d'information sont autorisées*" [job advertisements and applications through the means of information channels are authorised] – Belghazi (2012). Given the weak regulatory framework surrounding temporary agency work (see Chapter 2), the fact that private employment agencies in Tunisia currently operate outside the law, and that they are frequently seen with suspicion by trade unions (Angel-Urdinola et al., 2013), it is important that the rights and obligations of all parties, including those using these services, be clarified. Morocco, for instance, ratified ILO Convention No. 181 with the help of some leading global private employment agencies and the latter have ever since been pushing for better regulation as well as setting industry standards, working with unions, and providing the government with labour market intelligence (Ahmed, 2011). In addition, the Moroccan Government benefits from the ratification in that it allows it to attract investments in priority sectors such as offshore services and manufacturing (Ahmed, 2011). On the downside, although ANAPEC (the public employment service) now works in partnership with private recruitment firms (Subrahmanyam, 2011), there is still too little communication in Morocco between the various stakeholders, and the public employment service is seen as a rival rather than as a partner (Ahmed, 2011). This highlights the important role of government in co-ordinating the co-operation between public and private employment services.

### *Tunisia is already undertaking steps to work closer together with NGOs in the delivery of active labour market programmes*

As part of the 2012 ALMP reform to be implemented from January 2015 onwards and set out in Decrees No. 2012-2369 of 12 October 2012 and No. 2013-3766 of 18 September 2013), the Tunisian Government has made room for active labour market policies to be sourced out to non-governmental organisations. This is the case for competency assessments and training programmes under the *Chèque d'Amélioration de l'Employabilité* (e.g. job search training, communication and social skills training, etc.) as well as entrepreneurship training and coaching programmes under the *Programme d'Appui aux Promoteurs des Petites Entreprises* [Small Entrepreneur Support Programme]. A list of eligible NGO's will be drawn up by the Director General of ANETI based on the advice received from a technical committee, the composition and terms of reference of which will be decided upon by the Minister of Employment. This technical committee shall review all bids received in response to a call to tender published in the media. The decisions of the technical committee shall be based on the type of actions to be carried out, how and under what conditions, the expected results, as well as the monitoring and evaluation required. NGO's winning a contract shall be paid by the National Employment Fund according to performance agreements setting out the expected results as well as the indicators to be used for measuring performance. In the meantime, some memoranda of understanding with NGO's to allow them to deliver ALMPs have already been signed. One example is the partnership signed in July 2013 between the MFPE and the International Youth Foundation (IYF) to allow the latter to carry out activities to strengthen the skills of jobseekers and to build the capacity of local NGO's providing support services to youth, partly under the umbrella of the *Programme d'Encouragement à l'Emploi*. Another example is the agreement signed on March 2014 between ANETI and two NGO's (ADRA and INJAZ) to allow them to provide training and workshops to jobseekers registered with the public employment service (see Box 3.8).

**Box 3.8. Partnerships with NGOs in delivering employment services**

**International Youth Foundation**

The International Youth Foundation (IYF) is an NGO which was set up in 1990 and now operates in close to 80 countries around the world. IYF came to Tunisia in 2012 (after the revolution) and set up the TunisiaWorks initiative, a two-year programme that builds the capacity of local organisations and institutions to improve the employment prospects of Tunisian youth. TunisiaWorks offers employability, entrepreneurship, and civic engagement training and support to unemployed youth and aspiring entrepreneurs in Beja, Bizerte, Jendouba, and Tunis.

In July 2013 IYF signed a memorandum of understanding with the *Ministère de la Formation Professionnelle et de l'Emploi* (MFPE) [Ministry of Vocational Education and Employment], which will enhance the partnership between the two organisations. As part of this agreement, IYF commits to contributing to the design and implementation of a jobseeker support programme in Tunisia. In particular, in the context of the *Programme d'Encouragement à l'Emploi* [Employment Incentive Programme], IYF will assist in improving the employability of participants with the goal of their integration into salaried work or self-employment. More generally, IYF will help define quality standards for NGO's delivering employment support services as well as contribute to capacity-building within these organisations. In return, the MFPE will share information with IYF concerning possible collaborations as well as the list of jobseekers eligible for training and support services.

Only ten months after the signing of the MoU, IYF has worked together with nine local NGOs to support and train nearly 3 000 youths. In addition, the programme has resulted in the setting up of a local team with the necessary skills to accompany jobseekers and has strengthened the capacity of local NGO's. It has also supported the emergence of a public-private partnership that has encouraged the exchange of best practices in the area of youth employability.

**Box 3.8. Partnerships with NGOs in delivering employment services** *(cont.)*

**ADRA and INJAZ**

In March 2014, Tunisia's public employment service (ANETI) signed a tripartite agreement between itself and two NGO's: ADRA (an international NGO) and INJAZ (a local organisation). ADRA's focus is on vocational training for the poor to help them find a durable path out of poverty, whereas INJAZ's mission is more specifically focused on getting youth to become productive members of society, and this through the provision of educational programmes aimed at encouraging entrepreneurship and improving their professional skills. As part of the agreement, the NGO's agree to: i) provide training and workshops for jobseekers to improve their soft skills (including communication, time management and conflict management), as well as job search and entrepreneurship skills; and ii) help young people acquire work experience through internships in the private sector. In return, ANETI ensures that jobseekers are made aware of the programmes run by the NGO's, and share any information conducive to possible collaborations.

*Source:* www.iyfnet.org; Memorandum of Understanding between the Ministry of Vocational Education and Training and Employment and International Youth Foundation signed 2 July 2013, Tunis; Tripartite Agreement between ANETI, ADRA and INJAZ signed 3 March 2014, Tunis.

The increased engagement of non-governmental organisations in the delivery of active labour market programmes is a welcome development, partly because this will strengthen a civil society which, under the pre-revolution regime, was rarely allowed to be active and independent. While engaging NGO's is also a practical solution to ANETI's lack of capacity outlined above, it cannot entirely substitute for the value-added that experienced international private employment agencies could bring. The best way forward is therefore likely to contain a combination of public, for profit and not-for-profit organisations, building on the strengths of each to achieve the best employment outcomes for clients as possible.

## Nurturing entrepreneurship

Micro-enterprises and self-employment play an important role in job creation in Tunisia. Rijkers et al. (2013) estimate that two out of every five jobs created over the period 1996-2010 were in one-person firms (self-employment) and Belghazi (2012) similarly argues that the growth of micro-enterprises accounts for nearly half of jobs created. That said, Tunisia ranked only 64th out of the 67 countries that participated in the 2012 Global Entrepreneurship Monitor survey according to the measure of early stage entrepreneurial activity: only 5% of the adult population were involved in setting up a business or were owners of a new business (Figure 3.3). There are also significant gender differences, with men being 2.4 times more likely than women to start a business (Belkacem and Mansouri, 2013). Young people are also much less likely to be involved in entrepreneurship. While this is true in around the world, only 2% of people aged 18 to 24 in Tunisia were involved in creating a business in 2012 (Belkacem and Mansouri, 2013). These findings are confirmed by ILO and ONEQ (2014), who show that only a very small portion of young people in Tunisia are self-employed.

These statistics highlight the importance of putting in place adequate support structures for young people wanting to set up their own business. Indeed, compared to their peers in OECD countries, fewer young people in Tunisia say they receive access to training and finance. While Tunisia has a relatively well-developed start-up support system, with the provision of information, training, finance and follow-up services in the first two years of operation, considerable duplication exists in the provision of such services, suggesting that efficiency gains could be made. More could be done also to provide medium- to long-term assistance to young entrepreneurs, as well as additional support for women who face multiple obstacles in setting up a business.

**Figure 3.3. Total early-stage entrepreneurial activity (TEA), Tunisia, and selected OECD, MENA and large emerging economies, 2012**

Percentage of people aged 18-64 who are either a nascent entrepreneur or owner-manager of a new business[a]

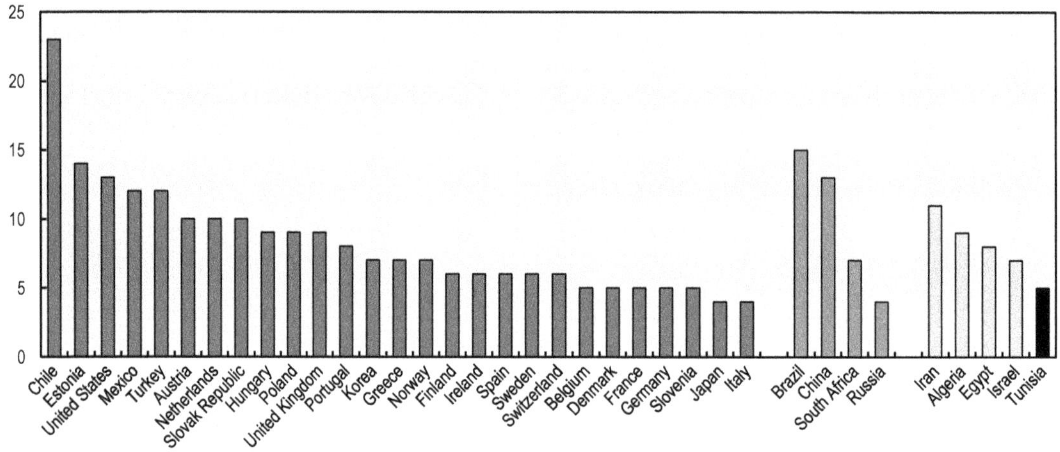


*a)* A nascent entrepreneur is defined as someone actively involved in setting up a business they will own or co-own; this business has not paid salaries, wages, or any other payments to the owners for more than three months. An owner-manager of a new business is defined as someone owning and managing a running business that has paid salaries, wages, or any other payments to the owners for more than three months, but not more than 42 months.

*Source*: Global Entrepreneurship Monitor (2013), *GEM 2012 Global Report*.

ANETI, through the *Programme d'Appui aux Promoteurs des Petites Entreprises* (PAPPE) [Small Entrepreneur Support Programme] provides jobseekers who want to set up their own business with the necessary information, training, advice and counselling, as well as financial support. Access to these services is provided through ANETI's 11 *Espaces Entreprendre* [Entrepreneurship Spaces]. While these *Espaces Entreprendre* primarily address the (young) unemployed, they are not the only structures in Tunisia providing such services: the country also boasts a *Centre d'Affaires* [Business Centre][25] in each of its 24 governorates, as well as *pépinières* [incubators][26] and *Espaces Tremplin*[27] [Springboard to Entrepreneurship]. This multitude of support structures raises the question of effective collaboration between them, as well as the risk of duplication in an environment characterised by scarce resources. For example, there is very little difference between the support provided by the Business Centres and the *Espaces Entreprendre*. This duplication is recognised by both the support developers and educators that are responsible for assisting students and directing them on where to get support. To further compound this, the *Banque Tunisienne de Solidarité* (BTS) [Tunisian Solidarity Bank] also plans on launching entrepreneurship support services.

The provision of information, advisory and consultancy services is one of the most common elements of business support. It provides guidance on the implications, rewards and risks of starting a business, as well as helping to diagnose problems and building the knowledge necessary to run a business. In the *Espaces Entreprendre*, individuals have access to a database with start-up ideas, a library containing technical and legal documents, the internet, as well as group information sessions and assistance with developing their ideas. The latter may take the form of three-day training courses such as the *Méthode*

*Originale de Recherche Active d'Idées Nouvelles pour Entreprendre* (MORAINE) [Original and Active Research Method for New Entrepreneurship Ideas] and *Trouvez une Idée d'Entreprise* (TIE) [Find a Business Idea].[28] For those who have identified an idea, more advanced training in entrepreneurial methods is provided through three-week programmes such as the *Création d'Entreprises Formation d'Entrepreneurs* (CEFE) [Business Start-up Entrepreneur Training] and the *Créez Votre Entreprise* (CREE) [Set Up Your Business]. Individuals can also take on an internship of up to one year to acquire and/or improve the skills required to set up their own business. Some additional support is available for those who have recently set up their business, such as supplementary management training (*Gérez Mieux votre Entreprise* [Manage Your Business Better]) and individual technical support (12 days of an expert's time within the first two years of the start-up date).[29] ANETI also enters into partnerships with non-governmental organisations to provide continued support to entrepreneurs during the first two years of operation. Beyond the initial years, however, very little further support is available for entrepreneurs (e.g. lack of long-term coaching) and the quality of the existing support varies substantially by region. Moreover, the current support system lacks cohesion and more can be done to ensure that young entrepreneurs can receive appropriate support at the right time. In other words, the current support system does not effectively ensure that an entrepreneur receives support at all stages of launching and growing a business: generating ideas, starting a business and developing and growing their business. In addition, while comprehensive entrepreneurship training appears to be available for unemployed youth through ANETI, a more comprehensive approach should be put in place – in particular exposure to such training earlier on in the educational cycle. Indeed, a much smaller proportion of youth who had not set up their own business in Tunisia say they had access to training than youth in OECD countries (Figure 3.4).

**Figure 3.4. Youth having access to training on how to start a business, Tunisia, OECD, and selected emerging and MENA countries, 2012**

As a percentage of youth who are not business owners

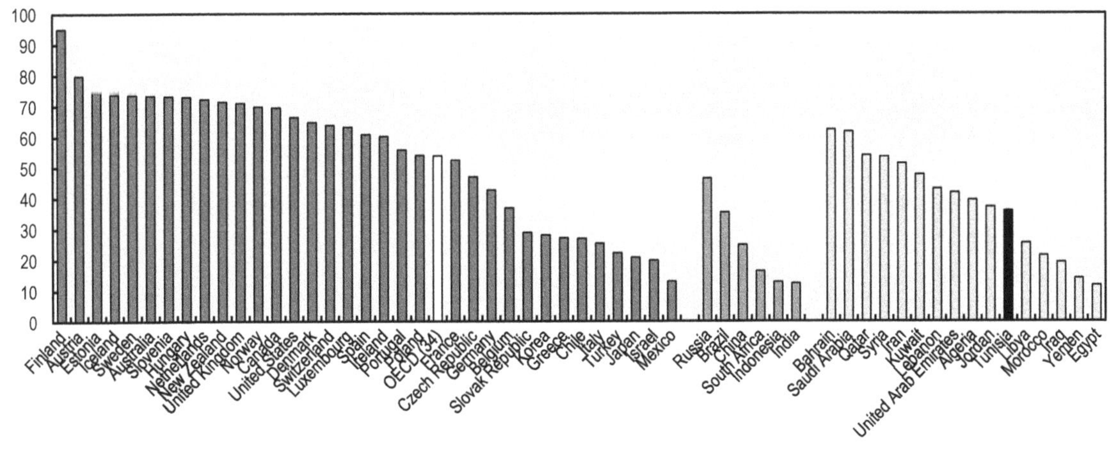


*Source*: OECD calculations based on Gallup World Poll data.

In addition to training, the PAPPE provides financial support to those setting up their own enterprise. This financial assistance takes two forms. First, PAPPE participants are entitled to a monthly stipend (TND 200 in the case of higher education graduates, and TND 100 for all others) for a period of twelve months during the first two years after the business start-up. Second, while loans for micro-projects do not require any collateral, larger loans (exceeding TND 20 000) require a 10% self-financing component (see Box 3.9) and many young people do not have the necessary resources for this (ANETI, 2014). More than half of projects accompanied by ANETI fail to obtain financing due to this restriction (Belghazi, 2012). Indeed, when asked whether youth are asked whether they have access to the money needed to start a business, youth in Tunisia are much less likely to respond in the affirmative than youth in OECD countries (Figure 3.5) and ILO and ONEQ (2014) estimate that approximately half of self-employed youth used their own savings to set up a business and a further 37% relied on their families. To address this obstacle, ANETI awards up to TND 5 000 to each entrepreneur, as long as they provide proof of the necessary competencies, training or experience and dedicate themselves full-time to their project. In addition to these grants, loans have been available (*A'timed el Intilak* [Seed Funding]) since 2011 to complete the financing required in order to obtain a small enterprise loan from the BTS. These *A'timed el Intilak* loans are interest-free and need to be repaid over a period of five years. Like most of Tunisia's active labour market programmes (ALMPs), entrepreneurship financing discriminates by level of education, with more generous funding being available to higher education graduates. It is a slight oddity that the size of the loan awarded should depend more on an individual's qualifications than on the merit of the business idea.

### Box 3.9. The *Banque Tunisienne de Solidarité* (BTS)

The BTS, created in 1997, provides loans for micro-projects (new start-ups or extensions) of suitably qualified individuals who do not have the necessary collateral to obtain a loan from a private bank. These loans are to be repaid over a period of between six months and seven years (11 years in the case of FONAPRAM[1] projects) and cover values of up to TND 10 000 in the case of non-university graduates, TND 20 000 in the case of university graduates, and TND 33 000 in the case of FONAPRAM activities. Interest is charged at a rate of 5%, with a grace period of between 3-12 months depending on the nature of the project and the extent of self-financing. The BTS also operates through independent micro-finance organisations that hand out credits of up to TND 5 000 and are expected to achieve an 80% recovery rate. Currently, 280 such organisations exist.

In addition to micro-finance, the BTS offers larger loans of up to TND 100 000[2] for setting up small enterprises, with interest charged at a 7.5% and a grace period lasting two years. For these loans, applicants need to put down a guarantee of 10% of the required capital from their own sources. This requirement indirectly discriminates against young people who frequently do not have any savings. While micro-loans do not require any collateral and are therefore more likely to be accessed by young people, they could lead to undercapitalised ventures with low survival prospects because of their relatively small values.

The beneficiaries of the BTS are generally young graduates of higher education institutions or from vocational training. From 1998 until 2011 BTS approved 15 000 loans, 30% of which have defaulted. An even higher default rate is expected for 2011 and beyond because of the revolution.

1. The *Fonds National de Promotion de l'Artisanat et des Petits Métiers* [National Fund for the Promotion of Crafts and Small Enterprises] was launched in 1981 to help individuals set up crafts and small trade businesses through the provision of low-interest loans.

2. The *Banque de Financement des Petites et Moyennes Entreprises* (BFPME) [Small and Medium Enterprise Financing Bank] provides loans for larger ventures (between TND 100 000 and TND 5 million).

**Figure 3.5. Youth reporting to have access to the money needed to start a business, Tunisia, OECD and selected emerging and MENA countries, 2012**

As a percentage of youth who are not business owners

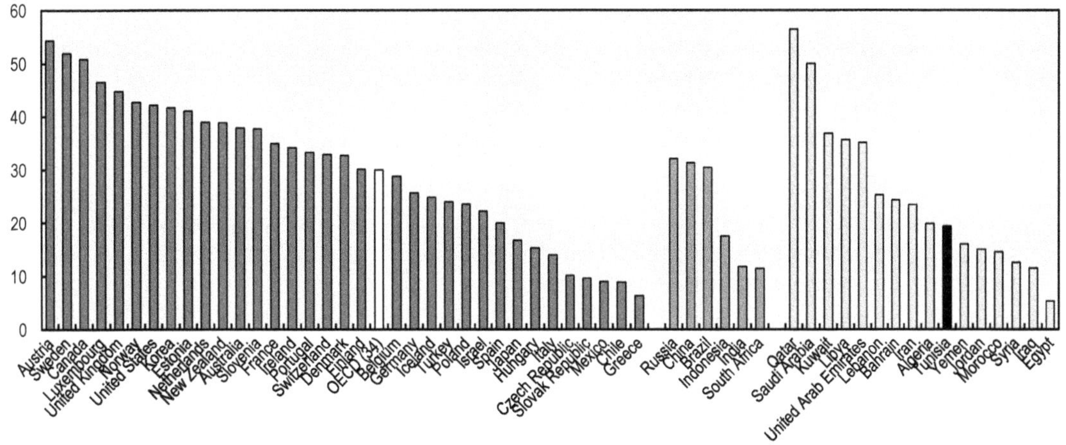


*Source:* OECD calculations based on Gallup World Poll data.

In addition to some of the limitations of entrepreneurship support outlined above, and also given the poor labour market outcomes of women outlined in Chapter 1, more could be done in Tunisia to assist potential female entrepreneurs. Indeed, according to a OECD and IDRC (2012) study on *New Entrepreneurs and High Growth Enterprises in the Middle East and North Africa*, low enterprise activity rates in the region are in part due to the low levels of participation of women in the formal economic sphere, as both employees and business leaders. As outlined by ILO (2011), women entrepreneurs face numerous obstacles in Tunisia, including: i) cultural barriers to starting a business; ii) a lack of collateral for bank loans because little property is in their name; and iii) a general scarcity of women in the workforce and in management positions. An evaluation of active labour market programmes in Tunisia (ONEQ, 2012) concludes that efforts to promote entrepreneurship have been more effective in the case of men than for women: despite more women than men participating in entrepreneurial training activities, fewer of them receive a bursary to set up a project (i.e. women are less likely to move to the realisation of their business idea).

More research is needed in the case of Tunisia to identify the real causes of lower female entrepreneurship and support evidence-based policy decisions. Indeed, the barriers could be complex and, without a good understanding of what they are, it will be difficult to develop successful policies. One step in the right direction would be to set up a single body responsible for co-ordinating the promotion of women's enterprise development – similar, for example, to the Office of Women's Business Ownership in the United States or the German National Agency for Women Start-up Activities and Services (OECD, 2012c) – as well as to develop a comprehensive policy to tackle the core barriers to developing female entrepreneurship. Depending on the exact barriers identified, interventions could include: raising awareness of successful female entrepreneurs and women role models; training programmes to build women's financial literacy and their ability to develop sound business plans and pitch them to potential lenders; promoting businesswomen's associations and including more women on the boards of chambers of commerce and industry to get the voice of women entrepreneurs heard in policy circles; and improving women's access to finance. In this respect, practices in Bangladesh, India, Malaysia, Pakistan and Turkey could be useful models for Tunisia to explore (OECD, 2012c) – although many MENA countries have also introduced measures recently (see Box 3.10).

**Box 3.10. Improving access to finance for female entrepreneurs: Recent measures taken by MENA countries**

Tailored approaches can be effective in improving the provision of financing for female entrepreneurs, and governments and financial institutions can work together in this respect. Public and private financial institutions can administer publically supported programmes for women entrepreneurs, or agree on a targeted amount or percentage of yearly lending to be disbursed to women-owned and managed businesses. Some recent actions, often supported by MENA governments, seek to improve financing for women-led SMEs:

- The Jordan Enterprise Development Corporation (JEDCO) has a small business grant programme that will raise the loan amount to 90% of the project cost for women entrepreneurs (because of their higher level of difficulty in offering collateral for traditional loans), whereas the loan will only cover 60-80% of the project cost for male entrepreneurs.
- The Women's Higher Technical Institute in the UAE, affiliated with the Technical and Vocational Training Corporation (TVTC), grants loans of up to 200 000 Saudi Riyals to its graduates who decide to start their own small businesses. This is complementary to the teaching programme which offers entrepreneurship courses to encourage new graduates to become entrepreneurs.
- In 2011, the Ministry of Women's Affairs in Iraq convinced the Iraqi Ministers Council to grant loans to finance small businesses, giving priority to women who support their families.
- In Morocco, the ANPME implemented the "Women Business Financing" project which included efforts to sensitise financial institutions to the needs of women clients and recommended that banks engage in gender sensitisation training for their front office staff. Commercial bank credit is still difficult to access, but some banks have initiated targeted marketing campaigns to reach out to the women's market.
- Bank Muscat, the leading financial services provider in Oman, has developed unique products for women, and its SME department supports various programmes to build the skills of businesswomen across all SME sectors. The Bank also funds business incubators for women.
- In 2011, the Association of Algerian Women Managers and Entrepreneurs (AME) entered into an agreement with the CIDEAL Foundation in Spain and the El Baraka Bank in Algeria to launch a project granting micro-finance to AME's members with flexible repayment terms over a five-year period. The CIDEAL Foundation will fund the project, AME will be the guarantor for the portfolio of projects and provide assistance to the women clients in developing and realising their business plans, and El Baraka Bank will deliver the loans. The larger objective of the project is to increase the participation of Algerian women in economic development and diversification.
- The Small Enterprise Development Fund (SEDF) in Yemen offers a Women Entrepreneur Credit Programme specifically designed for the micro-finance needs of home production.

*Source*: OECD (2012), *Women in Business: Policies to Support Women's Entrepreneurship Development in the MENA Region*, OECD Publishing, Paris, http://dx.doi.org/10.1787/9789264179073-en.

## Helping young families balance work and childcare responsibilities

The need for family-friendly policies in Tunisia manifests itself most visibly in the low labour force participation rates of young women discussed in Chapter 1. Indeed, one in five young women (aged 15-29) who were not in work nor looking for work (but would have liked to work given the opportunity) give family responsibilities as a reason for being out of work (compared to 0% of men in the same situation).[30] Although female labour force participation in Tunisia has increased significantly from 5.6% in 1966 (Gouider, 2010) to 25.6% in 2013[31] – reflecting the improved legal status of women (*Code du Status Personnel*

[Code of Personal Status][32] of 1956), the introduction of discrimination provisions in the Labour Code (Article 5bis[33] added in 1993), as well as gains in educational attainment for girls – the labour force participation rate of women (young and old) remains extremely low in Tunisia by international standards. Given that young women in Tunisia generally have higher educational attainment than young men, such low participation rates present a significant waste of human capital.

While there are many factors that help explain women's continued absence from the labour market worldwide (including cultural factors, discrimination, as well as workplace practices – see Box 3.11 for an overview of the literature), there is ample scope in Tunisia to improve social policies to help women participate more actively in the labour market and allow them to combine work with caring responsibilities more effectively. In particular, employment-protected paid maternity and paternity leave, affordable good-quality early childhood education and care, flexible work arrangements, and tax-benefit systems that do not harm work incentives, can help fathers and mothers find a healthy balance between working hours and family responsibilities, and will reduce barriers to (female) labour force participation in particular.

**Box 3.11. What explains differences in female labour force participation across countries and time?**

Analysis presented in Chapter 1 showed how young female labour force participation varies significantly across countries. Similarly, female labour force participation rates have often changed dramatically within countries over time. While Tunisia's female labour force participation rate is low by OECD standards, it has increased significantly in the past 50 years. In addition, women in Tunisia are considerably more likely to be active than women in other most other MENA countries. What explains such large differences in female labour force participation rates between countries, as well as within countries over time? This box aims to summarise some of the key findings from the literature on this topic. While historical and cultural factors are likely to be important, these are not set in stone. Indeed, the state and structure of the economy have played an important role in determining the extent of female participation in the labour force, as have technological changes, both at home and in the workplace. That said, there is also significant evidence to show that education, social and labour market policies play a critical role in helping women find their way to the labour force.

**History and culture**

Some commentators have argued that low female labour force participation rates reflect deep-rooted anti-egalitarian views. Fortin (2005), for example, looks at 25 OECD countries over the period 1990-1995-1999 and finds that anti-egalitarian views (as measured by the extent of agreement with statements such as "when jobs are scarce, men should have more right to a job than women") stand out as the most powerful explanatory factor of cross-country differences in female employment rates. Family attitudes and, in particular, preferences for nuclear and extended family relations, also lower the labour supply of women (Algan and Cahuc, 2007). That such preferences are deep-rooted has been demonstrated by a series of studies that looked at female immigrants in the United States and related their labour force participation rates to those of women in the home country, and found a very strong relationship between the two – suggesting that there exists a permanent portable factor (culture) that is not captured by observable human capital measures (Antecol, 2000; Fernández, 2007). Some have traced back such attitudes to historical factors that have shaped the division of labour between men and women. For example, Alesina et al. (2013) argue that descendants of societies that traditionally practiced plough cultivation (which required manual strength and therefore favoured men over women) today have less equal gender norms, as measured by reported gender-role attitudes and female participation in the workplace. However, such historical factors are not irreversible, and shocks to the system have been shown to dramatically alter gender roles in the labour market. One example of this is the significant shift brought about in female labour supply as a result of the military mobilisation for World War II (Acemoglu et al., 2002). In addition, men whose mothers were drawn into the labour force as a result of this mobilisation were, in turn, more likely to marry women who also work (Fernández et al., 2004).

## Box 3.11. What explains differences in female labour force participation across countries and time? *(cont.)*

**Economic and technological changes**

An influential theory argues that there is a U-shaped relationship between female labour force participation and economic development (i.e. at low levels of development, female labour force participation would fall with economic growth, whereas after a certain level of development, it would start increasing again) – Goldin (1995). However, this theory has been challenged by more recent analysis that found the relationship to be feeble and dependent on the data sources used (Gaddis and Klasen, 2014). Gaddis and Klasen do find some evidence, however, that structural change has an effect on female labour force participation – which echoes other studies that have found that the expansion of the service sector has been closely accompanied by a rise in the female labour supply (Thévenon, 2013). In addition to longer term economic changes, female labour force participation can respond to short-term business cycles, with married women increasing their labour supply when their husbands become unemployed – a phenomenon known as the added worker effect (Woytinsky, 1942).

In addition, technological change has fundamentally altered the role of women in society. For example, Albanesi and Olivetti (2007) show how improved medical knowledge and obstetric practices reduced the time cost associated with women's reproductive role, as well as how the introduction of formula milk reduced women's comparative advantage in infant care. Goldin (2004) argues that the contraceptive pill gave young women the ability to delay marriage and child-bearing and plan for a career and the consumer goods revolution was conducive to liberating women from the home (Greenwood et al., 2005).

**Education, social and labour market policies**

While female labour force participation may be strongly rooted in cultural factors and also determined by wider economic changes, there is now a considerable body of evidence to show that education, social and labour market policies play a critical role and, therefore, that governments concerned about low female labour force participation can bring in policies to address the issue. That educational attainment of women is a crucial determinant of female labour force participation is a widely known fact (Fortin, 2005; Thévenon, 2013). However, without trying to downplay the importance of education, the evidence also suggests that the latter in itself will not be sufficient to address the problem. In the context of MENA countries, for example, Shalaby (2014) notes that, despite a substantial reduction in the gender gap in education and literacy rates, women's economic participation in the region remains the lowest in the world. The international evidence suggests that, in addition to education, social and labour market policies are equally important. For instance, Cipollone et al. (2013) analyse 15 EU countries over a period of 20 years and find that labour market reforms and changes in social policies explain almost 25% of the actual increase in labour force participation for young women, and more than 30% for highly educated women, and Del Boca and Locatelli (2006) come to a similar conclusion on the contribution of social policies. In particular, a large empirical literature provides evidence of the importance of family-friendly policies in increasing female labour force participation (Blau and Kahn, 2013). The provision of childcare stands out as one of the most effective policies in this area (Apps and Rees, 2004), but equally parental leave and policies more generally to alleviate the financial burden of child-rearing are important. The rise in female labour force participation has also been associated with the increase in part-time employment (Thévenon, 2013; Buddelmeyer et al., 2004) as well as changes in the tax treatment of second earners in a household compared with single earnings (Jaumotte, 2003). Finally, there is no doubt that the passing of anti-discriminatory laws has played a crucial role in promoting female labour force participation – however, because of the nature of such interventions, hard evidence of their impact is often hard to obtain (Goldin, 2004).

## *Child-related leave entitlements are low*

Maternity, paternity and parental[34] leave consist of a period of employment-protected leave of absence for employed parents around childbirth. While such leave of absence has intrinsic benefits for the well-being of both the child and the mother, it also tends to yield positive effects on labour market outcomes of women in the longer-term because they allow for a greater degree of job continuity (or encourage them to seek a job in the first place).

There are, of course, trade-offs in deciding the length of absence to be awarded: while labour market prospects of women initially improve with the length of leave awarded, after a certain threshold negative effects set in as women become increasingly detached from the labour market and their skills depreciate.

Although this threshold is difficult to ascertain in practice Thévenon and Solaz (2014) estimate it at about two years of paid leave for OECD countries while Huerta et al. (2011) suggest up to one year (although these estimates are based on a study of just five OECD countries).

Either way, estimates vary across countries and depend on the availability of other public services such as childcare that help parents balance work and family commitments. Paternity and parental leave (i.e. leave which can be shared between both parents) have also been introduced in many OECD countries in order to encourage parents to play a more equal role in work and family life.

In Tunisia child-related leave consists of maternity leave for mothers and paternity leave for fathers, with no other forms of leave available as is common in most OECD countries. Maternity leave for private sector employees[35] in Tunisia lasts 30 calendar days, but can be extended by another 15 days upon presentation of a medical certificate.

Pay during maternity leave is equivalent to two thirds (66.7%) of the mother's wage, capped at twice the minimum wage (SMIG), provided the mother has worked at least 80 days during the four calendar quarters (one year) preceding the delivery. Mothers have no unpaid leave entitlement.

Paternity leave in Tunisia is just one day to be taken in the seven days following childbirth, and is paid at 100% of the wage of the father. Again, there is no unpaid leave entitlement. These leave entitlements are particularly low by OECD standards (Figures 3.6 and 3.7).[36]

Across OECD countries mothers are entitled to 54.6 weeks leave on average (of which 27.7 unpaid) while fathers are entitled to 7.6 weeks (of which 3.6 unpaid) – however, these averages do not include the third of OECD countries that do not offer fathers any leave (whether paid or unpaid).

**Figure 3.6. Paid leave for mothers[a] in full-rate[b] and unpaid[c] equivalent, Tunisia[d] and OECD[e] countries, 2011**

Duration in weeks

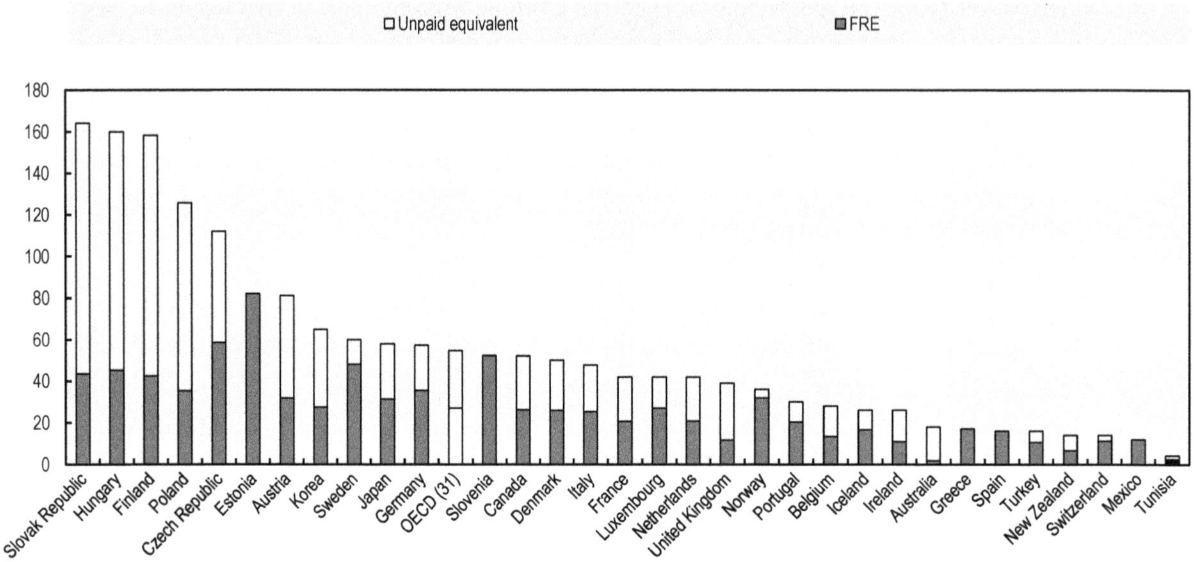


*a)* Paid leave available to mothers includes all leave that mothers are entitled to including leave that may also be taken alternatively by fathers. It therefore includes paid maternity, parental and homecare leave where applicable.

*b)* Full-rate equivalent (FRE) leave duration is calculated as: Duration of leave in weeks * average payment received by the claimant. This is a theoretical measure and parents do not necessarily have the option of taking reduced duration of leave at a payment rate of 100%.

*c)* Unpaid leave equivalent duration is calculated as: Duration of paid leave in weeks (regardless the level of payment) – FRE weeks.

*d)* For Tunisia, paid maternity leave is calculated using an average monthly gross wage of TND 667.65 (OECD calculation based on CRES and ILO, 2012, "Enquête sur la structure des salaires, Tunisie 2011. Rapport Final", CRES, Tunis), and the SMIG of May 2011 of TND 286.

*e)* In the United States maternity leave does not exist and as a consequence this country is not included in this figure.

*Source*: International Network on Leave and Policies (www.leavenetwork.org/); ILO Social Security database (www.ilo.org/dyn/sesame/IFPSES.SSDBMENU); European Commission Social Security systems database – MISSOC (www.missoc.org/MISSOC/MISSOCII/MISSOCII/index.htm); Social Security Programs Throughout the World (www.ssa.gov/policy/docs/progdesc/ssptw/).

**Figure 3.7. Paid leave for fathers[a] in full-rate[b] and unpaid[c] equivalent, Tunisia and OECD[d] countries, 2011**

Duration in weeks

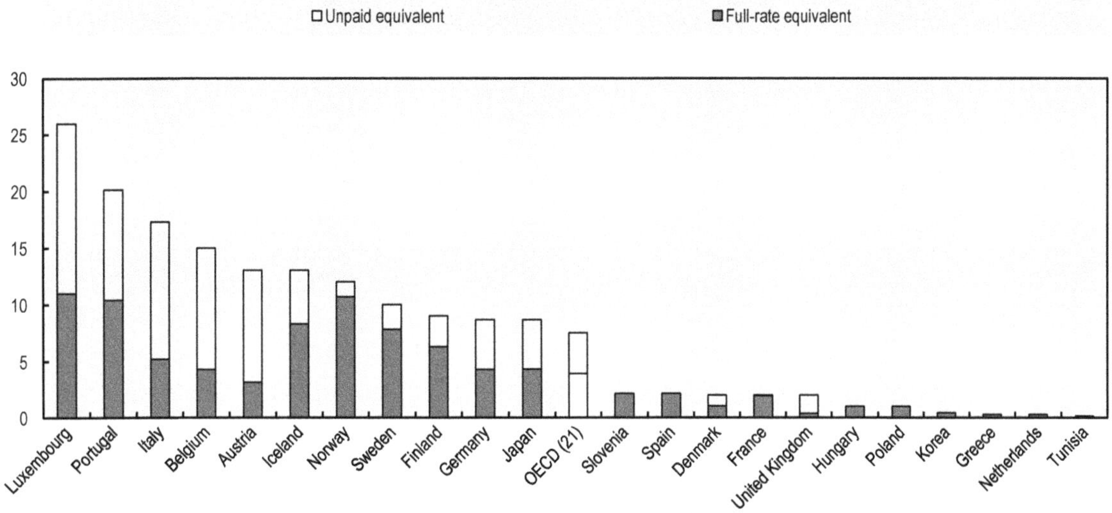


*a)* Paid leave for the exclusive use of fathers refers to leave that only the father is entitled to (or leave which allows for bonus leave or payment), thus includes paternity leave, any parental leave reserved for fathers and sharing requirements for bonus leave.

*b)* Full-rate equivalent (FRE) leave duration is calculated as: Duration of leave in weeks * average payment received by the claimant. This is a theoretical measure and parents do not necessarily have the option of taking reduced duration of leave at a payment rate of 100%.

*c)* Unpaid equivalent leave duration is calculated as: Duration of paid leave in weeks (regardless the level of payment) – FRE weeks.

*d)* In Australia, Canada, the Czech Republic, Estonia, Ireland, Mexico, New Zealand, the Slovak Republic, Switzerland, Turkey and United States paternity leave does not exist and as a consequence these countries are not included in this figure.

*Source*: For OECD countries, *OECD Family Database 2014*, www.oecd.org/social/soc/oecdfamilydatabase.htm (accessed 20 February 2014); for non-OECD countries: World Bank Group (2014), *Women, the Business, and the Law: Creating Economic Opportunities for Women (database)*, http://wbl.worldbank.org/data (accessed 20 February 2014).

The analysis above suggests that there is considerably scope for increasing maternity and paternity leave in Tunisia, and introducing parental leave that can be shared by parents. This would give mothers more continuity in the labour market, increase their labour force participation, as well as allow them to share the burden of childcare more equally with fathers.

### *Affordable and good-quality early childhood education and care is lacking*

Childcare is another key factor in the determination of maternal employment behaviour during the early years. In OECD countries, the increase in female labour force participation since the 1960s went hand-in-hand with the development of work/family life balance policies, of which access to affordable childcare of good quality was an important element (OECD, 2011b). In the context of Tunisia, it has also been argued that the lack of childcare is a key barrier to a better work/life balance for women and, therefore, to their increased labour force participation (Gouider, 2009).

Pre-school education in Tunisia (ages 3-5) is provided in one of two types of institution: i) *jardins d'enfants* [nursery schools] which are supervised by the *Ministère de la Jeunesse, du Sport, de la Femme et de la Famille* [Ministry for Youth, Sport, Women and Families], and which can either be private, *collectivités locales* [semi-public], or run by *associations specialises* [special associations]; and ii) *Kouttab* schools which are under the supervision of the *Ministère des Affaires Religieuses* [Ministry of Religious Affairs] and initiate children to the teachings of the Quran. In 2013, there were 3 767 pre-school institutions in Tunisia, including both nursery and *Kouttab* schools (Ministère des Affaires de la Femme et de la Famille, 2014) – up from 2 422 in 2004 (Observatoire de l'Enfance, 2010). In addition, five-year olds can attend an *année préparatoire* [preparatory year], which is under the responsibility of the *Ministère de l'Éducation* [Ministry of Education] and is provided either in public primary schools, or in private/semi-private institutions. While this preparatory year is considered part of the basic education cycle, it is neither compulsory, nor is free access guaranteed to all (Education Act of 23 July 2002).[37] The proportion of children (aged 3-5) in pre-school education is relatively low, at 44.3% compared to 76.9% on average across the OECD (Figure 3.8). With regards to care for younger children (0-2), crèches in Tunisia are very rare (there were only 293 registered institutions in 2013, up from 102 in 2004)[38] and they only enrolled 0.4% of the relevant age group in 2006 (Gouider, 2010).

**Figure 3.8. Average enrolment rate of children aged three to five years of age in pre-school educational programmes, Tunisia and OECD countries, 2010[a] or latest year available**

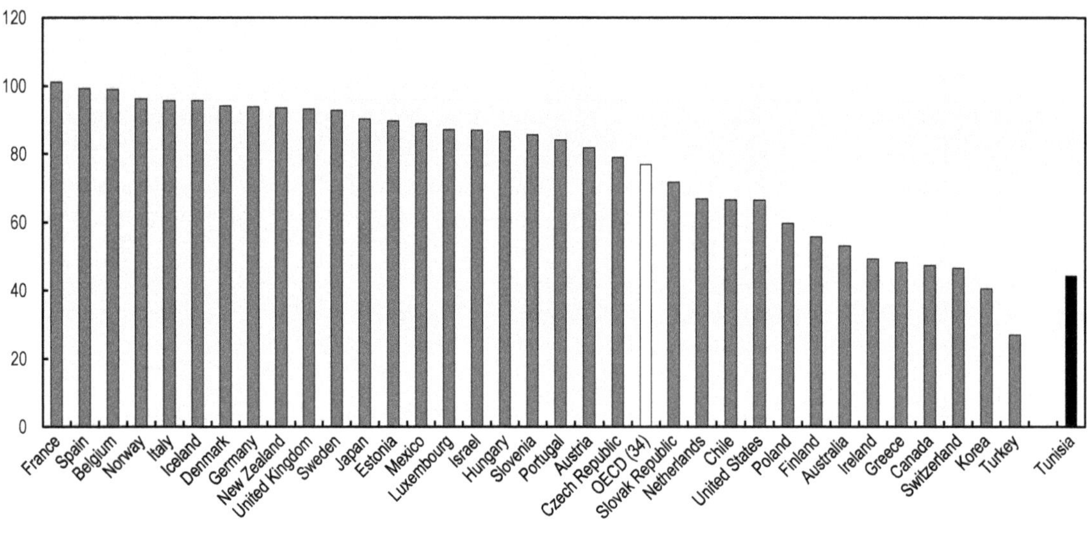


*a)* Data for Latvia, Romania, Bulgaria and Lithuania refer to 2008; data for Malta refer to 2005; data for Korea refer to 2009.

*Source:* OECD (2014), "Enrolment in Childcare and Pre-Schools", *OECD Family Database*, OECD Publishing, Paris, www.oecd.org/els/soc/PF3_2_Enrolment_in_childcare_and_preschools_1May2014.pdf; for Tunisia, MDCI, INS and UNICEF (2013), Tunisie: Suivi de la situation des enfants et des femmes, Enquête par grappes à indicateurs multiples 2011-2012 [Tunisia: Monitoring the Status of Women and Children, Multiple Indicator Cluster Survey 2011-2012], Tunis.

While some have argued that the lack of childcare arrangements in Tunisia reflects a lack of demand related to cultural preferences for raising children in the family,[39] cost is likely to play an important role as well. Nearly all childcare provision in Tunisia is private, with little government support available to help parents meet those costs. In the case of formal sector (and often non-agricultural) workers, family allowances (*allocations familiales*) are available for the first three children,[40] equivalent to 18%, 16% and 14% of a worker's quarterly earnings for the first, second and third child, respectively, but limited at TND 21.960, TND 19.520 and TND 17.080 per quarter (approximately EUR 10.15, EUR 9.03 and EUR 7.9 respectively) – i.e. they are very small. These values are increased by an additional TND 9.375, TND 18.750 and TND 23.475 per quarter for the first, second and third child, respectively, in the case of single earner families (or approximately EUR 4.34, EUR 8.67 and EUR 10.85 respectively). Finally, some specific help with childcare costs (TND 15, or EUR 6.94 a month for up to 11 months for each eligible child) is available for employees earning less than two times the minimum wage (SMIG) and whose children are aged between two and 36 months. In comparison to an estimated cost of nursery care of TND 70-80 (EUR 32-37) per month and per child (excluding canteen costs),[41] these payments are relatively small and young parents (aged under 28) are not eligible for any of these benefits anyway. High childcare costs combined with little financial support from the government might therefore partly explain why only 13% of 3-5 year-olds in the poorest quintile attend pre-school education, compared to 81% of children of the same age in the richest quintile (MDCI, INS and UNICEF, 2013) – and more should be done to support parents, particularly the poorest amongst them, in meeting childcare costs.

Similarly, lack of provision, particularly in less populated areas, is likely to be another barrier: 60% of 3-5 year-olds in urban areas attend pre-school, compared to only 17% of children in rural areas. While some programmes are in place to provide care for children from poor families (e.g. the *Union Tunisienne de Solidarité Sociale*[42] [Tunisian Union for Social Solidarity] welcomed 11 600 children in 269 centres located in the most deprived areas of the country – Ministère des Affaires Sociales, 2011) – such efforts are likely to fall short of the potential demand that exists for these services. More should be done, therefore, to expand access to early childhood education and care, and particularly for the poorest families, if significant progress is to be made on female labour force participation and early drop-out of young women from the labour force is to be avoided.

### *Few youth work part-time*

The possibility to work part-time gives parents more control over their working time and, therefore, allows them to more easily combine work with family commitments. Research shows that the increase in part-time work in OECD countries during the years 1980-2007 was closely related to the increase in female employment over the same time period (OECD, 2012d). In addition, there is evidence that part-time workers suffer less from stress and health worries than their full-time counterparts (OECD, 2010). On the down-side, part-time work in many countries remains predominantly a female matter, and part-time work is rarely a stepping-stone to full-time employment. There is also a penalty associated to part-time work, as such workers tend to have lower hourly earnings, receive fewer training and promotion opportunities, have less job security, have reduced pension entitlements, etc. (OECD, 2012d). So, while part-time work may help increase the proportion of women in the labour force, it also risks trapping them in jobs with fewer career prospects.

In Tunisia, part-time employment is largely regulated by a 1996 amendment to the Labour Code, in which it is defined as employment not exceeding 70% of the normal working time predominant in the firm. Part-time workers have the same rights as full-time workers but, although they are fully covered for sickness and work accidents, all other benefits (e.g. leave) are proportional to the time worked. Workers who started working part-time for pregnancy or caring reasons (for children aged under 6 or sick/disabled family members) have the right to re-enter a full-time working pattern in case full-time vacancies corresponding to their profile arise. In addition, a law introduced in 2006 (2006-58 of

28 July) institutes a special part-time regime allowing mothers with children under the age of 16 working in the public sector to work part-time for a period of three years while receiving two thirds of their salary and preserving all rights to promotion, leave, and social security coverage. Each mother can benefit up to three times from this regime, and can return to the full-time regime at any point she wishes.

The incidence of part-time employment amongst young workers in Tunisia is low at around 6%, and is surprisingly higher for young men (6.9%) than for young women (3.5%) – Figure 3.9. For older age groups (25-64), however, women are significantly more likely to work part-time than men (17.7% v. 9.1%) – suggesting that women take on part-time work as they start having families and children. This incidence of part-time work is still relatively low by OECD standards, however, and may be related to the lack of incentives offered to employers to offer part-time working conditions (Mzid, 2009). While some policies in Tunisia are intended to boost part-time employment, they also have the unintended consequence of placing women in the role of carer. The 2006 special part-time regime, for example, is not open to men and therefore implicitly expects women to work part-time when children are born, at the expense of their future career. Measures should therefore be taken to reduce the gap in part-time employment between men and women.

**Figure 3.9. Incidence of part-time[a] work among youth, Tunisia, OECD and other selected countries, 2012[b]**

As a proportion of those in dependent employment

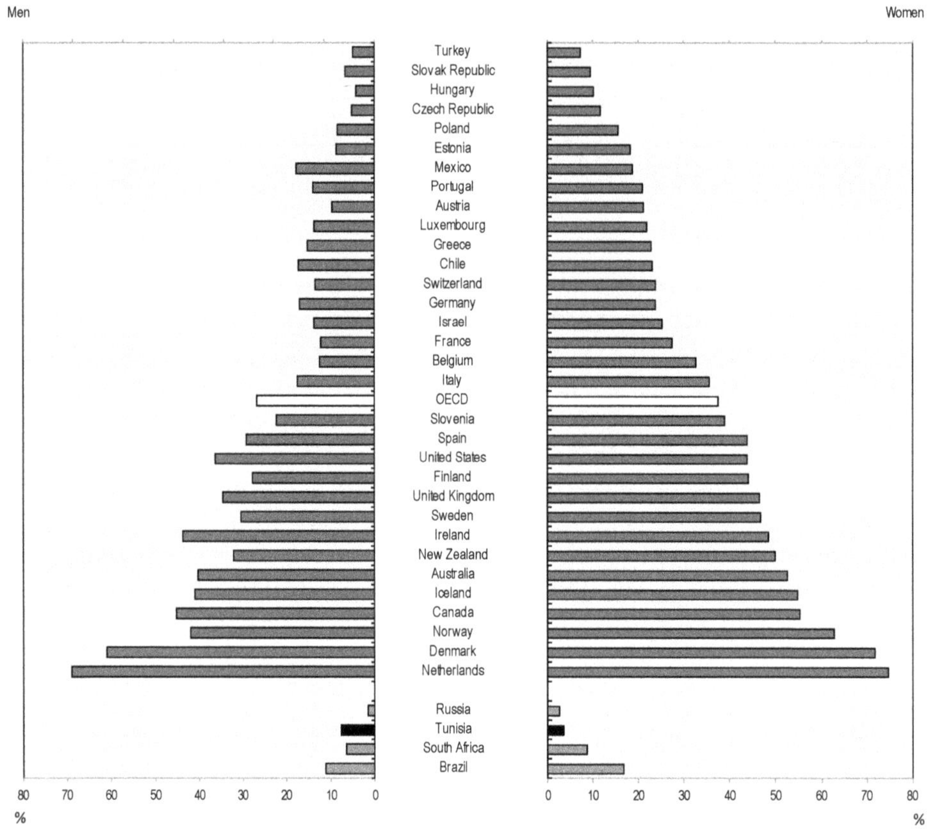


*a)* Part-time employment refers to persons who usually work less than 30 hours per week in their main job.

*b)* Data available for Tunisia corresponds to 2010.

*Source*: *OECD Employment and Labour Market Statistics*, www.oecd-ilibrary.org/employment/data/oecd-employment-and-labour-market-statistics_lfs-data-en; and OECD calculations based on the *Enquête Nationale sur la Population et l'Emploi* (ENPE) [National Population and Employment Survey] for Tunisia.

### *A tax-benefit system which tends to cast women in the role of second earners or carers*

In more developed countries, tax-benefits systems have been recognised to play a key role in parental work and care decisions. In particular, an individual's financial gain from taking up a job is affected by the amount of tax and other charges due on earnings as well as by the loss of social benefits when moving into work. In some cases, the net payoff from work may actually be negative. Given that many social transfers are specifically targeted towards low-income households, especially if children are present, parents in these households are most likely to face weak financial incentives to work. In some OECD countries, including Australia, Belgium, Denmark, Germany, Iceland, and Poland, financial incentives to move into work for spouses are particularly weak (OECD, 2007).

While the situation in Tunisia is slightly different, partly because tax-benefit systems are less developed, many aspects of the welfare system still reinforce the status of women as dependent on men (whether they be fathers or husbands) and/or as the *de facto* carers, and therefore could reduce their incentives to work. The special part-time work scheme for women has already been mentioned, but a few additional examples will help illustrate the point. For instance, while family allowances are, in general, paid to families with children up to the age of 16, girls are eligible until the age of 21 if they assume responsibility for looking after their siblings in their mother's absence. In the case of health insurance, while dependent boys are eligible up to the age of 20, girls are as long as they are not earning their own income or are not married, irrespective of their age. A final example is a special early retirement scheme (at age 50) for mothers (not fathers) employed in the non-agricultural sector and who have at least three children.[43] While taken on their own such treatments of women in the tax-benefit system are unlikely to create disincentives to work, collectively they create a system that does not treat women as equal to men and, while reflecting cultural expectations, place women in a dependent role in society rather than as active participants in the labour market. Similar assessments have been made of, for example, Turkey's social security system which, through gender-differentiated treatment in the policies of survivor benefits and healthcare, reduces women's reliance on the market and consolidates their status as second-earners or caretakers (Bozçağa, 2013). Increased participation of women in the labour market in Tunisia will therefore require a move towards a tax-benefit system where both parents have broadly similar financial incentives to work.

# Notes

1. Around 40% of youth are unemployed and, of those in employment, 50% are active in the informal sector. Given that around 14% of youth are students (and therefore covered by social security) this means that up to two thirds of youth will be not be contributing to and benefiting from social insurance (excluding students).

2. The actual incidence of poverty has been the topic of heated debates in Tunisia in recent years, with allegations that figures published during the Ben Ali presidency were massaged. An in-depth study into the issue (INS, 2012) has attempted to put the record straight, and has concluded that the poverty rate in Tunisia in 2010 was 15.5%. A household was deemed poor if its annual per capita consumption fell below the official poverty line of TND 1 277 in cities and TND 820 in rural areas. This rate was down from 23.3% in 2005 and 32.4% in 2000. No estimates are available for the poverty rate amongst youth. However, given their higher rates of unemployment and informality, as well as a lack of social security coverage, the poverty rate among youth is likely to be considerably higher. Importantly, INS (2012) found that poverty decreases with education, and that the population group dependent on a head of household with university level education does not know poverty. This further highlights the inequity of the government's employment programmes, which are primarily focused on university graduates.

3. Dependent children include those who are minors (up to the age of 20), disabled children, and girls as long as they are not earning their own income or are not married, irrespective of their age (CNAM, n.d.).

4. Spouses are also entitled to health care.

5. Estimates were obtained by comparing the employed population according to the *Enquête Nationale sur la Population et l'Emploi* (ENPE) [National Population and Employment Survey] with the number of contributors to social security.

6. In addition, it should be remembered that youth participating in active labour market policies will not be contributing to social security either. While it is true that these youth are at least covered by health insurance, they are not saving up towards any old age pension. With the ALMP reform, this situation is set to change.

7. These values reflect gross wages. The true comparison should be based on net wages, however these are not available from the SWTS. OECD estimates (applying a model for salaried non-agriculture workers) suggest that the net wages of youth working in the formal sector would be equivalent to TND 422 – which is still significantly higher than the average wage reported by youth working in the informal sector.

8. For example, the Ministère des Affaires Sociales (2011) describes a positive discrimination programme aimed at giving unemployed graduates coming from families in receipt of the *Programme National d'Aide aux Familles Nécessiteuses* (PNAFN) [National Support Programme for Disadvantaged Families] privileged access to public employment. The eligibility criteria include the length of time spent unemployed.

9. Anecdotally, an additional concern in Tunisia has been the increase in the black economy, and smuggling in particular, which has risen very sharply since the revolution as a result of a weakening of custom controls and existing distortions in product markets, including the system of price controls. Such opportunities in the black economy clearly weaken the incentive to get a formal job, especially in rural regions where the latter are scarcer.

10. This regime is based on self-declared turnover, without even the need to keep accounts. The tax rate is set at 2-2.5% of turnover. According to El Elj (2014), this has led to an explosion in the number of self-employed registering for this tax regime, paying on average only TND 92 per year in taxes.

11. This measure was to a large extent part of an attempt to increase "flexicurity" in the Tunisian labour market – i.e. where workers are protected, not jobs. The introduction of the unemployment benefit occurred at the same time as the reductions in employment protection introduced by the 1994 and 1996 revisions of the labour code (Destremau, 2006).

12. In China, unemployment insurance was introduced in the 1980s. Since 1999, all urban workers including those in state-owned enterprises, civil servants and private sector employees, have been covered by unemployment insurance. Employers contribute the equivalent of 2% and employees 1% of their wages, and with funds are usually managed by county or city level governments. The benefit level is not linked to earnings, yet payable for a relatively long period (up to 104 weeks) – Qian (2014). In Brazil, unemployment insurance was introduced in 1986, and has existed in its present form since 1994. UI covers individuals in the (formal) private sector who lose their work through unjustified dismissal. Recipients are entitled to between three and five monthly payments depending on their employment record over the last three years: three instalments for 6 to 11 months of employment; four instalments for 12 to 23 months of employment; and five instalments for 24 or more months of employment. In order to be eligible, the claimant needs to have completed at least six months of consecutive employment, and not have received unemployment benefits in the last 16 months. The minimum value of the benefit is set equal to the minimum wage, whilst any amount payable above that will depend on the worker's average salary in the last three months of employment, but is capped at BRL 1 235.91 (2013), or approximately EUR 433 or 1.82 times the Brazilian minimum wage (OECD, 2014a).

13. No law regulates the PNAFN. It was introduced by means of two Ministerial Circulars – No. 18 of 4 June 1986 and No. 5 of 16 May 1998.

14. One source (albeit dating back to 2008) mentions at least one visit per family per year (Mission permanente de Tunisie auprès de l'Office des Nations unies à Genève et des Organisations internationales en Suisse, 2008).

15. In the case of Tunisia, the most sensitive subsidy is the one on bread (Silva et al., 2012), as witnessed by the 1984 "bread riots" (Meddeb, 2010) and those experienced in late 2007/early 2008 (Subrahmanyam and Castel, 2014).

16. Another potential negative consequence of such programmes may be stigma effects.

17. The National Employment Fund was established in 1999 and is managed through a special account of the Treasury. It finances the active labour market programmes managed by ANETI (e.g. SIVP, SCV, CAIP, etc.) (75.9% of allocations in 2012), some micro credits managed by the Tunisian Solidarity Bank (BTS) (13.5% of allocations) as well as regional employment programmes managed by the Regional Councils (10.6% of allocations) under the heading of the *Contrat Emploi Solidarité*.

18. The purpose of the Employment Solidarity Contract (Decree No. 2009-349 of 9 February 2009) was to introduce an element of local flexibility in the provision of active labour market programmes. Each year, an agreement would be reached between the Regional Councils, the central government as well as other entities involved, and which sets out the programmes to be funded as well as the participants targeted. The type of activities funded included subsidised internships in small and medium enterprises, job-readiness training as well as public works programmes. Participants with a university degree received a monthly stipend of between TND 150 and TND 250 (for a period of up to three years), while those without university degree received a payment not exceeding TND 130 (for a period of maximum one year). Public works programmes accounted for the bulk of CES beneficiaries. Many of the CES programmes were similar to, and often duplicated, the ALMPs provided by ANETI. This duplication, together with the lack of monitoring as well as political capture of these programmes has led to calls that they (with the exception of the public works programmes) be abolished and merged with the standard programmes already managed by ANETI (Belghazi, 2012). The ALMP reform of 2012 maintains a regional element to ALMPs through the *Programme de Partenariat avec les Régions pour la Promotion de l'Emploi* [Partnership Programme with the Regions for Employment Promotion], and leaves open the question of what types of activities will be funded through this instrument.

19. These demands by public works participants to be absorbed as regular staff in the public sector may put a spanner in the works of future such programmes. It is important to communicate that such programmes are provided as social protection mechanisms, and not as public employment generation. Implementing such programmes via NGO's may offer a political way out of this impasse.

20. In addition, Tunisia experimented with mobile employment services (Benmimoun, 2010) – however, it would seem that these are no longer operational, partly because of a deteriorating security climate in some of Tunisia's more remote areas.

21. For university graduates the coverage rate of ANETI – defined as the number of registered jobseekers (taken from ANETI administrative records) divided by the number of unemployed (calculated based on the *Enquête Nationale sur la Population et l'Emploi*) – fluctuated between 36.1% and 50.9% in 2013, while the equivalent figures for non-graduates were 17.1% and 25.9%, respectively. These rates fluctuate quite a bit and are much higher during periods of public recruitment rounds.

22. This caseload may be over-estimated, however, because many registered jobseekers are not actively looking for work and should, therefore, be removed from the roster.

23. The efficiency of the matching process could also be increased by the introduction of an organising framework for occupations, which links the occupational classification to a competency framework. Such a framework would set the base for linking various occupations to specific skills and can assist in identifying further training needs. While Tunisia introduced an occupational classification in 1997 (*Nomenclature Nationale des Professions*) through Law No. 97-2452 of 15 December, a detailed description of occupations is still lacking. A *Dictionnaire National des Emplois et des Professions* (National Dictionary of Jobs and Occupations) has been in development within the MFPE since 2002, but has not yet become operational.

24. Since recently, the national identity number of new contributors to the social security system has been registered, which permits their records to be linked to those of ANETI on ALMPs. In the longer run, however, the Tunisian social security system, with the assistance of the World Bank, is working on developing a unique identifier which can

be attributed to each Tunisian at birth and which will be used for linking such data instead of the national identity number.

25. The target groups of Business Centres are graduates from university and vocational training. The majority of clients come from trade and services and plan a micro business; frequently, they return after some time to re-orient their venture. The Business Centres draw on external experts for their services, including one coach from a higher education institution (HEI), who work one day per week for the centres.

26. Incubators are located at HEIs and are financed by the *Agence de Promotion de l'Industrie et de l'Innovation* [Agency for the Promotion of Industry and Innovation] (APII). In addition to space, they offer low threshold services for graduate entrepreneurs. The majority of incubator clients are not freshly graduated, but come back several years after their studies. Each incubator has one coach from university. Sometimes they are also coaching for the Business Centre, thus in principal offering a mechanism for a more formalised referral system from HEIs to incubators.

27. The *Espaces Tremplin* are resource centres within VET training centres that are dedicated to business creation and support for entrepreneurs. Future entrepreneurs are offered comprehensive advice, guidance, counselling and information on setting up their own enterprise. These centres offer internet areas, meeting rooms and a series of offices with computer tools as well as documentation and activity areas.

28. While many of these supports help young entrepreneurs, the approaches taken are not always consistent with international good practice. For example, using a database of start-up ideas is contrary to the notion of entrepreneurship. A better approach would be to help new entrepreneurs generate and develop their own business ideas rather than selecting a generic idea from a list.

29. Although in practice this measure was rarely implemented.

30. OECD calculations based on the ILO's School-to-Work Transition Survey for Tunisia (2013).

31. OECD calculations based on INS (2014).

32. The Code of Personal Status of 1956 consists of a set of laws laying down the rights and responsibilities of women and men in the areas of marriage, divorce, custody and inheritance. It significantly changed the legal status of women in Tunisia, banning polygamy and granting women and men the same divorce rights. The inheritance law is the only law in the Code of Personal Status that favours men over women. It stipulates that a male heir receives twice as much as females, in accordance with Islamic Sharia law, unless a will specifies exactly how a parent's estate is to be divided among children.

33. "Il ne peut être fait de discrimination entre l´homme et la femme dans l´application des disposition du présent code et des textes pris pour son application" [There may be no discrimination between men and women in the application of the provisions of this Code and its implementing texts]. Article introduced on 5 July 1993. That said, the Labour Code itself places restrictions on the type of work that women are allowed to perform, in particular physically demanding work and night shifts. These restrictions could be argued to be an additional barrier to female employment in Tunisia.

34. Maternity (or pregnancy) leave refers to employment-protected leave of absence for employed women at around the time of childbirth, or adoption in some countries. Paternity leave is the same, but for fathers. Parental leave, on the other hand, refers to employment-protected leave of absence for employed parents, which is often

supplementary to specific maternity and paternity leave periods, and usually, but not in all countries, follows the period of maternity/paternity leave. Entitlement to the parental leave period is either for each parent or for the family, but entitlement to public income support is often family-based, so that in general only one parent claims such income support at any one time (OECD, 2012c).

35. Maternity leave in the public sector is more generous, lasting two months and paid at 100% of the mother's wage, with no earnings ceiling.

36. The calculations underlying these figures are based on the following set of assumptions: both parents normally earn the average wage; parents meet the usual employment conditions to be eligible for leave payment (e.g. minimum required period of work before the birth of a child); mother and child are healthy with no birth-related complications; it is the birth of the first child; mothers maximise their leave over fathers, but combined leave is also maximised, i.e. parents share leave if bonus months are on offer; parents take the highest paid option and, following that, they maximise leave; options that require employers' permission and cannot be strictly decided upon by a family are not included as they are not seen as a family option (thus, collective bargaining options are excluded unless data show that it is almost universal); the employment protection refers to the option of returning to a job of the same category and hence referred to as "employment-protected"; if there is separate legislation for the public and private sectors, then the private sector option is considered as it normally holds more workers; unless specifically mentioned, incomes and wages are assumed to refer to gross earnings.

37. Although there was a presidential programme in place to try and generalise the preparatory class to all eligible children by the end of 2009 (*Programme Présidentiel Relatif à la Généralisation Complète de l'Année Préparatoire à la Fin de 2009*) (Observatoire de l'Enfance, 2010).

38. Ministère des Affaires de la Femme et de la Famille (2014) and Observatoire de l'Enfance (2010), respectively. In practice, however, some nurseries will also provide crèche services, and these will not be recorded separately.

39. See Angel-Urdinola and Leon-Solano (2013) for some interesting statistics with regards to the role of family duties and female labour force participation in MENA countries.

40. Eligible children include: those aged under 16; those aged under 18 in an apprenticeship and not earning more than 75% of the SMIG; those aged under 21 and regularly attending a secondary, tertiary, technical or professional education institution; girls aged under 21 if she replaces and fulfils the role of her mother towards her brothers and sisters; all disabled children or those suffering from a terminal illness.

41. Chraiet (2012). No official estimates are available.

42. The UTSS is a non-governmental organisation set up in 1964 and financed through voluntary donations (M'barek, 2010).

43. An early retirement scheme at age of 50 existed also not long ago in Greece, but has been removed recently

# *References*


Acemoglu, D., D.H. Autor and D. Lyle (2002), "Women, War, and Wages: The Effect of Female Labor Supply on the Wage Structure at Midcentury", *Journal of Political Economy*, Vol. 112, No. 3, pp. 497-551.

Adamecz, A. (2013), "Performance Management in Public Employment Services: Benchmarking, Clustering and Individual Performance Management – Follow-up Visit Report", European Commision, Brussels.

AfDB – African Development Bank (2012), *Programme d'Appui à la Relance Économique et au Développement Inclusif: Rapport d'Évaluation, Octobre 2012* [Economic Recovery and Inclusive Development Support Programme: Evaluation Report, October 2012], African Development Bank, Tunis.

Ahmed, G. (2011), "Private Employment Agencies in Morocco", *ILO Working Papers*, ILO, Geneva.

Albanesi, S. and C. Olivetti (2007), "Gender Roles and Technological Progress", *NBER Working Papers*, No. 13179, National Bureau of Economic Research, Cambridge, United States.

Alesina, A., P. Giuliano and N. Nunn (2013), "On the Origins of Gender Roles: Women and the Plough", *Quarterly Journal of Economics*, Vol. 128, No. 2, pp. 469-530.

Algan, Y. and P. Cahuc (2007), "The Roots of Low European Employment: Family Culture?", in J. Frankel and C. Pissarides (eds.), *NBER International Seminar on Macroeconomics 2005*.

ANETI – National Employment and Self-Employment Agency (2014), "L'expérience tunisienne dans le domaine de création d'entreprises" [The Tunisian experience in the field of business start-ups], Presentation given during the OECD fact-finding mission in December 2013, Ministère de la Formation Professionnelle et de l'Emploi, Tunis.

Angel-Urdinola, D.F. (2013), "Un coup de pouce privé pour les programmes argent-contre-travail en Tunisie" [A private boost for cash-for-work programmes in Tunisia], blogs.worldbank.org (accessed 18 April 2014).

Angel-Urdinola, D.F. and A. Kuddo (2010), "Key Characteristics of Employment Regulation in the Middle East and North Africa", *World Bank Social Protection and Labour Discussion Papers*, No. 1006, World Bank, Washington, DC.

Angel-Urdinola, D.F. and R. Leon-Solano (2013), "A Reform Agenda for Improving the Delivery of ALMPs in the MENA Region", *IZA Journal of Labor Policy*, Vol. 2, No. 13, Springer Open, pp. 1-25.

Angel-Urdinola, D.F. and R. Leon-Solano (2011), "The AMAL Program: 'Hope' for Unemployed Youth in the MENA Region", *World Bank MENA Knowledge Papers*, No. 88, World Bank, Washington, DC.

Angel-Urdinola, D.F. and K. Tanabe (2012), "Micro-determinants of Informal Employment in the Middle East and North Africa Region", *World Bank Social Protection and Labour Discussion Papers*, No. 1201, World Bank, Washington, DC.

Angel-Urdinola, D.F., A. Hilger and R. Leon-Solano (2013), "Public Employment Programs in Tunisia", in D.F. Angel-Urdinola, A. Kuddo and A. Semlali (eds.), *Building Effective Employment Programs for Unemployed Youth in the Middle East and North Africa*, World Bank, Washington, DC.

Antecol, H. (2000), "An Examination of Cross-country Differences in the Gender Gap in Labor Force Participation", *Labour Economics*, Vol. 7, No. 4, Elsevier, pp. 409-126.

Apps, P. and R. Rees (2005), "Gender, Time Use and Public Policy Over the Life Cycle", *Discussion Papers*, No. 500, Centre for Economic Policy Research, Australian National University.

Azevedo, V. and M. Robles (2013), "Multidimensional Targeting: Identifying Beneficiaries of Conditional Cash Transfer Programmes", *Social Indicators Research*, Vol. 112, No. 2, Springer Netherlands, pp. 447-475.

Belghazi, S. (2012), *Évaluation stratégique du Fonds national pour l'Emploi* [Strategic Evaluation of the National Employment Fund], Report commissioned by the World Bank, Washington, DC.

Belkacem, L. and F. Mansouri (2013), *2012 GEM Tunisia: National Report*, Global Entrepreneurship Monitor, Sousse.

Ben Braham, M. (2012), "La protection sociale en Tunisie: État des lieux et perspectives" [Social protection in Tunisia: State of affairs and prospects], *Notes de synthèse*, Initiative pour le Développement Économique et Social (IDEES), Tunis.

Ben Cheikh, N. (2013), "L'extension de la protection sociale à l'économie informelle à l'épreuve de la transition en Tunisie" [The challenge of extending social protection to the informal sector in a Tunisia in transition], *CRES Working Papers*, CRES, Tunis.

Ben Mahmoud, M. (2011), "Tunisie – Le taux de pauvreté entre le maquillage et l'exagération" [Tunisia – Poverty estimates between make-up and exageration], *Business News*, www.businessnews.com.tn/Tunisie---Le-taux-de-pauvret%C3%A9-entre-le-maquillage-et-lexag%C3%A9ration,519,25024,1, 31 May.

Benmimoun, M. (2010), "Les services publics de l'emploi d'Afrique et l'information sur le marché du travail" [Public employment services in Africa and labour market information], Presentation given in Kinshasa, 22-25 September.

Blau, F.D. and L.M. Kahn (2013), "Female Labor Supply: Why Is the US Falling Behind?" *NBER Working Paper Series*, No. 18702, Cambridge, United States.

Bozçağa, T. (2013), "Women and the Welfare State Regime of Turkey", *Turkish Policy Quarterly*, Vol. 11, No. 4, pp. 177-188, Istanbul.

Buddelmeyer, H., G. Mourre and M. Ward (2004), "Recent Developments in Part-time Work in EU-15 Countries: Trends and Policy", *IZA Discussion Papers*, No. 1415, Bonn.

Butta, P., R. Murgai, M. Ravallion and D. van de Walle (2012), "Does India's Employment Guarantee Scheme Guarantee Employment?", *Economic & Political Weekly*, Vol. 47, No. 16, pp. 55-64.

Chraiet, A. (2012), "Tunisie: Rentrée des crèches et jardins d'enfants – Comme les grands" [Tunisia: Back to school for crèches and nurseries – Like the big ones], *La Presse*, 3 September 2012, Tunis.

Cipollone, A., E. Patacchini and G. Vallanti (2013), "Women Labor Market Participation in Europe: Novel Evidence on Trends and Shaping Factors", *IZA Discussion Papers*, No. 7710, Bonn.

CNAM – Caisse Nationale d'Assurance Maladie (n.d.), "Assurance Maladie" [Health Insurance], www.cnam.nat.tn/ (accessed 28 May 2014).

CRES – Centre des Recherches et d'Études Sociales, and ILO – International Labour Organization (2012), "Enquête sur la structure des salaires, Tunisie 2011, Rapport Final" [Salary Survey, Tunisia 2011, Final Report], Centre des Recherches et d'Études Sociales, Tunis.

Del Boca, D. and M. Locatelli (2006), "The Determinants of Motherhood and Work Status: A Survey", *IZA Discussion Papers*, No. 2414, Bonn.

Destremau, B. (2006), *La protection sociale en Tunisie: Nature et cohérence de l'intervention publique* [Social Protection in Tunisia: Nature and Consistency of Public Intervention], Centre National de la Recherche Scientifique, Paris.

El Elj, M. (2014), "Fiscalité et secteur informel: Des freins à la croissance de la PME tunisienne" [The tax system and the informal sector: A break on the growth of Tunisian SMEs], Initiative pour le Développement Économique et Social (IDEES), Tunis.

Fernández, R. (2007), "Women, Work, and Culture", *Journal of the European Economic Association*, Vol. 5, No. 2-3, pp. 305-332.

Fernández, R., A. Fogli and C. Olivetti (2004), "Mothers and Sons: Preferences Formation and Female Labor Force Dynamics", *Quarterly Journal of Economics*, Vol. 119, No. 4, pp. 1249-1299.

Fiszbein A. and N. Schady (2009), *Conditional Cash Transfers: Reducing Present and Future Poverty*, Policy Research Report, World Bank, Washington, DC.

Fortin, N.M. (2005), "Gender Role Attitudes and the Labour-market Outcomes of Women Across OECD Countries", *Oxford Review of Economic Policy*, Vol. 21, No. 3, pp. 416-438, Oxford University Press, Oxford.

Gaddis, I. and S. Klasen (2014), "Economic Development, Structural Change, and Women's Labor Force Participation", *Journal of Population Economics*, Vol. 27, No. 3, pp. 639-681.

Gatti, R., D.F. Angel-Urdinola, J. Silva and A. Bodor (2011), "Striving for Better Jobs: The Challenge of Informality in the Middle East and North Africa Region", *MENA Knowledge and Learning Quick Notes Series*, No. 49, World Bank, Washington, DC.

Global Entrepreneurship Monitor (2013), *GEM 2012 Global Report*.

Goldin, C. (2004), "From the Valley to the Summit: A Brief History of the Quiet Revolution that Transformed Women's Work", *Regional Review*, Quarter 1, Federal Reserve Bank of Boston, Boston.

Goldin, C. (1995), "The U-shaped Female Labor Force Function in Economic Development and Economic History", in T.P. Schultz (ed.), *Investing in Women's Human Capital and Economic Development*, University of Chicago Press, Chicago.

Gouider, A. (2010), "Les faits stylisés relatifs à l'emploi des femmes en Tunisie" [Stylised facts about female employment in Tunisia], *European Journal of Social Law*, Vol. 3, No. 8, CNCSIS, Târgovişte, pp. 114-132.

Gouider, A. (2009), "Déterminants de l'activité des femmes sur le marché du travail tunisien et discrimination par genre" [Determinants of female labour force participation in Tunisia and gender discrimination], Paper prepared for the GDRI DREEM conference on Inequalities and Development in Mediterranean Countries, May 21/22/23, 2009, Istanbul.

Greenwood, J., A. Seshadri and M. Yorukoglu (2005), "Engines of Liberation", *Review of Economic Studies*, Vol. 72, No. 1, pp. 109-133.

Handoussa, H. and Z. Tzannatos (eds.) (2002), *Employment Creation and Social Protection in the Middle East and North Africa*, American University of Cairo Press, Cairo, New York.

Huerta, M., W. Adema, J. Baxter, M. Corak, M. Deding, M.C. Gray, W-J. Han and J. Waldfogel (2011), "Early Maternal Employment and Child Development in Five OECD countries", *OECD Social, Employment and Migration Working Papers*, No. 118, OECD Publishing, Paris.

ILO – International Labour Organization (2013), "The Community Work Programme: Building a Society that Works", *Employment Working Papers*, No. 149, ILO, Geneva.

ILO (2011), *Tunisia – A New Social Contract for Fair and Equitable Growth Studies on Growth with Equity*, ILO, Geneva.

ILO (2007), *Guide to Private Employment Agencies: Regulation, Monitoring and Enforcement*, ILO, Geneva.

ILO (2006), *Labour Inspection*, International Labour Organisation, Geneva.

ILO – International Labour Organization, and ONEQ – Observatoire National de l'Emploi et des Qualifications (2014), *Transition vers le marché du travail des jeunes femmes et hommes en Tunisie* [School-to-Work Transitions of Young Women and Men in Tunisia], Work4Youth Publication Series, No. 16, ILO, Geneva.

INS – Institute National de la Statistique (2014), "Emploi" [Employment], *Données Démographiques et Sociales*, www.ins.nat.tn/indexfr.php (accessed 30 July 2014).

INS – Institut National de la Statistique (2012), *Measuring Poverty: Inequalities and Polarization in Tunisia 2000-2010*, INS, Tunis.

INS – Institut National de la Statistique, CRES – Centre des recherches et des études sociales and AfDB – African Development Bank (2013), *Analyse de l'Impact des Subventions Alimentaires et des Programmes d'Assistance Sociale sur la Population Pauvre et Vulnérable* [An Analysis of the Impact of Food Subsidies and Social Assistance Programmes on the Poor and Vulnerable Population], Institut National de la Statistique, Tunis.

IPEA – Institute for Applied Economic Research (2013), *Programme Bolsa Família: Uma Década de Inclusão e Cidadania* [The Bolsa Família Programme: A Decade of Inclusion and Citizenship], IPEA, Brasília.

Jaumotte, F. (2003), "Female Labour Force Participation: Past Trends and Main Determinants in OECD Countries", *Economics Department Working Papers*, No. 376, OECD Publishing, Paris.

Lieuw-Kie-Song, M., K. Philip, M. Tsukamoto and M. Van Imschoot (2010), "Towards the Right to Work: Innovations in Public Employment Programmes (IPEP)", *Employment Working Papers*, No. 69, ILO, Geneva.

Limam, R. (2012), *La redistribution des revenus* [The redistribution of income], Institut Tunisien de la Compétitivité et des Études Quantitatives, Tunis.

M'barek, E. (2010), *Les Effets du système de protection sociale sur la réalisation des objectifs du Millénaire de Développement: Le cas de la Tunisie* [The Impact of the Social Protection System on the Attainment of the Millennium Development Goals: The Case of Tunisia], United Nations Economic Commission for Africa, Tunis.

MDCI – Ministère du Développement et de la Collaboration Internationale, INS – Institute National de la Statistique, and UNICEF – United Nations Children's Fund (2013), *Tunisie: Suivi de la situation des enfants et des femmes. Enquête par grappes à indicateurs multiples 2011-2012* [Tunisia: Monitoring the Status of Women and Children, Multiple Indicator Cluster Survey 2011-2012], Tunis.

Meddeb, H. (2010), "La Tunisie, pays émergent?" [Tunisia: An emerging economy ?], *Sociétés Politiques Comparées*, No. 29, Fonds d'Analyse des Sociétés Politiques, Paris.

Ministère des Affaires de la Femme et de la Famille (2014), "Childhood Institutions in Numbers (Public and Private Sectors) " (in Arabic), Tunis, www.femme.gov.tn/fileadmin/_temp_/etab_enfance-prives__etatiques.pdf.

Ministère des Affaires Sociales (2014), "Social Statistics Yearbook 2012" [in Arabic], www.social.gov.tn/fileadmin/user1/doc/annuairestatsocial2012.pdf (accessed 11 February 2014).

Ministère des Affaires Sociales (2011), *Les programmes sociaux de lutte contre la pauvreté et l'amélioration des conditions de vie* [Social Programmes in the Fight Against Poverty and the Improvement of Living Conditions], Ministère des Affaires Sociales, Tunis.

Mission Permanente de Tunisie auprès de l'Office des Nations Unies à Genève et des Organisations Internationales en Suisse (2008), "Réponse du Gouvernement tunisien au questionnaire relatif aux programmes de transferts financiers adressé aux gouvernements par l'Experte indépendante sur la question des droits de l'homme et l'extrême pauvreté" [Response of the Tunisian Government to the questionnaire on cash transfer programmes addressed to governments by the independent expert on the question of human rights and extreme poverty], Ministère des Affaires Étrangères, Genève.

Murgai, R., M. Ravallion and D. van de Walle (2013), "Is Workfare Cost-effective Against Poverty in a Poor Labor-surplus Economy?", *Policy Research Working Papers*, No. 6673, World Bank, Washington, DC.

Mzid, N. (2009), "Droit du travail, entreprise et flexibilité de l'emploi" [Labour law, companies and labour market flexibility], Mimeo, University of Sfax, Tunisia.

Nicoletti, G. and S. Scarpetta (2005), "Product Market Reforms and Employment in OECD Countries", *OECD Economics Department Working Papers*, No. 472, OECD Publishing, Paris, http://dx.doi.org/10.1787/463767160680.

Observatoire de l'Enfance (2010), "Résumé Exécutif du Rapport National sur la Situation de l'Enfance en Tunisie 2009" [Executive Summary of the National Report on the Status of Children in Tunisia 2009], Observatoire d'Information, de Formation, de Documentation et d'Études pour la Protection des Droits de l'Enfant, Ministère des Affaires de la Femme, de la Famille, de l'Enfance et des Personnes Agées, Tunis.

OECD (2014a), *Investing in Youth: Brazil*, OECD Publishing, Paris, http://dx.doi.or/10.1787/9789264208988-en.

OECD (2014b), "Enrolment in Childcare and Pre-Schools", *OECD Family Database,* OECD Publishing, Paris, www.oecd.org/els/soc/PF3_2_Enrolment_in_childcare_and_preschools_1May2014.pdf.

OECD (2013a), "Building Tax Culture, Compliance and Citizenship: A Global Source Book on Taxpayer Education – Draft for Consultation", OECD Publishing, Paris, www.oecd.org/ctp/tax-global/sourebook-taxpayer-education.pdf.

OECD (2013b), *Strengthening Social Cohesion in Korea*, OECD Publishing, Paris, http://dx.doi.or/10.1787/9789264188945-en.

OECD (2013c), *OECD Economic Surveys: Colombia 2013: Economic Assessment*, OECD Publishing, Paris, http://dx.doi.or/10.1787/eco_surveys-col-2013-en.

OECD (2013d), "Activating Jobseekers: Lessons from Seven OECD Countries", *OECD Employment Outlook 2013*, Chapter 3 in *OECD Employment Outlook 2013*, OECD Publishing, Paris, http://dx.doi.org/10.1787/empl_outlook-2013-en.

OECD (2012a), "Net Replacement Rates for Six Family Types: Initial Phase of Unemployment", *Benefits and Wages: Statistics*, www.oecd.org/els/benefitsandwagesstatistics.htm (accessed 2 June 2014).

OECD (2012b), *Activating Jobseekers: How Australia Does It*, OECD Publishing, Paris, http://dx.doi.org/10.1787/9789264185920-en.

OECD (2012c), *Women in Business: Policies to Support Women's Entrepreneurship Development in the MENA Region*, OECD Publishing, Paris, http://dx.doi.org/10.1787/9789264179073-en.

OECD (2012d), *Closing the Gender Gap: Act Now*, OECD Publishing, Paris, http://dx.doi.org/10.1787/9789264179370-en.

OECD (2011a), "The Labour Market Effects of Social Protection Systems in Emerging Economies", Chapter 2 in *OECD Employment Outlook 2011*, OECD Publishing, Paris, http://dx.doi.org/10.1787/empl_outlook-2011-en.

OECD (2011b), *Doing Better for Families*, OECD Publishing, Paris, http://dx.doi.org/10.1787/9789264098732-en.

OECD (2010), *OECD Employment Outlook 2010 – Moving Beyond the Jobs Crisis*, OECD Publishing, Paris, http://dx.doi.org/10.1787/empl_outlook-2010-en.

OECD (2008), "Declaring Work or Staying Underground: Informal Employment in Seven OECD Countries", Chapter 2 in *OECD Employment Outlook 2008*, OECD Publishing, Paris, http://dx.doi.org/10.1787/empl_outlook-2008-en.

OECD (2007), *Babies and Bosses: Reconciling Work and Family Life*, OECD Publishing, Paris, http://dx.doi.org/10.1787/9789264032477-en.

OECD (2004), "Informal Employment and Promoting the Transition to a Salaried Economy", Chapter 5 in *OECD Employment Outlook 2004*, OECD Publishing, Paris, http://dx.doi.org/10.1787/empl_outlook-2004-en.

OECD and IDRC – International Development Research Centre (2012), *New Entrepreneurs and High Growth Enterprises in the Middle East and North Africa*, OECD Publishing, Paris, http://dx.doi.org/10.1787/9789264179196-en.

ONEQ – Observatoire National de l'Emploi et des Qualifications (2012), *Rapport de Suivi des Programmes Actifs d'Emploi: Réalisations de l'Année 2012* [Monitoring Report of Active Labour Market Programmes: 2012 Achievements], ONEQ, Tunis.

Pagés, C., J. Rigolini and D. Robalino (2013), "Social Insurance, Informality and Labor Markets: How to Protect Workers While Creating Good Jobs", *IZA Discussion Papers*, No. 7879, Bonn.

Perry, G.E. et al. (2007), *Informality: Exit and Exclusion*, World Bank, Washington, DC.

Qian, J. (2014), "Unemployment Insurance in China", *EAI Background Brief No. 903*, www.eai.nus.edu.sg/BB903.pdf.

Redjeb, M.S. and M. Ghobentini (2005), "L'intermédiation sur le marché du travail en Tunisie" [Intermediation in the Tunisian labour market], *Cahiers de la stratégie de l'emploi* (Employment Strategy Papers), No. 2005/19, ILO, Geneva.

Rijkers, B., H. Arrouri, C. Freund and A. Nucifora (2013), "Structural Stagnation: Firm-level Evidence on Job Creation in Tunisia", Paper prepared for the 8th IZA/World Bank Conference on Employment and Development, 22/23 August, Bonn.

Shalaby, M. (2014), "The Paradox of Female Economic Participation in the Middle East and North Africa", *Baker Institute Issue Briefs*, 3 July, Rice University.

Silva, J., V. Levin and M. Morgandi (2012), *Inclusion and Resilience: The Way Forward for Social Safety Nets in the Middle East and North Africa*, International Bank for Reconstruction and Development/The World Bank, Washington, DC.

Stanwix, B. and C. Van Der Westhuizen (2012), *Predicted Poverty Impacts of Expanding the Community Work Programme in South Africa: An Analysis of Income Poverty and Inequality*, Development Policy Research Unit, Cape Town.

Stovicek, K. and A. Turrini (2012), "Benchmarking Unemployment Benefit Systems", *Economic Papers*, No. 454, European Commission, Brussels.

Subbarao, K., C. del Ninno, C. Andrews and C. Rodríguez-Alas (2013), *Public Works as Safety Net: Design, Evidence, and Implementation*, World Bank, Washington, DC.

Subrahmanyam, G. (2011), "Tackling Youth Unemployment in the Maghreb", *African Development Bank Economic Briefs*, AfDB, Tunis.

Subrahmanyam, G. and V. Castel (2014), "Labour Market Reform in Post-transition North Africa", *Economic Brief*, African Development Bank, Tunis.

Thévenon, O. (2013), "Drivers of Female Labour Force Participation in the OECD", *OECD Social, Employment and Migration Working Papers*, No. 145, OECD Publishing, Paris.

Thévenon, O. and A. Solaz (2014), "Parental Leave and Labour Market Outcomes: Lessons from 40 years of Policies in OECD Countries", *Documents de Travail*, No. 199, Institut National d'Études Démographiques, Paris.

UGTT – Union Générale des Travailleurs Tunisiens (2008), "Mutations du Marché du Travail, la Précarité et ses Impacts en Tunisie – Résultats d'une Enquête Quantitative et Qualitative dans le Grand Tunis" [Labour Market Transformations, Precarity and their Impact in Tunisia – Results from a Quantitative and Qualitative Survey in Greater Tunis], UGTT, Tunis.

Vaidya, K. (2013), "Towards Acceptable Wages for Public Employment Programmes: A Guide for Conducting Studies for Wage Setting and Estimating Labour Supply Response", *Employment Working Papers*, No. 150, ILO, Geneva.

Vawda, S., M. Prinsloo, A. Mostert and N. Mazibuko (2013), *The Community Work Programme*, Trade and Industrial Policy Strategies, Pretoria.

Venn, D. (2012), "Eligibility Criteria for Unemployment Benefits: Quantitative Indicators for OECD and EU Countries", *OECD Social, Employment and Migration Working Papers*, No. 131, OECD Publishing, Paris, http://dx.doi.org/10.1787/5k9h43kgkvr4-en.

Venn, D. (2009), "Legislation, Collective Bargaining and Enforcement: Updating the OECD Employment Protection Indicators", *OECD Social, Employment and Migration Working Papers*, No. 89, OECD Publishing, Paris, http://dx.doi.org/10.1787/223334316804.

World Bank (2013), *Vers une meilleure équité: Les subventions énergitiques, le ciblage et la protection sociale en Tunisie* [Towards Greater Equity: Energy Subsidies, Targeting and Social Protection in Tunisia], Report No. 82712-TN, World Bank, Tunis.

Woytinsky, W.S. (1942), *Three Aspects of Labor Dynamics*, Committee on Social Security, Social Science Research Council, Washington, DC.

Zribi, M. and H. Bouktif (2011), "L'approche tunisienne en matière de justice sociale et lutte contre la pauvreté et l´exclusion" [The Tunisian approach to social justice and the fight against poverty and exclusion], Séminaire international justice sociale et lutte contre l´exclusion dans un contexte de transition démocratique [International seminar on social justice and the fight against social exclusion in the context of a democratic transition], Ministère des Affaires Sociales, 21/22 September 2011, Tunis.

# *Chapter 4*

## Vocational education and training in Tunisia

*This chapter examines the vocational education and training system in Tunisia, assessing strengths and challenges. Currently the system fails to provide youth with a sufficiently smooth transition into the labour market, and inadequately meets the needs of employers. The two main challenges are: i) the lack of attractiveness of vocational education and training in Tunisia, including the negative effects of the low status collèges techniques, and the underdevelopment of high quality options at the upper secondary level; and ii) the mix of provision (as between fields of study) is driven mainly by the capacity of the system, and it may not reflect the needs of the economy. This chapter recommends the implementation of a set of mutually reinforcing policy reforms, including a strategic expansion of VET at the upper secondary level and stronger mechanisms to engage employers. Finally, the chapter also looks at the provision of entrepreneurship training within the VET system, and identifies scope for improving both quality and accessibility of provision.*

## Introduction

Participation in vocational training plays an important role in helping youth acquire the skills needed to gain a firm foothold in the labour market, thus improving their chances of a successful professional career (OECD, 2010a; Eichhorst et al., 2012). There is evidence that high-quality vocational education pathways, particularly in upper-secondary education, can help engage youth who have become disaffected with academic education, improve graduation rates and ensure smooth transitions from school to work.[1] In emerging and less developed countries, VET is increasingly perceived as a tool to respond to changing labour market needs, while at the same time supporting social cohesion (Fredriksen and Tan, 2008). This will include the need to support Tunisia's transition to a green economy, insofar as greening the economy can be expected to alter the skill requirements of the labour market (Chapter 5). This will mean an increasingly responsive VET system. Furthermore, progress in expanding basic education in emerging and less developed countries has been typically associated with rapid increases in the number of young people who complete basic education and seek opportunities for further education and training, including VET (Tan and Nam, 2012). There is evidence of good labour market returns from VET programmes, including in African countries.[2]

Despite several strong points, the Tunisian VET system also faces challenges. Vocational education and training is widely perceived as an unattractive option in comparison to academic qualifications. In part, the low profile and reputation of the vocational tracks in Tunisia reflect the widespread preference for public sector jobs, for which the entry requirement is typically an academic university qualification. Indeed, many students undergo a VET programme involuntarily – generally because they have been redirected towards this stream of the education system after a failure – rather than as a deliberate choice, facilitated by a professional orientation. In turn, given that these students tend to be the ones falling behind in the academic track and are likely to come from more disadvantaged families, the lack of an attractive and well-performing VET system acts as a factor that perpetuates labour market and social marginalisation. In this framework, a more effective VET system can generate substantial gains, measurable not only in terms of better use of available human resources but also the improved opportunities for vulnerable groups. The disconnection of VET from the needs of the labour market, and fragmentation of programme options further erode its status and visibility.

This chapter also discusses entrepreneurship training in VET. As argued elsewhere in this report, entrepreneurship and self-employment can offer an important source of jobcreation for youth – conditional upon the existence of adequate training and support systems. Creating an entrepreneurial mindset needs to start early, however, and the education system plays a critical role in raising awareness about the potential of entrepreneurship as a career opportunity and to provide training and education to support entrepreneurship and business creation. There is also scope for improving the general framework for entrepreneurship training in VET by encompassing a focus on *green* entrepreneurship. Special attention could be devoted to providing entrepreneurship training on green job skills, including green skills in business start-up training, and incubating companies with a potential to deal with environmental issues.

There is a relatively long history of supporting entrepreneurship in the VET system in Tunisia. A number of international projects were launched in the 1990s and 2000s, which led to the development of entrepreneurship learning material and training for entrepreneurship trainers. However, this approach was not sustainable and all projects ended after their initial funding ceased. A positive outcome of this experience is that much of the necessary strategic framework is still in place and many of the entrepreneurship support structures and institutions continue to exist. This provides a solid base to build on for moving forward. However, there are substantial variations in the quality and accessibility of entrepreneurship training within the VET system, often depending on the region and the presence of entrepreneurship champions within the individual training centres. The key challenges going forward include: i) the lack of common understanding of the objectives of entrepreneurship promotion; ii) co-ordination challenges between the various stakeholders and the lack of strategic vision; and iii) the need to improve current methods of teaching entrepreneurship.

This chapter first outlines the structure of the education system in Tunisia, including basic, secondary, and higher education. It then focuses on vocational education and training (VET), describing its main features and recent reforms. Finally, it turns to a discussion of entrepreneurship training in VET. The main findings are as follows:

- ***There is a strong case for improving the vocational education and training system in ways that strengthen the labour market outcomes of young people.*** For instance, it is especially important to reduce early tracking practices between *collèges techniques* [technical colleges] and general lower secondary education, to expand the system at the upper secondary level, keeping quality assurance mechanisms strong, and to introduce opportunities of transition between academic and vocational tracks. In addition there are concerns about the quality of vocational programmes. The low status *collèges techniques* [technical schools] options, and the underdevelopment of high quality options at the upper secondary level are different aspects of this challenge.

- ***More effective and less fragmented provisions to reflect the needs of the labour market would generate substantial employment gains while preserving opportunities of access to education.*** In Tunisia, the government would like to make the VET system more responsive to the needs of employers. At the moment, signals of labour market needs are weak in the VET system and employer engagement is very limited. Employers and graduates are often not well-informed about what VET programmes offer. Weaknesses in governance, fragmentation and lack of co-ordination add to the problem. These factors further erode VET visibility and utilisation.

- ***Several mutually reinforcing policy reforms need to be implemented to improve quality, enhance employer engagement and to make VET more attractive.*** These include the development of high quality options at the upper secondary level, and the merger of *collèges techniques* [technical schools] with general *colleges* [academic schools]; stronger career guidance mechanisms, based on solid data, and smoother transition arrangements between vocational and academic programmes; as well as mechanisms to better engage employers, more co-ordination across ministries with responsibilities for VET, and the introduction of mandatory work-based learning in post-secondary VET.

- ***There is scope for improving both the quality and accessibility of entrepreneurship training provision in the VET system.*** First, the objectives of entrepreneurship training need to be clarified and agreed upon between all stakeholders. Second, Tunisia should develop a national strategy outlining how entrepreneurship could be supported within the vocational training systemand clearly identifying the roles of each actor and outlines the short-and long-term objectives. Finally, there is a need to increase the availability of support for trainers by making entrepreneurship training more available and by improving teaching material.

A stronger VET system is a key part of the solution to improve youth labour market outcomes, but it will not help all youth unless it is complemented by other measures, including the labour market and social reforms to help Tunisia youth to get a first foothold on the career ladder that appear discussed in Chapter 2 and Chapter 3.

**Box 4.1. Key recommendations**

On making VET more attractive:

- The integration of the lower secondary technical track into general lower secondary education.
- A strategic expansion of VET at the upper secondary level, linked to strong quality assurance mechanisms.
- The introduction of careers guidance in all lower secondary schools. Better data should be made available to support students' choice, and balance the strong preference for academic routes.
- Improved articulation between vocational and academic programmes (including access to higher education to VET graduates, and pathways between BTS and *licences appliquées*).

On the mix of provision and involvement of the social partners:

- An extension of mandatory work-based learning to the *licences appliquées.*
- Stronger mechanisms to engage employers, and to balance student preferences with employer needs, based on labour market data.
- A co-ordination body to reduce the fragmentation of VET across ministries and improve the responsiveness of the system.

On improving entrepreneurship training within VET:

- A national strategy should be developed to guide the improvement of entrepreneurship support services in VET, clearly defining roles as well as short- and long-run objectives, and encompassing different levels of support for different groups of potential entrepreneurs.
- Entrepreneurship training, including green orientations, should go beyond the provision of introductory modules on entrepreneurship to support learners in developing entrepreneurial mind-sets and increasing their opportunities to practice entrepreneurial behaviours.
- More support should be made available to trainers by making entrepreneurship training more available and by improving teaching material. Training for trainers should be available as part of ongoing career development training as well as initial training for trainers. This should be complemented by creating mechanisms that facilitate the exchange of good practices among trainers and by them with additional supports such as teaching manuals.
- Co-ordination of public business development services should be improved and the linkages with the training centres strengthened.

## The Tunisian vocational education and training system and where it sits within the wider education system

The education system of Tunisia has four levels: pre-primary[3], basic (including primary and lower secondary), upper secondary, and higher education. The complete school career includes 13 years of primary and secondary schooling for students aged 6 to 19 (see Figure 4.1).

**Figure 4.1. The Tunisian education and training system**

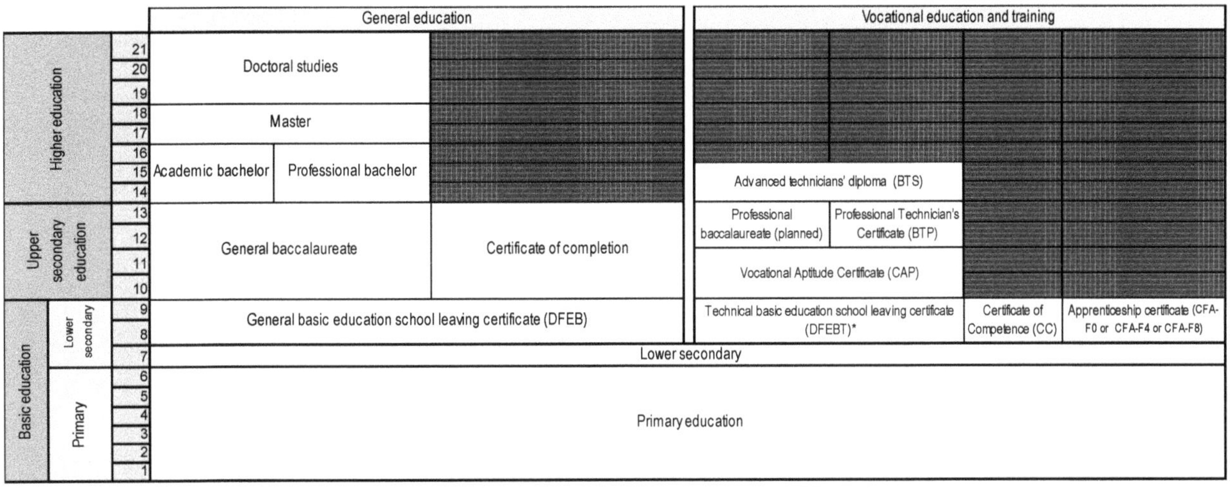


* While holders of the technical DFEBT have in the past only been able to pursue the vocational upper secondary tracks, since 2013/14 they may enter general upper secondary education, provided they meet the grade and age requirements.

*Source:* Updated figure based on figure provided by Ministry of Education (2013), "National Background Report : Renforcer l'employabilité des jeunes pendant la transition de la Tunisie vers une économie verte: Questionnaire de l'OCDE".

## *Basic education in Tunisia*

According to the Law on Orientation Regarding Education, modified in 2008 (Law No. 2008-09 of 11 February 2008), *enseignement de base* [basic education] is compulsory and lasts nine years (Tunisian Republic, 2008a). It aims to train students to develop their potential and to allow them to pursue either general education or vocational education and training and to integrate into society (UNESCO, 2012, p. 17). Basic education comprises two complementary cycles at primary ($1^{th}$-$6^{th}$) and lower secondary level ($7^{th}$-$9^{th}$).

### *Primary education*

The first six years of schooling ($1^{st}$-$6^{th}$ year) take place in primary schools for students aged 6 to 11. In 1990/91 only 88% of children aged 6-11 years attended the first cycle of basic education (year 1-6), with a higher enrolment rate for boys than for girls (92% compared to 84%). Enrolment in primary education is now nearly universal, reaching 99% in 2012/13 (National Institute of Statistics, 2014) (see Figure 4.2). In the school year 2011/12 around 1 million students (48% girls) attended years 1-6 of basic education, representing 10% of Tunisia's total population (Ministry of Education, 2013b; UNESCO, 2014a; National Institute of Statistics, 2014). Since 2006/07, an examination has tested students' competencies in Arabic, French, Mathematics and Sciences at the end of their fourth school year (UNESCO, 2012).

**Figure 4.2. Percentage of students aged 6-11 years in the 1st cycle of basic education**

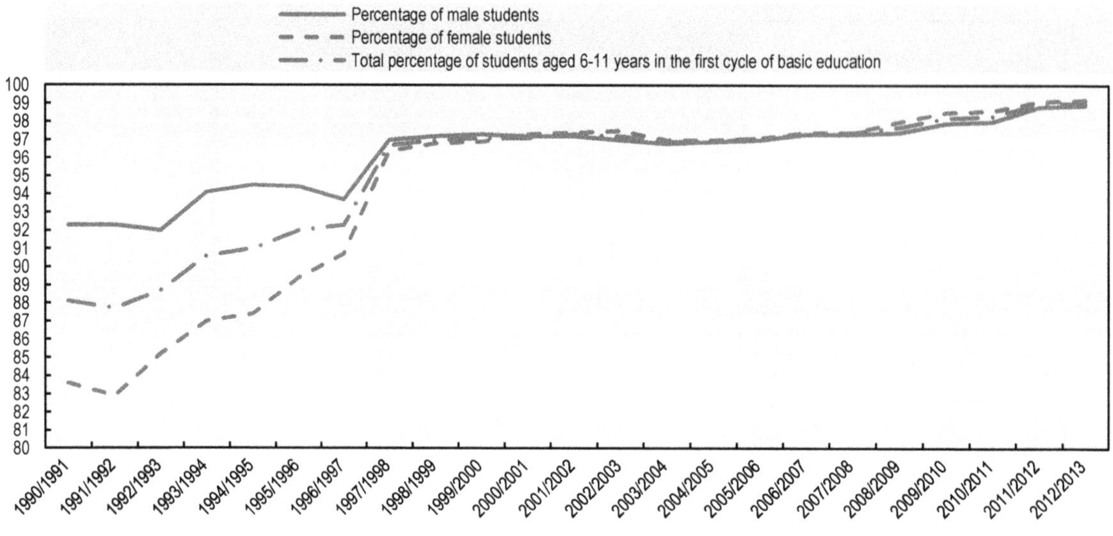


*Source*: National Institute of Statistics (2014), "Statistiques", www.tunisie-statistiques.tn/plateforme/detail.php?id=198.

Despite the significant progress achieved to raise overall education outcomes – the literacy rate in Tunisia's population increased from 15% in 1956 to 80% in 2012 (Tuniscope, 2012) – large variations remain, between men and women, age groups, and urban and rural areas (UNESCO, 2013). In 2011, the literacy rate was 97% for those aged 15-24 years (with less than 2% difference between girls and boys) compared to only 80% for the entire adult population aged over 15 years (with a 16% lower literacy rate among women) (UNESCO, 2014b).

In the first cycle of basic education, the repetition rate of students in primary education ($1^{st}$-$6^{th}$ year) fell from 29% in 1970 to 6% in 2010 (UNESCO, 2014a). Similarly, the dropout rates in primary education have decreased and the transition rate from primary to lower secondary education ($7^{th}$-$9^{th}$ years) has been 91-99% over the past five years (Ministry of Education, 2013c; UNESCO, 2013).

## *Lower secondary education*

The second basic education cycle, called *cycle préparatoire* [preparatory cycle], from age 12 to 14 lasts three years ($7^{th}$-$9^{th}$) and is offered at lower secondary preparatory schools (*collèges* or *écoles préparatoires*). Since 2007/08, this second cycle has been split from year 8 onwards into two course types both lasting two years. Students can choose between general education and a technical vocational education track offered at *collèges techniques* [technical schools] (see section on vocational education and training below). In the school year 2010/11, around 17 000 students attended the technical preparatory cycle compared to 470 000 students in the general preparatory cycle (Ministry of Education, 2013b) (see Table 4.1).

**Table 4.1 Students in basic education (year 1-9) in 2011**

| | Students in basic education (year 1-9), 2011 | Percentage of girls |
|---|---|---|
| Total students (year 1-9) | 1 501 015 | 48% |
| First cycle (year 1-6): primary education | 1 014 836 | 48% |
| Second cycle (year 7-9): lower secondary education | 486 179 | 49% |
| of which in technical preparatory cycle | 16 811 | 22% |
| of which in general preparatory cycle | 469 368 | 50% |

*Source*: National Institute of Statistics (2014), "Statistiques", www.tunisie-statistiques.tn/plateforme/detail.php?id=198; Ministry of Education (2013), "Statistiques scolaires: Année scolaire 2011/12", Direction Générale des Études de la Planification et des Systèmes d'Information.

One of the key objectives of the government's strategy launched in 2010 was to have 50% of students (in the 7th year of education) enrolled in a technical preparatory cycle by 2014-15. In the *Programme d'Appui à l'Éducation, la Formation Professionnelle, l'Enseignement Supérieur en Lien avec l'Employabilité des Jeunes Diplômés* (PEFESE) [Programme to Support Education, Vocational Training, Higher Education and the Employability of Graduates] this target is set to 10% in 2010-11, 15% in 2011-12 and 20% in 2012-13. The first evaluation of the programme, conducted in July 2012, revealed that the number of student enrolling in technical colleges at the end of the 7th year of education remains very low (ETF, 2012).

After these nine years of basic education, students sit a national exam which leads, depending on their course choice in the 8$^{th}$ year, to the *Diplôme de Fin d'Études de l'Enseignement de Base General, DFEB/ de Base Technique, DFEBT* [the general or the technical basic education school leaving certificate]. In 2011, the pass rate was 90% for the DFEBT and 83% for the DFEB (see Table 4.2). The general DFEB gives access to general upper secondary education. While holders of the technical DFEBT have in the past only been able to pursue the vocational upper secondary track (see section on vocational education and training below), since 2013/14 they have been able to enter general upper secondary education, provided they meet the grade and age requirements.

**Table 4.2. Students in year 9 of basic education in 2011**

| | Students in year 9 of primary education, 2011 | Pass rate | Percentage of those passing who were girls |
|---|---|---|---|
| Total students in year 9 | 133 700 | 83% | 49% girls |
| Technical year 9 leading to the technical basic education school leaving certificate (DFEBT) | 6 700 | 90% | 24% girls |
| General year 9 leading to the general basic education school leaving certificate (DFEB) | 127 000 | 83% | 50% girls |

*Source*: Ministry of Education (2013), "Statistiques scolaires: Année scolaire 2011/12", Direction Générale des Études de la Planification et des Systèmes d'Information.

The average dropout rate in the general preparatory cycle (7th-9th year) was 9% in 2010/11, with the highest drop-out rate in 7$^{th}$ year (14%) (see Ministry of Education, 2013b). Dropout rates in the technical preparatory cycle (7$^{th}$-9$^{th}$ year) are not available. According to data from PISA 2012, 33% of the 15-year old Tunisian students had already repeated at least one year of education, against an OECD average of 12% (OECD, 2013a).

The Programme for International Student Assessment (PISA) 2012 survey shows that the quality of education in Tunisia is quite low. Half of Tunisian 15-year-olds had a reading proficiency level below Level 2 of the five PISA literacy levels, which means that they were capable of completing only the least complex reading tasks, such as locating a single piece of information, identifying the main theme of a text or making a simple connection with everyday knowledge. Tunisia's students' performance in reading is well under the OECD country average as well as under the average of the other higher middle income countries. However, there have been improvements in the system as suggested by the fact that in 2003, two out of three students were under Level 2 (see Figure 4.3) (OECD, 2013a).

**Figure 4.3. Evolution of percentage of students below Level 2 in reading in PISA 2003 through 2012 in higher middle income countries**

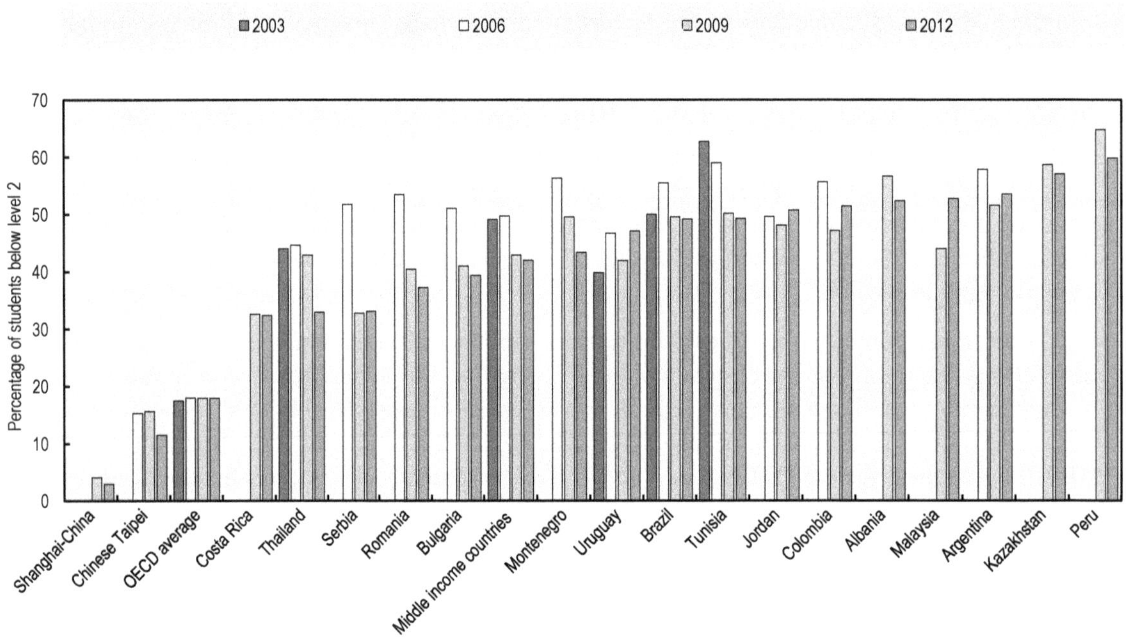


*Source*: OECD (2013), *PISA 2012 Results: What Students Know and Can Do (Vol. I)*, Annex B1.3 Results (tables): A profile of student performance in reading, Table I.4.1b.

## *Upper secondary education*

Students can either pursue a vocational upper secondary track (see the section on vocational education and training below) or a general upper secondary education track. In 2010/11, 89% were enrolled in general upper secondary programmes and 11% in upper secondary vocational programmes leading to a *Certificat d'Aptitude Professionnel, CAP* [the vocational aptitude certificate] or a *Brevet de Technicien Professionnel, BTP* [the professional technician's certificate] (Ministry of Education, 2013b; Ministry of Vocational Training and Employment, 2011a) (see Table 4.3).

**Table 4.3. Upper secondary education in Tunisia, 2011**

Number of students

| Programme | Students in upper secondary education | of which % of VET students | of which % of general education students |
|---|---|---|---|
| Students in upper secondary VET (qualifications: CAP, BTP) | 57 859 | 100% | 0% |
| Students in general upper secondary education (qualification: baccalaureate) | 466 939 | 0% | 100% |
| Total students in upper secondary education | 524 798 | 11% | 89% |

*Source*: Ministry of Education (2013), "Statistiques scolaires: Année scolaire 2011/12", Direction Générale des Études de la Planification et des Systèmes d'Information; Ministry of Vocational Training and Employment (2011), "La formation professionnelle en chiffre: Décembre 2011", Observatoire National de l'Emploi et des Qualifications, www.mfpe.gov.tn/fileadmin/user_upload/PDF/statistique/publication/statistiques_de_la_formation_professionnelle_2011.pdf.

The general upper secondary education track is divided into two cycles (of two years), both offered in *lycées* (upper secondary schools). The first cycle of general upper secondary education comprises a first year, in which all students follow a common general academic curriculum, and a second year, after which students specialise in either literature, sciences, economics and management, mathematics, technical studies, informatics or sport. The language of instruction is French in technical, scientific and mathematics fields, and Arabic in all other subjects (OECD, 2013b). The second cycle of general academic upper secondary education also lasts two years and offers seven specialisations.

In 2010/11, 22% of the 936 000 enrolled students pursued experimental sciences, followed by humanities (21%), economics and management (19%), mathematics (15%), technical sciences (12%), computer sciences (10%), and sports (1%) (Ministry of Education, 2013b).

At the end of the fourth year of general upper secondary education ($13^{th}$ year) students sit the *examen national du baccalauréat général* [the national general baccalaureate]; successful completion gives access to university and post-secondary education institutions. Those who do not pass the exam receive a certificate of completion, which can be used for employment, for access to private education institutions, or for accessing professional education and training education (OECD, 2013b) (see Figure 4.1).

The number of students successfully sitting the *examen national du baccalauréat* has increased. While in 1985 only 40% of the 12 000 students sitting the upper secondary school leaving exam succeeded, in 2011, 64% of the 79 000 students taking the exam did so (Ministry of Education, 2013b, p. 134) (see Box 4.2. for information on previous OECD analysis on Tunisia's general secondary education).

**Box 4.2. Previous OECD analysis and recommendations for Tunisia's general secondary education**

Although the objective of this chapter is to address vocational education challenges, general education clearly plays an essential role in raising the level on ambitious of education reform. In particular, the OECD Integrity Scan of Tunisia (OECD, 2013b) has focussed on the potential contribution of the reforms of general secondary education. In a number of subjects, many secondary school students in Tunisia have to "shift" learning away from their classrooms to various forms of out-of-school instruction in order to succeed in school: 70% of 15-year-olds in the country participate in out-of-school lessons (9th highest of all 54 countries for which PISA provides data) (OECD, 2013b). In this context, which reveals a problem of lack of trust in the public secondary schools, the Integrity Scan provides a comprehensive strategy for improving the general secondary education system. In a snapshot, the key elements of such a broad strategy include an effort to improve the system of quality assurance, which could also give priority to an in-depth review of the baccalaureate exam. Serious consideration should also be given to the need to strengthen the accountability of teachers and schools vis-à-vis the education authorities and stakeholders. This could includes the introducion of a code of professional conduct, along with measures to improve the school inspection system.

To ensure ownership, the Integrity Scan recommends that these reform steps be approached following an as inclusive as possible approach, with all sides concerned (parents, students, authorities, employers, educational professionals and the wider public) being involved in the debate about what needs to be done. One way to generate such an open debate is by starting from the outcomes of an independent review to assess the underlying reasons for the low effectiveness of classroom learning. Such an independent review could be carried out by an external body.

*Source*: OECD (2013), "Integrity Scan of Tunisia", OECD-CleanGovBiz: Integrity in Practice, OECD Publishing, Paris, www.oecd.org/cleangovbiz/Tunisia-Integrity-ScanEN.pdf.

## *Post-secondary education (excluding VET)*

University education in Tunisia is open to all holders of the national baccalaureate. The Tunisian university system underwent reform in 2006/07 to implement the three-tier Bologna system and now offers three-year bachelors programmes, two-year master degrees and five-year doctorate programmes (UNESCO, 2012).

The university sector has rapidly expanded. The number of students increased from 96 000 students (42% girls) in 1993/94 to 330 000 (61% girls) in 2012/13 with an average of 76 000 new enrolments per year over the last ten years (National Institute of Statistics, 2014). In 2012/13 93% attended public institutions and most were enrolled in undergraduate programmes with IT, business or technological curricula (Ministry of Higher Education and Scientific Research, 2013).

Tunisia's post-secondary sector currently includes 178 free public institutions, of which 155 institutions are under the direct supervision of the Ministry of Higher Education. Moreover, there are 20 university-level private institutions, six higher institutes of teacher training, and 24 *Instituts Supérieurs des Études Technologiques*, ISETs [higher institutes of technological studies]. The latter were created in 1992 with a view to improving graduate employability (OECD, 2013b; Ministry of Vocational Training and Employment, 2010a).

In Tunisia, many graduates of higher education are facing difficulties accessing the labour market. As mentioned in Chapter 1, one striking aspect of Tunisia's youth labour market is that the more educated young people have a higher risk of unemployment compared to their less educated peers. According to calculations based on the *Enquête Nationale sur la Population* [National Population and Employment Survey], in 2012, 62% of tertiary graduates were unemployed compared to an unemployment rate of 38% among

15-24 year-old with secondary and 30% among 15-24 year-old with primary education (see Figure 1.5 in Chapter 1).

Various studies have highlighted a growing disparity in employment opportunities of different education and training qualifications at the postsecondary level. For example, a study by the Ministry of Employment and Profession Insertion of Youth and the World Bank (2009) based on longitudinal data since 2004 shows significant imbalances between supply and demand for skills at the postsecondary level. Some qualifications and fields of studies are characterised by long-term unemployment and inactivity. The study finds that unemployment rates are particularly high among graduates from Masters in Law and *Brevet de Technicien Supérieur* [Higher Technician Certificate] in commerce and management. On the other hand, insertion into the labour market seems to be easier for engineers, with the exception of specialists in agriculture (see Table 4.4.). These findings suggest that there may be some mismatch between individuals' skills and employers' needs.

**Table 4.4. Labour market outcomes of post-secondary graduates**

| | In employment | | Unemployed | | Inactive | | Sample size |
|---|---|---|---|---|---|---|---|
| | 18 months after graduation | 3.5 years after graduation | 18 months after graduation | 3.5 years after graduation | 18 months after graduation | 3.5 years after graduation | |
| ***Brevet de Technicien Supérieur [Higher Technician Diploma]*** | 29 | 48 | 43 | 33 | 14 | 7 | 12 682 |
| Commerce and management | 26 | 44 | 49 | 37 | 12 | 8 | 3 864 |
| Technical fields | 28 | 48 | 40 | 31 | 16 | 7 | 6 070 |
| Health care and social care | 47 | 51 | 37 | 31 | 6 | 6 | 1 338 |
| Other fields | 25 | 51 | 47 | 35 | 18 | 6 | 1 410 |
| ***Maitrise [Masters]*** | 28 | 51 | 36 | 29 | 25 | 11 | 21 706 |
| Languages | 36 | 62 | 41 | 27 | 15 | 6 | 3 199 |
| Social sciences | 31 | 38 | 41 | 40 | 21 | 15 | 1 755 |
| Technical engineering fields | 40 | 65 | 27 | 19 | 25 | 7 | 1 488 |
| Sciences | 40 | 47 | 34 | 40 | 22 | 9 | 2 195 |
| Commerce, economics and management | 20 | 48 | 36 | 27 | 29 | 10 | 8 741 |
| Law | 13 | 28 | 42 | 39 | 39 | 24 | 1 849 |
| IT | 45 | 79 | 23 | 14 | 19 | 5 | 975 |
| Other fields | 35 | 57 | 38 | 24 | 24 | 15 | 1 505 |
| ***Engineering*** | 47 | 76 | 14 | 9 | 22 | 10 | 2 509 |
| Agriculture and food processing industry | 24 | 51 | 20 | 15 | 37 | 22 | 455 |
| Technical engineering fields | 50 | 82 | 13 | 8 | 17 | 8 | 438 |
| IT, telecom, electricity and electronics | 61 | 91 | 10 | 5 | 17 | 2 | 616 |
| ***Other*** | | | | | | | |
| Architecture | 19 | 25 | 8 | 4 | 9 | 4 | 71 |
| Medical studies | 29 | 45 | 18 | 17 | 13 | 5 | 825 |
| Fine arts | 26 | 42 | 21 | 23 | 33 | 14 | 315 |
| Teacher training | 100 | 100 | 0 | 0 | 0 | 0 | 797 |

*Note* : The *maîtrise* qualification [masters] requires four years of studies.

*Source*: Ministry of Employment and Professional Insertion of Youth and the World Bank (2009), "Dynamiques de l'emploi et adéquation de la formation parmi les diplômés universitaires: insertion des jeunes diplomés de l'enseignement supérieur promotion 2004 analyse comparative des résultats de deux enquètes (2005 et 2007)", www-wds.worldbank.org/external/default/WDSContentServer/WDSP/IB/2009/11/12/000020953_20091112162329/Rendered/PDF/515650ESW0P1111CH0Rapport0Dynamique.pdf.

The problem of a mismatch between the offer of university programmes and labour market needs is common to many countries. In many African countries, in particular, university systems have traditionally focused on educating for the public employment sector, with little concern for the needs of the private sector. Often a degree from a tertiary institution is an entry requirement for government employment, with little attention paid to a specific skill set. An *African Economic Outlook* survey found that tertiary graduates in technical fields, such as engineering and information technology, have less problems finding employment than those from the social sciences and humanities, which have high unemployment rates throughout the African continent (AfDB, OECD, UNDP, UNECA, 2012) (see Box 4.3. for information on previous OECD analysis on Tunisia's tertiary education system).

**Box 4.3. Previous OECD analysis and recommendations on Tunisia's tertiary education system**

According to the "OECD Integrity Scan of Tunisia" (2013b, p. 157), the rising enrolment rates at university are in strong contrast to the deteriorating preparedness of secondary school graduates for university studies – a problem confirmed by PISA results and a consequence of missing investment in quality assurance that should accompany the growing enrolment rates.

One issue at stake is that, young Tunisians who want to study at university have to go through a central student admission system which, on the basis of their grades in the final upper secondary school exam, proposes them a course of study. Only a minority of best-performing students can choose their preferred discipline. The majority of students in the middle and lower range of the performance spectrum has to consider taking a place in the (remaining) disciplines, which may be of little value in the labour market. These second best alternatives are numerous, given that for long study places have been opened independently of the needs of the labour market and in disciplines that cost less (philosophy is, for example, cheaper than engineering in terms of equipment requirements). Such conditions limit students' motivation and lower their academic ambitions. Stakeholders report that sometimes even those who are good enough to choose "better" subjects such as chemistry and pharmacy, medicine or engineering, follow their parents' wishes which often do not coincide with the students' interests and competences. Unfortunately, no career guidance system is in place that could help students find their best suited field of study and help adjust family expectations.

Confronted with these difficulties in tertiary education, the "OECD Integrity Scan of Tunisia" (2013b, p. 159) recommends that higher education authorities consider a reform of the current system of access to university. A more adequate and precise selection process coupled with sound career guidance would help to better detect students' abilities and academic aptitudes. This would ensure that the preferences of potential students are better met and that students take better informed decisions. Moreover, to improve the labour market relevance of study programmes, their overall quality, and the information provided to students, Tunisia should move ahead with the creation of the independent national evaluation and accreditation agency, which has already been envisaged in 2012.

*Source*: OECD (2013), "Integrity Scan of Tunisia", OECD-CleanGovBiz: Integrity in Practice, OECD Publishing, Paris, www.oecd.org/cleangovbiz/Tunisia-Integrity-ScanEN.pdf.

## *Overview of vocational education and training*

According to Article 1 of the Law on Vocational Education and Training adopted in 2008, vocational education and training (VET) aims, in co-ordination with the other educational sectors and employment, to qualify learners on the professional, social and cultural level, to develop their professional capacities, and to provide the economy with the right workforce to improve productivity and competitiveness (Tunisian Republic, 2008b, Article 1).

The number of students enrolled in vocational training has increased over the last decade (see Figure 4.4), during which period efforts have been undertaken to expand the capacity of the public VET system, through the creation of new VET centres and the restructuring of several existing ones. These efforts are seen to have played a role in the increase of the flow of new entrants (ONEQ and ILO, 2014). However the number of graduates has not kept pace with the increase in the number enrolled, which points to an increasingly number of dropout outs.

**Figure 4.4. Number of learners and graduates in vocational education, 2001-10**

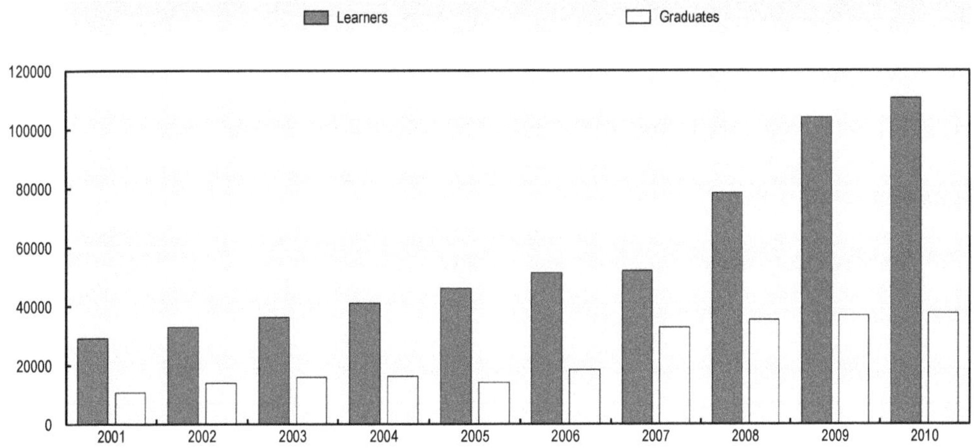


*Source*: Chahed, M.Y. (2013), "Skills for Entrepreneurship [Tunisia]: Le renforcement de la culture entrepreneuriale dans le cursus de la formation professionnelle dispensée dans les centres de l'Agence tunisienne de la formation professionnelle (ATFP)", Rapport Final de Mission, Project by the OECD, GIZ, ETF.

The Tunisian VET system includes initial and continuing VET (see Table 4.5 for student numbers in 2011) (see below for further information on continuing VET).

**Table 4.5. Students enrolled in VET in Tunisia, 2011**

| Education level | Programme leading to: | Students in VET, 2011 | Percentage of total VET students |
|---|---|---|---|
| Lower secondary | Basic technical education school leaving certificate (DFEBT) | 16 811 | 6% |
| Upper secondary | Vocational aptitude certificate (CAP) | 26 745 | 10% |
| | Professional technician's certificate (BTP) | 31 114 | 12% |
| Post secondary | Advanced technician's diploma (BTS) | 14 104 | 5% |
| | Professional bachelor (Licence appliquée) | 14 1647 | 54% |
| All levels | Total students in accredited VET courses | 230 421 | 87% |
| All levels | Total students in non-accredited VET courses | 33 556 | 13% |
| All levels | Total students in VET | 263 977 | 100% |

*Source*: Ministry of Vocational Training and Employment (2011), "La formation professionnelle en chiffre: Décembre 2011", Observatoire National de l'Emploi et des Qualifications, www.mfpe.gov.tn/fileadmin/user_upload/PDF/statistique/publication/statistiques_de_la_formation_professionnelle_2011.pdf; Ministry of Education (2013), "Statistiques scolaires: Année scolaire 2011/12", Direction Générale des Études de la Planification et des Systèmes d'Information; Ministry of Higher Education and Scientific Research (2013), "Features of Higher Education and Scientific Research: Academic Year 2012-2013", Studies, Planning and Programming Office.

Around 370 types of vocational programmes are provided in 13 different fields of study with a prominence of electricity and electronics, textile, mechanical engineering, construction and tourism (see Figure 4.5) (Ministry of Vocational Training and Employment, 2011a; Ministry of Vocational Training and Employment, 2010b).

In 2011, a total of 72 000 VET students pursued programmes in these 13 sectors leading to the upper secondary *Certificat d'Aptitude Professionelle*, CAP [the vocational aptitude certificate], the upper secondary *Brevet de Technicien Professionnel*, BTP [the professional technician's certificate] and the post-secondary *Brevet de Technicien Supérieur*, BTS [advanced technician's diploma]; 89% of these VET students attended public and 11% private institutions, with the private sector only offering programmes in six different fields (Ministry of Vocational Training and Employment, 2011a) (see Figure 4.5).

In 2011, 26% of all VET students attended the private vocational sector and 112 of the 900 private vocational institutions were certified (Chahed, 2013; Ministry of Vocational Training and Employment, 2011a).

**Figure 4.5. Students in 13 sectors of public and private VET leading to a CAP, BTP or BTS in 2011**

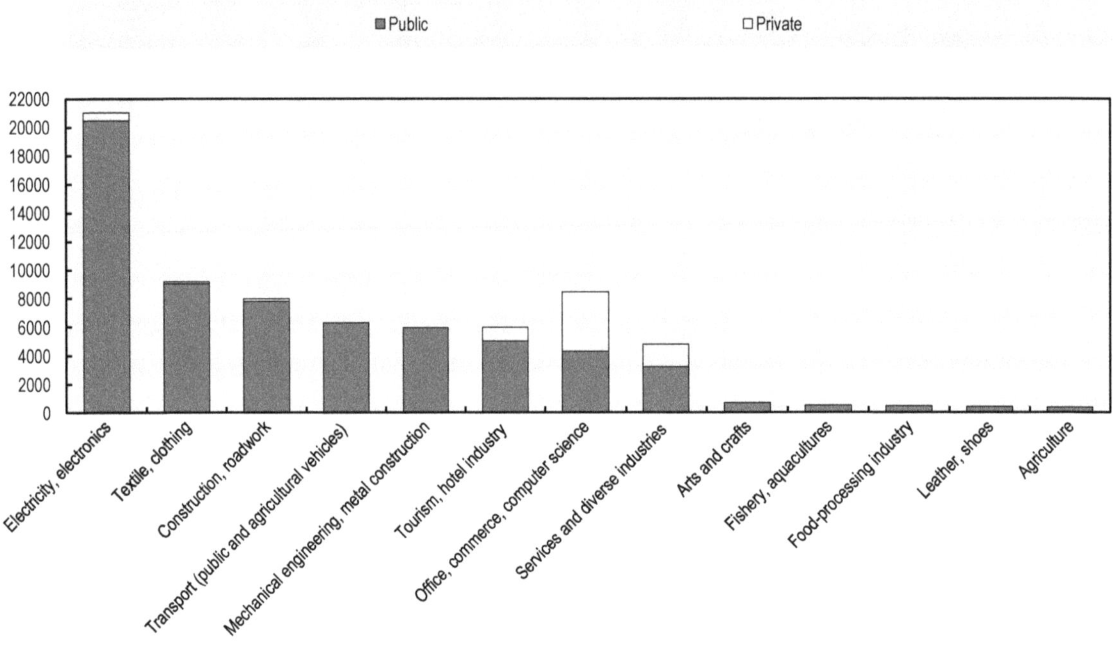


*Source*: Ministry of Vocational Training and Employment (2011), "La formation professionnelle en chiffre: Décembre 2011", Observatoire National de l'Emploi et des Qualifications, www.mfpe.gov.tn/fileadmin/user_upload/PDF/statistique/publication/statistiques_de_la_formation_professionnelle_2011.pdf.

*Lower secondary VET*

At lower secondary level, students can pursue the technical preparatory cycle ($8^{th}$-$9^{th}$ school year of basic education) at *collèges techniques* [technical schools] leading to the *Diplôme de Fin d'Études de l'Enseignement de base technique,* DFEBT [the technical basic education school leaving certificate]. In 2011, 6% of all VET students pursued the DFEBT programme at lower secondary level (Ministry of Vocational Training and

Employment, 2011a; Ministry of Education, 2013b; Ministry of Higher Education of Scientific Research, 2013) (see Table 4.5 for student numbers in VET).

Those students who do not achieve the education level of 9th year of basic education but have completed 7th year can obtain the *Certificat de Compétence* [the competence certificate] if they meet the specific requirements or if they successfully pass an assessment test (Chahed, 2013) (see Figure 4.1).

*Upper secondary VET*

During the first cycle of upper secondary VET, holders of both the *Diplôme de Fin d'Études de l'Enseignement de base général,* DFEB/*de base technique,* DFEBT [the general or the technical basic education school leaving certificate] can attend a two-year programme at training centres in order to obtain the *Certificat d'Aptitude Professionelle,* CAP [the vocational aptitude certificate] (Ministry of Vocational Training and Employment, 2014).

During the second cycle of upper secondary VET, both holders of the CAP and learners who have completed the second year of general upper secondary education can enter the two-year programme at training centres under the Ministry of Vocational Training and Employment that culminates in the *Brevet de Technicien Professionnel,* BTP [the professional technician's certificate] (see Figure 4.1). Data provided by the MVET show that in 2011 57 859 people were enrolled in professional upper secondary education, of which 31 114 in BTP programmes and 26 745 in CAP programmes (Ministry of Vocational Training and Employment, 2011a).

Holders of the BTP and of the *Brevet de Technicien Supérieur,* BTS [advanced technician's diploma] (see section on post-secondary VET below) can directly take the exam for the professional baccalaureate in order to gain access to university education (see Figure 4.1) (Ministry of Vocational Training and Employment, 2014; Tunisian Republic, 2008b). However, the professional baccalaureate has not yet been introduced, and its implementation is currently under deliberation.

## *Post-secondary VET*

At post-secondary level, holders of the general baccalaureate and, under certain conditions, holders of the BTP can obtain the *Brevet de Technicien Supérieur,* BTS [the advanced technician's diploma] in *Institut Supérieurs d'Études techniques,* ISETs [higher institutes of technological studies] or the *licence appliquée* [professional bachelor] at higher education institutions under the supervision of the Ministry of Higher Education (Ministry of Vocational Training and Employment, 2014). In 2011, 5% of all VET students attended BTS programmes, and 54% were enrolled in professional bachelors courses (Ministry of Vocational Training and Employment 2011a; Ministry of Education, 2013b; Ministry of Higher Education and Scientific Research, 2013) (see Table 4.5 for student numbers in VET).

## *Non-accredited VET*

While the DFEBT, CAP, BTP, BTS, and the professional bachelor are accredited certificates, a second group of certificates, the so-called *certificats non diplômants* (non-accredited certificates) exists. They include the above-mentioned *Certificat de Compétences,* CC [the Certificate of Competence], and the *Certificat de Fin d'Apprentissage,* CFA-F0/ CFA-F4/ CFA-F8 [Apprenticeship Certificate]. They are offered to students who have not achieved the educational level of 9th year of basic education.

Students can obtain the CC if they have completed the 7th year of basic education and meet specific requirements or successfully pass an assessment test (Chahed, 2013). While the CFA-F0 is granted to students who have completed an apprenticeship, the CFA-F4/8 is given to apprentices who have additionally attended four or eight training hours per week in training centres (see Figure 4.1). In 2011, 13% of all students in VET pursued programmes leading to a non-accredited certificate (see Table 4.6) (Ministry of Vocational Training and Employment, 2014).

**Table 4.6. Students pursuing non-accredited VET diplomas, 2011**

| Programme | Students pursuing non-accredited VET diplomas, 2011 |
|---|---|
| Certificate of Competence (CC) | 5 994 |
| Apprenticeship Certificate (CFA-F4) | 4 701 |
| Apprenticeship Certificate (CFA-F8) | 22 861 |
| Total students | 33 556 |

*Source*: Ministry of Vocational Training and Employment (2011), "La formation professionnelle en chiffre: Décembre 2011", Observatoire National de l'Emploi et des Qualifications, www.mfpe.gov.tn/fileadmin/user_upload/PDF/statistique/publication/statistiques_de_la_formation_professionnelle_2011.pdf.

## *Continuing Vocational Education and Training*

Under Article 26 of the Law on Vocational Education and Training (revised in 2008), continuing VET aims to develop the knowledge and professional skills of workers in different economic sectors in order to keep them up-to-date with changes in technology and production, to enhance the enterprises' competitiveness, and to give workers and the unemployed the opportunity to progress professionally or to learn a new profession (Tunisian Republic, 2008b).

Continuing VET in Tunisia includes two types: i) continuing VET organised by companies to ensure a certain skill level of their personnel in order to remain competitive; ii) continuing VET offered by private and public education institutions to improve the chances of professional progression. These programmes lead to the same certificates and diplomas as in VET (Tunisian Republic, 2008b).

The Tunisian authorities have several instruments to encourage enterprise training: the tax credit (*crédit d'impôt,* also called the *avance sur la taxe de formation professionnelle* – TFP); the drawing right (*droit de tirage*); and Article 39 of the Investment Incentives Code (*code d'incitation aux investissements*). The tax credit equals (a maximum of) 60% of the payroll tax paid by the company during the year preceding the training. This measure allows companies to directly use the tax credit for training expenses, rather than going through slower administrative processes. Only companies paying the TFP, whose contribution is equal or superior to TND 1 000 per year, are eligible for the tax credit. The drawing right allows enterprises to receive direct funding by the state to finance training activities for their staff. Article 39 of the Investment Incentives Code (*code d'incitation aux investissements*) provides funding for training staff in companies making a technology investment to either master new technologies, improve productivity, or enhance local integration. In addition to continuing training organised by companies, continuing vocational training is also offered to workers by private and public education insitutions, and the state typically pays for such training (Ministry of Vocational Training and Employment, 2012).

### *Assessment of outcomes: Labour market returns to VET*

Bellakhal and Mahjoub (2013) use a 2001 tracer survey of around 500 initial vocational education graduates (primarily CAP, BTS and BTP) to look at their employment and wage outcomes three years after graduation (as compared to a control group who did not benefit from such programmes, but would have been eligible to). They find that participation in VET increases both the likelihood of employment and wages. Nevertheless, descriptive statistics obtained from Tunisia's *Enquête Nationale sur la Population et l'Emploi* (ENPE) [National Population and Employment Survey] suggest that VET students (CAP, BTS and BTP) have higher unemployment rates than those who have completed just primary and secondary education, similar to those who have a tertiary education degree (see Table 4.7).

**Table 4.7. Unemployment rates by level of education, Tunisia, 2010**

Percentage of the labour force

| Highest qualification achieved | Unemployment rate |
|---|---|
| None | 5% |
| Primary | 9% |
| Secondary | 13% |
| Tertiary | 24% |
| CAP | 21% |
| BTP | 22% |
| BTS | 25% |
| TOTAL | 14% |

*Source*: OECD calculations based on the Enquête Nationale sur la Population et l'Emploi (ENPE) [National Population and Employment Survey].

While wage data in Tunisia are difficult to obtain, OECD calculations based on a recent ILO School-to-Work Transition Survey (STWS, 2013) suggests that those who graduated from vocational education earn about as much as graduates from academic secondary education (approximately TND 370 per month) – but significantly less than graduates from tertiary education (between TND 650 and 700, depending on the length of studies). The relatively poor labour market outcomes of VET graduates are likely to reflect two factors: first, a selection effect with only the weakest students being channelled through VET; and second the poor quality of VET education itself.

## While a range of actions have already been taken to improve the Tunisian VET system, achievements remains mixed

### *Work-based learning, including apprenticeship programmes, plays a role in VET*

Looked at across countries, work-based learning plays an essential role in high quality vocational programmes. It can take different forms, ranging from short periods of job-shadowing for school students to full apprenticeships (OECD, 2010a). It is a powerful tool for developing both hard and soft skills, for transitioning students into employment, engaging employers and linking the mix of provision to employer needs. In Tunisia apprenticeship and *alternance* [a combination of school-based and work-based modules leading to qualifications which is offered by the Ministry of Vocational Training and Employment], have had a legislative basis since the late 1950s. At the same time there have been notable efforts to formalise informal apprenticeship arrangements, to make them lead to recognised qualifications (Sultana and Watts, 2007; Chelbi and Ficatier, 2010).

Work-based learning is used in programmes under the Agence Tunisienne de Formation Professionel, which operates under the auspicies of the Ministry of Vocational Training and Employment. The apprenticeship programmes require that one day a week is spent in a training centre and the remaining days in the workplace. These programmes represent around 11% of all vocational training places for young people. In addition, *programmes d'alternance* [school and work-based programmes], which are offered from CAP to BTS level, represent around 75% of vocational education participants (Sweet, 2013). In 2011, more than nine out of ten pupils under ATFP had benefited from some type of placement with employers (Ministry of Vocational Training and Employment, 2012).

In principle, at least, work placements are linked to quality assurance mechanisms (a trainer from the training centres is supposed to supervise the student in the workplace, and a logbook allows the monitoring of the students' tasks during the placement). *Licences co-construites* [co-designed bachelors], are offered in universities, which are designed with employers, and include substantial periods spent in the company (but they are quite small in numbers). In practice, however, there are serious concerns about the quality of preparation of trainers within companies (Ministry of Vocational Training and Employment, 2012). In addition, a recent Survey carried out by the ILO shows that while young Tunisians attach value to work-based learning, apprenticeship is still partially implemented, with about one out of four youth declaring that an apprenticeship with an employer would have been useful for them to find a job (see Figure 4.6).

**Figure 4.6. Education and training that would be most useful in finding work (self-reported opinion)**

Percentage of non-working youth available to work previous week, by gender

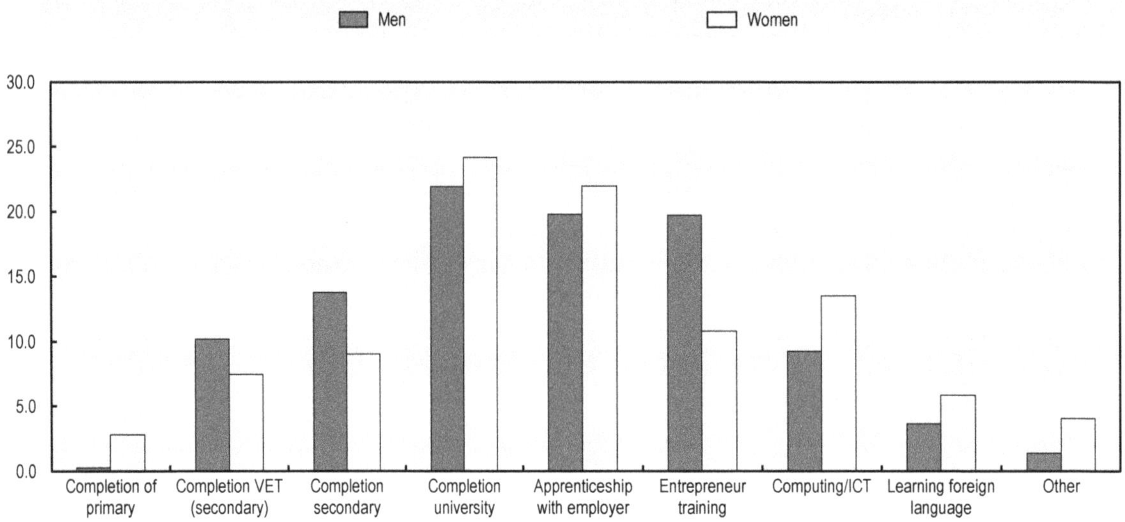


*Source*: OECD analysis of the ILO's School-to-Work Transition Survey (SWTS) for Tunisia (2013).

Evidence from a number of countries suggests that making work-based learning a mandatory element of vocational programmes is feasible and has multiple benefits for both students and employers (see Box 4.4). In Tunisia, vocationally-oriented programmes (*licences appliquées* [professional bachelors]) at universities are not subject to any formal requirements for work-based learning, and while the latter is commonly offered in some fields, it is generally taken up voluntarily by students. Work-based learning opportunities seem to be absent in *collèges techniques* [technical schools] under the Ministry of Education. Taken together, this evidence suggests that there remains considerable scope for strengthening work-based learning in Tunisia. To this end, the Tunisian Government should make work-based learning a substantial part of *licences appliquées*, as is already the case in programmes under the ATFP, and some type of work experience should also be introduced into the *collèges techniques* curriculum (if these are not merged into the general *collèges*, as recommended later on).

**Box 4.4. The principle of mandatory work-based learning**

Many institutions tend to operate in silos, and education and training institutions are no exception. Reaching out to employers means breaking out of these silos. It also means overcoming a natural resistance on the part of classroom teachers to the idea that students can learn much in the workplace that they cannot learn so readily in the classroom. So institutions naturally need strong incentives to establish partnerships with employers to facilitate an effective workplace learning element in programmes. Employers also need incentives. Sometimes employers believe (often wrongly) that offering work placements is an unnecessary cost, that they can reasonably avoid, while still benefiting by recruiting from the graduates of a vocational programme.

Against this background, making work placements mandatory can operate as a game-changer. It means that programmes will only be funded when training institutions develop and maintain the active partnerships that support work placements. Under these conditions training providers will see employer partnerships as central to their mission, while employers will see that, unless they are willing to offer work placements, the programme from which they draw their recruits may close or contract, and the government funding shift to another sector, or another region. Many currently reluctant employers will choose to offer work placements under these conditions, assuming that they value the training programmes.

Potentially it also means that some programmes that are of so little interest to employers that they will not offer placements may have to consider reducing training places, or even close. This gives employers a desirable influence over the mix of training provision, allied with the principle that the greatest influence goes to those employers that are prepared to contribute most, by way of the offer of work placements. A number of countries, such as Spain, Romania and Denmark, and more recently Sweden, have effectively transitioned their post-secondary VET systems to ones involving mandatory workplace training. In Spain, in both upper secondary and post-secondary programmes, workplace training normally takes place through a compulsory three-month module at the end of the programmes. In Sweden, all two-year higher (post-secondary) vocational programmes have a considerable amount of work-based learning (at least 25% of total programme hours), usually in several blocks. This mandatory work-based component of all programmes allows good co-operation between education providers and employers. The work-based components are designed so that students apply concepts learned in the study programme at the workplace, with specific attention given to the links between theory and practice. The education provider is responsible for quality assurance of the selected workplace programme and many education providers choose to appoint a placement co-ordinator to facilitate the process. In Denmark, work placement has been mandatory in all programmes since August 2009, to ensure that all programmes are professionally oriented and of relevance for the employers and thus the students. All "academy" post-secondary two-year programmes include three months of workplace training and all "professional bachelors" programmes, include at least six months workplace training.

*Source*: OECD (2014), *Skills beyond School: Synthesis Report*, OECD Reviews of Vocational Education and Training, OECD Publishing, Paris, http://dx.doi.org/10.1787/9789264214682-en.

## *Tunisia's post-secondary VET[4] sector is comparatively large by the standards of middle income countries*

In Tunisia, more than one in two university students study in *licences appliquées* [professional bachelor] as opposed to the more academic *licences fondamentales* [academic bachelor] (see Table 4.8). At least formally, these programmes present the advantage that they are geared towards the labour market, even though there remain doubts about the real vocational orientation of the *licences appliquées*. Nevertheless, assessed in terms of number of students, Tunisia appears to have a fairly well-developed post-secondary VET sector, unlike many other middle income countries (British Council, 2013). Particularly in Africa, for example, the focus in recent decades has been more on access and participation in primary and secondary education, focusing on academic programmes, rather than on the development of vocational tracks, especially at the post-secondary level.[5] Egypt and South Africa, both reviewed in the OECD *Skills beyond School* project, have more limited short-cycle professional participation than Tunisia, with university sectors and bachelor's degrees appearing to dominate provision. For these countries the OECD has recommended strategic expansion of the sector (OECD, 2014a).

**Table 4.8. Post-secondary education in Tunisia, 2011**

Student of numbers

| Programme | Students in post secondary education, 2011 | of which % of VET students | of which % of general education students |
|---|---|---|---|
| Students in post-secondary VET (qualifications: BTS, professional bachelor) | 155 751 | 100% | 0% |
| Students in academic post-secondary education (qualification: academic bachelor) | 88 675 | 0% | 100% |
| Total students in post-secondary education | 244 426 | 64% | 36% |

*Source*: Ministry of Vocational Training and Employment (2011), "La formation professionnelle en chiffre: Décembre 2011", Observatoire National de l'Emploi et des Qualifications, www.mfpe.gov.tn/fileadmin/user_upload/PDF/statistique/publication/statistiques_de_la_formation_professionnelle_2011.pdf; Ministry of Education (2013), "Statistiques scolaires: Année scolaire 2011/12", Direction Générale des Études de la Planification et des Systèmes d'Information.

Post-secondary vocational programmes often play an important role in OECD country skills systems. In the United States, around 12% of the labour force has a post-secondary "certificate" as their highest qualification, and certificate graduation rates are burgeoning – tripling in recent years; a further 10% have associate degrees. In France, in 2010-11 almost 360 000 students were enrolled in two-year professional programmes (*Brevet de technicien supérieur* and *Diplôme universitaire de technologie*), representing one-third of the students entering post-secondary education (OECD, 2014a). In Colombia, in 2010, enrolments in the technological and professional programmes represented one-third of all undergraduate enrolments (OECD/International Bank for Reconstruction and Development/World Bank, 2013).

### *Recent steps to implement a national qualifications framework*

Many OECD and non-OECD countries are currently implementing qualification frameworks, or have done so recently. In Tunisia, the recent move to implement a new national qualifications framework (*Classification Nationale des Qualifications* – CNQ, 2009), was intended to promote lifelong learning, help employers better understand qualifications, and make explicit how qualifications relate to each other. It involves seven qualifications levels (Ministry of Vocational Training and Employment, 2012). The new frameworks has the potential to support access to the vocational education and training systems, by making the value of different qualifications more clearly recognisable by students, employers and other stakeholders. International experience suggests that, when underpinned by a strong methodology for allocating qualifications to levels, supported by key stakeholders, and backed by complementary measures to unify the VET system and improve transitions, national qualifications frameworks can facilitate lifelong learning, and improve access to higher level education (OECD, 2010a). Box 4.5 briefly reviews the examples of such frameworks in Belgium (Flanders) and in South Africa.

**Box 4.5. Qualifications frameworks**

In **Belgium (Flanders)**, the development of a qualifications framework since 2009 aims to make qualifications more transparent and comparable. The intention of the framework is to clarify which programmes lead to the same qualification level and to the same job, making qualifications equivalent regardless of where the students have been taught – in a centre for adult education, a university college, or a competence centre. It will also give more visibility to the different qualifications for both students and employers. In the case of new qualifications, creating a new professional qualification starts with an assessment of how the qualification will translate into an education programme and identifies providers best suited to deliver the programme. The fact that the qualifications are defined by competences should help to support recognition of prior learning.

**South Africa** implemented a national qualification framework in 1995. It is intended to: i) create an integrated national framework for learning achievements; ii) facilitate access to mobility and progression within education, training and career paths; iii) enhance the quality of education and training; and iv) accelerate the redress of past unfair discrimination.

Recent reforms in the framework aimed to simplify it and limit the proliferation of qualifications. It identifies ten levels of learning achievement, and includes three sub-frameworks covering: i) General and Further Education and Training Qualifications; ii) Higher Education Qualifications; and iii) Trades and Occupations Qualifications. It is expected that these reforms should help to improve articulation, and to support more effective career guidance and recognition of prior learning, while also improving co-ordination across the different institutions and shareholders involved in the educational system.

*Source*: OECD (2014), *Skills beyond School: Synthesis Report*, OECD Reviews of Vocational Education and Training, OECD Publishing, Paris, http://dx.doi.org/10.1787/9789264214682-en.

## *Efforts are made to develop Recognition of Prior Learning (RPL)*

In most countries the requirement for getting a particular qualification is to undergo a defined programme of study within a given institution. However, this approach has become a source of concerns for many countries, which increasingly question its rigidity. Increasingly, therefore, countries are implementing smoother learning recognition approaches, which enable job seekers to put a stronger emphasise on the actual work experience and training of job candidates, rather than the formal learning routes followed and outcomes, In this light, Box 4.6 presents the two interesting experiences being pursued by the United Sates and Iceland.

In Tunisia, there are efforts to promote RPL within the framework of the National qualifications framework – a process of certifying pre-existing skills and knowledge, to make skills visible to other actors, such as employers and education and training institutions. A pilot was launched in 2005-07 in the fashion and auto-mechanic sectors (but with no formal evaluation of the results) (Ministry of Vocational Training and Employment, 2012).

Systematic RPL involves a number of practical advantages. Through course exemptions it can reduce the direct and opportunity costs of formal learning, while at the same time, improving labour market outcomes reflecting, for example, the possibility to carry out hiring strategies that are better informed and more focussed on the actual skills of job candidates. Furthermore, it supports social inclusiveness, by allowing adults with limited formal education to get recognition for the competences acquired while working, thereby helping them to advance their careers. Finally, it also works as a tool to reward learning and the skills, both acquired in informal settings. Unfortunately, examples from other countries show that educational institutions and employers sometimes have inadequate incentives to take advantage of this approach.

**Box 4.6. Recognition of Prior Learning (RPL) in the United States and Iceland**

In the **United States**, RPL has historical roots in the experience of World War II veterans who were granted college credits in recognition of their military training. Half of all colleges and universities in the United States have been estimated to offer RPL in some form, though it may not always be marketed effectively. A recent review of state policies highlighted the role played by state-level initiatives in building interest in RPL. In Tennessee the funding formula was altered so as to give colleges greater incentives to develop their use of RPL and therefore improve completion rates.

In **Iceland**, recent legislation contains provisions on individual entitlement to RPL at upper secondary level. It is seen as a means of combating dropout. RPL is aimed at people with poor formal education, allowing those who wish to return to upper secondary school to shorten the length of the required programme. The 12 lifelong learning centres around the country and the two centres for certified trades co-operate in pursuing RPL projects. On average a participant going through a validation process within the certified trades ends up with 28 units of credit recognised through RPL (the carpentry programme for example involves 100 units in total). Over the period 2007-09, 492 individuals had their competences recognised in this way, the majority within the certified trades.

*Source*: OECD (2014), *Skills beyond School: Synthesis Report*, OECD Reviews of Vocational Education and Training, OECD Publishing, Paris, http://dx.doi.org/10.1787/9789264214682-en.

### *The "Chèques de formation" are a novel way to expand provision and promote innovation in delivery*

In Tunisia, the "*chèques de formation*" represents an innovative way to expand provision through the private sector, in fields where labour market demand is relatively high. The use of these vouchers is linked to the accreditation of programmes within private centres, which reduces the risk of low quality. Students studying in public centres in "priority" fields receive a monthly allowance of TND 60. This is an innovative way to provide delivery, while at the same time allowing to better matching labour market needs.

This echoes the different approaches being adopted across countries to increase efficiency in training delivery, sometimes using market mechanisms, or exploiting an existing private market in training provision. Very often, private providers (both for- and not-for-profit) occupy a particular niche in provision. Sometimes they fill a gap in public provision – for example, in the Netherlands, the public sector faces barriers in delivering part-time programmes to adults, and as a result these are mostly offered through private providers. In Austria, Germany and Switzerland, private providers offer many preparatory courses leading to professional examinations, although evaluation of outcomes is critical in order to ensure the effectiveness of programmes (OECD, 2014a).

In Tunisia, evaluations still encompass a very limited set of employment outcomes, without quantifying the general effectiveness of service provision, which raises concerns about the quality of some of the private providers. In England, for example, the government inspection body, *Ofsted*, operates very widely, inspecting provision funded by public resources regardless of whether it is delivered by a private or a public training provider or indeed an employer (Musset and Field, 2013). This arguably allows for a better understanding of provisions that work and why they work better.

## Measures dealing with structural challenges must be taken

There is a clear hierarchy in the different tracks of education in Tunisia, with the prevailing logic of selection, manifested in rigid tracking in secondary education and high-stakes examinations, contributing to the low status of VET. Collectively this state of affairs sends a message that VET should only cater for a minority of students who have been unsuccessful academically, potentially reducing the take up of VET. It also perpetuates the widespread preference for academic programmes, which in turn discourages the expansion of the vocational sector at the upper secondary level despite the potential for this stream of the system to enhance employability. For instance, the quality of general education in Tunisia has been considered as relatively low compared to other middle income countries. This is shown by Tunisia's PISA scores (Figure 4.3).

In order to address this situation, in November 2013, the Ministry of Vocational Training and Employment in co-operation with various stakeholders put forward a set of guidelines and an action plan for a national reform of the vocational education and training system (Ministry of Vocational Training and Employment, 2013). The proposed reform is based on the four following objectives: i) The national VET system of vocational training should be well integrated into the national system of human resource development; ii) The effectiveness and efficiency of the training process should be guaranteed; iii) A national governance system of VET should be established, which responds to the aspirations of individuals, businesses, society, and the different regions; and iv) A system of funding of vocational training should be developed that facilitates lifelong learning and meets the needs of individuals, companies, and the different regions (Ministry of Vocational Training and Employment, 2013). While setting these objectives is a valuable first step the most demanding challenge will lie in implementation.

### *Addressing the problem of early tracking*

In Tunisia students get tracked between "*collèges techniques*" and general lower secondary schools at age 12 while the median age of first formal selection is 15 years old in OECD countries (OECD, 2012). International evidence shows that early tracking exacerbates differences in learning between students, and that it can have negative consequences for subsequent education and labour market outcomes. Student outcomes can also be improved by making the composition of peer groups less homogeneous to allow lower ability students to benefit from the interactions with better performing students. Indeed, data from PISA confirm that countries characterised by a more "grouped" education system – where students are placed between different types of schools and/or into different tracks within schools, based on individual performances – end up perpetuating inequality of performance between students, without significant gains in terms of overall performance (Hanushek and Woessmann, 2006). Countries with early tracking have performed less well on average in PISA than those with more comprehensive education systems.

Moving from a lower to a higher track approach is always difficult and there is no one-fits-all approach. Strategies depend upon the educational institutional setting and the governance capacity of the country. In the context of Tunisia, there seems to be a potential for measures aimed to integrate the lower secondary technical track into the general lower secondary education track. Linked to an active expansion of VET system at the upper secondary level, this would give both impetus and clarity to VET. There are relatively few students in *collèges techniques* in Tunisia, which suggests that a merger would cause little disruption. There appears to be a potential for creating a dialogue around this reform option in Tunisia (NA, 2012).

### *Towards a strategic vision to strengthen career guidance*

In turn, the low status of the VET system in Tunisia, acts as a brake to the further expansion of the upper secondary VET sector, which is small by international standards. Around 10% of the total number of upper secondary students is enrolled in VET programmes in Tunisia, which compares with an average for the OECD countries of close to 50% (see Figure 4.7). Indeed, academic routes continue to be perceived as leading to better labour market outcomes in Tunisia, compared to VET programmes. A recent study by the ONEQ and the ILO (2014) shows that only 10% of unemployed men and 5% of unemployed women find vocational education and training useful to find a job in Tunisia. Conversely, 23% of unemployed men and 28% of unemployed women believe that higher education is useful to find a job. In part, this hierarchy reflects the widespread preference for public sector jobs in Tunisia, for which the entry requirement is typically an academic university qualification (AfDB, 2012; World Bank, 2013; Yaagoubi et al., 2013).

**Figure 4.7. Enrolment in upper secondary education by programme orientation, 2011**

Percentage of students enrolled in general or vocational education and training programmes

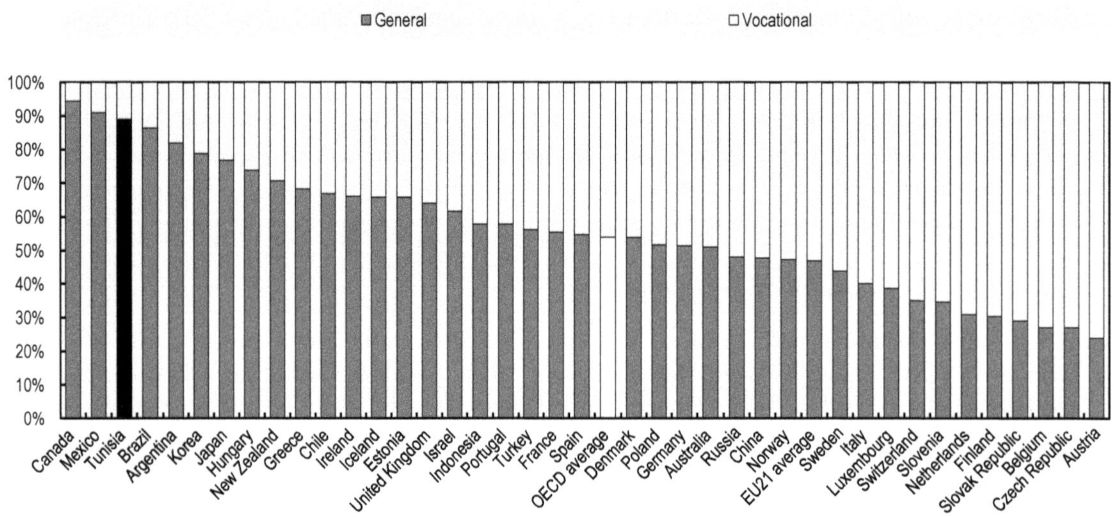


*Source*: OECD (2013), *Education at a Glance 2013: OECD Indicators*, Indicator C1, Table C1.3 "Upper secondary and post-secondary non-tertiary enrolment patterns (2011)", OECD Publishing, Paris, http://dx.doi.org/10.1787/eag-2013-en; for Argentina, China, Indonesia, Saudi Arabia and South Africa: UNESCO (2014), Institute for Statistics World Education Indicators Programme, database consulted on May 20th 2014; Ministry of Vocational Training and Employment (2011), "La formation professionnelle en chiffre: Décembre 2011", Observatoire National de l'Emploi et des Qualifications, www.mfpe.gov.tn/fileadmin/user_upload/PDF/statistique/publication/statistiques_de_la_formation_professionnelle_2011.pdf; Ministry of Education (2013), "Statistiques scolaires: Année scolaire 2011/12", Direction Générale des Études de la Planification et des Systèmes d'Information.

One explanation of the small size of the sector at the upper secondary level is the lack of adequate career guidance arrangements, resulting in few students being aware of the VET options available. The problem of poor career guidance outcomes for young Tunisian is not new. The first major reform of Tunisia's education system in 1958 already encompassed an emphasis on guidance, which was expected to serve as a tool in human resource planning. The education reform of 2002 highlighted the role of guidance even further by stating that "to be able to choose consciously his or her educational or vocational course, a student has the right to receive wide and complete information on any matters related to school or university education". More recently, the Ministry of Education has created a body of school and university advisers responsible for "informing and advising students and their families concerning the education system, universities and vocational opportunities in different sectors". In order to be part of this body, experienced teachers have received specialised training. Also the PEFESE programme has stressed the importance to urgently strengthen the role of career guidance, including through organising events both at the national and regional level devoted to the dissemination of information regarding VET programmes. Despite these repeated efforts, however, career guidance continues to be very poorly integrated in the Tunisian school system, leading to massive inflows of ill-informed students into universities (UTICA, 2012).

Although many other factors are likely to be behind the high dropout rate from VET programmes, the weakness of guidance arrangements and lack of information about these programmes likely play an important role in Tunisia (Table 4.9). Among those having recently dropped-out from a VET programme in Tunisia, 62% have declared that the programme from which they have subsequently dropped out was chosen following a personal decision, in the absence of counselling (Ministry of Vocational Training and Employment, 2011b). Indeed, evidence for the OECD countries shows that a wrong career choice is an important factor in explaining the disengagement of students from their vocational training programme (OECD, 2012). This is the important reason explaining why a country such as Denmark has decided to reinforce the guidance system as a ways to tackle high dropout rates in both upper-secondary and post-secondary education. Education institutions must, by law, refer students that wish to drop out or change programmes to regional guidance centres. Municipalities are legally obliged to make contact with, and offer guidance to, young people that are not working and not enrolled in education at least twice a year up to the age of 19; some municipalities extend the system beyond this (Field et al., 2012).

**Table 4.9. Dropout rates in vocational education and training (VET)**

| | Students enrolled (2007) | | | | Drop-out rates | | | |
|---|---|---|---|---|---|---|---|---|
| | CAP | BTP | BTS | total | CAP | BTP | BTS | Total |
| Tunisian Agency for Vocational Training | 14 011 | 13 393 | 4 217 | 31 621 | 32.3% | 33.1% | 33.7% | 33.4% |
| Extension and Agricultural Training Agency | 654 | 649 | | 1 303 | 27.5% | 5.4% | | 16.5% |
| Ministry of National Defence | 198 | 471 | | 669 | 41.4% | 14.2% | | 22.3% |
| Tunisian National Tourism Office | 440 | 889 | 240 | 1 569 | 15.5% | 22.2% | 45.0% | 23.8% |
| Ministry of Public Health | | 2 126 | | 2 126 | | 1.6% | | 1.6% |

*Source*: Ministry of Vocational Training and Employment (2011), "Le décrochage de la formation professionnelle en Tunisie: raisons et parcours professionnels", Observatoire National de l'Emploi et des Qualifications.

Still, the work done at the OECD for the series *Learning for Jobs* (OECD, 2010a) suggests that an effective career guidance service can be difficult to implement. While service provision is frequently fragmented and under-resourced, it also tends to be dominated by a counselling approach which often suffers a lack of adequate knowledge of labour market opportunities. Sometimes, it even has an academic bias, given that the service remains often delivered by academically trained teachers. As discussed in Box 4.7 a systemic approach is needed to develop a well performing career guidance service.

**Box 4.7. Career guidance and advisors in Scotland**

Scotland has a well-developed and comprehensive system of career guidance, offered in various institutions such as schools, colleges, local authorities and Job Centres. Multiple institutions involved in career guidance and different channels of provision allow the system to reach out to different groups, including young people seeking entry to further and higher education, and unemployed persons.

Contrary to other OECD countries where there is no specific profession of career advisors (career guidance being provided by school teachers and psychologists), Scotland recognises that "career guidance is a distinct, defined and specialist profession which demands a unique set of core skills and expects all career guidance practitioners to be professionally qualified". The Scottish approach to career management involves helping individuals to understand their strengths, the objectives that they wish to set for themselves and the networks and resources that will help them reach these objectives. The aim is therefore to help individuals to plan their career independently by equipping them with relevant tools and knowledge. Career services also include support from Career Coaches who engage with young people through talks, group sessions and individual coaching. Young people who need support to make a successful transition into employment receive one-to-one sessions, as does any young person who needs additional advice.

Co-ordination of services can be a challenge in a system involving many providers, but in Scotland Skills Development Scotland acts as the strategic leader, collaborating closely with schools, colleges, local authorities and other bodies and organisations such as employer representatives.

*Source*: Kuczera M. (2013), *A Skills beyond School Commentary on Scotland*, www.oecd.org/edu/skills-beyond-school/ASkillsBeyondSchoolCommentaryOnScotland.pdf.

Access to certain practical information is also essential to accompany students in their career decisions. Career guidance services that are well-informed about labour market returns (in particular wage returns which will be higher in areas of skills shortage) reduce the discrepancies in the supply and demand of workers by field of study. When career guidance services are not available, students tend to rely on informal sources, such as family and friends who may lack reliability and impartiality. Better data can be provided either through one-off surveys of those leaving vocational programmes (see Box 4.8), or by tracking cohorts of individuals through vocational programmes into employment (Sedrine, 2006).

**Box 4.8. Destinations surveys**

In Australia the Student Outcomes Survey is conducted annually among students who completed some vocational training. Conducted by the National Centre for Vocational Education and Research since 1997, it is funded by the Australian Government and provides information on the employment and further study outcomes, the relevance and benefits of training, and student satisfaction. The information collected supports the administration, planning and evaluation of the VET system.

In Ireland, the School Leavers Survey is based on a national sample of school leavers, contacted nine months after leaving school. Face-to-face interviews, used in this survey since its beginning in 1980, have become more difficult as a result of declining response rates and high costs. Therefore the 2007 School Leavers Survey used a mix of approaches. The selected individuals were asked to complete an online questionnaire and could also ask for a paper copy. Participants were offered an incentive to complete the questionnaire, with their names being entered in a draw for prizes. Those who were particularly difficult to reach (e.g. early school leavers) were followed up by telephone initially and then face to face.

*Source*: OECD (2010), *Learning for Jobs*, OECD Reviews of Vocational Education and Training, OECD Publishing, Paris, http://dx.doi.org/10.1787/9789264087460-en.

### *Creating pathways between vocational and academic tracks*

Weak articulation arrangements, which result in barriers between vocational and academic programmes, further hinder the attractiveness of VET in Tunisia, although measures have been introduced recently to create such pathways. As mentioned above, the 2008 reform sets formal pathways at all three levels (see Figure 4.1). While a welcome development, the pathways are not yet operational, which in parts reflects the fragmentation of the Tunisian governance system, particularly the split of responsibilities between ministries (see below the section on governance).

The vocational baccalaureate, introduced in the 2008 law, is a fundamental pillar of access to higher education for VET graduates as it would allow BTP holders to take the exam for the professional baccalaureate to gain access to higher education, but has not yet been implemented (Ministry of Vocational Training and Employment, 2012; Chelbi and Ficatier, 2010). In practice, it is not possible for upper secondary VET graduates to gain access to universities. There are also obstacles for students when transitioning from BTS to university.

## There remains large scope for improving the mix of provision to meet employers' needs

With vocational provision being largely dominated by supply and capacity factors, alongside student preferences which largely rest on individual decisions taken without career guidance, unsurprisingly the room for improving the VET system in such a way to meet the labour market needs is large in Tunisia. The engagement of social partners – both employers and unions – is essential to this end. There is also the possibility to orient the engagement of social partners in the context of the Tunisian transition to a green economy. The VET system needs to work with employers and unions in the light of common strategies for change, for example with regards to greening tourism, organic agriculture, or construction. Still, employers and graduates are often ill-informed about what programmes the VET system is actually able to. Weaknesses in governance and fragmentation in the system adds to the challenge. These factors, combined with the preference for academic routes and public sector jobs, further erode the visibility of vocational education and its utilisation.

Several studies have highlighted a growing disparity in employment opportunities based on different education and training qualifications at the post-secondary level, including VET options. For example, the study of the Ministry of Employment and Professional Insertion of Youth and the World Bank (2009) based on longitudinal data (tracer study from the 2004 cohort) shows the existence of imbalances between supply and demand for skills at the post-secondary level. Some qualifications and fields of studies are characterised by long duration unemployment and withdrawal from activities. They find that unemployment rates are particularly high among BTS graduates of agriculture, commerce and administration (Ministry of Employment and Professional Insertion of Youth and the World Bank, 2009).

This evidence points to a discrepancy between the mix of specialties taught and market needs in BTS programmes,[6] and particularly the inadequacy of the acquired training in relation to certain job profiles. Indeed, Tunisia's employers have frequently complained about their very limited capacity to help shaping the content programmes (Chelbi and Ficatier, 2010). While sporadically employers work with the ministries in charge of VET, there are no systematic consultation mechanisms. For example, some sectoral branches are quite active in the skills system (electricity and electronics, tourism, construction, agriculture and fishery) but elsewhere engagement is weak (UTICA, 2012). Also at the local level, VET institutions have weak connections with companies, which is seen as an important factor behind the high number of unfilled training places in many education and training facilities. Both UTICA and CONNECT, the employers' organisations, should be more systematically involved in the content of new programmes and their updating, to make the system more responsive. The technical clusters in Egypt provide an interesting example to help these reflections (see Box 4.9).

**Box 4.9. The Integrated Technical Education Cluster Initiative in Egypt**

In Egypt, the importance of a comprehensive VET offer for students and employers is well-recognised. The Integrated Technical Education Cluster Initiative, ITEC, represents a valuable effort to provide VET of high quality, clearly articulated across different educational levels and designed to be more responsive to employers' skills needs. The key point of this cluster model is to ensure that resources are integrated to achieve the highest level of utilisation and set up a clear progression path to higher technical skills for students – that must be also transparent and understandable to employers. These clusters have four components: a technical secondary school; a technical institute; an advanced technical institute; and a vocational training centre. Crucially, the curricula and programme design of these clusters at all levels is meant to be inspired by local labour market needs. The first cluster has been established in Cairo (Ameeria).

*Source*: Alvarez-Galván, J. (2014), A *Skills beyond School Review of Egypt*, OECD Reviews of Vocational Education and Training, OECD Publishing, Paris, http://dx.doi.org/10.1787/9789264209626-en.

One key finding of the *OECD Learning for Jobs* work is that the challenge of ensuring that vocational education and training systems respond effectively to the needs of the labour market is common to all countries. Given that the benefits of VET are realised both by students and employers, it is important to shape the VET system in such a way to reflect both employer demand and student preferences. Each country thus has to exert a careful balancing act between such preferences, which do not necessarily coincide. Students' choices, for example, are often driven by the presumption to acquire a status, rather than a set of skills which are attractive to the labour market.

In addition, the optimal balance will depend upon who pays: the mix of government, student and employer contributions. For example if most of the costs fall on students – as in some forms of post-secondary training in some countries – then it is reasonable to expect that student choice will dominate the mix of provision. But in Tunisia, the cost of providing VET at upper secondary level mainly falls on the government rather than employers. One very constructive way for employers to make more of a contribution to training, and at the same time obtain many benefits for themselves, might be through the provision of workplace training and experience, which they already do quite successfully in the programmes under the ATFP, but that could be replicated in the rest of the system, in particular in the *licences appliquées* (professional bachelors) in universities. In this context, Box 4.10 provides some interesting examples of mechanisms to influence the mix of provision, drawing from the experience of OECD countries.

**Box 4.10. Mechanisms for balancing students preferences and employers needs**

Some specific mechanisms can help to balance student preferences and employers' needs, such as:

- Linking programmes and places to employers' willingness to provide workplace learning.
- Assessing existing shortages and future skill needs through consultations with employers and unions and/or through systematic forecasts or assessments.
- Providing effective career guidance that includes good information about labour market prospects.
- Using financial incentives to encourage students to train in specific areas, to boost the amount of workplace learning offered, or to expand off-the job training opportunities to address demand.
- Financial incentives or competition between providers can stimulate a quick response although obtaining new equipment and qualified staff may be expensive and take time.

*Source*: OECD (2010), *Learning for Jobs*, OECD Reviews of Vocational Education and Training, OECD Publishing, Paris, http://dx.doi.org/10.1787/9789264087460-en.

## Reforms should be supported by significant measures to improve the governance of the VET system

Effective governance of VET provisions is also indispensable. It can generate significant gains, though, for example, ensuring that service provisions remains adaptable and fully responsive to local needs, which is essential to reduce waste in equipment purchases, as well as the recruitment of VET teachers with the right competences. However, achieving these outcomes in Tunisia requires a certain number of adjustments, across a range of institutional levels, as, for example, between national and local authorities and across ministries of the central administration. A well-defined governance structure will also involve the consultation with the social partners, which is essential to ensure that schools ultimately chose to specialise in the most promising fields, instead of every school providing a comprehensive range of programmes. Finally, to be fully effective VET provisions and outcomes need to be properly evaluated.

### *While the responsibilities for VET are highly centralised across level of governments they remain fragmented across ministries*

One important issue for concerns is that in Tunisia the governance of the VET system is much centralised (design of the programme, curriculum development, and implementation), which reduces the involvement of the local authorities in the management and administration of the system (ETF and MFPE, 2014). At present, the limited responsibilities of the regions are essentially confined to data collection and representative functions of the central ministries. Also the opportunities for collaborations with the social partners at the local level are limited in Tunisia (Ministry of Vocational Training and Employment, 2012).

Recent reforms have aimed at tackling these challenges and promoting co-ordination between ministries, regions and VET centres. Devolution of some of responsibilities from ANETI and ATFP to regional branches is also under consideration. The new VET strategy of the government (*Plan d'orientation 2014-2018*), aims to provide VET centres with greater autonomy and improved responsiveness to changing needs. This would be particularly welcome from the perspective of the move towards green growth, which the government sees as a priority (cf. Chapter 5).

At the level of the central administration, while the Tunisian VET system is primarily administered by the Ministry of Vocational Training and Employment (Tunisian Republic, 2008, p. 683; OECD, 2013b, p. 143), some of these powers are shared with the Ministry of Education (*Ministère de l'Education)* as well as the Ministry of Higher Education and Scientific Research *(Ministère de l'Enseignement Supérieur et de la Recherche Scientifique*), which acts as a source of fragmentation. For, example, the Ministry for Higher Education has responsibilities for the VET programmes offered in universities (*licences appliquées*) and the Ministry for Education is responsible for the *collèges techniques* [technical schools].

Course design and instructor training are provided by the *Centre National de Formation des Formateurs et d'Ingenierie de Formation,* CENAFFIF, [the National Centre for Training of Trainers and Training Course Design]. In the sphere of agriculture, the *Institut national pédagogique et de formation continue agricole,* INOFCA [National Institute for Agricultural Education and Continuing Training] performs that role in collaboration with CENAFFIF. Continuing training initiated by businesses and individuals is a matter for the *Centre National de la Formation Continue de la Promotion Professionnelle,* CNFCPP [the

National Centre for Continuing Training and Career Development], whose task is to administer funding programmes and instruments (Chahed, 2013).

The *Agence Tunisienne de Formation Professionnelle*, ATFP [the Tunisian Agency for Vocational Training] under the auspices of the Ministry of Vocational Training and Employment was established in 1993 to provide and evaluate initial training for young people and adults. It supervises 136 of the 214 public vocational training centres (Ministry of Vocational Training and Employment, 2011a). In 2011, of all 98 000 VET students in the public VET sector, the majority (95%) pursued their vocational training in these 136 training centres (Ministry of Vocational Training and Employment, 2011a). While the public vocational training centres under the ATFP focus on industrial activities, since September 2012, there have been four priority sectors, namely building and construction, general engineering and steel construction, electricity and electronics, and tourism and hotel business (Chahed, 2013).

Specific vocational programmes falling under the jurisdiction of ministries other than the Ministry of Vocational Training and Employment are offered in tourism by eight centres of the *Office National du Tourisme Tunisien,* ONTT [Tunisian National Tourism Office] under the authority of the National Office of Tunisian Tourism; in agriculture and water resources by 39 centres managed by the *Agence de la Vulgarisation et de la Formation Agricole*, AVFA [the Agricultural Extension and Training Centre] under the Ministry of Agriculture; in health by 19 centres under the authority of the Ministry of Health; and in defence industries by 12 centres which are operated by the Ministry of Defence (Chahed, 2013; Ministry of Vocational Training and Employment, 2011a). In 2011, overall these vocational programmes were offered at 78 of the 214 public vocational training centres (Ministry of Vocational Training and Employment, 2011a).

A more federated governance structure could be envisaged, in this context, consistent with the analysis being carried out by the Tunisian Government with the funding of the European Commission [*PEFESE, Programme d'Appui à l'Education, la Formation Professionnelle, l'Enseignement supérieur en Lien avec l'Employabilité des Jeunes Diplômés*]. This is also the aim of the High Council for Human Resources Development (*Conseil Supérieur pour le Développement des Ressources Humaines*), which is leading the policy reflection about how to implement in practice the spirit of the works under the PEFESE programme (Sawy et al., 2012; Ministry of Vocational Training and Employment, 2012).

### *Strong co-ordination mechanisms with key stakeholders*

The involvement of the social partners is also important in order to ensure the creation of a VET system that is more responsive to labour market needs. In this regards, the international experience suggests that arrangements for employer engagement might range from advisory boards to decision-making bodies. However, whatever role employers might play, their contribution must be meaningful and significant to the system. If they participate in advisory groups, the information provided by employers should truly reflect their workforce skills needs; if they participate in decision-making bodies, these bodies must have a real impact on VET. The connection between employers and VET is fundamental to the success of this system. Box 4.11 provides some examples of institutional arrangements.

### Box 4.11. Bodies for co-ordination: National approaches

In **Switzerland**, the involvement of professional organisations (trade and employer organisations and trade unions) in VET policy making is required by law. Professional organisations have the leading role in the content and examination process of both secondary and post-secondary programmes. Professional organisations draft core curricula for professional college programmes, which are then approved by the Swiss federal authorities. National examinations leading to a federal diploma are also led by professional organisations that ensure that diplomas are relevant to the needs of the profession and the labour market. Professional organisations draft examination rules, which cover admission requirements, occupational profiles, the knowledge and skills to be acquired, qualification procedures and the legally protected title. They also conduct examinations. The role of Swiss authorities (at Confederation level) includes approving examination rules, supervising examinations and issuing federal diplomas.

In **the United Kingdom**, the UK Commission for Employment and Skills (UKCES), launched in April 2008, aims to increase the employer voice in the United Kingdom's VET system and promote investment in skills to drive growth. It is led by commissioners from large and small employers, trade unions and the voluntary sector. It also includes representatives of further and higher education institutions and from Northern Ireland, Scotland and Wales. Its strategic objectives are: to provide world-class labour market intelligence which helps businesses and people make the best choices for them; to work with sectors and business leaders to develop and deliver the best solutions to generate greater employer investment in skills; and to maximise the impact of changed employment and skills policies and employer behaviour to help drive jobs, growth and an internationally competitive skills base. The UKCES also funds and manages the Sector Skills Councils.

In **Denmark**, both the employers' and the employees' sides are very engaged in the planning, design and the steering of the system. The involvement of social partners and other stakeholders is reflected in a special council, with responsibility for the post-secondary level, set up by the Minister for Education in 2008. It advises on the development of post-secondary VET programmes, the mix of provision, work placements, and quality assurance. The social partners may also be represented in the educational advisory committees which the institutions set up within the various disciplines of their programmes. The committees advise on the quality and relevance of existing and future programmes of study (Danish Agency for Higher Education and Educational Support, 2012).

*Source*: OECD (2014), *Skills beyond School: Synthesis Report*, OECD Reviews of Vocational Education and Training, OECD Publishing, Paris, http://dx.doi.org/10.1787/9789264214682-en.

One concrete option could be the creation of a consultation body aimed at engaging the social partners, without damaging local innovation. The frameworks in Denmark and Switzerland build on strong industrial bodies (employers' organisations and trade unions) and a long tradition of engagement in VET. Conversely the employer-led UKCES is a recent creation, but involves high-level representatives of large companies and SMEs, as well as trade unions and other stakeholders.

The body should include relevant ministries, the social partners, representatives from the main institution networks and key providers (including private) and have responsibility for giving policy advice to government, and to ensure more strategic co-ordination of the VET system. It should cover both post-secondary and upper secondary vocational programmes as well as programmes offered for adults by different ministries to ensure co-ordination between the sectors, and a more seamless transition from upper secondary to post-secondary levels for students. Such a body would pursue objectives such as:

- Fostering consolidation when synergies and economies of scale are possible during the integration of *collèges techniques* and general *colleges*.
- Planning the development of more upper secondary VET programmes,

- Improving articulation and transitions from upper secondary VET to post-secondary programmes and from post-secondary VET to academic bachelors programmes.

Although a similar body does not exist in Tunisia, at present, it is contemplated by the new VET strategy (*Plan d'orientation 2014-2018*), which envisages the creation of a national consultation body for human resources development, composed of representatives of public and private education system, social partners and the civil society.

### *Monitoring and evaluation to better inform the decision-making process*

Monitoring is a key to decide which provisions should be expanded, adapted or even ended, and which intervention might work best. Yet important knowledge gaps remain in Tunisia. Data collection, monitoring and evaluation of vocational education and training, in particular, are poorly developed, which undermines the effectiveness of governance. Despite recent efforts to support data collection and evaluation of the VET system, the monitoring and information system remains insufficient. A new approach, *gestion budgétaire par objectif* (GBO) (fiscal management by objectives), has been adopted since 2008 in the field of vocational education and training (ETF and MFPE, 2014. However, the implementation of such approach has been delayed due to poor implementation by concerned institutions.

In this context, only sporadic performance evaluations of the VET system are available, typically carried out by foreign development agencies (for example in 2013 by the *Agence Française de Développement*). For instance, the monitoring of the school-to-work transition of VET graduates in Tunisia is not rigorous and systematic. The latest comprehensive evaluation assessment dates back to 2000, and was conducted in collaboration with the World Bank. In order to address this challenge, the new VET strategy (*Plan d'orientation 2014-2018*) includes the design of an information system aiming to track down VET students in their school-to-work transition and evaluate the performance of the VET system.

In this context, creating a self-evaluation monitoring approach seems desirable if the long-run efficiency of the VET system is to be improved. Useful practical recommendations on this front could probably be built upon the work that OECD and the World Bank (2013) have been carrying out, particularly in light of the important measurement efforts that such a shift will involve (i.e., training, data and greater involvement of the national statistical office). This work presents a conceptual framework for choosing the most appropriate skills indicators to guide skills development policies and to benchmark country performance. Based on this framework an initial set of internationally comparable indicators is proposed. The conceptual framework developed consists of five inter-related domains of indicators, including: *contextual factors,* which drive both the supply of and demand for skills; skill acquisition which covers investments in skills, the stock of human capital and its distribution; *skill requirements*, which measure the demand for skills arising in the labour market; the degree of *matching*, which captures how well skills obtained through education and training correspond to the skills required in the labour market; and *outcomes*, which reflect the impact of skills on economic performance and employment and social outcomes.

It is worth mentioning, however, that first steps towards a self-evaluation monitoring approach have already been undertaken in Tunisia. A self-evaluation monitoring approach was adopted within the framework of the Tunisian co-operation with the European Training Foundation (ETF). Within the Vocational Education and Training system, a project run by the European Union-funded program PEFESE is currently underway.

## A focus on strengthening entrepreneurship support in VET

This section makes a zoom on the specific challenge of improving the provision of entrepreneurship training within the VET system in Tunisia. Given its potential role in job creation, entrepreneurship has become a policy priority in Tunisia in recent years in response to growing labour market challenges. However, as indicated in Chapter 3 of this report, the level of entrepreneurship activities in Tunisia is very low, and this calls for a greater role for the education system in raising awareness about the potential of entrepreneurship as a career opportunity and to provide training and education to support entrepreneurship and business creation.

VET can play a significant role in helping many youth acquire entrepreneurship skills, including green skills, given its proximity to the business sector. Entrepreneurship skills refer to entrepreneurial mind-sets and attitudes, as well as the set of skills that are needed to start and successfully operate a business. These include, for example, planning and goal setting, opportunity seeking, negotiation, growth management, leadership and network building (OECD, 2010b; OECD/Euroepan Commission, 2013). Entrepreneurship skills typically increase the chances of successfully starting and operating a business, but can also be applied more broadly. For example, they can be applied in social entrepreneurship and volunteer activities and employers often value these skills in their employees, suggesting that developing entrepreneurship skills can make an individual more employable.

### *Past experiences*

Policy support for entrepreneurship in the VET system dates back to the beginning of the 1990s. In 1991, the 8th Tunisian economic development plan (1992-96) outlined the creation of regional centres for small businesses located in different regions to encourage young people to carry out their projects. This allowed the government to support regions with their development management and assist with the mobilisation of available resources. This was followed by a number of initiatives for the entrepreneurship development in the vocational training and training system. These initiatives were financially supported and organised by international donors.

Although these past experiences were short-term projects, a number of lasting benefits were realised. First, these projects introduced and promoted entrepreneurship within the VET system, leading to a recognition of the importance and potential for entrepreneurship within the VET context. Second, the entrepreneurship projects were conducted in training centres across all regions of Tunisia. This signalled to the entire VET system that entrepreneurship is an important topic and provided an opportunity to all training centres, including those in outlying regions, to support young entrepreneurs and contribute to the local economy.

These past experiences also provided some key lessons for future entrepreneurship training projects in the Tunisian VET system. First, More efforts are needed to ensure that projects are sustainable so that they can build a critical mass of people with entrepreneurship skills and to have an impact on the local economy. Past training projects were implemented with funding from foreign donors and they ended when foreign funding ceased. Second, there is a need to systemically adapt training projects to local circumstances, while also to learn from other entrepreneurship training experiences. Projects implemented by sponsors did not consider previous training projects, nor the local contexts. Each sponsor came and implemented pre-set programmes without consideration for a long-term strategy. None of these projects performed any monitoring or evaluation activities and it is therefore difficult to learn about the impact of the training projects.

## *Current institutional framework*

Entrepreneurial competences and skills are now core learning outcomes of formal education in Tunisia. As indicated in *Loi No. 2008-09 du 11 février 2008*, students and learners across all levels of education should be able to recognise opportunities and implement projects as an individual or as part of a group. This provides a mandate for supporting entrepreneurship in the VET system.

At the level of national policy making, five ministries have a direct role in promoting and supporting competences for entrepreneurship in the Tunisian VET system. The principle ministry concerned with the promoting entrepreneurship in VET is the Ministry of Vocational Training and Employment (MFPE), which supports entrepreneurship in collaboration with its two agencies – the Tunisian Agency for Vocational Training (ATFP) and the National Centre for Training for Trainers and Training Development (CENAFFIF). The Ministries of Tourism, Agriculture, Health, and Defence also have a role to play in this implementing this mandate as each of these ministries is responsible for several VET centres and collaborates with the MFPE on course content and pedagogy. Moreover, each ministry hase separate business creation and support organisations that work with learners.

## *Outstanding challenges*

Despite these foundations, a few important challenges remain, including: a lack of consensus on the objectives of entrepreneurship training; co-ordination difficulties between the various stakeholders and the lack of strategic vision; and a need to update methods for teaching entrepreneurship.

### *The objectives of entrepreneurship training*

A first challenge is that the different players involved (learners, trainers, training centre management and representatives of local business support providers) do not have a common understanding of the objectives of entrepreneurship promotion. For most, the promotion of self-employment is the ultimate goal. The understanding of entrepreneurship amongst these groups is more that of a process linked to the management of a specific business, rather than an effort structured around the aims of creativity, innovation, business development and growth. The enhancement of capabilities and competences to turn opportunities into commercial actions are not considered to be an objective.

This understanding limits entrepreneurship promotion in VET to a small target group of those interested in starting their own business and excludes it from improving the learners' employability and assisting with their transition to the labour market (Gatti et al., 2013). The MFPE and ATFP, however, do consider these as key objectives for entrepreneurship promotion. This suggests a difference of approaches between , on the one hand, the national ministries and agencies and, on the other hand, the training centres which needs to be addressed to achieve an effective entrepreneurship support system.

Moving forward, the mandate of the Tunisian Agency for Vocational Training (ATFP) with respect to entrepreneurship training should be expanded. This increased role should go beyond the provision of introductory modules on entrepreneurship to support learners in developing entrepreneurial mind-sets and increasing their opportunities to practice entrepreneurial behaviours. This will require support from the National Centre for Training for Trainers and Training Development (CENAFFIF), which provides training for trainers. Both the ATFP and CENAFFIF will require additional resources to carry out a broader mandate.

### *Co-ordination difficulties and the need for strategic vision*

There are also challenges in implementing and co-ordinating entrepreneurship activities in the VET training centres. This requires co-operation at the level of the national ministries but there is currently no mechanism to support this. This implementation and co-ordination challenge becomes even greater when other stakeholders are considered. For example, *centres d'affaires* are business support organisations that are under the Ministry of Industry and are an important actor in local entrepreneurship eco-systems (see Box 4.12 for more information on centres d'affaires and other business start-up support structures). In many OECD countries, these types of organisations work collaboratively with training centres to provide complementary business support to the entrepreneurship training offered by the training centres. However, such formal partnership arrangement would require an agreement between the Ministry of Industry and other ministries that are responsible to for VET training centres.

**Box 4.12. Entrepreneurship and business start-up support structures for VET learners**

***Centres d'affaires*** (i.e. business centres): The business centres are under the responsibility of the Ministry of Industry. Clients are therefore not limited to VET learners. Business centres offer various support services, including formal coaching arrangements and support in accessing financing.

***Espace entreprendre***: These workspaces are under the responsibility of ANETI and are therefore not targeted at VET learners. However, learners, particularly those receiving training through ANETI, use them. These spaces offer a variety of training and coaching and mentoring services.

***Espace tremplins***: These workspaces were started with funding from the French Ministry of Immigration, Integration, National Identity and Solidarity Development. These spaces aim to create an entrepreneurial spirit within the VET centres and the local region. In practical terms, they raise awareness about entrepreneurship and provide some training sessions. These spaces were launched in 2010.

***Pépinières*** (i.e. business incubators): As part of the vocational training strategy and guidance for the five-year period 2009-14, the President of the Republic ordered the creation of business incubators in each vocational training centre to support young people who want to create their own businesses and to support the project leaders in the development stage and to facilitate their integration into the economic fabric. These centres offer training and personalised support for clients. Incubators typically specialise in services that are targeted to the training centre and the needs of the region.

There is therefore a need to develop a national strategy that outlines how entrepreneurship should be supported within the vocational training system. The development of such a mandate should be managed and implemented through a national steering group, chaired by the Ministry of Vocational Training and Employment. The objective of the national strategy should be to clearly define entrepreneurship within the context of vocational training in Tunisia, identify the roles for each actor and outline the short- and long-term objectives.

Improved co-ordination is also needed between training centres and business start-up support structures. International experience suggests that this can be accomplished by ensuring that training centres have partnership with other stakeholders such as business incubators, chambers of commerce, higher education institutions and financial institutions. In Tunisia, many support services exist separately with very few examples of linkages between providers and the training centres (Box 4.12). As a result, learners have a low level of awareness about all of the support that is available to them.

Moreover, closer linkages are needed between VET training centres and the two public banks that are active in lending to small businesses (BFPME and BTS). The linkages could help learners in the VET system access financing for start-up through financial literacy education and training on the requirements to access start-up capital. Personal contacts can facilitate this linkage but a more institutionalised approach is needed to share resources and to build up local entrepreneurship ecosystems.

One interesting example of good practice in the matter of co-ordination is TKNIKA, which is a public agency that oversees 63 technical and vocational training colleges in the Basque region of Spain (see Box 4.13). It is a public agency with the responsibility for co-ordinating entrepreneurship activities in all of training colleges, as well as building relationships with other local, regional and international partners. Moreover, it is responsible for building relationships with universities and integrating new technologies within vocational training colleges.

**Box 4.13. TKNIA in Spain**

TKNIKA was established in 2005 by the Department of Training, Linguistic Policy and Culture of the Basque Government as a public agency to oversee vocational education and training (VET) in the Basque region and its 63 technical and vocational training colleges. TKNIKA operates under the direct supervision of the Deputy Ministry of Vocational Training and Lifelong Learning as the innovation tool for the Basque Vocational Training System.

TKNIKA promotes innovation in VET, both in how schools are organised and in how technology is incorporated into the learning. The aim is to introduce new technologies and innovations, emerging from universities, research centres and companies into the technical and vocational training colleges.

Another important activity for TKNIKA is the promotion of entrepreneurship. TKNIKA works with all the trainers in charge of entrepreneurial training at VET centres on two main programmes that can be considered as complementary. Those two main programmes deal with entrepreneurship training, *ikasenpresa* (Entrepreneurship for Learning), as part of the study curricula, and *urratsbat* (in one step) in business start-up support. The latter is implemented in partnership with the local entrepreneurship support ecosystems around the technical and vocational training colleges.

To date, 7 253 learners participated in training activities to raise and nurture entrepreneurial culture, and 965 companies were started. More than 43 529 learners received training in entrepreneurial competences, 762 business projects received coaching, 412 of them became real businesses with a success rate of 76% and 616 jobs created.

Key success factors include the leadership of the ministry leading to the involvement of the relevant actors and the nurturing and upholding of their enthusiasm around VET, innovation and entrepreneurship. The ministry has provided consistency and stability for TKNIKA over several political cycles. Through its quality management system, TKNIKA also promotes an efficient and effective VET system.

*Source:* OECD (2014), "Supporting Entrepreneurship in the Vocational Training System in Tunisia: An Assessment of Entrepreneurship Support in Vocational Training Centres under the Tunisian Agency for Vocational Training (ATFP)", LEED Working Paper, OECD Publishing, Paris, http://dx.doi.org/10.1787/20794797.

### *Current methods of teaching entrepreneurship*

A final challenge consists in increasing the availability of support for trainers by making entrepreneurship training more available and by improving teaching material. Training for trainers should be available as part of ongoing career development training. This should be complemented by creating mechanisms that facilitate the exchange of good practices among trainers and by them with additional supports such as teaching manuals.

Entrepreneurship training is often included in national curricula for vocational training in the European Union and other developed countries (Cedefop, 2011). Teaching and engaging learners in entrepreneurship continues to increasingly use practical projects and hands-on activities that facilitate learning-by-doing and real life "immersion" projects (Cedefop, 2011). The most commonly used methods of teaching entrepreneurship in VET in OECD countries include traditional lectures, computer simulations and business games, learner companies, project and group work, company visits, and work placements. Setting-up practice firms and learner companies are also sufficiently widespread, particularly in VET. These activities are often integrated into the compulsory curriculum, but can also be optional or extra-curricular activities of the school. Less frequently used techniques in VET are coaching and mentoring, role playing, discussions and brainstorming, and case studies.

Current course offerings in Tunisia are loosely based on the FORTI programme which was designed in the 1990s. The FORTI programme follows the logic of learning through action as it attempts to facilitate a process of Action (experimentation) – Analysis (summary) – Generalisation (connecting to the real world) – Application (new behaviour), which is in line with the entrepreneurial process. The aim of entrepreneurship training is largely focussed on creating new businesses and self-employment among the learners. The modules and courses mainly tackle the issues of business start-up and small business management and are delivered mostly by entrepreneurship trainers through relatively traditional teaching methods, i.e. lectures. Very little attention is paid to entrepreneurship awareness programmes or modules to increase learners' interest in entrepreneurship.

The ATFP has produced a teaching module for entrepreneurship culture, but it is not well developed nor heavily used in practice. The vocational training centres recognise the need to develop an entrepreneurial culture in their centres but this requires more of an active learning approach that gives learners experience with entrepreneurial behaviour. Teaching methods that support this such as case-studies, learner companies, role play exercises, business games and simulations, company visits and competitions are not often used in Tunisian training centres.

While the use of FORTI material iswelcome, there is a need to develop an updated systematic approach to delivering entrepreneurship training in VET. Furthermore, most trainers currently in charge of entrepreneurship training in training centres have not received any training of how to apply the FORTI programme in their teaching. The FORTI programme as such is appreciated and often referred to, but it is acknowledged that it needs to be updated and properly disseminated in order to be effective. Trainers need specific knowledge, skills and resources to be able to use the innovative, learner-centred and active learning methods conducive to entrepreneurship training. In addition to engaging in specific training, trainers also need to have continuous access to good practice examples, peer advice and learning opportunities as well as didactic materials that they can use to implement their entrepreneurial learning activities. It is therefore important to establish platforms where trainers can access and share such resources.

Initial steps to address this challenge have been taken. CENAFFIF has recently offered a training consisting of five modules starting with initiation to entrepreneurship and ending with a module on how to teach entrepreneurship training as continued professional development. In 2013, 14 trainers received this training and it is expected that six to ten of these participants will become trainers of trainers. However, more training and support is needed. The trainers' teaching material needs to be updated based on the common definitions and objectives. It needs to touch upon both entrepreneurship training pedagogy and content to effectively support entrepreneurship trainers in their teaching. After the support material has been updated it needs to be clearly communicated to and disseminated in VET centres. Further, this should be complemented with additional supports such as a trainer networks, peer learning opportunities and good practice guides. The Danish Foundation for Entrepreneurship can serve as a good model for how this can be accomplished (see Box 4.14).

**Box 4.14. The Danish Foundation for Entrepreneurship**

To ensure the integration of entrepreneurship in the Danish training system, the Danish Foundation for Entrepreneurship – Young Enterprise (FFE-YE) was established in 2010. The overall aim of FFE-YE is to ensure that more learners on every training level are introduced to – and participate in – entrepreneurship training, thus ensuring the integration of entrepreneurship in the Danish training system. FFE-YE targets both learners and trainers.

In order to operationalise this objective, FFE-YE has established a model that functions as a framework for the development of learning outcomes for entrepreneurship training – and on which FFE-YE base their training for trainers. The model contains four dimensions which are all contributing to the development of entrepreneurial skills:

- *Action*: the ability and desire to implement value-creating initiatives, to realise these initiatives through co-operation, networking and partnerships, to communicate in a purposive way and to organise, specify, plan and lead activities, to analyse and handle risk
- Creativity: the ability to discover and create ideas and opportunities, to combine knowledge, experience and personal resources, to create and revise personal perceptions, to experiment and improvise
- Environment: as knowledge about and understanding of the world, locally as well as globally, the ability to analyse a context socially, culturally and economically
- Attitude: the personal and subjective resources with which learners meet challenges and tasks, faith in one's own ability to act in the world and thus to realise dreams and plans, the ability to accept and learn from others' and own failures.

FFE-YE offers a number of services to build the capacities of VET trainers to engage in and deliver entrepreneurship training:

1. Workshops based on the understanding and implementation of the above four progression model dimensions:
   - An understanding of the dimensions
   - A discussion of the relevance for each school and trainer of the start and ending points on the scales in the four dimensions
   - Each trainer reflects on his/her own preferred implementation model.
2. Introduction to relevant programmes developed for teaching entrepreneurship to learners at VET schools.
3. Access to a knowledge centre, where trainers can download teaching materials for whole modules on entrepreneurship, get access to a tool box containing scripts for innovations camps, competitions and other entrepreneurship activities aimed at vocational training, information on international collaborative projects on entrepreneurship and much more.
4. Introduction to the entrepreneurship network for trainers, NEIS. This network reaches trainers from all training levels incl. VET, and is an inspiring meeting ground for all. Through this network the trainers are acquainted with pedagogical tools for their entrepreneurship training, and trainers share experience throughout the training system.

*Source:* OECD (2014), "Supporting Entrepreneurship in the Vocational Training System in Tunisia: An Assessment of Entrepreneurship Support in Vocational Training Centres under the Tunisian Agency for Vocational Training (ATFP)", LEED Working Paper, OECD Publishing, Paris, http://dx.doi.org/10.1787/20794797.

Another significant challenge faced in Tunisia is measuring the impact of the entrepreneurship training. Often a business start-up is considered as an ultimate goal for entrepreneurship training. As actual start-up decision and related activities very seldom immediately follow entrepreneurship training, entrepreneurial intentions have been widely used as a proxy for entrepreneurial learning outcomes. However, entrepreneurship training can also have goals other than starting up a company (e.g. awareness raising, entrepreneurial behaviour in any context). Previous research (Henry et al., 2005) suggests that entrepreneurship training assessments need to be sensitive to thebroader goals set for entrepreneurship courses and programmes (Hytti and O'Gorman, 2004). A good model that could be implemented in Tunisia is the measurement tool that has been developed in Finland (see Box 4.15). This tool provides a good framework for developing and collecting basic indicators that will allow for the measurement of the impact of entrepreneurship training.

**Box 4.15. Measurement Tool for Entrepreneurship Training in Finland**

Measurement Tool for Entrepreneurship Training was developed as a four-year project during which indicators and a related manual was prepared for entrepreneurship training. The indicators in the tool are built to support the work of trainers, principals and decision-makers, and to guide entrepreneurship training.

The outcome of the project is a measurement tool for entrepreneurship training and a related manual, which unfold the concept of entrepreneurship training and support the implementation of the tool. The tool explains in specific terms the trainer's work as an entrepreneurship educator, provides guidelines for teaching and its organisation and it is a tool for school quality management and its development. With the tool, trainers can evaluate the contents, modes of operation, and methods of teaching. It highlights the well-functioning aspects of the trainers' entrepreneurship training and provides them with tips for developing their performance further. The tool may also be employed by decision-makers as they assess the state of entrepreneurship training in their various settings.

*Source:* OECD (2014), "Supporting Entrepreneurship in the Vocational Training System in Tunisia: An Assessment of Entrepreneurship Support in Vocational Training Centres under the Tunisian Agency for Vocational Training (ATFP)", LEED Working Paper, OECD Publishing, Paris, http://dx.doi.org/10.1787/20794797.

# Notes

1. Quintini and Manfredi (2009) discuss different transition patterns from school to work across OECD countries. They note that in countries with regulated labour markets and strong apprenticeship systems, such as Germany, about 80% of school leavers succeed in integrating into the labour market. Such countries contrast with countries with regulated labour markets but without strong work-based training integrated into the formal school system, such as Italy and Spain where more than a third of young people end up in unemployment or inactivity (Quintini and Manfredi, 2009). VET is also crucial to develop a highly skilled labour force, with a range of mid-level trade, technical, professional and management skills alongside those high-level skills associated with university education (OECD, 2014a).

2 An analysis of labour force surveys and household surveys reported higher marginal returns for vocational training than general secondary education in five out of eight African countries (AfDB, OECD, UNDP, UNECA, 2012). Kuépié, Nordman and Roubaud (2009) show that returns to vocational education are higher than those to general secondary education in urban West Africa.

3 Pre-primary education falls beyond the scope of this chapter. However, pre-primary education is to some extent discussed in Chapter 3 under family policies.

4 Post-secondary vocational education and training includes the programmes and qualifications that prepare students for particular occupations or careers, that are beyond upper secondary level, and that would normally require at least six months full-time preparation. Higher level vocational qualifications, including professional bachelor degrees, are included in this definition (OECD, 2014a).

5. In most MENA countries, while foreign languages are increasingly being taught, the composition of post-compulsory education programmes continues to favour humanities and arts over scientific fields of study. On average, about two-thirds of university students in MENA countries major in these fields. This is higher than the averages of East Asia and Latin America. In Djibouti, Morocco, Oman, and Saudi Arabia, students in education, humanities, and social sciences are 71%, 75%, 75%, 76%, and 76% of university students, respectively (World Bank, 2008).

6. The same study shows some evidence of a poor match between the field of study and the field of work and consequent job downgrading. One out of three people with a BTS worked in a field other than that of their qualification in 2007. Those most affected are graduates of commerce and management (almost 40%) (Ministry of Employment and Professional Insertion of Youth and the World Bank, 2009).

# *References*

AfDB (2012), "Tunisie: Défis Économiques et Sociaux Post – Révolution", www.afdb.org/fileadmin/uploads/afdb/Documents/Publications/Tunisie%20D%C3%A9fis%20%C3%89conomiques%20et%20Sociaux.pdf.

AfDB, OECD, UNDP, UNECA (2012), "Education and Skills Mismatch – African Economic Outlook", www.africaneconomicoutlook.org/en/theme/youth_employment/education-skills-mismatch/, (accessed 2 June 2014).

Alvarez-Galván, J. (2014), A *Skills beyond School Review of Egypt*, OECD Reviews of Vocational Education and Training, OECD Publishing, Paris, http://dx.doi.org/10.1787/9789264209626-en.

Belkacem, L. and F. Mansouri (2013), "2012 GEM Tunisia: National Report", www.gemconsortium.org/docs/download/3197.

Bellakhal, R. and M.-B. Mahjoub (2013), "The Impact of Tunisian Vocational Training Programs on Employment and Wage", unpublished working paper, March 2014.

British Council (2013), "Graduate Employability in the Middle East and North Africa: Post-Arab Spring", www.britishcouncil.org/employability_report.pdf.

Cedefop – European Centre for the Development of Vocational Training (2011), *Guidance Supporting Europe's Aspiring Entrepreneurs. Policy and Practice to Harness Future Potential*, Publications Office of the European Union, Luxembourg.

Chahed, M.Y. (2013), "Skills for Entrepreneurship [Tunisia]: Le renforcement de la culture entrepreneuriale dans le cursus de la formation professionnelle dispensée dans les centres de l'Agence tunisienne de la formation professionnelle (ATFP)", Rapport Final de Mission, Project by the OECD, GIZ, ETF.

Chelbi, A. and Y. Ficatier (2010), "Capitalisation des démarches pour la mise en oeuvre des projets de formation professionnelle : cas de la Tunisie et du Maroc", Département de la Recherche, Division Evaluation et capitalisation, Agence Française de Développement.

Danish Agency for Higher Education and Educational Support (2012), *Skills beyond school: OECD Review of Post-Secondary Vocational Education and Training – National Background Report for Denmark*, Copenhagen.

Dunkel, T. and I. Le Mouillour (2009), "Through the Looking Glass: Diversification and Differentiation in Vocational and Training and Higher Education", *Modernising Vocational Education and Training, Fourth Report on Vocational Training Research in Europe*, Background Report, Vol. 2, CEDEFOP, www.cedefop.europa.eu/EN/publications/5073.aspx.

Eichhorst, W. et al. (2012), "A Roadmap to Vocational Education and Training Systems around the World", IZA Discussion Papers No. 7110, IZA, Bonn.

ETF – European Training Foundation (2012), *Le Processus de Turin*, ETF, Turin.

ETF and MFPE (2014), *Le Processus de Turin 2014 – Pays : Tunisie*, European Training Foundation (ETF), Ministère de la Formation Professionnelle et de l'Emploi (MFPE), Tunis.

Field, S. et al. (2012), *A Skills beyond School Review of Denmark,* OECD Reviews of Vocational Education and Training, OECD Publishing, Paris, http://dx.doi.org/10.1787/9789264173668-en.

Fredriksen, B. and J.-P. Tan (2008), "East Asia Education Study Tour: An Overview of Key Insights", in B. Fredirksen and J.-P. Tan (eds.), *An Africa Exploration of the East Asian Education Experience*, World Bank, Washington, DC.

Gatti, R., M. Morgandi, R. Grun, S. Brodmann, D. Angel-Urdinola and J.M. Moreno (2013), *Jobs for Shared Prosperity: Time for Action in the Middle East and North Africa,* World Bank Publications.

Global Entrepreneurship Monitor (2012), "GEM 2012 Global Report", available at www.gemconsortium.org/docs/2645/gem-2012-global-report.

Hanushek, E. and L. Woessmann (2006), "Does Educational Tracking Affect Performance and Inequality? Differences-in-Differences Evidence across Countries", *Economic Journal*, Vol. 116, pp. 63-76.

Henry, C., F. Hill and D. Leitch (2005), "Entrepreneurship Education and Training: Can Entrepreneurship Be Taught?", Part I, *Education + Training*, Vol. 47, No. 2, pp. 98-111.

Hytti, U. and C. O'Gorman (2004), "What is 'Enterprise Education'? An Analysis of the Objectives and Methods of Enterprise Education Programmes in Four European Countries", *Education + Training*, Vol. 46, No. 1, pp. 11-23.

Kuczera, M. (2013), *A Skills beyond School Commentary on Scotland*, www.oecd.org/edu/skills-beyond-school/ASkillsBeyondSchoolCommentaryOnScotland.pdf.

Kuépié, M., C.J. Nordman and F. Roubaud (2009), "Education and Earnings in Urban West Africa", *Journal of Comparative Economics*, Vol. 37, No. 3.

La Presse.tn (2013), "Tunisie: Élèves des collèges techniques – Admission en première année secondaire", *La Presse.tn*, 30 May 2013, http://fr.allafrica.com/stories/201305301147.html.

Ministry of Education (2013a), "National Background Report : Renforcer l'employabilité des jeunes pendant la transition de la Tunisie vers une économie verte, Questionnaire de l'OCDE".

Ministry of Education (2013b), "Statistiques scolaires: Année scolaire 2011/12", Direction Générale des Études de la Planification et des Systèmes d'Information.

Ministry of Education (2013c), "Statistiques scolaires: Année scolaire 2012/13", Direction Générale des Études de la Planification et des Systèmes d'Information.

Ministry of Employment and Professional Insertion of Youth and the World Bank (2009), "Dynamiques de l'emploi et adéquation de la formation parmi les diplômés universitaires: insertion des jeunes diplomés de l'enseignement supérieur promotion 2004 analyse comparative des résultats de deux enquètes (2005 et 2007)", www-wds.worldbank.org/external/default/WDSContentServer/WDSP/IB/2009/11/12/000020953_20091112162329/Rendered/PDF/515650ESW0P1111CH0Rapport0Dynamique.pdf.

Ministry of Higher Education and Scientific Research (2013), *Features of Higher Education and Scientific Research: Academic Year 2012-2013,* Studies, Planning and Programming Office.

Ministry of Vocational Training and Employment (2014), "Formation professionnelle initiale en Tunisie", www.emploi.gov.tn/fr/formation-professionnelle/formation-initiale/.

Ministry of Vocational Training and Employment (2013), "Réforme du dispositif national de la formation professionnelle", Document d'orientation et Plan d'opération 2014-2018, Ministry of Vocation Training and Employment, Tunis.

Ministry of Vocational Training and Employment (2012), "Analyse du système et des politiques d'enseignement et de formation professionnels de la Tunisie", réalisée dans le cadre du processus de Turin avec l'appui de ETF.

Ministry of Vocational Training and Employment (2011a), "La formation professionnelle en chiffre: Décembre 2011", Observatoire National de l'Emploi et des Qualifications, www.mfpe.gov.tn/fileadmin/user_upload/PDF/statistique/publication/statistiques_de_la_formation_professionnelle_2011.pdf.

Ministry of Vocational Training and Employment (2011b), "Le décrochage de la formation professionnelle en Tunisie: Raisons et parcours professionnels", Observatoire National de l'Emploi et des Qualifications.

Ministry of Vocational Training and Employment (2010a), "Torino Process 2010, Self-Assessment Summary", European Training Fund, Turin.

Ministry of Vocational Training and Employment (2010b), "Formation Professionnelle: Nomenclature des Secteurs", www.emploi.gov.tn/fileadmin/user_upload/Formation_Professionnelle/PDF/Nomenclature_Secteurs-Specialites_GP_Ar-Fr.pdf.

Musset, P. and S. Field (2013), *A Skills beyond School Review of England*, OECD Reviews of Vocational Education and Training, OECD Publishing, Paris, http://dx.doi.org/10.1787/9789264203594-en.

NA (2012), "L'enseignement technique, le maillon faible", *Direct Info*, 12 June 2012, http://directinfo.webmanagercenter.com/2012/06/11/social-education-lenseignement-technique-le-maillon-faible-du-systeme-educatif/.

National Institute of Statistics (2014), "Statistiques", www.tunisie-statistiques.tn/plateforme/detail.php?id=198.

OECD (2014a), *Skills beyond School: Synthesis Report*, OECD Reviews of Vocational Education and Training, OECD Publishing, Paris, http://dx.doi.org/10.1787/9789264214682-en.

OECD (2014b), "Supporting Entrepreneurship in the Vocational Training System in Tunisia: An Assessment of Entrepreneurship Support in Vocational Training Centres under the Tunisian Agency for Vocational Training (ATFP)", LEED Working Paper, OECD Publishing, Paris, http://dx.doi.org/10.1787/20794797.

OECD (2013a), *PISA 2012 Results: What Students Know and Can Do (Vol. I),* OECD Publishing, Paris, http://dx.doi.org/10.1787/9789264208780-en.

OECD (2013b), "Integrity Scan of Tunisia", OECD-CleanGovBiz: Integrity in Practice, OECD Publishing, Paris, www.oecd.org/cleangovbiz/Tunisia-Integrity-ScanEN.pdf.

OECD (2013c), *Education at a Glance 2013: OECD Indicators*, OECD Publishing, Paris, http://dx.doi.org/10.1787/eag-2013-en.

OECD (2012), *Equity and Quality in Education: Supporting Disadvantaged Students and Schools*, OECD Publishing, Paris, http://dx.doi.org/10.1787/9789264130852-en.

OECD (2010a), *Learning for Jobs, OECD Reviews of Vocational Education and Training*, OECD Publishing, Paris, http://dx.doi.org/10.1787/9789264087460-en.

OECD (2010b), *SMEs, Entrepreneurship and Innovation*, OECD Publishing, Paris, http://dx.doi.org/10.1787/9789264080355-en.

OECD (2009), *The Role of Agriculture and Farm Household Diversification in the Rural Economy: Evidence and Initial Policy Implications*, OECD Publishing, Paris, www.oecd.org/agriculture/44559905.pdf.

OECD and the World Bank (2013), *Indicators of Skills for Employment and Productivity: A Conceptual Framework and Approach for Low-income Countries*, OECD and World Bank, www.g20dwg.org/documents/pdf/view/352/.

OECD/European Commission (2013), *The Missing Entrepreneurs: Policies for Inclusive Entrepreneurship in Europe*, OECD Publishing, Paris, http://dx.doi.org/10.1787/9789264188167-en.

OECD/International Bank for Reconstruction and Development/World Bank (2013), *Reviews of National Policies for Education: Tertiary Education in Colombia 2012*, OECD Publishing, Paris, http://dx.doi.org/10.1787/9789264180697-en.

ONEQ – Observatoire National de l'Emploi, and ILO – International Labour Organization (2014), *Transition vers le marché du travail des jeunes femmes et hommes en Tunisie*, ONEQ and ILO.

Quintini, G. and T. Manfredi (2009), "Going Separate Ways? School-To-Work Transition in The United States and Europe", *OECD Social, Employment and Migration Working Papers No. 90*, OECD, Paris, http://dx.doi.org/10.1787/221717700447.

Sawy, K., C. Farr and S. Newera (2012), "Saving Vocational Education in a New Arab World", Knowledge@Wharton, Lauder Global Business Insight Report 2012, University of Wharton.

Sedrine, S.B. (2006), "Career Guidance in the MEDA Region: Country Report on Tunisia", European Training Foundation, Turin.

Sultana, R. and A. Watts (2007), "Career Guidance in the Mediterranean Region", European Training Foundation, Turin.

Sweet, R. (2013), "Work-based Learning: Why? How?", *Revisiting Global Trends in TVET: Reflections on Theory and Practice*, UNESCO-UNEVOC International Centre for Technical and Vocational Education and Training.

Tan, J.-P. and Y.-J. Nam (2012), "Pre-Employment Technical and Vocational Education and Training: Fostering Relevance, Effectiveness, and Efficiency", in R. Almeida et al. (eds.), *The Right Skills for the Job?: Rethinking Training Policies for Workers,* World Bank, Washington, DC.

Tuniscope (2012), "Le véritable taux d'analphabétisme est de 20,3%", www.tuniscope.com/index.php/article/12446/actualites/societe/analphabetisme-531719.

Tunisian Republic (2008a), "Loi n° 2008-09 du 11 février 2008, modifiant et complétant la Loi d'orientation n° 2002-80 du 23 juillet 2002, relative à l'éducation et à l'enseignement scolaire", *Journal officiel, 2008-02-15,* No. 14, pp. 681-682, www.ilo.org/dyn/natlex/docs/SERIAL/78124/83306/F1975788623/TUN-78124.pdf.

Tunisian Republic (2008b), "Loi n° 2008-10 du 11 février 2008, relative à la formation professionnelle", *Journal Officiel de la République Tunisienne*, No. 15, www.ilo.org/dyn/natlex/docs/SERIAL/78125/83307/F1245596670/TUN-78125.pdf.

UNESCO (2014a), "Social Indicators", http://data.un.org/CountryProfile.aspx?crName =Tunisia#Social.

UNESCO (2014b), "Dataset Education, Series Literacy Rates", UNESCO Institute of Statistics (UIS).

UNESCO (2014c), "Statistiques", www.unicef.org/french/infobycountry/Tunisia_statistics. html.

UNESCO (2014d), "Institute for Statistics World Education Indicators Programme", Database consulted on May 20th 2014.

UNESCO (2013), "Education (all Levels) Profile – Tunisia", *UIS Statistics in Brief*, UNESCO Institute of Statistics (UIS).

UNESCO (2012), "Données mondiales de l'éducation: Tunisie, 2010/11", 7e édition, 2010/11, Bureau International d'Éducation.

UTICA – Union Tunisienne de l'Industrie, du Commerce et de l'Artisanat (2012), "UTICA's 2020 Strategy for VET", www.fedelec-uaf.tn/Actualites%20FEDELEC/Vision%20UTICA%202020-%20Version%2023%20decembre%202012.pdf.

World Bank (2013), *Jobs for Shared Prosperity Time for Action in the Middle East and North Africa,* http://elibrary.worldbank.org/doi/pdf/10.1596/9780821397190_FM.

World Bank (2008), "New Challenges Facing the Education Sector in MENA", *MENA Development Report: The Road Not Travelled – Education Reform in the Middle East and Africa*, International Bank for Reconstruction and Development/The World Bank, Washington, http://dx.doi.org/10.1596/978-0-8213-7062-9.

Yaagoubi, M. et al. (2013), "Analyse du système éducatif Tunisien", Organisation International du Travail pour la Promotion de l'emploi productif et le travail décent des jeunes en Tunisie.

# *Chapter 5*

# Creating jobs for Tunisian youth in the green economy: Anticipating skills and developing entrepreneurship

*This chapter examines the opportunities for the creation of jobs for young people in the green economy and actions which can build skills and entrepreneurship around these opportunities. The economy will inevitably become greener, either through the influence of external factors, i.e. climate change, pressure on non-renewable resources and the related adaptation policies, or through a domestic strategy in the direction of sustainable development. This will have implications for vocational education and training (VET), both in terms of the skills which will be in demand, and the opportunities for entrepreneurship. Greening of the economy will not have the same effect on all sectors, and a number of areas are examined where there will be opportunities for the creation of new jobs, including for youth through the creation of green jobs. Capturing such opportunities will require clear government strategies, prioritisation and action.*

## Introduction

Previous chapters have discussed the key policy approaches to increase the employability of young people. At the same time, it is also essential to consider the complementary issue about the creation of new employment opportunities, and in particular the opportunities stemming from the transition to a green economy. While some opportunities may arise regardless of actions by the government, an appropriately conducive strategy needs to be implemented and ensure good co-ordination between different Ministries.

There is a general presumption that the world will experience green growth going forward and that, in order to prepare for this, countries will have to adjust their policies and priorities in such a way to better reconcile economic growth, social justice and environmental concerns. Although most countries, including Tunisia, have some form of sustainable development strategy, retaining a balance between interests is a challenge to policy makers, particularly as it can be expected that there will be trade-offs between short-term economic effects and longer term social and environmental problems. At the same time, external factors , *i.e.* climate change and the related adaptation policies, will mean that there will be implications for employment whether this is through losses of jobs in declining and polluting industries, the creation of new employment types, or a change in the balance of skills required in particular sectors.

Policy makers can respond to these challenges in a variety of ways: by means of short-term adjustment measures; as part of a broader, long-term strategy for greening the economy; by concentrating actions on specific sectors where most change is likely to take place; or, indeed, by some combination of all three approaches. This chapter examines these policy approaches and their implications for Tunisia, specifically with regard to youth employment. In considering a sectoral approach, sectors of importance for Tunisia are chosen, where opportunities for enhancing youth employment appear to be particularly promising. In this light, the chapter discusses the variety of areas for policy action which would both enhance green growth and create opportunities for employment and entrepreneurship for young people.

The following conclusions can be derived from the chapter:

- ***Firstly, even if no policy action is taken to move towards sustainable development, Tunisia will confront the same challenges that all countries will be facing, as a result of global climate change trends and the pressures on non-renewable resources.*** Such challenges can be expected to result in the creation of new opportunities for workers, but also risks. In this context, a first essential pre-requisite for Tunisia will be to ensure that the appropriate set of well-functioning labour market institutions and skills policies are in place to enable the country to react to changes. Indeed, labour market and skills policies can make an important contribution to a successful transition by facilitating the structural change required to put green production practices in place.
- ***Policies should also seek to maximise the benefits of green growth for workers while giving assurance that unavoidable adjustment costs are shared fairly.*** Failure to meet these challenges could undermine political support for green growth policies. Given the high proportion of youth in the Tunisian population, their generation will be the first to benefit. Under the circumstances, a first stage would be to consider incorporating green skills in all curricula, to enable those who have been trained to be better able to adapt to changing circumstances.

- ***Furthermore, to successfully manage the transition towards a green economy the Tunisian Government will have to look at ways to build a comprehensive strategy, which will have to involve all ministries, as well as an effective social dialogue***. This will require further elaboration of the existing Sustainable Development Strategy and better clarity regarding institutional co-ordination.
- ***In addition, there are a number of specific areas where action could be taken to improve green employment and entrepreneurship***. The following areas have been chosen as ones where actions recommended in previous chapters will have the greatest impact and where there will be the best opportunities for youth employment. In these areas the transition to a green economy will either increase employment or significantly change the nature of jobs in the sector.
  - *Innovation and a clean-tech cluster.* Further actions can be taken to encourage graduate entrepreneurship, and to seek spin-outs from universities and research institutes. Opportunities to develop or attract businesses connected with existing green investments need to be explored more fully. A green focus could be given to entrepreneurship support, including that targeting the social enterprises, and higher education.
  - *Energy.* The existing and successful Prosol initiative could be continued and expanded to other areas of renewable energy. Barriers to the production of energy at a municipal level need to be considered.
  - *Waste and recycling.* Greater involvement of social enterprises in recycling and reuse could both increase employment and be used for training unemployed youth. Barriers to the use of social enterprises need to be addressed and the results of current actions to resolve issues of legal status and finance need to be followed through.
  - *Tourism.* Efforts to make existing tourism more sustainable need to be reinforced in the light of external pressures. Development of eco-tourism can bring employment to more remote areas, but requires better organisation and an overall strategy.
  - *Agriculture.* Organic agriculture represents an opportunity for both the environment and employment. Tunisia has an existing organic sector, but with appropriate public support its size and export potential could be increased.
  - *Construction.* Although for the construction sector itself there will likely be little net growth in employment, a need for policies to upgrade skills can be expected, while better management of resources (recycling of waste, and improving energy efficiency) will support jobs in other sectors.

There are synergies between these sectors suggesting that there exists considerable scope to green the Tunisian economy by addressing particular sectoral challenges as part of a holistic policy reform. The key building blocks of such a comprehensive reform agenda are summarised below (Box 5.1).

**Box 5.1. Key recommendations**

Given the challenges presented in this chapter, the OECD suggests that:

- Actions are taken to improve the effectiveness of the VET system and its ability to react to changing skills requirements. These are outlined further in chapter 4
- *Le Centre National de Formation de Formateurs et d'Ingénierie de Formation* (CENAFFIF) [The National Centre for Training of Trainers and Pedagogy] should review all curricula from the point of view of green employment, seeking to introduce appropriate green skills and through this the adaptability of the workforce.
- The existing Sustainable Development Strategy should be reviewed in particular to ensure that all key stakeholders are committed to its implementation, and that there are appropriate implementation and co-ordination institutions with the power to implement the strategy.
- Opportunities for employment through necessary public works, particularly with regard to addressing the problems of water supply, should be used as a way of increasing employment and training the unemployed.
- In order to maximise employment opportunities for young people, there should be a concentration on actions in fields where there will be either employment expansion or substantive changes to the nature of employment. These are likely to be innovation and high tech clusters, energy, waste and recycling, tourism, agriculture and construction. For the most effective results there will be a need to co-ordinate work between different Ministries. This should be done at two levels, on the one hand seeking better co-ordination within the government (including reviewing the Sustainable Development Strategy) and on the other hand promoting specific actions, possibly of a pilot nature, in order to gain experience and promote trust between different organisations.
- Existing support to entrepreneurship in universities should be extended by broadening the opportunities given to students to participate in entrepreneurship classes, while at the same time deepening the support given to the smaller number of students who try to start their own businesses. This will require changes within universities, including improvement of interdisciplinary working.
- Local supply chains for larger green investments should be developed by better targeting existing means of support (information, advice and training) to enterprises. This will include targeted support to enterprises which could form part of such a supply chain as well as more general actions to improve linkages with foreign direct investment, including information, provision of property, and structured networking between larger and smaller companies.
- The Prosol initiative should be continued and used as a model for corresponding schemes related to other forms of renewable energy.
- Consideration of local generation of energy should be considered (specifically through energy from waste), and barriers which prevent communes from taking this approach need to be examined and removed.
- The role of NGOs and social enterprises in the realisation of the strategy for integrated and sustainable waste management needs to be further supported. Existing funds for the support of social enterprises should be targeted more clearly with relation to opportunities related to recycling.
- The existing eco-label system should be further elaborated and enforced in the tourism sector in order to improve the environmental impact of mass tourism.
- A new eco-tourism strategy should be developed, based on engaging all key stakeholders and with a view to creating a network which can be used to implement the strategy.
- Further support should be given to the enlargement of the organic sector in agriculture. This will include better co-ordination of promotion of exports and better targeting of subsidies to areas where Tunisia is competitive, notably fruit and vegetables.
- A sustainability strategy should be developed for the construction sector, which will include the need for upgrading skills, incentives for the use of greener approaches (such as using recycled materials) and provisions for recycling construction and demolition waste (which should also be explicitly included as a target in the integrated waste management strategy).

## Labour market challenges during the transition towards green growth

The transition to green growth creates a number of general market challenges which will apply to Tunisia as they do to other countries. Recent analysis carried out at both the OECD and the European Commission shows that a successful transition towards a low-carbon economy will necessarily reshape the labour market, creating new opportunities for workers, but also risks. Labour market and skills policies can make an important contribution to a successful transition by facilitating the structural change required to put green production practices in place. Policies should also seek to maximise the benefits of green growth for workers while assuring that unavoidable adjustment costs are shared fairly. Failure to meet these challenges can undermine political support for green growth policies (OECD, 2011a; and European Commission, 2013)

Greening the economy will create additional employment in some sectors, but will also make some jobs obsolete and change the skill requirements of others. One of the main labour market impacts will be to alter the sectoral composition of employment, with "green" sectors growing rapidly and the most $CO_2$-intensive sectors needing to radically change their technologies or shed jobs in the transition towards green growth.

The international evidence so far available about labour market effects of green growth and related wage developments is not clear-cut. For example, recent simulations carried out by the OECD suggest that the net impact on overall employment is likely to be small. Even the more sizeable impacts on the industry mix of jobs (see Figure 5.1) will be small compared to the high underlying rates of labour reallocation generally observed in European countries during recent decades, including due to the impact of deepening globalisation. The main reason for this is that much of the economic restructuring implied by an aggressive green growth policy occurs within the energy sector and that sector employs only a small share of the total workforce. While certain green sectors, such as renewable energy, will grow at a rapid pace, the overall labour market impact will likely be modest due to the fact that employment in these sectors starts from such a low base.

As in the case of the ICT revolution, the shift towards greener production practices will lead to changes in skill requirements across the economy. However, unlike the ICT revolution there appear to be few uniquely "green skills"; the green skills that new labour market entrants will require can largely be acquired by incremental enrichment of established vocational education and training programmes, combined with some top-up training in the case of experienced workers. However, the strong increase in environmental patenting observed in some countries such as Germany, also suggests the importance of preparing the workforce for a period of rapid eco-innovation, including by raising science, technology, engineering and mathematics (STEM) skills.

The transition towards green growth will not only create new opportunities for workers, it will also create challenges, particularly for workers in the most carbon-intensive industries. Should many workers in these industries lose their jobs in the transition towards green growth, they are likely to face above-average adjustment costs since many of these industries are characterised by relatively low educated workers with a low level of labour mobility. Several are also highly localised. It should be underlined, however, that close to 90% of $CO_2$ emissions in the European Union are accounted for by a relatively small number of industries, which absorb just 14% of employment. Although relatively few workers appear to be at-risk, some of the workers in these industries will need targeted assistance, such as retraining to be able to work with cleaner technologies, or help finding new jobs in growing green sectors. These measures will be particularly important in several European countries where coal mining or heavily polluting heavy industry are still major sources of employment.

**Figure 5.1. Change in sectoral composition of employment**

**Panel A. Europe**

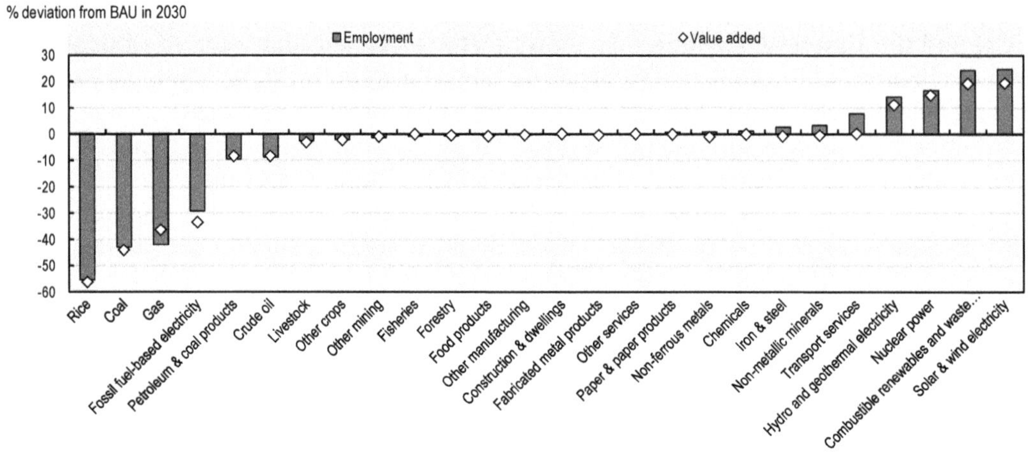


**Panel B. OECD**

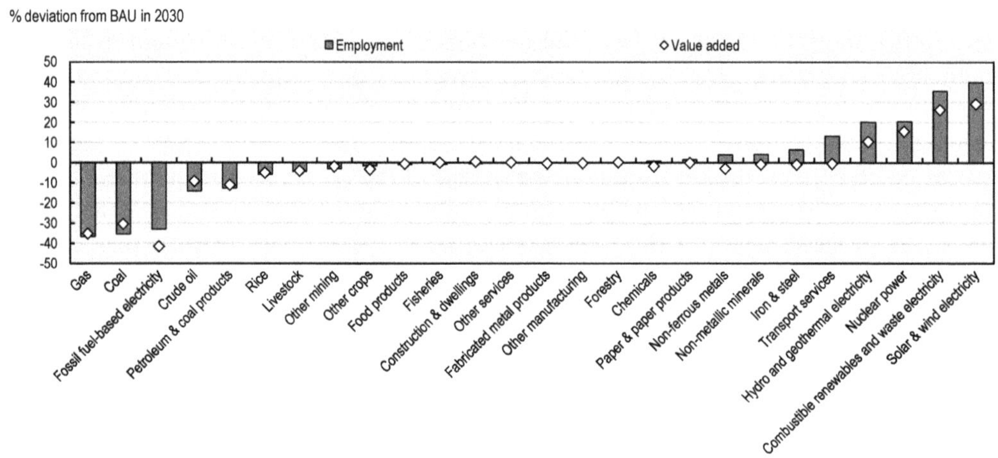


*Note*: The data charted represent the differences in 2030 between projected values under a business as usual (BAU) scenario, where climate mitigation policies reflect their current settings, with an alternative scenario where aggressive mitigations strategies are implemented via an emissions trading system

*Source*: OECD (2012), "The Jobs Potential of a Shift Towards a Low-carbon Economy", *OECD Green Growth Papers*, No. 2012/01, OECD Publishing, Paris, http://dx.doi.org/10.1787/5k9h3630320v-en.

The greening of the European economy is already generating significant numbers of new jobs in key sectors such as renewable energy, and will continue to do so in coming decades. There has also been acceleration in the development and application of new environmental technologies, which is creating new occupational specialties such as designers and operators of smart electrical grids, and opening up new export markets. For example, green technology innovation hubs have developed in the Copenhagen area and in several other EU countries, which are opening up new export markets and generating employment.

Overall the transition to greener growth is likely to involve distributional effects. While well-designed green growth policies should result in a higher level of well-being when all costs and benefits are considered, including the future beneficial effects of improved environmental quality, the associated adjustment costs will be largely borne by specific segments of the economy and their workers. This raises distributional concerns suggesting that appropriate supporting measures may be required to compensate those directly affected.

One important challenge, particularly in light of today's youth labour market conditions in Tunisia, will be to ensure that short-term problems associated with labour market transitions do not turn into long-term disadvantages. Key policy tools to help successfully manage the transition include:

- ***Reducing insecurity due to job displacement***. The transition will reinforce the need for achieving a workable model that combines a high degree of labour mobility with appropriate support for job losers. It will be especially important to provide effective employment support to displaced workers, even if this means higher spending on active labour market policies and in-work support in the short-term. This support can take the form of adequate income replacement benefits combined with effective activation measures for benefit recipients. Some workers will need targeted assistance, such as retraining to work with cleaner technologies or help finding new jobs in growing green sectors. Reconciling efficient flows of workers from declining to growing firms with income and employment security will be a crucial precondition to defuse political opposition to green growth policies.
- ***Fostering eco-innovation through education and training***. Developing stronger basic skills in core fields, including mathematics and science, will be essential for compulsory schooling. There is also a need for a more supportive and responsive VET system. At the same time, the general case for strengthening tertiary education and VET programmes in such a way to train quality graduates who can contribute directly or indirectly to innovation in their workplace and harness research excellence and links to industry is made even stronger in the light of green growth.
- ***Redistributive policies***. The priority must be to ensure that the tax and benefit system is made more supportive of employment. Putting into place a comprehensive green strategy will provide a unique opportunity to improve the effectiveness of tax and benefit systems. The available evidence across the OECD area demonstrates how the additional revenue from carbon pricing can be used to reduce the tax wedge on labour incomes, so as to promote job creation. However, a careful analysis of the tax/benefit system in a given country will be required to assess whether current distortions from labour taxation are severe enough that this would be the most valuable use of new tax revenues, as well as an assessment of how best to target reductions in labour taxation.
- ***Green-specific labour market and skill policies, especially to help meet new job skill needs***. An OECD questionnaire sent to labour and employment ministries reveals that about 60% of the responding countries have implemented at least one labour market measure targeted on green growth, with training being the most common type of measure. However, most of these measures are of small scale and were only recently introduced. The limited experience with implementing these policies suggests that they confront two particularly difficult challenges; detecting how green growth is changing labour demand and jobs skill requirements, and co-ordinating labour market and skill policies with environmental policy. This suggests that the role for green-specific measures is likely to emerge only

incrementally, as the environmental policy framework needed to support green growth develops and experience with managing the labour market dimension of the transition to green growth accumulates.

- ***Ensuring that the manner in which green growth is promoted will provide opportunities for new enterprises and employment.*** Different approaches to green growth will have different impacts on employment – for example, large scale infrastructure for renewable energy may be more efficient in power generation than local small-scale approaches, but at the same time may have less impact on employment either directly (e.g. solar maintenance engineers) or indirectly (manufacture of solar cells in Tunisia rather than importing them).
- ***Addressing the barriers that young people face in being able to compete in the market for green jobs.*** Those barriers which disproportionately affect young people, for example lack of experience and finance, need to be identified. In general, young people entering the labour market are likely to have the greatest opportunities in areas where there are changes in skills and ways of working or where there is rapid growth in employment which is unlikely to be taken up by existing workers. It should be noted, however, that unemployment is not only amongst youth and that older unemployed may in some cases be better placed to fill jobs created as part of the green economy.

Previous chapters of this report have given recommendations on appropriate actions in Tunisia to support these policies. In addition, one important conclusion of OECD works on the issue is that to successfully manage the transition towards green growth, governments must look at ways to build an effective social dialogue, which will have a key role to play in developing green growth policies and smoothly adapting labour markets to this emerging reality. The transition to green growth will be complex and the effort required to get it through will only be sustained if policy goals and strategies are developed through dialogue with all stakeholders. Social partners' deep knowledge of issues such as job skill requirements and best practices for implementing new technologies in the workplace will be invaluable in anticipating and managing the labour market dimension of the transition to green growth.

Worldwide changes in the environment can be expected to affect Tunisia, in ways that the government cannot ignore. For example, even though the price of oil is set internationally, it affects the financial incentives for domestic consumers to switch to renewable forms of energy. At the same time, climate change in Tunisia will result in higher temperatures and increased pressure on already over-stretched water supplies. These developments will provide opportunities (for solar power, for example) while also posing important policy challenges, such as water shortages, which could hinder mass tourism, facilities and expansion. Reallocation effects on both jobs and enterprises can also be expected. Responding to these exogenous changes will require adequate "change-proof" government policies with some of the actions involved being explored in further detail in the sections below. It can be seen that inaction will have opportunity costs – for example, slow and unplanned changes (partly due to sunk costs and vested interests) can result in the inefficient use of resources, while late adaptation may result in foregone opportunities from innovation and foreign direct investment, as other countries will take advantage of them.

The challenge of moving the Tunisian economy towards a path of sustainable growth is recognised by the authorities and it has been so for some time, at least formally. What has become increasingly clear is that the question about how best to embed sustainability in concrete policy actions, and across a broad range of economic areas, remains unaddressed (see also Adbessalem, 2014). It is important to urgently acknowledge the specific trade-offs associated with different aspects of a sustainable development strategy, in particular between economic growth, environmental sustainability, and employment and social factors. The development of such a broad strategy needs to take into account the views of a wide range of stakeholders, and the support of an enabling institutional setting where possible gaps can be addressed (see also Adbessalem, 2014). The gains of such a strategy will be higher the clearer the signals that the government will be able to send that it is serious about dealing with major environmental issue (OECD, 2011a).

In many countries, environmental externalities are under-priced or not priced at all and at the same time the dominance of existing technologies and systems can make it difficult for new technologies and approaches to compete. Tunisia has already made some progress in this respect in the field of renewable energy, but undoubtedly there are further areas where these issues need to be addressed.

## How will Tunisia's response to the challenges of green growth impact on employment?

Analysis suggests that there will be some employment growth from green factors in Tunisia, even if existing plans remain unchanged. For example, a study by GIZ indicates that the *Plan Solaire Tunisien* (PST) [Tunisian Solar Plan] will generate between 7 000 and 20 000 jobs in renewable energy by 2030, based on experience from other countries (GIZ, 2012). This makes for a considerable expansion, in light of the fact that fewer than 3 500 people are employed in the sector at present. In general, qualifications are specialisations within already existing qualifications: electricians specialised in photovoltaics (PV), plumbers in solar water heaters, etc. This can be covered by the existing system of education and training – with suitable adaptations to the curricula – noting that there is an existing higher education institute (the *Institut Supérieur des Sciences et Technologies de l'Énergie de Gafsa* [Higher Institute of Energy Science and Technology of Gafsa]), which can help create the specialists required.

The effect on youth employment is more difficult to assess. Indeed it can be expected that existing workers will be the primary beneficiaries of re-training programmes that will be implemented as demand changes. At the same time, the prospect that some new activities will emerge, which did not exist in more traditional industries, will open up new job opportunities for the younger generations to capture.

Nevertheless, the discussion in the previous section suggests that some caution should be applied when assessing the size of possible effects on overall employment. Analysis of developed economies reveals that even where these effects will be positive, the biggest impact will likely take the form of changes in the distribution of total employment across sectors, rather than in total employment (OECD, 2012a). This will clearly have implications for retraining, but also, and more generally, for the broader set of labour market activation policies that will have to be provided to existing workers to smooth their reallocation. In this context, Tunisia will need to form a clear vision of the sectors where change is most likely to take place, and where employment reallocation effects and/or the opportunities for new jobs are greatest. However, an important line of policy action should also be directed at improving the broad system of labour market institutions as a policy tool of early intervention and capacity building. The reforms put forward in Chapters 2 and 3 of this report provide a useful framework for complementary labour market and social policies to help Tunisia cope with the transition to a greener economy.

In approaching green growth, one additional important question for Tunisia will be about whether "green skills" form a bottleneck, *i.e.*, whether there are specific skills, which are needed for green growth and which did not previously exist. In this regard, a study on skills for green jobs in Tunisia concludes that there is a need for a wider overall strategy for VET, and adaptation of the curriculum by the addition of modules on environmental matters (MDGIF, 2013). In a time of change, a responsive and flexible VET system is essential, and needs to be demand driven (since not all changes are under direct governmental control). This means adjusting supply to meet demand, having the ability to forecast demand, and having the ability to adapt curricula to meet the detailed needs of new jobs based on existing skills.

Useful policy insights to improve Tunisia's VET system are discussed in Chapter 4 of this report. In a nutshell, the VET system will need to be adaptable, demand-driven, and able to forecast changes. Green skills/education should be considered as part of all curricula. CENAFFIF shows ability to specify new qualifications and curricula based on analysis when the expected demand is known (for example as part of the Prosol programme). Analysis in Chapter 4 suggests that there are still issues with regard to responding to market demands (rather than the requirements of centrally conceived programmes) and forecasting skills. Under these circumstances it is important to review all curricula and to insert appropriate green aspects into them, in order to prepare students for new green employment opportunities. In a similar vein, the Higher Education system will need to teach a wider range of skills and include support for students to be adaptable as they face the labour market.

At the same time, the support system for entrepreneurship will need to identify opportunities related to green growth and to ensure that new entrepreneurs have the right detailed advice and information. Removing barriers to entrepreneurship (availability of finance, training, information and advice) will be essential to strengthen the greening of the Tunisian economy. As with qualifications, there will be a need to complement ordinary measures of support for entrepreneurship with tailored advice, training and information to raise awareness of the opportunities related to green growth. A particularly important age group to target will be the youth.

A recent study shows that there is already institutional development in this direction with not only a National Strategy for Sustainable Development but also specific assistance available to SMEs from *Centre International des Technologies de l'Environnement de Tunis* (CITET) [Tunis International Center for Environmental Technologies] (information and training on environmental issues and regulations) and *L'Agence Nationale de Gestion des Déchets* (ANGeD) [National Waste Management Agency] (information and support on waste management for SMEs) (OECD et al., 2014). This report is part of a broader work programme financed by the Middle East and North Africa Transition Fund, whose aim is to provide grant funding to address the thematic areas covered by the G8 Deauville Partnership, which was launched in 2011. The other component is a technical assistance programme, which aims to implement a *Plateforme Emplois Verts* in the governorate of Bizerte and which is operated by the Ministry of Vocational Training and Employment with the technical assistance of the United Nations Office for Project Services (UNOPS), the operational arm of the United Nations (Box 5.2). The Bizerte pilot project is another concrete example of the institutional steps currently under implementation to create a favourable "green growth" momentum in Tunisia.

**Box 5.2. The *Plateforme Emplois Verts***

The *Plateforme Emplois Verts* under implementation in the governorate of Bizerte aims to introduce, within a period of 40 months, new practices for improving youth employability and facilitating the employment, in the green sector, of around 850 unemployed young graduates and establishing 50 small and medium-size clean-tech companies. Special attention is being placed on women who constitute the majority of unemployed young graduates. The component is inclusive of all the categories of unemployed young graduates and uses a participatory approach to facilitate contribution and participation for all actors concerned (public sector, civil society and private sector).

While Tunisia has already recognised the benefits of an overall strategy for sustainable development, with a provisional strategy already in place (MEDD, 2011), further detailed elaboration remains necessary to ensure that all line ministries are engaged in its implementation. There appears to be insufficient consideration of the possible negative short term impacts of concentration on sustainability (i.e. the balance between short-term growth and longer term sustainability). Box 5.3 presents a set of OECD good practices to guide the design of a strategy for sustainable development.

**Box 5.3. Good practices in national sustainable development strategies**

Although each green growth strategy will have to be tailored to the economic context, the institutional setting and the administrative capacity of the country, many pressures for change will be common across countries. An OECD review of good practice concludes that the following issues are important in the development of a national sustainable development strategy (OECD, 2006).

1. Policy integration – national strategies should give consideration to environmental, economic and social concerns in integrated approaches contained in national plans and reports.
2. Intergenerational timeframe – national strategies should adopt long-term timeframes which enable inclusion of intergenerational principles and indicators.
3. Analysis and assessments – integrated assessment tools should be used in national reports to identify the environmental, economic and social costs and benefits of policy and strategy options.
4. Co-ordination and institutions – a wide range of government departments and agencies should be involved in the formulation and implementation of national strategies, with overall responsibility in the office of the Prime Minister or equivalent.
5. Local and regional governance – local and regional authorities should be fully involved in the development of national strategies, with certain delivery aspects devolved to sub-national levels.
6. Stakeholder participation – stakeholders (e.g., business, unions, non-governmental organisations) should participate with government representatives in commissions responsible for developing and implementing national strategies.
7. Indicators and targets – strategies should be based on structured indicator systems (enumerated in national plans and reports) to assist in monitoring progress and to serve as quantitative targets.
8. Monitoring and evaluation – independent bodies or processes should be established to act as watchdogs monitoring implementation of national strategies and providing recommendations for their improvement.

While Tunisia has gone some distance in following these guidelines in its elaboration of a national sustainable development strategy, there still seem to be some gaps, in particular regarding policy integration and co-ordination, an unclear approach to work at the regional level, and a lack of data on monitoring and evaluation.

The approach needs more than a written strategy, however. The trade-offs between different aspects of sustainable development (economic growth, environmental protection, and social development) need to be both recognised explicitly and to involve appropriate mechanisms (stakeholder fora, inter-ministerial committees) where they can be discussed. For example, if employment and green growth are considered together this can have an effect on choice of projects by infrastructure ministries: a large solar plant will be green and may assist in green growth but will not have the employment impact of a larger number of small initiatives. Current strategies do not appear to provide a framework for this debate, even though there exists a *Commission Nationale de Développement Durable* (CNDD) [National Commission for Sustainable Development] and an *Observatoire Tunisien de l'Environnement et du Développement Durable* (OTED) [Tunisian Observatory on Environment and Sustainable Development]. However, this does not mean that work has not been done at a sectoral level. As Tunisia has become increasingly dependent upon imported fossil fuels, (since the 1990s), it has been a regional pioneer in the promotion of energy efficiency, as well as, more recently, in the realm of renewable sources of energy, where it leads the Arab world (see below). Measures have been introduced gradually to facilitate the private sector's participation in renewable energy sources and waste management. The government is also committed to reporting on the improvement of the framework for investment in support of green growth and to sharing the experience it has acquired (OECD, 2012b).

Direct support to facilitate the transition to green growth in SMEs appears generally absent, as are general actions to stimulate the green market (see also Abdessalem, 2014) (with some important exceptions such as Prosol – see Box 5.4). Strategies for strengthening the market to encourage green entrepreneurship through standards and regulations, and actions to influence consumer behaviour (through both pricing and softer instruments such as education and labelling) also need to be further developed.

A key area where there needs to be a public response is that of water resources, given that climate change is expected to result in a temperature rise of 2.1 degrees and a reduction of precipitation by 10-30% (both figures on a horizon of 2050). At the same time the sea level could rise by as much as 50 cm, causing real change to the ecology and uses of the coastline (MEDD, 2011). Tunisia's water resources are already stressed, so that action will be urgently required, including public works to address the infrastructural needs of change. Analysis suggests that there is a need for review of water policy, in particular because tariffs are set too low to allow for necessary investments within the current framework (OECD, 2012b). This should be an essential area to focus on in developing public works programmes (see Chapter 3), particularly in poorer regions of the country (ILO, 2011). Since the infrastructure framework hardly be improved in the most remote regions without public support, such programmes will have little distortionary effects on local labour markets.

All in all, further action needs to be taken to elaborate the national sustainable development strategy and this will include better clarity at the institutional level, showing how co-ordination will be made between ministries and how stakeholders, including those at a regional level, will be involved (see also Abdessalem, 2014). The development of skills to match a long-term sustainable development strategy will require the review of all curricula and consideration of how green considerations can influence them. Actions can be taken to stimulate demand for green jobs, in particular through promotion of green occupations within the educational system and by providing better information on green jobs and future trends. This needs to be done in the context of better skills-forecasting and reforms to the VET system to make it more demand-driven. Public works which will need to be expanded in response to climate change will contribute to job creation, particularly in poorer areas of the country, whose water resources will be disproportionately affected.

## Actions in particular sectors: where are the opportunities?

There are many areas for green growth but only a few have the potential to create employment for youth. This is because not all growth will create expansion in employment, and in some areas the jobs created are more likely to be taken by existing employees (with retraining).

- The greatest impact on youth employment is likely to be made in areas where there will be employment growth (see figure 5.1), areas where there is likely to be considerable change in the nature of employment which would not be covered by retraining existing employees, and areas where the skills required are likely to be those most prevalent amongst young people. Using this analysis, the following areas are recommended for action: ***The need for encouraging entrepreneurship, in particular in higher education, as a precondition for the development of innovative clean-tech companies***: chosen since it covers the target group of young people.
- ***Developments in energy***: chosen because this is an area where environmental and economic pressures mean that major change is necessary.
- ***Improving waste management***: chosen because this is already identified as a priority in Tunisia, where a strategy for improving environmental performance exists.
- ***Tourism***: chosen because this is a major industry in Tunisia and there are opportunities both for greening existing tourism and for the development of eco-tourism. In addition, existing environmental pressures, notably on water supply, could have an impact on the viability of current tourism approaches, so that change seems likely.
- ***Agriculture***: chosen because this is a major employer and because of its environmental impact, but also because there has been work done already on organic agriculture.
- ***Construction***: chosen because it is a major sector where upgrading of skills will be required, and which will have implications for employment in other sectors, in particular waste management, as resource efficiency becomes more important.

In pursuit of policies to achieve a balanced expansion of these areas, policy makers can draw on a wide range of tools including regulatory measures, as well policies to boost entrepreneurship and training. They also need to count on the support of policies to develop infrastructures – for example transport, water and water management – which represents important challenges in Tunisia. The success of these initiatives rests on the careful prioritisation of these sets of measures, and exploiting synergies and complementarities between them. This is particularly important given that the Tunisian Government is facing large fiscal imbalances that constrain the range of policy options available to it.

### *Entrepreneurship in Higher Education, Innovation and Clean-Tech*

Fostering innovation for green growth requires investment from both the public and private sectors, and, within this, support for general purpose technologies, as well as those specifically related to green sectors (OECD, 2011b). From the public side, Tunisia has moved some distance in this direction, as exemplified by the creation of the technopole at

Borj Cedra and its associated research institutes. However, the beneficial effects of these efforts on private sector investment appear to have been limited so far.

As noted in previous chapters, there is a need to improve the co-ordination of entrepreneurship support. Part of this should be a focus on green entrepreneurship since this is a potential area of market growth. For example, special attention could be devoted to spinning out new ideas from universities and research institutes, and incubating companies with a potential to deal with environmental issues. The technopole at Borj Cedra uses a similar approach. However, the results achieved so far, in terms of the number of new enterprises supported, are below expectations. Analysis of successful clusters in other countries shows that key challenges to be addressed include a weak entrepreneurial culture and incentives in research, limited capacity to involve and engage small firms, a lack of seed capital, and poor co-ordination of policies – all of which apply to Tunisia. By contrast, success clusters stories have included a mix of enabling factors, most notably, a critical mass of human capital, strong commitment of the public sector, and strong partnerships and leadership (OECD, 2009).

It should be noted that photovoltaic (PV) cell manufacture still relies on foreign imports with a limited or absent local supply chain (PV Magazine, 2012). It seems possible that new and innovative local companies which are spun out of the research institutes could fill this gap as part of wider actions to develop a local supply chain. This would help to reduce costs of manufacture, thus ultimately raising competitiveness. Developing a supply chain requires concerted efforts by local economic development agents in order to identify local companies and help them to network, but these actions are essential to instil the creation of a nascent cluster of mutually supportive companies.

The move towards green jobs can, in many areas, be further supported by social entrepreneurship, with waste management being one activity where the case for expanding social enterprises appears to be especially promising (see below). There has been renewed interest recently in Tunisia for engaging social enterprises and for the central role that they can play in the expansion of new waste management activities. To this end, several pilot projects have been launched in 2014, with the aim of gradually increasing their number and territorial coverage in the years to come. Two major barriers exist for social enterprise in addition to those of other enterprises:

- The most appropriate legal framework for the social enterprises remains to be determined. Although, in principle, social enterprises can be established using existing company law, a specific status would assist them in their operations by making it clear that they have a non-profit orientation. It is expected that a new law will be implemented soon.
- The problem of finance. In the past, the *Banque Tunisienne de Solidarité* (BTS) [Tunisian Solidarity Bank] has restricted its financing to private enterprises and individual entrepreneurs. However, BTS now has an allocation of TND 8 million from the Ministry of Employment, which could be destined to the expansion of the social enterprises.

All in all, while the infrastructure for improving graduate entrepreneurship is partly in place, there needs to be better organisation and strategic direction, alongside renewal of more general support for entrepreneurship. In respect of developing a clean-tech cluster, again the elements are in place (the technopole, connections with research, and an incubator), but as yet there is not a critical mass. Cluster development should be better co-ordinated with other investments (for example in PV cell manufacture) and greater attention paid to supply chain development. The supportive role played by social enterprises will be important but the current projects to clarify the legal status and provide finance need to be pursued.

## *Energy: capitalising on existing experience*

Tunisia is a net importer of oil and has been for more than a decade. This has given impetus to the move towards renewable energy sources and, indeed, Tunisia is a leader in the Arab world in this respect with more than 14% of total primary energy supply from renewables compared to an Arab average of 3.1%, see Figure 5.2 (AFED, 2013).

**Figure 5.2. Use of renewable energy in Arab countries, 2010**

Share of renewable energy in total primary energy supply

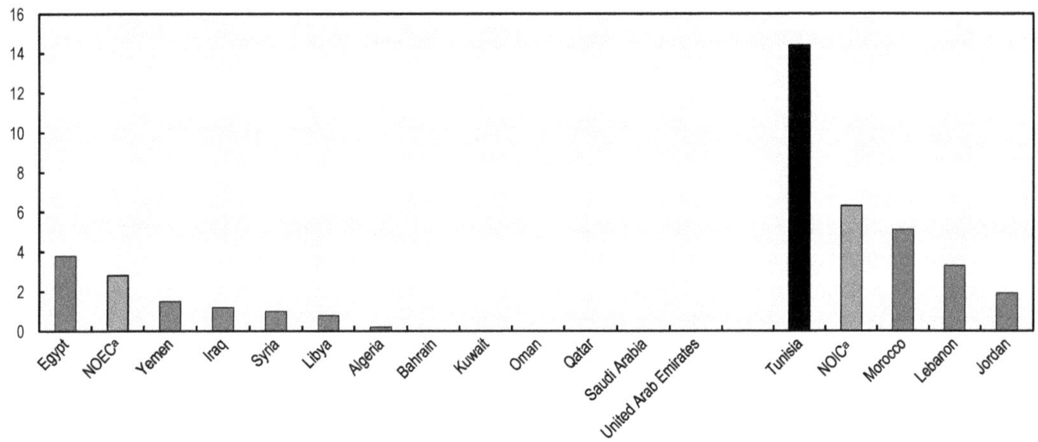


*a)* NOEC = Net Oil Exporting Countries. NOIC = Net Oil Importing Countries.

*Source*: AFED (2013), "Arab Environment: Sustainable Energy: Prospects, Challenges, Opportunities", 2013 Report of the Arab Forum for Environment and Development, Arab Forum for Environment and Development, Beirut.

Energy and the opportunities offered by renewable sources of energy are clearly important for Tunisia. These opportunities, for example those stemming from solar power, have been recognised for some time (OME, 2012). Specifically, the *Plan Solaire Tunisien* (PST), which was announced in 2009 aims to give a framework for investment both in improving use of renewable energy and in increasing energy efficiency.

Tunisia is well placed for solar power, while it also has appropriate sites for wind power. PST envisages some 40 projects, and an investment of EUR 2 000 million (of which EUR 1 390 million from the private sector) over the period to 2016. Many of the projects are large infrastructure projects which will create largely temporary employment opportunities, but attention is also paid to local energy production, including at the residential level. Specifically, as part of PST, Tunisia has developed the Prosol programme, which encourages the use of small scale solar thermal water heaters, allowing residential customers to pay back the capital cost of installation through their normal utility bills. This initiative has been very successful in terms of its capacity to widen solar power usage and, has resulted in a net gain to the public budget (see Box 5.4). Part of the programme has been focused on the creation of new incentives for the enterprises involved in installation and maintenance of the installations. Qualifications have been designed by CENAFFIF and training has been delivered by relying on the VET system. Prosol is still continuing, but consideration should be given to extending the same principle to other areas of renewable energy, for example Solar PV, wind, and insulation.

### Box 5.4. Prosol Programme in Tunisia

The Prosol programme in Tunisia is seen internationally as an example of good practice in extending the usage and market for residential solar water heaters (SWH).

Initially supported by foreign donors, one key factor explaining the success of Prosol lies in the capacity of the programme to remove some of the key barriers to the expansion of SWH. These were identified as: the distortion of the market caused by subsidies to fossil fuels; the lack of public resources; lack of awareness of the potential of the technology; difficulty of households in obtaining suitable credit for investment in SWH; the need for quality control of suppliers and installers. These barriers were addressed by:

- Levelling the playing field by offering subsidies to match the current unfair advantage of gas-fired systems;
- Building up both the demand and supply sides of the market through awareness campaigns, accreditation of suppliers, and establishment of a network of maintainers;
- Using the state utility provider (STEG) to act as debt collector and guarantor to address the absence of effective consumer credit.

An analysis of the results of the programme from 2005 to 2010 (Climate Policy Initiative, 2012) shows that the capacity of SWH installed increased fivefold and some 3 000 jobs were created in the solar thermal industrial cluster. These results appear to have been achieved with a net gain to the public budget, owing to a saving of USD 15.2 million, projected to rise to USD 101 million over the life span of the SWHs, more than the government's initial investment of USD 21.8 million. The imposition of quality standards through training and accreditation schemes proved effective with technology failures at only around 1%.

Prosol is an example of good government action and how this can effectively result in the introduction of a new technology at low cost, while at the same time creating new jobs in a green industry. The careful design of the programme, particularly the quality of installations, as well as the means of payment have been important factors. Repayment through STEG has been effective since the company can enforce debts through withholding of services.

Prosol for SWH has been seen to be a success and has shown a model which could be used for other technologies, most notably Solar PV. Taking this approach will be helped by an integrated set of actions including awareness, training, accreditation, and a system of debt collection.

The experience of PST illustrates well some of the challenges to be faced in increasing the use of renewable energy and through this the generation of employment. These include: the implicit subsidies to existing fossil fuels and the sunk cost in infrastructure; the use of centralised and larger infrastructure; and the ability to fund capital costs as sources of energy change. Opportunities relate to finding appropriate ways of financing locally produced energy. This can be at the residential level using programmes like Prosol, but there are also opportunities to develop renewable sources at the municipal level. This requires some freedom to act, either through the creation of municipal companies or via social enterprise. An example is shown in Box 5.5. Evidence suggests that green energy initiatives can drive job creation and new business opportunities if they are integrated into other local development activities but that fostering green energy initiatives requires inclusive governance arrangements (Martinez-Fernandez et al., 2013).

**Box 5.5. Locally produced energy from waste, Italy**

This example shows the way in which the municipality of Peccioli in the Tuscany region established a municipal company (Belvedere SpA) with the aim to address both environmental challenges and local employment needs.

At the end of the 1990s there was an unmanaged waste dump in Peccioli, located in a landfill site shared by six municipalities in the area. In spite of public opinion demanding its closure, eventually a plan was made to reclaim the previous landfill site, expand it, and recover new areas in order to cope with environmental problems. After discussion, a new intervention was proposed to produce large quantities of biogas that would justify the installation of a cogeneration plant. This plant would produce electricity for sale to the national electricity board, ENEL, as well as hot water for district heating distribution to the adjacent village of Legoli. Thanks to efficient environmental organisation and close working relations with the local population and public opinion, the Provincial Administration Authority decided on the Peccioli site as a "strategic plan". A new expansion project was set up to meet the needs of the provincial plan. Particular attention was paid to environmental issues, extremely important in a region with such a high tourist impact, which explains the high certification requirements imposed.

Belvedere Spa is the privately owned public company which has managed the Peccioli waste disposal plant since 1997. Starting as an "incubator business", it has created a range of business ventures and benefits in the form of a community company set in a small rural area with a population of only 5 000, where it has succeeded in lowering taxes and rates, and in expanding and improving local services. Thanks to a coherent strategy and far-sighted project planning, the company managed to reinforce local social identity and general consensus. One interesting aspect is the ownership structure of Belvedere SpA, whose capital stock belongs by 38% to small stockholders (mainly residents in the Peccioli Municipality), who play an active role in the company's management and profit distribution. Today, following two shareholding investments, the total number of stockholders has risen to 750, with total investments of EUR 4 200 000.

Another success factor, of possible relevance to Tunisia, is the importance to gain support from the local community, listening to its views about how to address environmental problems. If a similar model is to be followed in Tunisia, current centralisation, of decisions may need to be re-examined.

*Source* : www.belvedere.peccioli.net/

It can be expected that the size of investment envisaged under the *Plan Solaire Tunisien* (PST) will help the creation of a larger market for renewable energy and consequent establishment of suppliers of parts and services. For example, the existence of PST has already had some part in the establishment of a PV cell manufacturing plant (PV magazine, 2012). However, at this stage, outside the direct consequences of programmes (for example Prosol), there appears to have been little work done to develop a supply chain, which could create employment through import substitution. It seems likely that better results could be achieved by targeted actions to encourage supply chains, and to link investment in manufacture with research in universities.

To maximise employment results as part of a strategy to increase the use of renewable energy, programmes such as Prosol should be continued and extended to other forms of renewable energy. As this requires the willing support of the local communities, the current work to support social enterprises will also be important in giving opportunities for expansion in this sector.

### *Waste and recycling: Realising an existing strategy*

The need to improve the management of waste has also been acknowledged for some time, with the establishment of a managing authority (ANGeD) and a long-term strategy with targets for waste reduction and treatment. The current situation shows good control of landfills (see Figure 5.3), with 85% of waste ending up in sanitary landfills and only 10% in open dumps (one of the best records for Arab countries). On the other hand only very small amounts of waste are composted or recycled, showing further potential for development (SWEEP-Net, 2012).

**Figure 5.3. Treatment of municipal solid waste, end 2011**

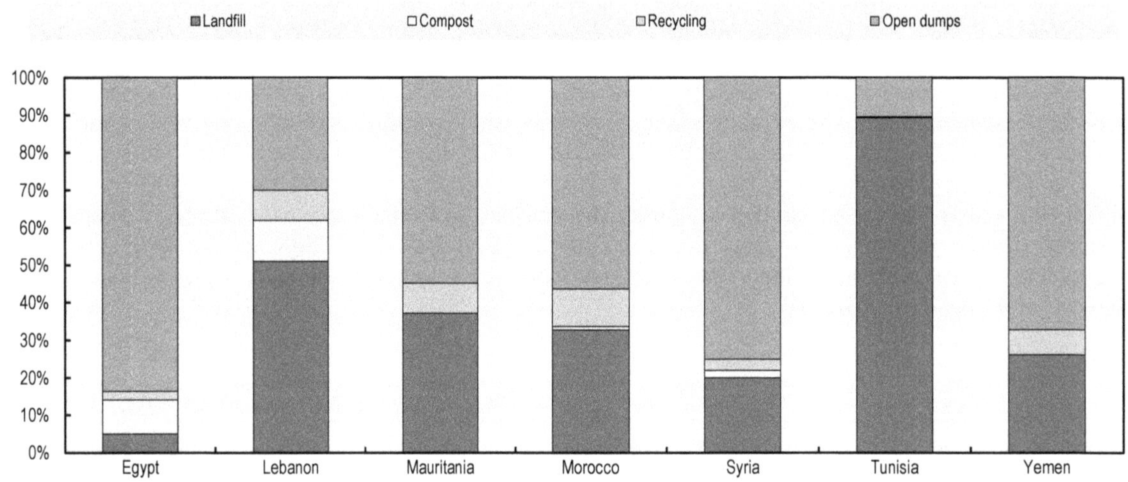


*Source*: SWEEP-Net (2012), "The Solid Waste Management Situation in Mashreq and Maghreb Countries: Update on the Challenges and Opportunities", Solid Waste Exchange of Information and Expertise Network.

Waste management has been guided by a strategy for integrated and sustainable waste management (*Stratégie de Gestion Integrée et Durable des Déchets* – SGIDD) [Integrated and Sustainable Waste Management Strategy]) and a corresponding programme of actions (*Programme National de Gestion Integrée et Durable des Déchets* – PRONGIDD) [National Programme for Integrated and Sustainable Waste Management]). This covers the period 2007-16 and has a set of ambitious targets, for example increasing the level of recycling in plastic waste (30% to 70%), used oil (40% to 85%), used tyres (0% to 50%), and electrical and electronic waste (0% to 70%). While some parts of the programme have stalled since 2011, in part reflecting difficulties with the public consultations needed to plan waste disposal sites, a number of actions have been taken, which may have positive effects on job creation. In particular, the programme envisages:

- A greater involvement of the private sector. A particular example of this is the Eco-lef scheme which gives funding to enterprises that collect and recycle plastic waste. By 2009, the programme had created 310 collection points of which 79% are privately owned, and 231 enterprises under a programme for employment reduction. The amount of waste collected has risen from 1 178 tonnes in 2001 to more than 15 000 tonnes in 2009. Some 70% of this is exported showing that the recycling is performed to an acceptable standard (Plan Bleu, 2011).
- An explicit commitment in the programme to act in partnership with NGOs, which could help to support the interactions with the local communities (ANGeD, 2006).

A major issue is that the responsibility for waste collection is at the commune level and, although this typically constitutes 30% of commune budgets, they are unable to collect local taxes to cover these (SWEEP-Net, 2010). GIZ and other donors have sought to create commune level waste management plans (PCGD) across the whole country. However, although the process is almost complete, the impact of these plans has been limited, mainly due to a lack of finance to implement the measures identified, as well as a lack of support from the elected municipal councils. It is also difficult to create a consensus in favour of innovative solutions at a time when the country is undergoing such an important political transition.[1]

The ambition to have a fully integrated waste management system is a good one, and continued progress in this direction will at the same time create employment. Nonetheless, such an approach tends to put excessive emphasis on the treatment and disposal of waste, rather than reuse and recycling. While reuse and recycling schemes can be part of a unified system, international experience suggests that they can be run more effectively at a local level, adapting to local conditions, and often operating as social enterprises (UNEP, 2005). This would probably match with the PCGDs, provided that appropriate finance is in place for implementation. An example of the type of projects which could be implemented, drawing from the UK experience, is shown in Box 5.6. It points to the crucial importance to provide adequate training for young people. This can help them to find employment in the wider economy.

### Box 5.6. Furniture Re-use Network in the United Kingdom

The Furniture Re-use Network (FRN) in the United Kingdom supports over 300 non-profit enterprises involved in promoting the re-use of household furniture and electrical appliances. Its members vary in size and scope, but have a common model based on:

- Use furniture and electrical items being donated free of charge (or for a nominal fee), but being collected by the enterprise.
- Refurbishment being performed by the enterprise, often through training of otherwise unemployed people and through this making them more employable (by giving them basic skills, understanding of employability requirements, and experience).
- Sale of refurbished items at low cost to needy families (based on different criteria depending on the area).

The enterprises are run as businesses, but receive implicit subsidy through the fact that the population are willing to donate items free of charge (because of the non-profit nature and social objectives of the enterprise) and through government schemes which support trainees.

FRN estimates that the sector employs 4 000 staff, provides training annually for 15 000 trainees, reuses 2.7 million items of furniture and electrical equipment – and diverts 110 000 tonnes of waste from landfill saving over 380 000 tonnes of $CO_2$.

A typical member of FRN is Changing Lives in Cheshire (CLiC) which employs 22 people, the majority of whom were previously unemployed, and recycled 140 tonnes of furniture and 40 tonnes of electrical goods.

This approach could be used in Tunisia if some key preconditions are met. The business model (obtaining items free of charge) depends upon the fact that the enterprises are recognised to have social objectives and to be non-profit, so a clear framework for social enterprise will be important. Successful enterprises in the network require local leadership and promotion, as well as clear business plans based on knowledge of government programmes for training and other subsidies which may be available. For Tunisia this may mean both specific training and support for those wishing to run social enterprises, and adaptation of government training schemes to fit into this type of operation

*Source*: Furniture Re-use Network (FRN) at www.frn.org.uk/; and Changing Lives in Cheshire at www.clic-changinglives.org.uk/about-us/.

Tunisia has been a leader in the Arab world in implementing an integrated waste management system. However, this could be taken further by mobilising social enterprises and further mobilising local private enterprises in the field of reuse and recycling. The current strategy and programme for integrated and sustainable waste management is well developed, but it sets very ambitious targets, which will need to be carefully monitored as progress is achieved. As already discussed, a rapid, clarification of the legal status of non-profit organisations would be essential to enable the sector to expand in line with targets. Some initiatives have been created to encourage social enterprise, including an incubator (Lab'ESS). However, a better guided approach might be needed to facilitate the creation of such enterprises in the activities where they have a stronger role to play (i.e. related to waste management) or with a specific format. While the current government seems to have already allocated the funding required, project design remains an issue, as suggested by a reported lack of viable projects.[2]

### *Tourism: a more sustainable approach*

Tourism is an important sector in Tunisia, representing 6.5% of GDP. The bulk of the available capacity rests on mass tourism, based on beach resorts, while opportunities for cultural, sport and eco-related tourism activities remain largely unexploited. As a result, comparison with other Mediterranean countries shows that on average receipts per tourist arrival in Tunisia are low (see Figure 5.4). Despite wide cyclical fluctuations in overall tourism receipts during the past years (-30% in 2011, +24% in 2012), per capita figures have not varied suggesting that the limited diversification of the structure of Tunisia's tourism represents a structural issue, with low value tourism or very short stays being significant. Therefore actions should be implemented to both rejuvenate existing attractions and to find new approaches if the resilience of the sector to cyclical demand fluctuations is to be strengthened.

**Figure 5.4. Receipts per tourist arrival in selected Mediterranean destinations, 2010-12**

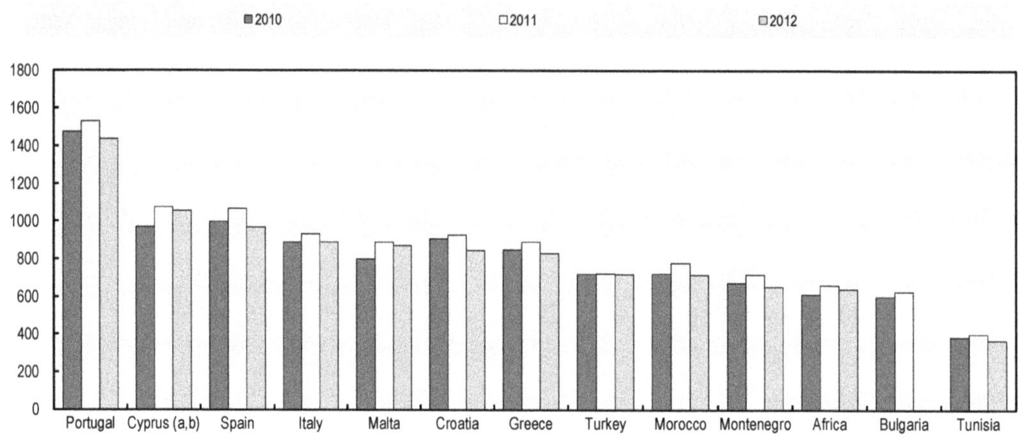


*a)* Note by Turkey: The information in this document with reference to "Cyprus" relates to the southern part of the Island. There is no single authority representing both Turkish and Greek Cypriot people on the Island. Turkey recognises the Turkish Republic of Northern Cyprus (TRNC). Until a lasting and equitable solution is found within the context of the United Nations, Turkey shall preserve its position concerning the "Cyprus issue".

*b)* Note by all the European Union Member States of the OECD and the European Union: The Republic of Cyprus is recognised by all members of the United Nations with the exception of Turkey. The information in this document relates to the area under the effective control of the Government of the Republic of Cyprus.

*Source:* OECD calculations from UNWTO (2013), "Tourism highlights", 2013 Edition, United Nations World Tourism Organisation.

Tourism is a major user of resources, particularly water, and energy, implying that any strategy for the future development of the sector will need to pay due attention to sustainability issues. Welcome actions have already been taken to introduce pricing mechanisms in water consumption and the pay-offs of these efforts are already visible. Indeed, even though overall consumption has grown steadily from 50.2 litres to 63.9 litres per head per day between 1997 and 2006, over the same period of time there have been major changes in tourist consumption per head per night, which has declined, thanks to the tariff changes. Even though more recent data are not available, this pattern suggests the strong responsiveness of the sector to pricing mechanisms on the use of recycling and reduction in usage. More should be done to ensure that overall daily water consumption is affected going forward. Similar encouraging developments can be seen with regards to electricity consumption (which has fallen from a peak of 20 KWh per tourist per night in 2003 to 16.7 KWh in 2005) and gas (1.6 KgEP in 2003 down to 1.4 KgEP in 2006). This progress was not, however, accompanied by a corresponding change in employment, indicating that in itself sustainability may not be a driver of employment growth (MEDD, 2010).

As mentioned previously, sustainability and green issues are not explicit objectives in the current strategy for the tourism sector (Berger, 2012). There are both opportunities and challenges to the development of sustainable tourism in Tunisia. The main drivers supporting a move towards more sustainable tourism practices are numerous and relate to consumer demand shifts; opportunities for increasing competitiveness; the adoption of more coherent policies and regulations to safeguard the environment; technology improvements; private efforts for environmental and social responsibility and natural resource conservation. By contrast, the major cross-cutting barriers involve: information gaps; the lack of a critical mass in industry capacity and networking; fiscal budgetary considerations which reduce the scope for public support of the sector; limited access to private financing; and the need for better aligning vocational education to changing needs. Taken together, these factors highlight the strong potential for greening tourism activities in Tunisia. At the same time, they also reveal that a comprehensive strategic response will need to be put in place in order to ensure that these opportunities are fully met (OECD, 2012c).

Currently the greening of tourism largely rests on voluntary actions undertaken by the private sector, partly encouraged by some by pricing mechanisms, with only a small proportion of hotels and tourist establishments acquiring "eco-label" certification. The Eco-label has been developed in the framework of ISO 14001 and requires progress related to a range of criteria. The growing number of such initiatives suggests that sustainability priorities will play an increasingly important guiding role in the way tourism develops (IPAG, 2014).

Eco-tourism has yet to have a significant impact, but its co-ordinated development could bring income and employment to some of the more remote and disadvantaged areas of the country. Although a strategy has been produced with the aid of GTZ (MEDD, 2008), this does not appear to have been put into practice and there is no overall organisation of eco-tourism. Greater involvement of stakeholders and development of networks will be necessary in order to expand this sector. This will require some adjustments in the current strategic orientations of the government which should be improved by making it more consensual. To this end, some useful practical insights about how to develop an action plan for eco-tourism in Tunisia more aligned with the objectives of a broad range of stakeholders can be drawn from the experience of Bulgaria (Box 5.7).

**Box 5.7. Eco-tourism strategy in Bulgaria**

Bulgaria faces similar problems in tourism to those of Tunisia – a concentration of mass tourism on holiday complexes on the beach, but at the same time a vast and largely unexploited natural and cultural heritage from the viewpoint of tourism. Bulgaria produced a national eco-tourism strategy and action plan in 2003. Important lessons come from the *process* of preparing the strategy, which has had an impact on the degree to which it is owned by key stakeholders (regional tourist associations and NGOs, ministries, municipalities, as well as actual tourism providers), with positive results in terms of actual implementation.

The plan was initiated by three ministries (Environment and Water, Economy, including Tourism, and Agriculture and Forests), formalised by a protocol on co-operation, including a strong commitment with regards to implementation. The process was supported by four foreign donors (USAID, UNDP, the World Bank, and the Swiss Agency for Co-operation and Development). Work proceeded at both local and national levels, including:

- Local pilots leading to the formation of local eco-tourism partnerships/associations, and providing a model for other areas.
- Establishment of a national eco-tourism working group, including not only the relevant ministries but also national and local tourism associations and NGOs.
- Setting up thematic working groups at national level (covering IT, product development and marketing, funding, enterprise development, institutional development, and regional development).
- Dividing the region into destination regions based on landscape types and clusters of protected areas and cultural sites.

The process took two years and included 400 individual and group meetings involving 800 different organisations and 140 municipalities. It was backed up by comprehensive market research, efforts to stimulate local interest and support, and extensive media coverage.

This experience suggests the essential role played by a strategy that aims at achieving the engagement of stakeholders. This contrasts with the situation in Tunisia where, although there is a written strategy for eco-tourism, it lacks detailed involvement of local actors with hardly any strong commitments to implementation.

*Source*: National Ecotourism Strategy and Action Plan for Bulgaria (2003); UNEP/WTO (2005), *Making Tourism More Sustainable: A Guide for Policy Makers.*

### *Agriculture: extending a lead in organic production*

The transition to a green economy clearly involves important implications for agriculture, a sector characterised by high employment levels and strong environmental impacts. Organic agriculture plays an important role in the green economy. This sector has been growing and has a full system of certification, which is recognised by the European Union, thereby allowing access to the EU market. Organic agriculture tends to be a relatively skills intensive activity, both reflecting the search for quality of output and the fact that it is often practised in vulnerable agriculture areas – due to higher temperatures, lower rainfall, and stresses on water supply. Although Tunisia is a respected international player in the field of organic agriculture – such as organic olive oil, for example – it still lags behind most European Union countries in terms of the percentage of agricultural land certified as organic, which suggests a strong case for harnessing new opportunities for expansion (see Figure 5.5).

**Figure 5.5. Percentage of agricultural land certified as organic, 2011**

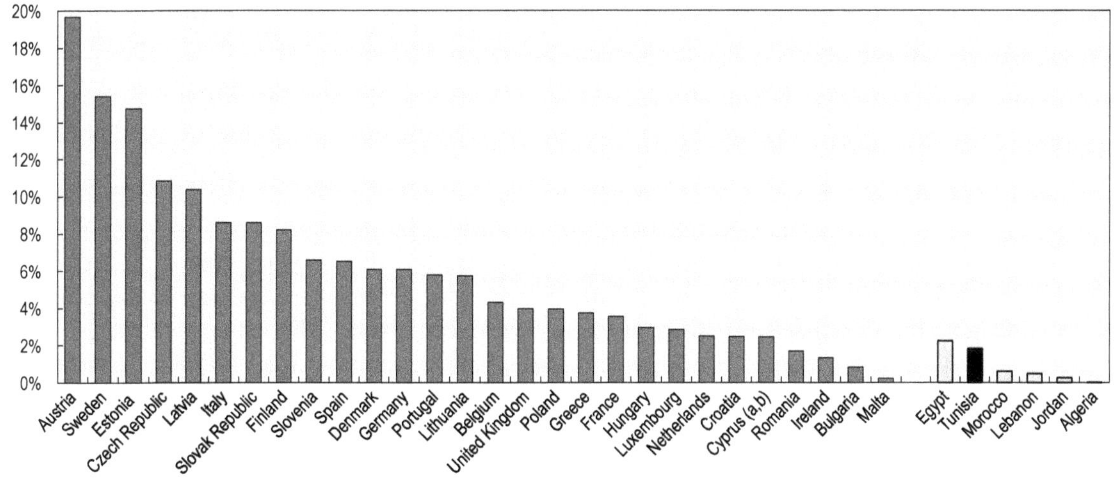


*a)* Note by Turkey: The information in this document with reference to "Cyprus" relates to the southern part of the Island. There is no single authority representing both Turkish and Greek Cypriot people on the Island. Turkey recognises the Turkish Republic of Northern Cyprus (TRNC). Until a lasting and equitable solution is found within the context of the United Nations, Turkey shall preserve its position concerning the "Cyprus issue".

*a)* Note by all the European Union Member States of the OECD and the European Union: The Republic of Cyprus is recognised by all members of the United Nations with the exception of Turkey. The information in this document relates to the area under the effective control of the Government of the Republic of Cyprus.

*Source*: FiBL & IFOAM (2013), *The World of Organic Agriculture 2013*, Frick and Bonn.

Encouragement of organic agriculture can be done in a number of ways. Policy options range from enabling initiatives (e.g. providing certification and labelling frameworks, research and extension services), to better enforcement (e.g. establishing regulations and standards); and support efforts (e.g. providing financial incentives, bringing together agents along the production chain to establish partnerships and procurement policies). Market-based policy approaches, including certification and labelling schemes are now in place in virtually all OECD countries, as they are in Tunisia. Several governments have undertaken information campaigns and promotional activities to encourage consumption of organic products. In a few countries, notably in Europe, government procurement policies encourage or require the purchase of organic food by public institutions such as schools and hospitals. In many OECD countries financial support is specifically provided to organic farmers, usually on a per-hectare basis. Financial support is still very limited in Tunisia, based on subsidies for equipment and for the process of certification.

While in OECD countries more publicly funded research efforts are now devoted to organic systems it still only accounts for a small share of overall research on agriculture. Some of the results of farm experiences and research into organic farming systems have been adopted by non-organic farming systems (e.g. ways to control pests without chemicals). Governments need to address the externalities in conventional agriculture to provide a better use of resources and a more level playing field for organic systems. Furthermore, policies that reward farming (both organic and non-organic) for any environmental benefits must be based on verifiable evidence, monitored and evaluated, and adapted in the light of changing evidence (OECD, 2003).

There is a strong case for shaping administrative simplification in ways that harness the potential for increasing the land area which is certified as organic. This could have important feedback effects on the growth of exports, particularly to the European Union. Current challenges relate to the costs of the process of conversion to organic farming (which can take two or three years). A very interesting example of an export-led strategy is provided by Chile, whose experience is outlined in Box 5.8.

Development of agriculture within the EU has been stimulated by the creation of Organic Action Plans at national and regional level. These are usually the result of many years of dialogue between government, the organic movement and the agricultural industry. An important factor in success has been the creation of clear and fully shared goals and timelines – the reason that Austria has the highest share of organically cultivated land within the EU is partly the fact that this is an explicit goal of an integrated action plan (an aim for 20% by 2013). Other targets include percentage of organic products in shops (Finland), percentage of organic products in government canteens (France), share of farms in total number of farms (Poland) and percentage of organic consumption produced nationally (England) (Gonzalvez et al., 2011). Currently Tunisia has an office responsible for organic agriculture, attached to the Ministry of Agriculture (the *Centre Technique de l'Agriculture Biologique* (CTAB) [Technical Center of Organic Agriculture]). A strategy was produced with the assistance of GTZ (GTZ, 2007), but the actual extent to which this strategy is being pursued in practice remains limited. A website was set up to assist the export of organic products but this appears to be out-of-date (still advertising events in 2012).[3]

**Box 5.8. Chile: Promotion of exports from organic agriculture**

As in many countries, there was considerable expansion of the organic sector in Chile in the early 21st century – between 1998 and 2004 the area under organic cultivation increased roughly tenfold. What is specific to Chile is the rapid expansion of organic exports, which have increased in value terms by more than four times between 1999 and 2004, with exports going worldwide, particularly to North America and to Europe.

Important factors in this success are:

- The creation of a sectoral organisation (the Chilean Organic Association – AAOCH) to promote the sector and recognised as the representative of the sector by governmental authorities. The Ministry of Agriculture has also established INDAP, the network of small organic farmers. The National Commission of Organic Agriculture was established in 2005 to co-ordinate development of the organic sector. It includes both public and private representatives and is chaired by the Vice Minister of Agriculture.
- A government control system in place, which allows for products to be certified and to fulfil standards required by destination markets.
- Integration of organic agriculture into national agricultural policy, which emphasises quality and sustainability.
- Co-ordination with ProChile (the export promotion agency, under the Ministry of Foreign Affairs), providing market information and support at important trade fairs.

Important lessons for Tunisia relate to the organisation of the sector and its representatives, and the co-ordination with general export promotion. Even though the EU market is close and Tunisian certification is recognised, Tunisia has a relatively low number of exporters and a much smaller proportion of producers export. Administrative simplification combined with better organisation could considerably increase access to foreign markets.

*Source*: UNCTAD-UNEP (2008), "Best Practices for Organic Policy: What Developing Country Governments Can Do to Promote the Organic Agriculture Sector", Prepared under the CBTF Project "Promoting Production and Trading Opportunities for Organic Agricultural Products in East Africa".

Agriculture remains an area with high employment potential and the greening of the economy will encourage a move towards organic production, which may be more labour intensive as well as being more sustainable. A more comprehensive strategy to support organic agriculture, including promotion of export in sectors where Tunisia has a competitive advantage, could increase the importance of the sector.

### *Construction: taking advantage of necessary changes*

Construction is both a major part of the economy and, at the same time, has major environmental effects, particularly with regard to disposal of waste, and the potential for energy efficiency measures. It is not certain that green construction will directly create significant numbers of new jobs, or jobs which will be relevant to youth (see Figure 5.1 above for predictions for Europe and OECD countries). To a large extent the process of change will concentrate on changing or upgrading the skills of existing workers at all levels (from labourers using new materials through to architects who design new buildings). There are, however, likely to spin-offs of jobs in other areas, in particular in the field of waste disposal and recycling, which is examined more generally above. Examination of European markets shows that the demand for green skills in construction is influenced primarily by the regulatory and incentive schemes introduced under energy and environmental policies but that, on the other hand, the number of jobs is not increased by such stimulation (Cedefop, 2012).

In order to stimulate green construction (and consequent improvement of skills in the sector and job opportunities in related sectors), it will be necessary to develop an integrated strategy covering not only skills and employment issues, but also issues such as design, innovation, use of materials, and waste disposal. An example of such a strategy can be seen in the United Kingdom (HMG, 2008). This shows the importance of consultation with the sector itself, include employers and trade associations.

It should be noted that a major driver towards sustainable construction strategies within the European Union has been the adoption of Europe-wide regulations. However, the progress actually achieved has varied across countries, particularly in waste disposal (CRW, 2010). Evidence suggests that information is also an important factor in success, for example in understanding the environmental impact of different approaches and materials, and facilitating the use of recycled materials in construction (Powell and Craighill, 2001).

It is perhaps surprising that the current SGIDD does not identify targets for recycling and disposal of Construction and Demolition Waste (CDW). The ANGeD website notes that construction is a major cause of the proliferation of uncontrolled landfills,[4] and gives details of a pilot project from 2004 to address the problem. However, detailed and up to date statistics appear unavailable. Management of CDW is important, since otherwise, as a major waste stream, it will cause stress on landfills designated for Municipal Solid Waste, while at the same time, there are a variety of possibilities for more appropriate treatment (UNEP, 2005).

The amount of CDW varies widely between countries, but in general prevention and reuse are unlikely to grow based purely on market forces. An example of the degree to which landfill can be avoided is provided by the Netherlands, where CDW is the second largest waste stream. In 2001, 90% of waste was used as secondary materials, with the rest being landfilled or incinerated (van Dijk et al., 2001), and the figure reached 95% by 2006 (CRW, 2010). These figures were achieved by a combination of different regulations as well as support for the industry in moving towards the use of secondary materials. In view of the number of uncontrolled landfills, it would be difficult for Tunisia to move quickly to a highly regulated approach, but development of a strategy for change, including incentives for use of secondary materials, could have a positive effect on the environment (and release space in existing landfills) while at the same time creating employment in recycling and treatment.

For Tunisia this shows the need for integrated strategies in areas of concern for greening the economy: in construction it will be important to produce a strategy for the sector which encompasses not only improving skills, but also all other aspects of construction, and which is elaborated in consultation with appropriate stakeholders. Issues related to re-use and recycling of construction waste will be important, and need to be integrated into the SGIDD, with appropriate regulations and actions designed to encourage resource efficiency.

### *Common approaches*

These sectors show some common features. In particular, experience of other countries suggests that government action in terms of regulations and incentives can have a major impact on behaviours in these sectors and hence their growth and employment for young people.

This report has evidenced a need for upgrading and adapting the skills supply in Tunisia as it makes the transition to a greener economy. At the same time, however, many Tunisian youth, and particularly the higher educated, face high levels of unemployment and inactivity. A comprehensive set of government actions are therefore required to produce effects in the sectors identified in this chapter through aiming to facilitate job creation and boosting demand for and supply of skills against a background of longer-term changes.

Implementation of changes does, however, present some challenges of co-ordination. There are initiatives which have worked well as being centrally driven (notably Prosol) but on the other hand many of the employment opportunities will happen at a local level and this will require the ability for people to act locally, including through the creation and operation of social enterprises, implying that encouragement of this approach will be important. This requires a degree of flexibility in the way in which training and enterprise support is delivered, and also encouragement of civil society to organise itself.

These factors indicate a need for an overall sustainable development strategy, which involves stakeholders from across government and joins concerns regarding environment with those of employment and social affairs and with economic growth. However, this needs to be complemented by actions in the specific sectors. These actions will again involve many stakeholders and can be used as pilots to learn both about the best way to use green growth for the production of youth employment and to explore better ways of co-operation between different stakeholders.

# Notes

1. www.sweep-net.org/pcgd-tunisia-current-situation.
2. www.babnet.net/cadredetail-75071.asp.
3. www.organic.com.tn/.
4. www.anged.nat.tn/index.php?option=com_content&view=article&id=118&Itemid=248&lang=en.

# *References*

Abdessalem, T. (2014), *Rapport sur les politiques d'économie verte inclusive et la transformation structurelle en Tunisie*, Preliminary version presented in "Atelier de validation du rapport de l'étude sur les politiques d'économie verte inclusive et la transformation structurelle en Tunisie", organised by the Commission économique pour l'Afrique des Nations Unies in collaboration with the Institut National de la Statistique de Tunisie, 21-22 October, Tunis.

AFED – Arab Forum for Environment and Development (2013), "Arab Environment: Sustainable Energy: Prospects, Challenges, Opportunities", 2013 Report of the Arab Forum for Environment and Development, Arab Forum for Environment and Development, Beirut.

ANGeD – Agence Nationale de Gestion des Déchets (2006), "Stratégie de gestion intégrée et durable des déchets, 2007-2016", Ministère de l'Environnement et du Développement Durable – Agence Nationale de Gestion des Déchets, Tunis.

Berger, R. (2012), "Plan de mise en oeuvre de l'étude stratégique du secteur touristique tunisien".

Cedefop – European Centre for the Development of Vocational Training (2012), *Green Skills and Environmental Awareness in Vocational Education and Training.*

Climate Policy Initiative (2012), "San Giorgio Group Case Study: Prosol Tunisia".

CRW – Construction Resources and Waste Platform (2010), "Construction Resources and Waste Roadmap: 2010 Update", Construction Resources and Waste Platform.

European Commission (2013), "Promoting Green Jobs throughout the Crisis: A Handbook of Best Practices in Europe", *European Employment Observatory Review.*

FIBL/IFOAM (2013), *The World of Organic Agriculture 2013*, Research Institute of Organic Agriculture (FIBL) and International Federation of Organic Agriculture Movements (IFOAM), Frick and Bonn.

GIZ – German Federal Enterprise for International Cooperation (2012), "Renewable Energy and Energy Efficiency in Tunisia – Employment, Qualification and Economic Effects".

Gonzalvez, V. et al. (2011), "Organic Action Plans in Europe", in H. Willer and L. Kilcher (eds.), *The World of Organic Agriculture – Statistics and Emerging Trends 2011*, IFOAM, Bonn, FiBL, Frick.

GTZ – German Organisation for Technical Cooperation (2007), "Stratégie nationale d'adaptation de l'agriculture tunisienne et des écosystèmes aux changements climatiques".

HMG – HM Government (2008), "Strategy for Sustainable Construction", HM Government in association with the Strategic Forum for Construction.

ILO – International Labour Organization (2011), "Local Investments for Climate Change Adaptation: Green Jobs through Green Works", ILO Regional Office for Asia and the Pacific, ILO, Geneva.

IPAG – Institut de Préparation à l'Administration Générale (2014), "Stratégie de 'tourisme durable': Validation empirique dans le Groupe TUI en Tunisie", IPAG Business School Working Paper No. 2014-264.

Martinez-Fernandez, C., S. Sharpe, M. Hughes and C. Avellaner de Santos (2013), "Improving the Effectiveness of Green Local Development: The Role and Impact of Public Sector-Led Initiatives in Renewable Energy", *OECD Green Growth Papers*, No. 2013-09, OECD Publishing, Paris.

MDGIF – MDG Achievement Fund (2013), "Étude sur les compétences pour les emplois verts en Tunisie", Millennium Development Goals Achievement Fund, Youth, Employment & Migration programme.

MEDD – Ministère de l'Environnement et du Développement Durable (2011), "Stratégie Nationale du Développement Durable", Version provisoire, Ministère de l'Environnement et du Développement Durable, Tunis.

MEDD (2010), "Le Tourisme Durable en Tunisie", Ministère de l'Environnement et du Développement Durable, Tunis.

MEDD (2008), "Etude stratégique sur le développement de l'écotourisme en Tunisie", Ministère de l'Environnement et du Développement Durable, Tunis.

OECD (2012a), "The Jobs Potential of a Shift Towards a Low-carbon Economy", *OECD Green Growth Papers*, No. 2012/01, OECD Publishing, Paris, http://dx.doi.org/10.1787/5k9h3630320v-en.

OECD (2012b), *OECD Investment Policy Reviews: Tunisia 2012*, OECD Publishing, Paris, http://dx.doi.org/10.1787/9789264179172-en.

OECD (2012c), "Green Innovation in Tourism Services", *OECD Tourism Papers*, No. 2013/01, OECD Publishing, Paris, http://dx.doi.org/10.1787/5k4bxkt1cjd2-en.

OECD (2011a), *Towards Green Growth*, OECD Green Growth Studies, OECD Publishing, Paris, http://dx.doi.org/10.1787/9789264111318-en.

OECD (2011b), *Fostering Innovation for Green Growth*, OECD Green Growth Studies, OECD Publishing, Paris, http://dx.doi.org/10.1787/9789264119925-en.

OECD (2009), *Clusters, Innovation and Entrepreneurship*, Local Economic and Employment Development (LEED), OECD Publishing, Paris, http://dx.doi.org/10.1787/9789264044326-en.

OECD (2006), "Good Practices in the National Sustainable Development Strategies of OECD Countries", OECD Publishing, Paris, www.oecd.org/greengrowth/36655769.pdf.

OECD (2003), *Organic Agriculture: Sustainability, Markets and Policies*, OECD Publishing, Paris, http://dx.doi.org/10.1787/9789264101517-en.

OECD et al. (2014), "Mise en oeuvre du 'Small Business Act' pour l'Europe dans le bassin méditerranéen au moyen orient et en Afrique du Nord 2014 : Profil SBA : Tunisie", OECD Publishing, Paris, www.oecd.org/mena/investment/BriefingforMinisters_FR.pdf.

OME – Observatoire Méditerranéen de l'Energie (2012), "Solar Thermal in the Mediterranean Region: Market Assessment", Report OME for GSWH-UNEP-UNDP.

Plan Bleu (2011), "Programme de Travail du Plan Bleu sur la Gestion des Déchets et les Flux de Matières : Études nationales et études de cas de la gestion des déchets urbains – Cas de la Tunisie".

Powell, J. and A. Craighill (2001), "Information: The Key to Sustainability in the Building Sector?", Report presented at the OECD workshop on the Design of Sustainable Building Policies 28-29 June 2001, Paris.

PV Magazine (2012), "Export-driven PV Plans for Tunisia: Interview with Khaled Nasraoui, Co-founder and Deputy CEO of Tunisian-based Producer Aurasol", 3rd September 2012, www.pv-magazine.com/news/details/beitrag/interview--export-driven-pv-plans-for-tunisia_100008275/.

SWEEP-Net (2012), "The Solid Waste Management Situation in Mashreq and Maghreb Countries: Update on the Challenges and Opportunities".

SWEEP-Net (2010), "Rapport pays sur la gestion des déchets solides en Tunisie".

UNCTAD-UNEP (2008), "Best Practices for Organic Policy: What Developing Country Governments Can Do To Promote the Organic Agriculture Sector", Prepared under the CBTF Project "Promoting Production and Trading Opportunities for Organic Agricultural Products in East Africa".

UNEP – United Nations Environment Programme (2005), *Solid Waste Management.*

UNEP/WTO (2005), *Making Tourism More Sustainable: A Guide for Policy Makers*.

UNWTO – United Nations World Tourism Organisation (2013), "Tourism Highlights, 2013 Edition", United Nations World Tourism Organisation.

Van Dijk, K. et al. (2001), "Strategy for Reuse of Construction and Demolition Waste: Role of Authorities", HERON, Vol. 46, No. 2.

# ORGANISATION FOR ECONOMIC CO-OPERATION AND DEVELOPMENT

The OECD is a unique forum where governments work together to address the economic, social and environmental challenges of globalisation. The OECD is also at the forefront of efforts to understand and to help governments respond to new developments and concerns, such as corporate governance, the information economy and the challenges of an ageing population. The Organisation provides a setting where governments can compare policy experiences, seek answers to common problems, identify good practice and work to co-ordinate domestic and international policies.

The OECD member countries are: Australia, Austria, Belgium, Canada, Chile, the Czech Republic, Denmark, Estonia, Finland, France, Germany, Greece, Hungary, Iceland, Ireland, Israel, Italy, Japan, Korea, Luxembourg, Mexico, the Netherlands, New Zealand, Norway, Poland, Portugal, the Slovak Republic, Slovenia, Spain, Sweden, Switzerland, Turkey, the United Kingdom and the United States. The European Commission takes part in the work of the OECD.

OECD Publishing disseminates widely the results of the Organisation's statistics gathering and research on economic, social and environmental issues, as well as the conventions, guidelines and standards agreed by its members.

OECD PUBLISHING, 2, rue André-Pascal, 75775 PARIS CEDEX 16
(81 2014 30 1 P) ISBN 978-92-64-19082-5 – 2015-02

www.ingramcontent.com/pod-product-compliance
Ingram Content Group UK Ltd.
Pitfield, Milton Keynes, MK11 3LW, UK
UKHW051500290926
15471UKWH00008B/1312

9 789264 190825